W9-BNE-947

JONES & BARTLETT LEARNING INFORMATION SYSTEMS SECURITY & ASSURANCE SERIES

Managing Risk in Information Systems

DARRIL GIBSON

JONES & BARTLETT
LEARNING

World Headquarters
Jones & Bartlett Learning
40 Tall Pine Drive
Sudbury, MA 01776
978-443-5000
info@jblearning.com
www.jblearning.com

Jones & Bartlett Learning Canada
6339 Ormindale Way
Mississauga, Ontario L5V 1J2
Canada

Jones & Bartlett Learning
International
Barb House, Barb Mews
London W6 7PA
United Kingdom

Jones & Bartlett Learning books and products are available through most bookstores and online booksellers. To contact Jones & Bartlett Learning directly, call 800-832-0034, fax 978-443-8000, or visit our website, www.jblearning.com.

Substantial discounts on bulk quantities of Jones & Bartlett Learning publications are available to corporations, professional associations, and other qualified organizations. For details and specific discount information, contact the special sales department at Jones & Bartlett Learning via the above contact information or send an email to specialsales@jblearning.com.

Production Credits
Chief Executive Officer: Ty Field
President: James Homer
SVP, Chief Operating Officer: Don Jones, Jr.
SVP, Chief Technology Officer: Dean Fossella
SVP, Chief Marketing Officer: Alison M. Pendergast
SVP, Chief Financial Officer: Ruth Siporin
SVP, Business Development: Christopher Will
VP, Design and Production: Anne Spencer
VP, Manufacturing and Inventory Control: Therese Connell
Editorial Management: High Stakes Writing, LLC, Editor and Publisher: Lawrence J. Goodrich
Reprints and Special Projects Manager: Susan Schultz
Associate Production Editor: Tina Chen
Director of Marketing: Alisha Weisman
Associate Marketing Manager: Meagan Norlund
Cover Design: Anne Spencer
Composition: Mia Saunders Design
Cover Image: © ErickN/ShutterStock, Inc.
Chapter Opener Image: © Rodolfo Clix/Dreamstime.com
Printing and Binding: Malloy, Inc.
Cover Printing: Malloy, Inc.

ISBN: 978-0-7637-9187-2

Library of Congress Cataloging-in-Publication Data
Unavailable at time of printing

6048
Printed in the United States of America
14 13 12 11   10 9 8 7 6 5 4

Contents

CHAPTER 4   **Developing a Risk Management Plan   85**

To my wife, who has enriched my life
in so many ways over the past 18 years.
I'm looking forward to 18 more.

Preface

Purpose of This Book

This book is part of the Information Systems Security & Assurance Series from Jones & Bartlett Learning (*www.jblearning.com*). Designed for courses and curriculums in IT Security, Cyber Security, Information Assurance, and Information Systems Security, this series features a comprehensive, consistent treatment of the most current thinking and trends in this critical subject area. These titles deliver fundamental information-security principles packed with real-world applications and examples. Authored by Certified Information Systems Security Professionals (CISSPs), they deliver comprehensive information on all aspects of information security. Reviewed word for word by leading technical experts in the field, these books are not just current, but forward-thinking—putting you in the position to solve the cyber security challenges not just of today, but of tomorrow, as well.

This book provides a comprehensive view of managing risk in information systems. It covers the fundamentals of risk and risk management and also includes in-depth details on more comprehensive risk management topics. It is divided into three major parts.

Part 1, Risk Management Businesses Challenges, addresses many of the issues relevant to present-day businesses. It covers details of risks, threats, and vulnerabilities. Topics help students understand the importance of risk management in the organization, including many of the techniques used to manage risks. Many of the current laws are presented with clear descriptions of how they are relevant in organizations. It also includes a chapter describing the contents of a risk management plan.

Part 2, Mitigating Risk, focuses on risk assessments. Topics presented include different risk-assessment approaches including the overall steps in performing a risk assessment. It covers the importance of identifying assets and then identifying potential threats, vulnerabilities, and exploits against these assets. Chapter 9 covers the different types of controls that you can use to mitigate risk. The last two chapters in this part identify how to plan risk mitigation throughout the organization and convert the risk assessment into a risk management plan.

Part 3, Risk Mitigation Plans, cover the many different elements of risk mitigation plans such as a business impact analysis and a business continuity plan. The last two chapters cover disaster recovery and computer incident recovery team plans.

Learning Features

The writing style of this book is practical and conversational. Each chapter begins with a statement of learning objectives. Step-by-step examples of information security concepts and procedures are presented throughout the text. Illustrations are used both to clarify the material and to vary the presentation. The text is sprinkled with Notes, Tips, FYIs, Warnings, and sidebars to alert the reader to additional and helpful information related to the subject under discussion. Chapter Assessments appear at the end of each chapter, with solutions provided in the back of the book.

Chapter summaries are included in the text to provide a rapid review or preview of the material and to help students understand the relative importance of the concepts presented.

Audience

The material is suitable for undergraduate or graduate computer science majors or information science majors, students at a two-year technical college or community college who have a basic technical background, or readers who have a basic understanding of IT security and want to expand their knowledge.

Acknowledgments

I would like to thank Jones & Bartlett Learning for this opportunity to write a detailed and practical information security textbook. I would also like to thank Jeff T. Parker, the technical reviewer, for his outstanding feedback and recommendations, and Kim Lindros the project editor. Kim managed the project from beginning to end, reviewing and ferrying all of the pieces that flowed between me and Jones & Bartlett Learning. Kim was a pleasure to work with and made even the most challenging elements of this project simpler. Thanks again, Kim!

About the Author

Darril Gibson is the CEO of Security Consulting and Training, LLC. He regularly teaches, writes, and consults on a wide variety of security and technical topics. He's been a Microsoft Certified Trainer for more than 10 years and holds several certifications, including MCSE, MCDBA, MCSD, MCITP, ITIL v3, Security+, and CISSP. He has authored, coauthored, or contributed to 10 books including the successful *Security+: Get Certified, Get Ahead*.

PART ONE

Risk Management Business Challenges

Risk Management Fundamentals

RISK MANAGEMENT IS IMPORTANT to the success of every company—a company that takes no risks doesn't thrive. On the other hand, a company that ignores risk can fail when a single threat is exploited. Nowadays, information technology (IT) systems contribute to the success of most companies. If you don't properly manage IT risks, they can also contribute to your company's failure.

Effective risk management starts by understanding threats and vulnerabilities. You build on this knowledge by identifying ways to mitigate the risks. Risks can be mitigated by reducing vulnerabilities or reducing the impact of the risk. You can then create different plans to mitigate risks in different areas of the company. A company typically has several risk mitigation plans in place.

Risk management is presented in three parts in this textbook. Part 1 is titled "Risk Management Business Challenges." It lays a foundation for the book, with definitions of many of the terms and techniques of risk management. It finishes with details on how to develop a risk management plan. Part 2 is titled "Mitigating Risk." This section covers risk assessments. Once you identify risks, you can take steps to reduce them. It ends with methods for turning a risk assessment into a risk mitigation plan. Part 3 is titled "Risk Management Plans." Here you learn how to create and implement several different plans, such as the business continuity plan and the disaster recovery plan.

This book can help you build a solid foundation in risk management as it relates to information system security. It won't make you an expert. Many of the topics presented in a few paragraphs in this book can fill entire chapters or even entire books. You'll find a list of resources at the end of the book. Use these resources to dig deeper into the topics that interest you. The more you learn, the closer you'll be to becoming the expert that others seek to solve their problems.

Chapter 1 Topics

This chapter covers the following topics and concepts:

- What risk is and what its relationship to threat, vulnerability, and loss is
- What the major components of risk to an IT infrastructure are
- What risk management is and how it is important to the organization
- What some risk identification techniques are
- What some risk management techniques are

Chapter 1 Goals

When you complete this chapter, you will be able to:

- Define risk
- Identify the major components of risk
- Describe the relationship between threats and vulnerabilities, and impact
- Define risk management
- Describe risk management's relationship with profitability and survivability
- Explain the relationship between the cost of loss and the cost of risk management
- Describe how risk is perceived by different roles within an organization
- Identify threats
- List the different categories of threats
- Describe techniques to identify vulnerabilities
- Identify and define risk management techniques
- Describe the purpose of a cost-benefit analysis (CBA)
- Define residual risk

What Is Risk?

Risk is the likelihood that a loss will occur. Losses occur when a **threat** exposes a **vulnerability**. Organizations of all sizes face risks. Some risks are so severe they cause a business to fail. Other risks are minor and can be accepted without another thought. Companies use risk management techniques to identify and differentiate severe risks from minor risks. When this is done properly, administrators and managers can intelligently decide what to do about any type of risk. The end result is a decision to avoid, transfer, mitigate, or accept a risk.

The common themes of these definitions are threat, vulnerability, and loss. Even though the common body of knowledge (CBK)— see note—doesn't specifically mention loss, it implies it. Here's a short definition of each of these terms:

- **Threat**—A threat is any activity that represents a possible danger.
- **Vulnerability**—A vulnerability is a weakness.
- **Loss**—A loss results in a compromise to business functions or assets.

Risks to a business can result in a loss that negatively affects the business. A business commonly tries to limit its exposure to risks. The overall goal is to reduce the losses that can occur from risk. Business losses can be thought of in the following terms:

- Compromise of business functions
- Compromise of business assets
- Driver of business costs

Compromise of Business Functions

Business functions are the activities a business performs to sell products or services. If any of these functions are negatively affected, the business won't be able to sell as much. The business will earn less revenue, resulting in an overall loss.

Here are a few examples of business functions and possible compromises:

- Salespeople regularly call or e-mail customers. If the capabilities of either phones or e-mail are reduced, sales are reduced.
- A Web site sells products on the Internet. If the Web site is attacked and fails, sales are lost.
- Authors write articles that must be submitted by a deadline to be published. If the author's PC becomes infected with a virus, the deadline passes and the article's value is reduced.

- Analysts compile reports used by management to make decisions. Data is gathered from internal servers and Internet sources. If network connectivity fails, analysts won't have access to current data. Management could make decisions based on inaccurate information.

- A warehouse application is used for shipping products that have been purchased. It identifies what has been ordered, where the products need to be sent, and where they are located. If the application fails, products aren't shipped on time.

Because compromises to any of these business functions can result in a loss of revenue, they all represent risks. One of the tasks when considering risk is identifying the important functions for a business.

The importance of any business function is relative to the business. In other words, the failure of a Web site for one company may be catastrophic if all products and services are sold through the Web site. Another company may host a Web site to provide information to potential customers. If it fails, it will have less impact on the business.

Compromise of Business Assets

A business asset is anything that has measurable value to a company. If an asset has the potential of losing value, it is at risk. Value is defined as the worth of an asset to a business. Value can often be expressed in monetary terms, such as $5,000.

Assets can have both tangible and intangible values. The **tangible value** is the actual cost of the asset. The **intangible value** is value that cannot be measured by cost, such as client confidence. Generally acceptable accounting principles (GAAP) refer to client confidence as goodwill.

Imagine that your company sells products via a Web site. The Web site earns $5,000 an hour in revenue. Now, imagine that the Web server hosting the Web site fails and is down for two hours. The costs to repair it total $1,000. What is the tangible loss?

- **Lost revenue**—$5,000 times two hours = $10,000
- **Repair costs**—$1,000
- **Total tangible value**—$11,000

The intangible value isn't as easy to calculate but is still very important. Imagine that several customers tried to make a purchase when the Web site was down. If the same product is available somewhere else, they probably bought the product elsewhere. That lost revenue is the tangible value.

However, if the experience is positive with the other business, where will the customers go the next time they want to purchase this product? It's very possible the other business has just gained new customers and you have lost some. The intangible value includes:

- **Future lost revenue**—Any additional purchases the customers make with the other company is a loss to your company.
- **Cost of gaining the customer**—A lot of money is invested to attract customers. It is much easier to sell to a repeat customer than it is to acquire a new customer. If you lose a customer, you lose the investment.

- **Customer influence**—Customers have friends, families, and business partners. They commonly share their experience with others, especially if the experience is exceptionally positive or negative.

Some examples of tangible assets are:

- **Computer systems**—Servers, desktop PCs, and mobile computers are all tangible assets.
- **Network components**—Routers, switches, firewalls, and any other components necessary to keep the network running are assets.
- **Software applications**—Any application that can be installed on a computer system is considered a tangible asset.
- **Data**—This includes the large-scale databases that are integral to many businesses. It also includes the data used and manipulated by each employee or customer.

One of the early steps in risk management is associated with identifying the assets of a company and their associated costs. This data is used to prioritize risks for different assets. Once a risk is prioritized, it becomes easier to identify risk management processes to protect the asset.

Driver of Business Costs

Risk is also a driver of business costs. Once risks are identified, steps can be taken to reduce or manage the risk. Risks are often managed by implementing countermeasures or controls. The costs of managing risk need to be considered in total business costs.

If too much money is spent on reducing risk, the overall profit is reduced. If too little money is spent on these controls, a loss could result from an easily avoidable threat and/or vulnerability.

Profitability Versus Survivability

Both **profitability** and **survivability** must be considered when considering risks.

- **Profitability**—The ability of a company to make a profit. Profitability is calculated as revenues minus costs.
- **Survivability**—The ability of a company to survive loss due to a risk. Some losses such as fire can be disastrous and cause the business to fail.

In terms of profitability, a loss can ruin a business. In terms of survivability, a loss may cause a company never to earn a profit. The costs associated with risk management don't contribute directly to revenue gains. Instead, these costs help to ensure that a company can continue to operate even if it incurs a loss.

When considering profitability and survivability, you will want to consider the following items:

- **Out-of-pocket costs**—The cost to reduce risks comes from existing funds.
- **Lost opportunity costs**—Money spent to reduce risks can't be spent elsewhere. This may result in lost opportunities if the money could be used for some other purpose.
- **Future costs**—Some countermeasures require ongoing or future costs. These costs could be for renewing hardware or software. Future costs can also include the cost of employees to implement the countermeasures.
- **Client/stakeholder confidence**—The value of client and stakeholder confidence is also important. If risks aren't addressed, clients or stakeholders may lose confidence when a threat exploits a vulnerability, resulting in a significant loss to the company.

Consider antivirus software. The cost to install antivirus software on every computer in the organization can be quite high. Every dollar spent reduces the overall profit, and antivirus software doesn't have the potential to add any profit.

However, what's the alternative? If antivirus software is not installed, every system represents a significant risk. If any system becomes infected, a virus could release a worm as a payload and infect the entire network. Databases could be corrupted. Data on file servers could be erased. E-mail servers could crash. The entire business could grind to a halt. If this happens too often or for too long the business could fail.

What Are the Major Components of Risk to an IT Infrastructure?

When you start digging into risk and risk management, you'll realize there is a lot to consider. Luckily, there are several methods and techniques used to break down the topics into smaller chunks.

One method is to examine the seven domains of a typical IT infrastructure. You can examine risks within each domain separately. When examining risks for any domain, you'll look at threats, vulnerabilities and impact. The following sections explore these topics.

Seven Domains of a Typical IT Infrastructure

There are a lot of similarities between different IT organizations. For example, any IT organization will have users and computers. There are seven domains of a typical IT infrastructure.

Figure 1-1 shows the seven domains of a typical IT infrastructure. Refer to this figure when reading through the descriptions of these domains.

When considering risk management, you can examine each of these domains separately. Each domain represents a possible target for an attacker. Some attackers have the skill and aptitude to con users so they focus on the User Domain. Other attackers may be experts in specific applications so they focus on the System/Application Domain.

> **NOTE**
>
> These seven domains are also explored in Chapters 7, 8, and 10. Chapter 7 covers these domains as they relate to asset and inventory management. Chapter 8 covers them as they relate to threat assessments. Chapter 10 covers them as they relate to risk management.

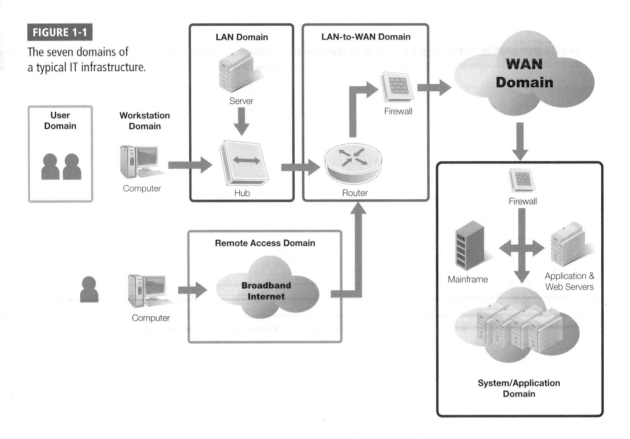

FIGURE 1-1

The seven domains of a typical IT infrastructure.

An attacker only needs to be able to exploit vulnerabilities in one domain. However, a business must provide protection in each of the domains. A weakness in any one of the domains can be exploited by an attacker even if the other six domains have no vulnerabilities.

User Domain

The User Domain includes people. They can be users, employees, contractors, or consultants. The old phrase that a chain is only as strong as its weakest link applies to IT security too. People are often the weakest link in IT security.

You could have the strongest technical and physical security available. However, if personnel don't understand the value of security, the security can be bypassed. For example, technical security can require strong, complex passwords that can't be easily cracked. However, a social engineer can convince an employee to give up the password. Additionally, users may simply write their password down. Some users assume that no one will ever think of looking at the sticky note under their keyboard.

Users can visit risky Web sites, and download and execute infected software. They may unknowingly bring viruses from home via universal serial bus (USB) thumb drives. When they plug in the USB drive the work computer becomes infected. This in turn can infect other computers and the entire network.

Demystifying Social Engineering

Social engineering is a common technique used to trick people into revealing sensitive information. Leonardo DiCaprio played Frank Abagnale in the movie *Catch Me If You Can*, which demonstrated the power of social engineering. A social engineer doesn't just say "give me your secrets." Instead, the attacker uses techniques such as flattery and conning.

A common technique used in vulnerability assessments is to ask employees to give their user name and password. The request may come in the form of an e-mail, a phone call, or even person-to-person.

One common method used in vulnerability assessments is to send an e-mail requesting a user name and password. The e-mail is modified so that it looks as if it's coming from an executive. The e-mail adds a sense of urgency and may include a reference to an important project. From the user's perspective here's what they receive:

From: CEO

Subj: Project upgrade

All,

The XYZ project is at risk of falling behind. As you know this is integral to our success in the coming year. We're having a problem with user authentication. We think it's because passwords may have special characters that aren't recognized.

I need everyone to reply to this e-mail with your user name and password. We must complete this test today so please respond as soon as you receive this e-mail.

Thanks for your assistance.

When employees are trained to protect their password, they usually recognize the risks and don't reply. However, it has been shown that when employees aren't trained, as many as 70 percent of the employees may respond.

Workstation Domain

The workstation is the end user's computer. The workstation is susceptible to malicious software, also known as malware. The workstation is vulnerable if it is not kept up to date with recent patches.

If antivirus software isn't installed, the workstation is also vulnerable. If a system is infected, the malware can cause significant harm. Some malware infects a single system. Other malware releases worm components that can spread across the network.

Antivirus companies regularly update virus definitions as new malware is discovered. In addition to installing the antivirus software, companies must also update software regularly with new definitions. If the antivirus software is installed and up to date, the likelihood of a system becoming infected is reduced.

Bugs and vulnerabilities are constantly being discovered in operating systems and applications. Some of the bugs are harmless. Others represent significant risks.

Microsoft and other software vendors regularly release patches and fixes that can be applied. When systems are kept updated, these fixes help keep the systems protected. When systems aren't updated, the threats can become significant.

LAN Domain

The LAN Domain is the area that is inside the firewall. It can be a few systems connected together in a small home office network. It can also be a large network with thousands of computers. Each individual device on the network must be protected or all devices can be at risk.

Network devices such as hubs, switches, and routers are used to connect the systems together on the local area network (LAN). The internal LAN is generally considered a trusted zone. Data transferred within the LAN isn't protected as thoroughly as if it were sent outside the LAN.

As an example, sniffing attacks occur when an attacker uses a protocol analyzer to capture data packets. A protocol analyzer is also known as a sniffer. An experienced attacker can read the actual data within these packets.

> **NOTE**
>
> Many organizations outlaw the use of hubs within the LAN. Switches are more expensive. However, they reduce the risk of sniffing attacks.

If hubs are used instead of switches, there is an increased risk of sniffing attacks. An attacker can plug into any port in the building and potentially capture valuable data.

If switches are used instead of hubs, the attacker must have physical access to the switch to capture the same amount of data. Most organizations protect network devices in server rooms or wiring closets.

LAN-to-WAN Domain

The LAN-to-WAN Domain connects the local area network to the wide area network (WAN). The LAN Domain is considered a trusted zone since it is controlled by a company. The WAN Domain is considered an untrusted zone because it is not controlled and is accessible by attackers.

The area between the trusted and untrusted zones is protected with one or more firewalls. This is also called the boundary, or the edge. Security here is referred to as boundary protection or edge protection.

The public side of the boundary is often connected to the Internet and has public Internet Protocol (IP) addresses. These IP addresses are accessible from anywhere in the world, and attackers are constantly probing public IP addresses. They look for vulnerabilities and when one is found, they pounce.

A high level of security is required to keep the LAN-to-WAN Domain safe.

Remote Access Domain

Mobile workers often need access to the private LAN when they are away from the company. Remote access is used to grant mobile workers this access. Remote access can be granted via direct dial-up connections or using a virtual private network (VPN) connection.

A VPN provides access to a private network over a public network. The public network used by VPNs is most commonly the Internet. Since the Internet is largely untrusted and has known attackers, remote access represents a risk. Attackers can access unprotected connections. They can also try to break into the remote access servers. Using a VPN is an example of a control to lessen the risk. But VPNs have their vulnerabilities, too.

Vulnerabilities exist at two stages of the VPN connection:

- The first stage is authentication. Authentication is when the user provides credentials to prove identity. If these credentials can be discovered, the attacker can later use them to impersonate the user.
- The second stage is when data is passed between the user and the server. If the data is sent in clear text, an attacker can capture and read the data.

> **NOTE**
>
> VPN connections use tunneling protocols to reduce the risk of data being captured. A tunneling protocol will encrypt the traffic sent over the network. This makes it more difficult for attackers to capture and read data.

WAN Domain

For many businesses, the WAN is the Internet. However, a business can also lease semiprivate lines from private telecommunications companies. These lines are semiprivate because they are rarely leased and used by only a single company. Instead, they are shared with other unknown companies.

As mentioned in the LAN-to-WAN Domain, the Internet is an untrusted zone. Any host on the Internet with a public IP address is at significant risk of attack. Moreover, it is fully expected that any host on the Internet will be attacked.

Semiprivate lines aren't as easily accessible as the Internet. However, a company rarely knows who else is sharing the lines. These leased lines require the same level of security provided to any host in the WAN Domain.

A significant amount of security is required to keep hosts in the WAN Domain safe.

System/Application Domain

The System/Application Domain refers to servers that host server-level applications. Mail servers receive and send e-mail for clients. Database servers host databases that are accessed by users, applications, or other servers. Domain Name System (DNS) servers provide names to IP addresses for clients.

You should always protect servers using best practices: Remove unneeded services and protocols. Change default passwords. Regularly patch and update the server systems. Enable local firewalls.

One of the challenges with servers in the System/Application Domain is that the knowledge becomes specialized. People tend to focus on areas of specialty. For example, common security issues with an e-mail server would likely be known only by technicians who regularly work with the e-mail servers.

> **TIP**
>
> You should lock down a server using the specific security requirements needed by the hosted application. An e-mail server requires one set of protections while a database server requires a different set.

Availability

Threats, Vulnerabilities, and Impact

When a threat exploits a vulnerability it results in a loss. The **impact** identifies the severity
of the loss.

A threat is any circumstance or event with the potential to cause a loss. You can also
think of a threat as any activity that represents a possible danger. Threats are always
present and cannot be eliminated, but they may be controlled.

Threats have independent probabilities of occurring that often are unaffected by an
organizational action. As an example, an attacker may be an expert in attacking Web
servers hosted on Apache. There is very little a company can do to stop this attacker from
trying to attack. However, a company can reduce or eliminate vulnerabilities to reduce
the attacker's chance of success.

Threats are attempts to exploit vulnerabilities that result in the loss of **confidentiality,
integrity**, or **availability** of a business asset. The protection of confidentiality, integrity,
and availability are common security objectives for information systems.

Figure 1-2 shows these three security objectives as a protective triangle. If any side
of the triangle is breached or fails, security fails. In other words, risks to confidentiality,
integrity, or availability represent potential loss to an organization. Because of this,
a significant amount of risk management is focused on protecting these resources.

> **NOTE**
>
> Confidentiality,
> integrity, and
> availability are
> often referred to as
> the security triad.

- **Confidentiality**—Preventing unauthorized disclosure of information.
  Data should be available only to authorized users. Loss of confidentiality
  occurs when data is accessed by someone who should not have access to it.
  Data is protected using access controls and encryption technologies.
- **Integrity**—Ensuring data or an IT system is not modified or destroyed.
  If data is modified or destroyed, it loses its value to the company. Hashing
  is often used to ensure integrity.
- **Availability**—Ensuring data and services are available when needed.
  IT systems are commonly protected using fault tolerance and redundancy
  techniques. Backups are used to ensure the data is retained even if an entire
  building is destroyed.

A vulnerability is a weakness. It could be a procedural, technical, or administrative weakness. It could be a weakness in physical security, technical security, or operational security. Just as all threats don't result in a loss, all vulnerabilities don't result in a loss. It's only when an attacker is able to exploit the vulnerability that a loss to an asset occurs.

Vulnerabilities may exist because they've never been corrected. They can also exist if security is weakened either intentionally or unintentionally.

Consider a locked door used to protect a server room. A technician could intentionally unlock it to make it easier to access. If the door doesn't shut tight on its own, it could accidentally be left open. Either way, the server room becomes vulnerable.

> **TIP**
>
> The method used to take advantage of a vulnerability can also be referred to as an exploit.

The impact is the amount of the loss. The loss can be expressed in monetary terms, such as $5,000.

The value of hardware and software is often easy to determine. If a laptop is stolen, you can use the purchase value or the replacement value. However, some losses aren't easy to determine. If that same laptop held data, the value of the data is hard to estimate.

Descriptive terms instead of monetary terms can be used to describe the impact. You can describe losses in relative terms such as high, medium, or low. As an example, NIST SP 800-30 suggests the following impact terms:

High Impact—If a threat exploits the vulnerability it may:
- Result in the costly loss of major assets or resources
- Significantly violate, harm, or impede an organization's mission, reputation, or interest
- Or, result in human death or serious injury.

Medium Impact—If a threat exploits the vulnerability it may:
- Result in the costly loss of assets or resources
- Violate, harm, or impede an organization's mission, reputation, or interest
- Or, result in human injury.

Low Impact—If a threat exploits the vulnerability it may:
- Result in the loss of some assets or resources
- Or, noticeably affect an organization's mission, reputation, or interest.

Risk Management and Its Importance to the Organization

Risk management is the practice of identifying, assessing, controlling, and mitigating risks. Threats and vulnerabilities are key drivers of risk. Identifying the threats and vulnerabilities that are relevant to the organization is an important step. You can then take action to reduce potential losses from these risks.

It's important to realize that risk management isn't intended to be risk elimination. That isn't a reasonable goal. Instead, risk management attempts to identify the risks that can be minimized and implement controls to do so. Risk management includes several elements:

- **Risk assessment**—Risk management starts with a **risk assessment** or risk analysis. There are multiple steps to a risk assessment:

NOTE

Risk assessment is covered in more depth in chapters 5 and 6.

  - Identify the IT assets of an organization and their value. This can include data, hardware, software, services, and the IT infrastructure.
  - Identify threats and vulnerabilities to these assets. Prioritize the threats and vulnerabilities.
  - Identify the likelihood a vulnerability will be exploited by a threat. These are your risks.
  - Identify the impact of a risk. Risks with higher impacts should be addressed first.

- **Identify risks to manage**—You can choose to avoid, transfer, mitigate, or accept risks. The decision is often based on the likelihood of the risk occurring, and the impact it will have if it occurs.

- **Selection of controls**—After you have identified what risks to address, you can identify and select control methods. Control methods are also referred to as counter-measures. **Controls** are primarily focused on reducing vulnerabilities and impact.

- **Implementation and testing of controls**—Once the controls are implemented, you can test them to ensure they provide the expected protection.

- **Evaluation of controls**—Risk management is an ongoing process. You should regularly evaluate implemented controls to determine if they still provide the expected protection. Evaluation is often done by performing regular vulnerability assessments.

How Risk Affects an Organization's Survivability

Profitability and survivability were presented earlier in the chapter. You should also consider them when identifying which risks to manage. Consider both the cost to implement the control and the cost of not implementing the control. As mentioned previously, spending money to manage a risk rarely adds profit. The important point is that spending money on risk management can help ensure a business's survivability.

As an example, consider data and backups. Data is often one of the most valuable assets a business owns. It can include customer data. It can include accounting data such as accounts payable and accounts receivable. It can include employee data. The list goes on and on. This data is integral to success of a business, so it is often backed up regularly.

Imagine that a business spends $15,000 a year on data backups. This cost will not increase revenue or profits. Imagine that in a full year's time, data is never lost and the backups are never needed. If profitability is the only consideration, management may decide to eliminate this cost. Backups are stopped. The next year, data could be lost, causing the company to fail.

The cost does need to be considered against profitability, though. For example, if a company earns only $10,000 in profit a year, it doesn't make sense to spend $15,000 a year to protect the data.

On the other hand, imagine a company with $100,000 in annual profits. They choose
not to spend the $15,000 on backups. Then a virus spreads through the enterprise,
destroying all customer and accounting data. The company no longer has reliable records
of accounts receivable. No one has access to the customer base. This can be a business-
ending catastrophe.

Reasonableness

A company doesn't need to manage every possible risk. Some risks are reasonable to
manage while others are not.

Reasonableness is a test that can be applied to risk management to determine if the risk
should be managed. It's derived from the reasonable-person standard in law. In short, you
should answer this question. "Would a reasonable person be expected to manage this risk?"

Risks that don't meet the reasonableness test are accepted. For example, the threat
of nuclear war exists. A company could spend resources on building bomb shelters for
all employees and stocking them with food and water to last 30 years. However, this just
isn't reasonable.

As another example, consider a company located on the east coast of Florida.
Hurricanes are a very real threat and should be considered. However, the likelihood
of a major earthquake hitting the east coast of Florida is relatively minor and doesn't
need to be addressed. A business in San Francisco, however, has different concerns.
An earthquake there is a real threat, but a hurricane is not. So, for San Francisco, the
risk of a hurricane is readily accepted while risk of an earthquake may not be accepted.

Balancing Risk and Cost

The cost to manage the risk must be balanced against the impact value. The costs can
be measured in actual monetary values if they are available. You can also balance the
costs using relative values such as low, medium, and high.

Table 1-1 shows an example of how the relative values can be assigned. This matrix
was derived from NIST SP 800-30. Likelihood values are shown vertically, while impact
values are shown horizontally. If a threat has a 10 percent likelihood of occurring it is
assigned a value of Low. If the value is between 10 and 50 percent, the value is medium.

TABLE 1-1 A threat-likelihood-impact matrix.			
	LOW IMPACT 10	**MEDIUM IMPACT 50**	**HIGH IMPACT 100**
High threat likelihood 100 percent (1.0)	10 × 1 = 10	50 × 1 = 50	100 × 1 = 100
Medium threat likelihood 50 percent (.50)	10 × .50 = 5	50 × .50 = 25	100 × .50 = 50
Low threat likelihood 10 percent (.10)	10 × .10 = 1	50 × .10 = 5	100 × .10 = 10

TIP

You can create a more detailed likelihood-impact matrix. For example, instead of assigning values of low, medium, and high for the threat likelihood, you can assign actual percentages. This allows greater separation between the categories. Similarly, you can assign any number within a range to the impact. The matrix in the table uses a range of 10, 50, and 100, but you could use any numbers between 1 and 100, if desired.

If the value is between 51 and 100, the value is high. Similarly, the impact can be ranked as low, medium, and high.

The potential of some risks to occur is very high and the impact is high giving you an easy choice. For example, systems without antivirus software will become infected. The threat is common. The likelihood is high. If or when it happens, an infected system can result in the compromise or destruction of all the business's data. The impact is also high. This risk needs to be mitigated. The cost of antivirus software is far less than the impact costs. Therefore, antivirus software is commonly used in business.

Other times, the likelihood is low but the impact is high. For example, the risk of fire in a data center is low. However, the impact is high. A business will often have fire detection and suppression equipment to prevent the impact if a fire occurs. Insurance is also purchased to reduce the impact if a fire does cause damage.

Role-Based Perceptions of Risk

Ideally, all personnel within an organization will readily understand the threat to a company's health if risk is not managed. Unfortunately, risks and risk management are often perceived quite differently.

One of the challenges with effective risk management is achieving a proper balance between security and usability. Consider Figure 1-3. In the diagram on the left, the computers are completely locked down with a high level of security. Users are unable to use them to adequately perform their job. On the right, the computers are easy to use but security is neglected. In the middle, a balance between the two has been achieved.

FIGURE 1-3

Balancing security and usability in an organization.

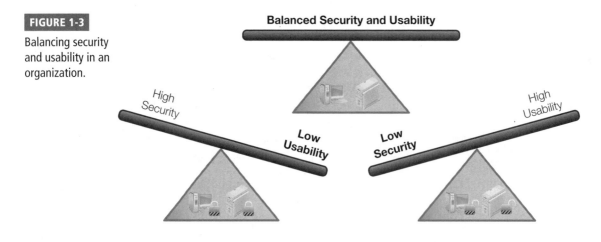

Balanced security rarely satisfies everyone. Security personnel want to lock systems down tighter. End users find the security controls inconvenient and want more usability. It is common for individuals in the followings roles to have different perceptions of risk:

- **Management**—Management is concerned mostly with profitability and survivability. Since attacks can result in loss of confidentiality, integrity, or availability, management is willing to spend money to mitigate risks. However, their view of the risk is based on the costs of the risk and the costs of the controls. Management needs accurate facts to make decisions on which controls to implement to protect company assets.

- **System administrator**—Administrators are responsible for protecting the IT systems. When they understand the risks, they often want to lock systems down as tight as possible. Administrators are often highly technical individuals. System administrators sometimes lose sight of the need to balance security costs with profitability.

- **Tier 1 administrator**—Tier 1 administrators are the first line of defense for IT support (thus the "tier 1" part of the name). When a user needs assistance, a tier 1 administrator is often called. They may be more concerned with usability than security or profitability. These administrators are given limited administrative permissions. They often view the security controls as hindrances to perform their job and don't always recognize the importance of the controls. For example, the need to use a change management process isn't always understood. A well-meaning technician may bypass a change management process to solve one problem but unintentionally create another problem. These unapproved changes can result in business losses.

- **Developer**—Some companies have in-house application developers. They write applications that can be used in-house or sold. Many developers have adopted a secure computing mindset. They realize that security needs to be included from the design stage all the way to the release stage. When developers haven't adopted a security mindset, they often try to patch security holes at the end of the development cycle. This patching mindset rarely addresses all problems, resulting in the release of vulnerable software.

- **End user**—End users simply want the computer to work for them. They are most concerned with usability. They often don't understand the reason for the security controls and restrictions. Instead, security is viewed as an inconvenience. Well-meaning users often try to circumvent controls so they can accomplish their job. For example, USB thumb drives often transport viruses without the user's knowledge. Companies frequently implement policies restricting the use of thumb drives. When a user needs to transfer a file from one computer to another, the USB thumb drive can be tempting.

> ▶ **TIP**
>
> You can restrict the use of thumb drives through a written policy telling people not to use them. You can also use technical controls to prevent use of thumb drives. Computer users can easily ignore a written policy, but they can't easily bypass a technical control. A best practice is to create and enforce both types of policies— written and technical.

You can address the perceptions of these different role holders through targeted training. Some training can include all employees; other training should be targeted to specific roles. Targeted training helps each role holder better understand the big picture. It can also help them understand the importance of security and its value to the success of the company.

People responsible for managing risks must take all perceptions into account. This is especially true if any of the controls can be bypassed.

For example, theft of laptops is a common problem for some companies. An employee can leave the laptop to take a break at a conference only to come back and find the laptop gone. This risk can almost be eliminated if the company purchases hardware locks. The lock can secure the laptop to a desk or other furniture. However, if users don't perceive the risk as valid, they may simply not use the lock. In addition to purchasing the lock, steps need to be taken to train the users.

Risk Identification Techniques

You learned about risk and losses earlier in this chapter. Risk is the likelihood that a loss will occur. Losses occur when a threat exposes a vulnerability. In order to identify risks, you'll need to take three steps:

- Identify threats
- Identify vulnerabilities
- Estimate the likelihood of a threat exploiting a vulnerability

The following sections explore these concepts.

Identifying Threats

A threat is any circumstance or event with the potential to cause a loss. Said another way, it is any activity that represents a possible danger. The loss or danger is directly related to one of the following:

- **Loss of confidentiality**—Someone sees your password or a company's "secret formula."
- **Loss of integrity**—An e-mail message is modified in transit, a virus infects a file, or someone makes unauthorized changes to a Web site.
- **Loss of availability**—An e-mail server is down and no one has e-mail access, or a file server is down so data files aren't available.

"Threat identification" is the process of creating a list of threats. This list attempts to identify all the possible threats to an organization. This is no small task. The list can be extensive.

Threats are often considered in the following categories:

- **External or internal**—External threats are outside the boundary of the organization. They can also be thought of as risks that are outside the control of the organization. Internal threats are within the boundary of the organization. They could be related to employees or other personnel who have access to company resources. Internal threats can be related to any hardware or software controlled by the business.

- **Natural or man-made**—Natural threats are often related to weather such as hurricanes, tornadoes, and ice storms. Earthquakes and tsunamis are also natural threats. A human or man-made threat is any threat from a person. Any attempt to sabotage resources is a man-made threat. Fire could be man-made or natural depending on how the fire is started.

- **Intentional or accidental**—Any deliberate attempt to compromise confidentiality, integrity, or availability is intentional. Employee mistakes or user error are accidental threats. A faulty application that corrupts data could be considered accidental.

One method used to identify threats is through a brainstorming session. In a brainstorming session, participants throw out anything that pops into their heads. All ideas are written down without any evaluation. This creative process helps bring up ideas that may be missed when a problem is only analyzed logically.

Some examples of threats to an organization include:

- An unauthorized employee trying to access data
- Any type of malware
- An attacker defacing a Web site
- Any DoS or DDoS attack
- An external attacker trying to access data
- Any loss of data
- Any loss of services
- A social engineer tricking an employee into revealing a secret
- Earthquakes, floods, or hurricanes
- A lightning strike
- Electrical, heating, or air conditioning outages
- Fires

> **TIP**
>
> A denial of service (DoS) attack is an attack that attempts to disrupt a service. A DoS attack results in the service being unavailable. A distributed denial of service (DDoS) attack originates from multiple attackers.

All these threats represent possible risks if they expose vulnerabilities.

Of course, you will identify different threats and vulnerabilities depending on the organization. Every organization has threats and vulnerabilities specific to them. In fact, a business with multiple locations may have some threats and vulnerabilities unique to one location.

Identifying Vulnerabilities

You learned earlier that a vulnerability is a weakness. When a threat occurs, if there is a vulnerability the weakness is apparent. However, before threats occur, you'll have to dig a little to identify the weaknesses. Luckily, most organizations have a lot of sources which can help you.

Some of the sources you can use are:

- **Audits**—Many organizations are regularly audited. Systems and processes are checked to verify a company complies with existing rules and laws. At the completion of an audit, a report is created. These reports list findings which directly relate to weaknesses.

- **Certification and accreditation records**—Several standards exist to examine and certify IT systems. If the system meets the standards, the IT system can be accredited. The entire process includes detailed documentation. This documentation can be reviewed to identify existing and potential weaknesses.

- **System logs**—Many types of logs can be used to identify threats. Audit logs can determine if users are accessing sensitive data. Firewall logs can identify traffic that is trying to breach the network. Firewall logs can also identify computers taken over by malware and acting as zombies. DNS logs can identify unauthorized transfer of data.

- **Prior events**—Previous security incidents are excellent sources of data. As evidence of risks which already occurred, they help justify controls. They show the problems that have occurred and can show trends. Ideally, weaknesses from a security incident will be resolved right after the incident. In practice, employees are sometimes eager to put the incident behind them and forget it as soon as possible. Even if documentation doesn't exist on the incident, a few key questions can uncover the details.

> ▶ **TIP**
>
> Some malware can take control of multiple computers and control them as robots. The controlling computer issues attack commands and the computers attack. The individual computers are referred to as "zombies." The network of controlled computers is called a "botnet."

- **Trouble reports**—Most companies use databases to document trouble calls. These databases can contain a wealth of information. With a little bit of analysis, you can use them to identify trends and weaknesses.

- **Incident response teams**—Some companies have incident response teams. These teams will investigate all the security incidents within the company. You can interview team members and get a wealth of information. These teams are often eager to help reduce risks.

Using the Seven Domains of a Typical IT Infrastructure to Identify Weaknesses

Another way of identifying weaknesses is by examining the seven domains of a typical IT infrastructure. These domains were presented earlier in this chapter. Each domain can be examined individually. Further, each domain can be examined by experts in that domain. The following list gives you some examples in each of these domains:

- **User Domain**—Social engineering represents a big vulnerability. Sally gets a call. "Hi. This is Bob from the help desk. We've identified a virus on your computer." Bob then attempts to walk Sally though a long detailed process and then says "Why don't I just fix this for you? You can get back to work. All I need is your password."

- **Workstation Domain**—Computers that aren't patched can be exploited. If they don't have antivirus software they can become infected.

- **LAN Domain**—Any data on the network that is not secured with appropriate access controls is vulnerable. Weak passwords can be cracked. Permissions that aren't assigned properly allow unauthorized access.

- **LAN-to-WAN Domain**—If users are allowed to visit malicious Web sites, they can mistakenly download malicious software. Firewalls with unnecessary ports open allow access to the internal network from the Internet.

- **WAN Domain**—Any public-facing server is susceptible to DoS and DDoS attacks. A File Transfer Protocol (FTP) server that allows anonymous uploads can host Warez from black-hat hackers.

- **Remote Access Domain**—Remote users may be infected with a virus but not know it. When they connect to the internal network via remote access, the virus can infect the network.

- **System/Application Domain**—Database servers can be subject to SQL injection attacks. In a SQL injection attack, the attacker can read the entire database. SQL injection attacks can also modify data in the database.

> **TIP**
>
> "Warez" (pronounced as "wares") is a term that describes pirated files. Examples included pirated games, MP3 files, and movies. A Warez site often includes hacking tools, which anyone can download, including hackers.

> **TIP**
>
> A "SQL injection attack" tries to access data from Web sites. SQL statements are entered into text boxes. If the Web site isn't programmed defensively, these SQL statements can be executed against a database. Some programs are available that can launch a SQL injection attack and retrieve an entire database.

This list certainly isn't complete. The number of vulnerabilities discovered in IT is constantly growing. The MITRE Corporation catalog **Common Vulnerabilities and Exposures (CVE)** includes more than 40,000 items.

Using Reason When Identifying Vulnerabilities

Reasonableness was covered earlier in this chapter. As a reminder, reasonableness answers the question, "Would a reasonable person be expected to manage this risk?" In this context, you can think of it as, "Would a reasonable person be expected to reduce this vulnerability?"

You should focus on vulnerabilities within the organization or within the system being evaluated. External vulnerabilities are often not addressed. For example, a server will likely fail if air conditioning fails. You would address this when identifying vulnerabilities for a server room. You wouldn't address for each of the 50 servers in the server room. Similarly, the commercial power may fail. You may address this by having uninterruptible power supplies (UPS) and generators. However, you don't need to identify alternatives for the commercial power company.

TABLE 1-2 Risk and trust levels of common network zones.		
THREAT	**VULNERABILITY**	**IMPACT**
An unauthorized employee tries to access data hosted on a server.	The organization doesn't use authentication and access controls.	The possible loss would depend on the sensitivity of the data and how it's used. For example, if the unauthorized employee accessed salary data and freely shared it, this could impact morale and productivity.
Any type of malicious software, such as viruses or worms, enters the network.	Antivirus software doesn't detect the virus.	The virus could be installed on systems. Viruses typically result in loss of confidentiality, integrity, or availability.
An attacker modifies or defaces a Web site.	The Web site isn't protected.	Depending on how the attacker modifies the Web site, the credibility of the company could be affected.
A social engineer tricks an employee into revealing a password.	Users aren't adequately trained.	Passwords could be revealed. An attacker who obtains a password could take control of the user's account.

Pairing Threats with Vulnerabilities

The third step when identifying risks is to pair the threats with vulnerabilities. Threats are matched to existing vulnerabilities to determine the likelihood of a risk.

The "Identifying Threats" section listed several threats. Table 1-2 takes a few of those threats and matches them to vulnerabilities to identify possible losses.

The following formula is often used when pairing threats with vulnerabilities.

Risk = Threat × Vulnerability

However, this isn't a true mathematical formula. Compare this to the formula for area: Area = Length × Width. Length has a numerical value. Width has a numerical value. The result is a number for Area.

Threat and vulnerability often don't have numerical values. The formula isn't intended to give a number as a result. Instead, it is designed to show the relationship between the two.

If you can identify the value of the asset, the formula is slightly modified to:

Total Risk = Threat × Vulnerability × Asset Value

Risk Management Techniques

After risks have been identified, you need to decide what you want to do about them. Risk management can be thought of as handling risk. It's important to realize that risk management is not risk elimination. A business that doesn't take any risks doesn't stay in business long. The cost to eliminate all risks will consume all the profits.

The ultimate goal of risk management is to protect the organization. It helps ensure a business can continue to operate and earn a profit. Risk management includes several steps. They include:

- Identifying risks
- Assessing risks
- Determining which risks will be handled and which risks will accepted
- Taking steps to reduce risk to an acceptable level.

When deciding how to handle a risk you can choose to **avoid, transfer, mitigate,** or **accept** the risk. These techniques are explained in the following section.

Avoidance

One of the ways you manage risk is by simply avoiding it. The primary reason to avoid a risk is that the impact of the risk outweighs the benefit of the asset.

An organization can avoid risk by:

- **Eliminating the source of the risk**—The company can stop the risky activity. For example, a company may have a wireless network that is vulnerable to attacks. The risk could be avoided by removing the wireless network. This can be done if the wireless network isn't an important asset in the company.

- **Eliminating the exposure of assets to the risk**—The company can move the asset. For example, a data center could be at risk because it is located where earthquakes are common. It could be moved to an earthquake-free zone to eliminate this risk. The cost to move the data center will be high. However, if the risk is unacceptable and the value of the data center is higher it makes sense.

Transfer

You can transfer risk by shifting responsibility to another party. This is most commonly done by purchasing insurance. It can also be done by outsourcing the activity.

- **Insurance**—You purchase insurance to protect your company from a loss. If a loss occurs, the insurance covers it. Many types of insurance are available, including fire insurance.

- **Outsourcing the activity**—For example, your company may want to host a Web site on the Internet. The company can host the Web site with a Web hosting provider. Your company and the provider can agree on who assumes responsibility for security, backups, and availability.

Mitigation

You reduce risk by reducing vulnerabilities, and risk mitigation is the primary strategy in this process. Risk mitigation is also known as reduction or treatment.

You reduce vulnerabilities by implementing controls or countermeasures. The cost of a control should not exceed the benefit. Determining costs and benefits often requires a cost-benefit analysis, which is covered later in this chapter.

Some examples of mitigation steps are:

> **TIP**
>
> Controls are often referred to as either preventive or detective. A "preventive control" attempts to deter or prevent the risk from occurring. Examples include increasing physical security and training personnel. "Detective controls" try to detect activity that may result in a loss. Examples include antivirus software and intrusion detection systems.

- **Alter the physical environment**—Replace hubs with switches. Locate servers in locked server rooms.
- **Change procedures**—Implement a backup plan. Store a copy of backups offsite, and test the backups.
- **Add fault tolerance**—Use Redundant Array of Independent Disks (RAID) for important data stored on disks. Use failover clusters to protect servers.
- **Modify the technical environment**—Increase security on the firewalls. Add intrusion detection systems. Keep antivirus software up to date.
- **Train employees**—Train technical personnel on how to implement controls. Train end users on social engineering tactics.

Often the goal is not to eliminate the risk but instead, to make it too expensive for the attacker. Consider the following two formulas.

- **Attacker's cost < attacker's gain**—When this is true, it is appealing to the attacker.
- **Attacker's cost > attacker's gain**—When this is true, the attacker is less likely to pursue the attack.

Cryptography is one of the ways to increase the attacker's cost. If your company sends data across the network in clear text, it can be captured and analyzed. If the company encrypts the data, an attacker must decrypt it before analyzing it. The goal of the encryption isn't to make it impossible to decrypt the data. Instead, the goal is to make it too expensive or too time-consuming for the attacker to crack it.

Acceptance

You can also choose to accept a risk. A company can evaluate a risk, understand the potential loss, and choose to accept it. This is commonly done when the cost of the control outweighs the potential loss.

For example, consider the following scenario: A company hosts a Web server used for e-commerce. The Web server generates about $1,000 per month in revenue. The server could be protected using a failover cluster. However, estimates indicate that a failover cluster will cost approximately $10,000. If the server goes down, it may be down for only one or two hours, which equates to less than $3. (Revenue per hour = $1,000 × 12 / 365 / 24 = $1.37.)

> **NOTE**
>
> A simple failover cluster could include two servers. One server provides the service to users and the other server acts as a spare. If the online server fails, the spare server can sense the failure and automatically take over.

The decision to accept a loss becomes easier if you have evaluated the costs against the benefits, which is known as a "cost-benefit analysis." A cost-benefit analysis is useful when choosing any of the techniques to manage risk.

Cost-Benefit Analysis

You perform a **cost-benefit analysis (CBA)** to help determine which controls or counter-measures to implement. If the benefits outweigh the costs, the control is often selected.

A CBA compares the business impact with the cost to implement a control. For example, the loss of data on a file server may represent the loss of $1 million worth of research. Implementing a backup plan to ensure the availability of the data may cost $10,000. In other words, you would spend $10,000 to save $1 million. This makes sense.

A CBA starts by gathering data to identify the costs of the controls and benefits gained if they are implemented.

- **Cost of the control**—This includes the purchase costs plus the operational costs over the lifetime of the control.

- **Projected benefits**—This includes the potential benefits gained from implementing the control. You identify these benefits by examining the costs of the loss and how much the loss will be reduced if the control is implemented.

A control doesn't always eliminate the loss. Instead, the control reduces it. For example, annual losses for a current risk may average $100,000. If a control is implemented, these losses may be reduced to $10,000. The benefit of the control is $90,000.

You can use the following formula to determine if the control should be used:

Loss before control − loss after control = cost of control

Imagine the company lost $100,000 last year without any controls implemented. You estimate you'll lose $10,000 a year if the control is implemented. The cost of the control is estimated at $10,000. The formula is:

$100,000 − $10,000 (cost of control) − $10,000 (expected residual loss) = $80,000

This represents a benefit of $80,000.

One of the biggest challenges when performing a CBA is getting accurate data. While current losses are often easily available, future costs and benefits need to be estimated. Costs are often underestimated. Benefits are often overestimated.

The immediate costs of a control are often available. However, the ongoing costs are sometimes hidden. Some of the hidden costs may be:

- Costs to train employees
- Costs for ongoing maintenance
- Software and hardware renewal costs

If the costs outweigh the benefits, the control may not be implemented. Instead, the risk could be accepted, transferred or avoided.

Residual Risk

Residual risk is the risk that remains after you apply controls. It's not feasible to eliminate all risks. Instead, you take steps to reduce the risk to an acceptable level. The risk that's left is residual risk.

Earlier in this chapter, the following two formulas were given for risk:

Risk = Threat × Vulnerability

Total risk = Threat × Vulnerability × Asset Value

You can calculate residual risk with the following formula:

Residual Risk = Total Risk − Controls

Senior management is responsible for any losses due to residual risk. They decide whether a risk should be avoided, transferred, mitigated or accepted. They also decide what controls to implement. Any resulting loss due to their decisions falls on their shoulders.

CHAPTER SUMMARY

Risks occur when threats exploit vulnerabilities, resulting in a loss. The loss can compromise business functions and business assets. Losses also drive business costs. Risk management helps a company identify risks that need to be reduced. The first steps in risk management are to identify threats and vulnerabilities. These can then be paired to help determine the severity of the risk.

You can manage risks by choosing one of four techniques: A risk can be avoided, transferred, mitigated, or accepted. The primary risk management technique is risk mitigation. Risk mitigation is also known as risk reduction or risk treatment. You reduce vulnerabilities by implementing controls.

KEY CONCEPTS AND TERMS

Accept	Impact	Risk assessment
Availability	Intangible value	Risk management
Avoid	Integrity	Survivability
Common Vulnerabilities and Exposures (CVE)	Mitigate	Tangible value
	Profitability	Threat
Confidentiality	Reasonableness	Total risk
Control	Residual risk	Transfer
Cost-benefit analysis (CBA)	Risk	Vulnerability

CHAPTER 1 ASSESSMENT

1. Which one of the following properly defines risk?

A. Threat × Mitigation
B. Vulnerability × Controls
C. Controls − Residual Risk
D. Threat × Vulnerability

2. Which one of the following properly defines total risk?

A. Threat − Mitigation
B. Threat × Vulnerability × Asset Value
C. Vulnerability − Controls
D. Vulnerability × Controls

3. You can completely eliminate risk in an IT environment.

A. True
B. False

4. Which of the following are accurate pairings of threat categories? (Select two.)

A External and internal
B. Natural and supernatural
C. Intentional and accidental
D. Computer and user

5. A loss of client confidence or public trust is an example of a loss of _____.

6. A _____ is used to reduce a vulnerability.

7. As long as a company is profitable, it does not need to consider survivability.

A. True
B. False

8. What is the primary goal of an information security program?

A. Eliminate losses related to employee actions
B. Eliminate losses related to risk
C. Reduce losses related to residual risk
D. Reduce losses related to loss of confidentiality, integrity, and availability

9. The _____ is an industry-recognized standard list of common vulnerabilities.

10. Which of the following is a goal of a risk management?

A. Identify the correct cost balance between risk and controls
B. Eliminate risk by implementing controls
C. Eliminate the loss associated with risk
D. Calculate value associated with residual risk

11. If the benefits outweigh the cost, a control is implemented. Costs and benefits are identified by completing a _____.

12. A company decides to reduce losses of a threat by purchasing insurance. This is known as risk _____.

13. What can you do to manage risk? (Select three.)

A. Accept
B. Transfer
C. Avoid
D. Migrate

14. You have applied controls to minimize risk in the environment. What is the remaining risk called?

A. Remaining risk
B. Mitigated risk
C. Managed risk
D. Residual risk

15. Who is ultimately responsible for losses resulting from residual risk?

A. End users
B. Technical staff
C. Senior management
D. Security personnel

Managing Risk: Threats, Vulnerabilities, and Exploits

A KEY STEP WHEN MANAGING RISKS is to first understand and manage the source. This includes threats and vulnerabilities, and especially threat/vulnerability pairs. Once you understand these elements, it's much easier to identify mitigation techniques. Exploits are a special type of threat/vulnerability pair that often includes buffer overflow attacks.

Fortunately, the U.S. federal government has initiated several steps to help protect IT resources. The National Institute of Standards and Technology has done a lot of research on risk management. The results of this research are freely available in the form of Special Publications. Additionally, the Department of Homeland Security oversees several other initiatives related to IT security.

Chapter 2 Topics

This chapter covers the following topics and concepts:

- What threats are and how can they be managed
- What vulnerabilities are and how can they be managed
- What exploits are and how can they be managed
- Which risk management initiatives the U.S. federal government sponsors

Upon completion of this chapter, you will be able to:

- Describe the uncontrollable nature of threats
- List unintentional and intentional threats
- Identify best practices for managing threats
- Identify threat/vulnerability pairs
- Define mitigation
- List and describe methods used to mitigate vulnerabilities
- Identify best practices for managing vulnerabilities
- Define exploit
- Describe perpetrators' role in vulnerabilities and exploits
- Identify mitigation techniques
- Identify best practices for managing exploits
- Identify the purpose of different U.S. federal government risk management initiatives

Understanding and Managing Threats

Chapter 1 provided an introduction to threats. It defined a threat as any activity that represents a possible danger. This includes any circumstances or events with the potential to adversely impact confidentiality, integrity, or availability of a business's assets.

Threats are a part of the equation that creates risk:

Risk = Vulnerability × Threat

Any attempt to manage risk requires a thorough knowledge of threats. This section includes the following three topics:

- The uncontrollable nature of threats
- Unintentional threats
- Intentional threats

The Uncontrollable Nature of Threats

It's important to realize a few basic facts about threats. These include:

- Threats can't be eliminated.
- Threats are always present.
- You can take action to reduce the potential for a threat to occur.

- You can take action to reduce the impact of a threat.
- You cannot affect the threat itself.

Consider the threat of a car thief. Car thieves steal cars, and you can't prevent that. However, you can take steps to either enhance or reduce the threat against your car. To increase the chances a thief steals your car, you can park your car in a busy parking lot. Leave the keys in it and the car running. Leave a $20 bill on the dashboard. Leave a few expensive items on the front seat. It's just a matter of time before your car is stolen.

However, you can take different steps to reduce the potential threat and impact. Remove the keys and lock the doors. Install a car alarm. Put valuables in the trunk. A car thief might still visit that parking lot, but it is less likely that your car will be stolen.

Sometimes a car thief looks for a specific model, year, and color of car. If your car is a match, the thief will likely steal it no matter what you do. If you never recover your car, your vehicle insurance will reduce the impact of your loss.

Threats to IT are similar. Lightning strikes hit buildings. Malware authors constantly write new programs. Script kiddies run malware programs just to see what they can do. Professional attackers spend 100 percent of their work time trying to break into government and corporate networks. You can't stop them.

However, there many things you can do to reduce the potential harm that the threat can do to your network. You can take steps to reduce the impact of the threat.

Unintentional Threats

Unintentional threats are threats that don't have a perpetrator. They don't occur because someone is specifically trying to attack. Natural events and disasters, human errors, and simple accidents are all considered unintentional.

There are four primary categories of unintentional threats. They are:

- **Environmental**—Threats affecting the environment. This includes weather events such as floods, tornadoes, and hurricanes. Earthquakes and volcanoes are environmental threats too. Illnesses or an epidemic can cause a loss to the labor force and reduce the availability of systems.

- **Human**—Errors caused by people. A simple keystroke error can cause incorrect or invalid data to be entered. A user may forget to enter key data. A technician could fail to follow a backup procedure resulting in an incomplete backup. An administrator may write incomplete or incorrect backup procedures. Undiscovered software bugs can also cause serious problems.

- **Accidents**—Anything from a minor mishap to a major catastrophe. A backhoe digging a new trench for new cables can accidentally cut power or data cables. An employee might start a fire in a break room accidentally.

- **Failures**—Equipment problems. A drive can crash. A server can fail. A router can stop routing traffic. The air conditioner might stop blowing cool air, causing multiple systems to overheat and fail. Any of these failures can result in the loss of availability of data or services.

▶ TIP

You can use a hot, warm, or cold site to provide an alternate location for IT functions. You will learn about hot, warm, and cold sites in Chapter 14.

Although these threats are unintentional, you can address them with a risk management plan. Here are some common methods:

- **Managing environmental threats**—You can purchase insurance to reduce the impact of many environmental threats. A business may decide to move to reduce the threat. For example, a business in the area of the Mount St. Helens volcano can relocate to avoid eruptions. Companies in a hurricane zone can transfer operations elsewhere.

- **Reducing human errors**—Automation and input validation are common methods used to reduce errors. Any process that can be automated will consistently run the same way. Input validation checks data to ensure it is valid before it is used. For example, if a program expects a first name, the input validator checks whether the data looks like a valid name. Rules for a valid first name may be no more than 20 characters, no numbers, and only specific special characters. Input validation can't check to ensure that data is accurate, but it can ensure that data is valid.

- **Preventing accidents**—Contact the 1-800-MISS-DIG company in Michigan, or similar companies or agencies in other states, to identify underground cables before digging. You can stress safety to prevent common accidents.

- **Avoiding failures**—Use fault-tolerant and redundant systems to protect against the immediate impact of failures. A RAID system can help ensure data availability, and failover clusters ensure users can access servers at all times.

Intentional Threats

Intentional threats are acts that are hostile to the organization. One or more perpetrators are involved in carrying out the threat. Perpetrators are generally motivated by one of the following:

- **Greed**—Many attackers want to make money through the attacks. Successful attackers can steal data and perform acts of fraud. Databases with customer data can be stolen to steal identities. Proprietary data can be stolen from competitors. Users can be tricked into giving up credentials used to access financial sites.

- **Anger**—When anger is the motivator, the attacker often wants the victim to pay a price. Anger can result in attempts to destroy assets or disrupt operations. Any of these types of threats result in a loss of availability.

- **Desire to damage**—Some attackers just want to cause damage. The result is the same as if an attacker is motivated by anger. The attack results in a loss of availability.

Although the above list helps you understand what motivates attackers, the items don't identify who the attackers are. Some people still have the image of a bored teenager launching random threats from his or her room. However, attackers are much more sophisticated today.

Some of the more common attackers today are:

- **Criminals**—More and more opportunities to make money from online attacks have resulted in a growth in criminal activity. This activity can be either fraud or theft. For example, "rogueware" is on the rise, in which a user is tricked into installing free antivirus software. However, what they actually install is malware. Then, they must pay to get it removed. Panda Labs reports that as many as 35 million computers are infected every month, giving cybercriminals as much as $34 million a month.

- **Vandals**—Some attackers are intent on doing damage: They damage just for the sake of damaging something. Their targets are often targets of opportunity.

- **Saboteurs**—A saboteur commits sabotage. This could be sabotage against a competing company or against another country. The primary goal is to cause a loss of availability.

- **Disgruntled employees**—Dissatisfied employees often present significant threats to a company. There are countless reasons why an employee may be dissatisfied: an employee did not receive a pay raise is one example. Employees with a lot of access can cause a lot of damage.

- **Activists**—Occasionally, activists present a threat to a company. Activists often operate with a mindset of "the end justifies the means." In other words, if your company does something the activist doesn't approve of, they consider it acceptable to attack.

- **Other nations**—International espionage is a constant threat. For example, information about the U.S. president's helicopter appeared on servers in Iran in 2009. This is widely believed to have been due to data leakage from a peer-to-peer (P2P) program. Many countries include cyber warfare as a part of their offensive and defensive strategies.

- **Hackers**—Hackers attempt to breach systems. Depending on the goal of the hacker, the motivation may range from innocent curiosity to malicious intent.

> ▶ **TIP**
>
> There is a technical difference between a hacker and a cracker. Hackers have historically been known as "white-hat hackers" or "ethical hackers"—the good guys. They hack into systems to learn how it can be done, but not for personal gain. Crackers have been known as "black-hat hackers" or "malicious hackers"—the bad guys. They hack into systems to damage, steal, or commit fraud. Many black-hat hackers present themselves as white-hat hackers claiming that their actions are innocent. However, most mainstream media put all hackers in the same black-hat category. The general perception is that all hackers are bad guys.

Best Practices for Managing Threats Within Your IT Infrastructure

There are many steps you can take to manage threats within your IT infrastructure. The following list represents steps that many IT security professionals consider best practices:

TIP

A security policy may include several individual policies. For example, it could include a password policy, an acceptable use policy, and a firewall policy.

NOTE

There is a subtle difference between the **principle of least privilege** and the **principle of need to know.** Privileges are associated with rights that grant a user authority to perform an action on a system, such as to shut it down or change the time. Need to know is associated with permissions assigned to files and folders. For example, read permission allows a user to open a file to read it.

- **Create a security policy**—Senior management identifies and supports the role of security, and creates a **security policy.** This policy provides a high-level overview of the goals of security but not details of how to implement security techniques. Managers use this policy to identify resources and create plans to implement the policy. Security policies are an important first step in reducing the impact from threats. Once the security policy is approved, it needs to be implemented and enforced.

- **Insurance**—Purchase insurance to reduce the impact of threats. Companies commonly purchase insurance for fire, theft, and losses to due to environmental events.

- **Use access controls**—Require users to authenticate. Grant users access only to what they need. This includes the following two principles:
  - *Principle of least privilege*—Grant users only the rights and privileges they need to perform their job and no more. This prevents users from accidentally or intentionally causing problems.
  - *Principle of need to know*—Grant users access only to the data they need to perform their job and no more. For example, a person may have a security clearance for Secret data. However, they don't automatically receive access to all Secret data. Instead, the person is granted access only to what they need for the job. This helps prevent unauthorized access.

- **Use automation**—Automate processes as much as possible to reduce human errors.

- **Include input validation**—Test data to determine if it is valid before any applications use it.

- **Provide training**—Use training to increase safety awareness and reduce accidents. You can also use training to increase security awareness to reduce security incidents.

- **Use antivirus software**—Make sure you install antivirus software on all systems. Schedule automatic virus definition updates to occur daily.

- **Protect the boundary**—Protect the boundary between the intranet and the Internet with a firewall, at a minimum. You can also use intrusion detection systems for an added layer of protection.

CSI Computer Crime and Security Survey 2009

The Computer Security Institute (CSI) completes an annual survey that identifies many of the trends related to IT security. A summary of the report is available for free download. Members of the CSI can download the full report at no charge.

Some of the notable findings in the 2009 report were:

- Losses due to financial fraud attacks increased from 12 percent to 19.5 percent.
- Denial of service (DoS) attacks increased from 21 percent to 29.5 percent
- Web defacement increased from 6 percent to 13.5 percent
- Password sniffing increased from 9 percent to 17.3 percent
- Wireless exploits were reduced to 7.6 percent from 14 percent.
- Twenty-five percent of the respondents felt that over 60 percent of their financial losses were due to employee user errors. These are losses from non-malicious employees.

The most expensive malicious incidents from any sources were identified as:

- Wireless exploits
- Theft of personally identifiable information (PII) or personal health information
- Financial fraud

Understanding and Managing Vulnerabilities

Chapter 1 provided an introduction to vulnerabilities. A vulnerability can be a weakness in an asset or the environment. You can also consider a weakness as a flaw in any system or any business process.

A vulnerability leads to a risk, but by itself it does not become a loss. The loss occurs when a threat exploits the vulnerability. This is also referred to as a threat/vulnerability pair. When the two are paired, a loss results.

Figure 2-1 shows the flow of a threat to a loss. You can use mitigation techniques to reduce the vulnerability, the loss, or both.

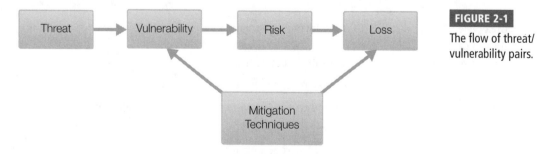

FIGURE 2-1

The flow of threat/ vulnerability pairs.

This section presents the following three topics:

- Threat/vulnerability pairs
- Vulnerabilities can be mitigated
- Mitigation techniques

Threat/Vulnerability Pairs

A **threat/vulnerability pair** occurs when a threat exploits a vulnerability. The vulnerabilities provide a path for the threat that results in a harmful event or a loss. It's important to know that both the threat and the vulnerability must come together to result in a loss.

Vulnerabilities depend on your organization. For example, if you're hosting public-facing servers, the servers have several potential weaknesses. However, if you don't have any public-facing servers, there aren't any vulnerabilities for the organization in this area. Thus, the risk is zero.

Table 2-1 shows some examples of threat/vulnerability pairs and the potential losses.

Table 2-1 only scratches the surface. The list of vulnerabilities for any single network can be quite extensive.

TABLE 2-1   Examples of threat/vulnerability pairs and potential losses.

THREAT	VULNERABILITY	HARMFUL EVENT OR LOSS
Fire	Lack of fire detection and suppression equipment	Can be total loss of business
Hurricane, earthquake, tornado	Location	Can be total loss of business
Malware	Lack of antivirus software Outdated definitions	Infection (impact of loss determined by payload of malware)
Equipment failure	Data not backed up	Loss of data availability (impact of loss determined by value of data)
Stolen data	Access controls not properly implemented	Loss of confidentiality of data
Denial of service (DoS) or distributed denial of service (DDoS) attack	Public-facing servers not protected with firewalls and intrusion detection systems	Loss of service availability
Users	Lack of access controls	Loss of confidentiality
Social engineer	Lack of security awareness	Loss depends on the goals and success of attacker

TABLE 2-2 Common threat/vulnerability pairs and possible mitigation steps.

THREAT	VULNERABILITY	MITIGATION
Fire	Lack of fire detection and suppression equipment	Install fire detection and suppression equipment Purchase insurance
Hurricane, earthquake, tornado	Location	Purchase insurance Designate alternate sites
Malware	Lack of antivirus software Outdated definitions	Install antivirus software Update definitions at least weekly
Equipment failure	Data not backed up	Backup data regularly Keep copies of backup off-site
Stolen data	Access controls not properly implemented	Implement both authentication and access controls Use principles of "need to know"
DoS or DDoS attack	Public-facing servers not protected with firewalls and intrusion detection systems	Implement firewalls Implement intrusion detection systems
Users	Lack of access controls	Implement both authentication and access controls
Social engineer	Lack of security awareness	Provide training Raise awareness through posters, occasional e-mails, and mini-presentations

2

Managing Risk

Vulnerabilities Can Be Mitigated

You can mitigate or reduce vulnerabilities, which reduces potential risk. The risk reduction comes from one of the following:

- Reducing the rate of occurrence
- Reducing the impact of the loss

It's rare that a threat is completely eliminated. Instead, it's more common that the risk is reduced to an acceptable level. As mentioned in Chapter 1, the remaining risk is referred to as the "residual risk." Table 2-2 matches the threat/vulnerabilities pairs from Table 2-1 with possible mitigation steps.

Mitigation Techniques

You can use a wide variety of mitigation techniques in any enterprise. As you explore the techniques in this section, keep the following elements in mind:

- The value of the technique
- The initial cost of the technique
- Ongoing costs

For example, antivirus software has an initial cost. This initial cost includes a subscription for updates for a period of time, such as a year. When the subscription expires, it must be renewed.

When estimating the value and cost of any of these techniques you can consider the value of the resource and the impact of the loss. For example, training in basic social engineering tactics may cost $10,000 a year. However, if users don't receive the training, the company may lose $100,000. The value of the training equates to $90,000.

There are other variables to consider when estimating the value of a mitigation technique. A company may have lost $100,000 last year. If people are trained, the company estimates it will only lose $5,000 this year. This would give a value of $85,000 to the training. This is calculated as: Last year's loss − training cost − this year's loss, or $100,000 −$10,000 − $5,000 = $85,000.

The following list identifies many common mitigation techniques you can use in any enterprise:

- **Policies and procedures**—Written policies and procedures provide standards. These standards make it clear what should be implemented and how. Many organizations start by creating a security policy as mentioned earlier. You should review policies and procedures on a regular basis.

- **Documentation**—Documentation is useful in a wide number of areas. Up-to-date documentation of networks makes problems easier to troubleshoot. Once problems occur, you can repair them more quickly. This results in improved availability times. As the network and systems change, you need to be sure to update documentation.

- **Training**—Training helps employees understand that security is everyone's responsibility. Some training is geared to all users; other training must be targeted to specific users. For example, you should train all end users about social engineers. Train administrators on current threats and vulnerabilities. Train management on risk management strategies. Training is an ongoing event—as things change, you should offer updated training classes.

- **Separation of duties**—The **separation of duties** principle ensures that any single person does not control all the functions of a critical process. It's designed to prevent fraud, theft, and errors. For example, accounting separates accounts receivable from accounts payable. One division accepts and approves bills. The other division pays the approved bills. You could say separation of duties also helps prevent conflicts of interest.

- **Configuration management**—When system configuration is standardized, systems are easier to troubleshoot and maintain. One method of **configuration management** is to use baselines. For example, you configure a system and then create a system image. You can deploy the image to 100 other systems, so every system is identical. Maintenance of each of these systems is the same. When technicians learn one system, they learn them all. Without a baseline, the systems may be configured 100 different ways. Technicians need to learn how each system is configured before they can provide effective support. Images are updated as the configuration changes.

  Configuration management also ensures that systems are not improperly modified. Most organizations have change management processes in place. This ensures that only authorized changes are made. Compliance auditing is done to ensure that unauthorized changes don't occur.

NOTE

Symantec's Ghost is a common tool used to deploy multiple clients. Ghost allows you to capture images and store them on DVD or on a Ghost casting server. You can then deploy the image to any client from the DVD. You can also cast the image to multiple clients simultaneously from the server.

- **Version control**—When multiple people work on the same document or the same application, data can be lost or corrupted. **Version control** systems are commonly used with the development of application. They track all changes and can reduce wasted time and effort, especially if changes had to be reversed. The process requires programmers to check out modules or files before modifying them. After the file is modified, it can be checked in and someone else can modify the file. Some version control software allows multiple changes to be merged into a single file.

- **Patch management**—Over time, you may discover bugs in software. Software bugs are vulnerabilities that can be exploited. When the bugs are discovered they are patched by vendors; however, attackers also find out about the bugs. Systems that aren't patched are vulnerable to attack. A comprehensive **patch management** policy governs how patches are understood, tested, and rolled out to systems and clients. It should also include compliance audits to verify that clients are current. Patch management can also include the ability to quarantine unpatched clients. Patch management is an almost continuous process.

NOTE

Microsoft releases patches on the second Tuesday of every month. This has become known as **Patch Tuesday**. When the patches aren't deployed, attackers can exploit the bugs.

- **Intrusion detection system**—An **intrusion detection system (IDS)** is designed to detect threats. It cannot prevent a threat. A passive IDS will log the event and may provide an alert. An active IDS may modify the environment to block the attack after it is detected. Many IDS systems use definitions the way antivirus software uses signatures. Network-based intrusion detection systems (NIDS) provide overall network protection. Host-based intrusion detection systems (HIDS) can protect individual systems.

- **Incident response**—When a company is prepared and able to respond to an incident, they have a better chance to reduce the impact. An important step when responding to an incident is containment, which ensures the incident doesn't spread to other systems. An incident response team tries to identify what happened. They look for the vulnerabilities that allowed the incident. They then seek ways to reduce the vulnerability in the future. On the other hand, some companies would like to quickly put the incident behind them. They try to fix the immediate issue without addressing the underlying problem. When you address an incident, the chance of its recurring are much lower.

- **Continuous monitoring**—Security work is never finished. Instead, you implement controls and then check and audit to ensure they are still in place. You deploy patches. Later, through compliance audits, you verify that all systems are patched. Through access controls you lock down systems and data. Later, you check to ensure they haven't been modified. You record a wide range of activity in logs and then monitor these logs for trends and suspicious events. Luckily there are many tools that you can use to audit and monitor systems within a network.

- **Technical controls**—Controls that use technology to reduce vulnerabilities. IT professionals implement the controls and computers enforce them. For example, after an IT professional installs antivirus software, the software prevents infections. Some other examples of **technical controls** include intrusion detection systems, access controls, and firewalls. As you discover new vulnerabilities you can implement new technical controls.

- **Physical controls**—**Physical controls** prevent unauthorized personnel from having physical access to areas or systems. For example, you should locate servers in server rooms and keep the server room doors locked. Place network devices in wiring closets and keep the wiring closet doors locked. Physical security can also include guards, cameras, and other monitoring equipment. For mobile equipment, such as laptops, you can use cable or hardware locks.

Best Practices for Managing Vulnerabilities Within Your IT Infrastructure

Vulnerabilities are the portion of the threat/vulnerability pair that you can control. Therefore, it's very important to take steps to manage vulnerabilities. Here are some of the best practices you can use to do this:

- **Identify vulnerabilities**—Chapter 1 described several tools you can use to identify vulnerabilities. For example, audits and system logs help identify weaknesses. Use all the available tools, and examine all seven domains of the typical IT infrastructure.

- **Match the threat/vulnerability pairs**—The vulnerabilities you want to address first are the ones that have matching threats. Some vulnerabilities may not have a matching threat. If so, the weakness may not need to be addressed. For example, you may have an isolated network used for testing that does not have any access to the Internet. Weaknesses that can be exploited only from Internet threats can't reach this network and may be ignored.

- **Use as many of the mitigation techniques as feasible**—Several mitigation techniques were listed in this section. It's certainly possible to use all of these techniques. Depending on your IT infrastructure, you may use more. With multiple techniques in place, you create multiple layers of security.
- **Perform vulnerability assessments**—Vulnerability assessments can help you identify weaknesses. You can perform them internally or hire external experts to perform them. Vulnerability assessments are covered in greater depth in Chapter 8.

Understanding and Managing Exploits

Losses occur when threats exploit vulnerabilities. If you want to reduce losses due to risks, you'll need to have a good understanding of what exploits are and how to manage them. This section covers the following topics:

- What an exploit is
- How perpetrators initiate an exploit
- Where perpetrators find information about vulnerabilities and exploits
- Mitigation techniques
- Best practices for managing exploits within your IT infrastructure

What Is an Exploit?

An **exploit** is the act of exploiting a vulnerability. It does so by executing a command or program against an IT system to take advantage of a weakness. The result is a compromise to the system, an application, or data. You can also think of an exploit as an attack executed by code.

In this context, an exploit primarily attacks a public-facing server. In other words, it attacks servers that are available on the Internet. Common servers are:

- Web servers
- Simple Mail Transport Protocol (SMTP) e-mail servers
- File Transfer Protocol (FTP) servers

Figure 2-2 shows how these public-facing servers are often configured in a network. They are placed within two firewalls configured as a **demilitarized zone (DMZ)**. A DMZ is also known as a buffer area, or a perimeter zone. The firewall connected to the Internet allows anyone to access these public-facing servers. The firewall connected to the internal network restricts traffic from the Internet.

Since the servers in the DMZ are public facing, they are accessible to anyone with a public Internet Protocol (IP) address. This includes attackers or black-hat hackers.

While internal servers are susceptible to attacks from employees, it isn't common for an employee to use an exploit to attack an internal server. Employees can attack and cause damage. However, it's much easier for an employee to steal data or perform acts of sabotage. An insider usually won't take the time to write a program to attack an internal system. Insiders have the advantage of at least some basic employee privileges and internal knowledge. It's also common that the internal network is trusted, so the company gives less attention to detecting threats or wrong behavior.

FIGURE 2-2

Public-facing servers
in a DMZ bounded
by two firewalls.

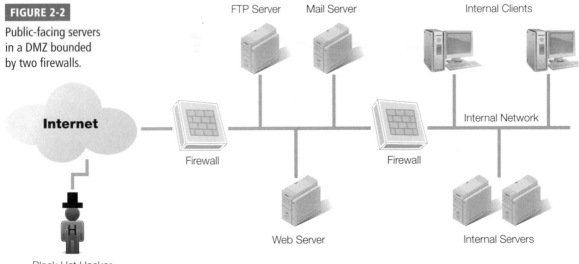

A **buffer overflow** is a common type of exploit. A buffer overflow can occur when an attacker sends more data or different data than a system or application expects. The vulnerability exists when the system or application is not prepared to reject it. This can cause the system to act unreliably. Additionally, if the exploit's creator was especially skilled, the exploit runs extra instructions, gaining the attacker additional privileges on a system.

> **NOTE**
>
> While a divide-by-zero error is simple to explain, it's unlikely this will cause a problem today. Most applications will detect the problem and never try to divide by zero. However, there are many more advanced errors that aren't predicted.

Normally, the system will validate data and reject data that isn't expected. Occasionally, a bug allows invalid data to be used.

For example, imagine a simple calculation: $X / Y = Z$. The program expects the value of X and Y to be provided. It will then divide the two to calculate the value of Z. However, if zero is given as the value of X or Y, Z cannot be calculated. You can't divide anything by zero. If the program didn't check to ensure that X and Y were valid numbers, the program could fail when zero is entered. If the error isn't handled gracefully, an attacker may be able to exploit the failure.

Buffer overflow errors allow attackers to insert additional data. This additional data can be malware that will remain in the system's memory until it's rebooted. It could insert a worm that spreads through the network. It could be code that seeks and destroys data on the system. It could cause the server to shut down and no longer be able to reboot.

When a vendor finds buffer overflow vulnerabilities, it patches the code to prevent the error in the future. You should download this patch and apply it to plug the hole.

The Nimda Virus

The Nimda virus is an example of an older virus that took advantage of a buffer overflow problem in Microsoft's Internet Information Services (IIS). This virus helps explain many of the lessons learned with IT risk management.

First, IIS was installed by default when Windows Server 2000 was installed. Since IIS was installed by default, it often wasn't managed. An unmanaged service is easier to attack.

When the buffer overflow was discovered, Microsoft released a patch. This patch corrected the problem as long as it was applied. However, patch management was in its infancy at that time. Many companies didn't have effective patch management programs, and many patches weren't applied. More so, a company may have wrongly concluded that since they weren't using IIS, it wasn't vulnerable.

Nimda was released on the Internet and had a multipronged approach. The buffer overflow allowed it to exploit an IIS system. It had a worm component that allowed it to seek and infect other systems on the internal network. It also looked for other IIS servers on the Internet susceptible to the same buffer overflow. Network activity slowed to a crawl and data was destroyed.

Two of the basic security practices that were reinforced by Nimda are:

- **Reduce the attack surface of servers**—Unneeded services and protocols should not be installed. If they have been installed, they should be removed. If IIS wasn't installed on a server, it couldn't have been attacked by Nimda.

- **Keep systems up to date**—If IIS servers had been updated with the released patch, they wouldn't have been susceptible to the attack.

Other exploits include:

- **SQL injection attacks**—SQL injection attacks take advantage of dynamic SQL. Many Web sites require users to enter data in a text box or Web address. If the user-supplied data is used directly in a SQL statement, a SQL injection attack can occur. Instead of giving the data that's expected, a SQL injection attack gives a different string of SQL code. This different code can compromise the database. SQL injection attacks are easy to avoid by using parameters and stored procedures which first review the code. However, all database developers aren't aware of the risks.

> **NOTE**
>
> Structured Query Language (SQL) is the language used to query and modify databases. It has specific rules that you must follow. Dynamic SQL is a SQL statement that accepts input from a user directly. For example, the statement may be SELECT FROM Users Where LName = 'txt.Name'. In this example, the value of txt.Name is retrieved from the text box named *txt.Name* and used when the program is run. Permitting input directly from a user and without any input filtering is not recommended.

- **Denial of service (DoS) attacks**—Denial of service (DoS) attacks are designed to prevent a system from providing a service. For example, a **SYN flood attack** is very common. Normally TCP uses a three-way handshake to start a connection. A host sends a packet with the SYN flag set. The server responds with the SYN and ACK flags set. The host then responds with the ACK flag set to complete the handshake. In the SYN flood attack, the host never responds with the third packet. It's as if the host stuck out his hand to shake, the server put his hand out, and then the host pulled his hand away. The server is left hanging. When this is repeatedly done in a short time period, it consumes the server's resources and can cause it to crash.

- **Distributed denial of service (DDoS) attacks**—Distributed denial of service (DDoS) attacks are initiated from multiple clients at the same time. For example, many criminals and attackers run botnets from a command and control center. A botnet controls multiple hosts as "clones" or "zombies." These clones can be given a command at any time to attack, and they all attack at the same time. The attack could be as simple as constantly pinging the same server. If thousands of clients are pinging a server at the same time, it can't respond to other requests as easily.

How Do Perpetrators Initiate an Exploit?

Most exploits are launched by programs developed by attackers. The attackers create and run the programs against vulnerable computers.

You've probably heard about **script kiddies.** These are attackers with very little knowledge, sometimes just young teenagers. However, they can download scripts and small programs and launch programs. They don't have to be very intelligent about computers or even about the potential harm they can do. Some programs are so simple, the script kiddie can just enter an IP address and click Go to launch an attack.

However, the attackers most companies are worried about are much more sophisticated. They have programming skills. They know how to target specific servers. They know methods to infiltrate networks. They erase evidence to cover their tracks. They are professional attackers.

Imagine a country hostile to the United States with extensive computer expertise. They could create their own internal secret department with separate divisions. Each division could be assigned specific jobs or tasks. Each of the divisions could work together to launch exploits as soon as they become known. This department could have the following divisions:

- **Public server discovery**—Every system on the Internet has a public IP address. This division could use ping scanners to identify any systems that are operational with public IP addresses. IP addresses are assigned geographically, so servers can also be mapped to geographical locations.

- **Server fingerprinting**—This division could use several methods to learn as much about the server as possible. They can use a ping to identify if the systems are running UNIX or Microsoft operating systems. They can use port scans to identify what ports are open. Based on what ports are open, they can identify the running protocols. For example, port 80 is the well-known port for Hypertext Transfer Protocol (HTTP), so if port 80 is open, HTTP is probably running. If HTTP is running, it is probably a Web server. The department can use other techniques to determine if it's an Apache Web server or an IIS Web server.

- **Vulnerability discovery**—Investigators and hackers in this division could constantly be on the lookout for any new weaknesses. They could just try new things to see what can be done. They could lurk on newsgroups to hear about new bugs that aren't widely known. They could even subscribe to professional journals or read blogs by IT security experts. When they discover a vulnerability, it could be passed on to programmers or attackers to exploit.

- **Programmers**—Once vulnerabilities are discovered, programmers can write code or applications to exploit them. It could be just a few lines of code that are embedded into a Web page and downloaded when a user visits the Web site. It could be a virus that is released to exploit the weakness. It could be an application that is installed on zombie computers and made ready to be launched in a botnet.

- **Attackers**—Attackers initiate the exploit. For example, attackers may discover a new vulnerability for Apache servers. The attackers may want to target servers in Washington D.C. They could get a list of servers in D.C. running Apache from other divisions. They can then launch an attack on those servers. This group could regularly launch attacks on older weaknesses that are patched on most computers. Say they launch an attack on 10,000 computers. Even if they have only a 1 percent success rate, they've exploited 100 computers.

> **NOTE**
> Attackers often use diversion when launching attacks. Instead of launching the attack from their own computer, they will often take control of one or more other computers on the Internet. They then direct the attack from that remote-controlled computer.

This secret department in a hostile country is presented as fictitious. However, cyberattacks from one country against another are not fiction. The news reports cyberattacks regularly. If you wanted to commit cyberwarfare against a hostile country, how would you do so? It's very possible you would design a similar department with similar divisions.

Even if it is a single perpetrator launching an attack, the steps listed above would be separated. The attacker would take time through reconnaissance to learn as much about a target as possible. The attacker may develop a program to automate the attack. The actual attack is usually quick.

It's important to realize that attackers very often spend 100 percent of their work time on attacks. Since many attacks often return significant amounts of money, they aren't shy about working more than 40 hours a week. They take time to discover targets. They take time to identify weaknesses. They take time to plan the attacks. When the opportunity presents itself, they swoop in and attack just as quickly as an owl will attack a field mouse.

Where Do Perpetrators Find Information About Vulnerabilities and Exploits?

There are a surprising number of sources for perpetrators to learn about vulnerabilities and exploits. A primary source is from security professionals sharing information with each other.

Of course, when a security professional writes about or discusses an exploit, the danger is that they are educating the enemy. This leads some people to say that the weaknesses shouldn't be discussed at all. However, when nothing is said, systems are attacked without IT professionals having a clue about the vulnerabilities.

The general mindset that currently prevails is that the vulnerabilities should be discussed with a focus on mitigation. In other words, don't publicly share so often the details on how to exploit a vulnerability. However, freely share the details on how to prevent the vulnerability.

Even sharing details about how to prevent a vulnerability, however, provides the attackers with information. They can use this to learn the weakness and exploit it. However, the alternative is worse. If information on how to reduce the weakness isn't shared, more systems will be wide open.

The following list identifies some sources that attackers can use to gain information.

- **Blogs**—Many security professionals regularly blog about their findings. When they suspect vulnerabilities, they often discuss them. Many full-time security professionals are cautious about what they post. They realize they have a mixed audience and try to avoid giving too many details.

- **Forums**—IT and security professionals often share ideas on different forums. Sometimes a user has a problem they don't understand, so the problem is posted on the forum. Some of these problems expose vulnerabilities that can be exploited.

- **Security newsletters**—Many security newsletters are regularly released to anyone on the e-mail list. Anyone can sign up. While the company uses a newsletter to advertise and promote their products, there is sometimes valuable content about threats and potential vulnerabilities. Even the newsletters published by the U.S. government can be used by attackers. Some of these newsletters are discussed later in this chapter, including how to subscribe.

- **2600: Hacker quarterly**—You can subscribe to this or pick up the printed version in some bookstores. They frequently include code and details that can be used to exploit vulnerabilities.

- **Common Vulnerabilities and Exposures (CVE) list**—The CVE is discussed in more detail later in this chapter. When someone discovers a vulnerability it can be submitted to the MITRE Corporation for inclusion in this list. The entry about the vulnerability will include information on resources where more details on the vulnerability can be learned.

- **Reverse engineering**—Patch Tuesday was mentioned earlier as the day that Microsoft releases patches. It is the second Tuesday of every month. The day after is known as **Exploit Wednesday** by some. Attackers often reverse-engineer the patches to discover the vulnerability. Once the weakness is understood, exploits are written to attack the weakness.

> **NOTE**
>
> Many corporate clients of Microsoft have advance notice that patches will be released. This allows the companies to perform advance testing of the patches. When the patches are formally released, the companies are ready to apply them immediately.

A good philosophy to adopt is this: If a known vulnerability exists, a bad guy knows about it. Remember, it only takes one bad guy who knows about the vulnerability to attack an unprotected system. You must protect all of the systems to stay protected.

Mitigation Techniques

Mitigation techniques are the individual steps you need to take to protect any system that is vulnerable. Together these steps are often referred to as **hardening a server.** Hardening a server makes it more secure from the default installation.

Some of the specific mitigation techniques you can take to protect public-facing servers are:

- **Remove or change defaults**—If an operating system or application has any defaults, ensure they are removed or changed as soon as the system is installed, for example, default passwords. It's also common to change the name of privileged accounts such as the Administrator account to prevent attempts to guess the password.

- **Reduce the attack surface**—The **attack surface** refers to how much can be attacked on a server. For example, if 10 services are running on a server, but you only need 7, you can reduce the attack surface by disabling the remaining 3 services. The overall attack surface is reduced by removing all unneeded services and protocols. If a service isn't needed it should be disabled. If the protocol isn't needed it should be removed. Every service and protocol that is running adds more risk to the system. When you remove unneeded ones, you reduce the risk without impacting the quality of the service.

- **Keep systems up to date**—Use a patch management system to ensure that systems are patched. Patches should be applied as quickly as possible after they are released. Every hour that passes gives the attackers more time to reverse engineer the patch and begin their attacks. Compliance audits can be used to ensure that patches are received and applied to all systems.

- **Enable firewalls**—Firewalls forming a DMZ filter traffic coming into the DMZ. However, you can also enable individual firewalls on each server as an added layer of protection.

- **Enable intrusion detection systems (IDSs)**—An active IDS can detect attacks and take steps to stop them.

- **Install antivirus software**—Antivirus software should be installed on all systems, including servers, even before they are first connected to the network. Many servers require different versions of antivirus software. For example, a Microsoft Exchange mail server needs a specialized version of antivirus software so the mail stores can be examined.

Best Practices for Managing Exploits Within Your IT Infrastructure

There are several best practices you can use to reduce your risks from exploits. Many of these are directly related to basic risk management practices.

- **Harden servers**—Methods were mentioned in the previous section. They include basic steps such as reducing the attack surface and keeping systems up to date.
- **Use configuration management**—Ensure systems are configured with consistent security settings. Use security baselines to ensure systems are configured the same way. A security baseline can come from an image created with a tool like Symantec's Ghost. You can also achieve it by applying settings to all systems with technology like Microsoft's Group Policy. Perform compliance audits to ensure that systems stay configured the same way.
- **Perform risk assessments**—These allow you to learn about the relevant threats and vulnerabilities. You can then identify and evaluate countermeasures. Risk assessments are covered in more depth in Part 2 of this book.
- **Perform vulnerability assessments**—Vulnerability assessments were mentioned earlier in this chapter. You can also use them as a best practice to manage exploits.

U.S. Federal Government Risk Management Initiatives

The U.S. federal government has taken many steps to help companies manage IT risks. The initiatives covered in this section are:

- The National Institute of Standards and Technology (NIST)
- The Department of Homeland Security (DHS)
- The National Cyber Security Division
- The United States Computer Emergency Readiness Team (US-CERT)
- The MITRE Corporation and the CVE list

Figure 2-3 shows the relationships among many of these organizations. There are two primary paths: One is under the U.S. Department of Commerce. The other is under the Department of Homeland Security.

NIST is directly under the Department of Commerce. The Information Technology Laboratory (ITL), part of NIST, publishes special publications. The Department of Homeland Security includes the Office of Cyber Security and Communications. Within this office is the National Cyber Security Division. The National Cyber Security Division provides funding for the civilian company the MITRE Corporation. MITRE maintains the Common Vulnerabilities and Exposures list. The US-CERT is located within the National Cyber Security Division.

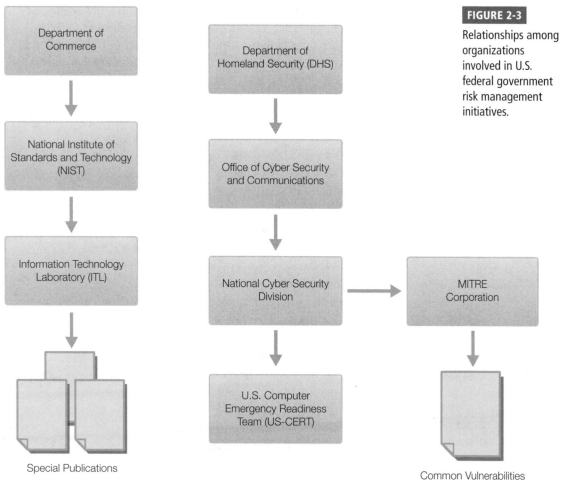

FIGURE 2-3

Relationships among organizations involved in U.S. federal government risk management initiatives.

2

Managing Risk

National Institute of Standards and Technology

The **National Institute of Standards and Technology (NIST)** is a division of the U.S. Department of Commerce. NIST's mission is to promote U.S. innovation and industrial competiveness. It does this by advancing measurement science, standards, and technology.

NIST includes the Information Technology Laboratory (ITL). ITL develops standards and guidelines. The goal is improved security and privacy of information on computer systems.

> **NOTE**
>
> ITL and ITIL are two different programs. The Information Technology Infrastructure Library (ITIL) was developed by the United Kingdom (UK). It is managed by the UK Office of Government Commerce (OGC). ITIL is a collection of books that provide guidance and best practices for the successful operation of IT. ITIL is presented in the Standards and Guidelines section of Chapter 3 of this book. The ITL managed by NIST is a U.S. program.

The Special Publication 800 (SP 800) series includes several reports that document ITL's work. It includes research, guidance, and outreach efforts in computer security. It is intended to be a collaborative effort combining the work of industry, government, and academic organizations. Many of the publications in the SP 800 series are available on the Internet.

The following list includes some of these. They are numbered sequentially. Lower numbered publications are older; higher numbered publications are newer. The newer publications are listed here first:

- SP 800-124, "Guidelines on Cell Phone and PDA Security"
- SP 800-123, "Guide to General Server Security"
- SP 800-121, "Guide to Bluetooth Security"
- SP 800-118, "Guide to Enterprise Password Management"
- SP 800-115, "Technical Guide to Information Security Testing and Assessment"
- SP 800-100, "Information Security Handbook: A Guide for Managers"
- SP 800-94, "Guide to Intrusion Detection and Prevention Systems"
- SP 800-61, "Computer Security Incident Handling Guide"
- SP 800-55, "Performance Measurement Guide for Information Security"
- SP 800-51, "Use of the Common Vulnerabilities and Exposures (CVE) Vulnerability Naming Scheme"

> **NOTE**
>
> You can access the full list of Special Publications including links to all of them from the NIST Web site at: *http://csrc.nist.gov/publications/PubsSPs.html*

- SP 800-50, "Building an Information Technology Security Awareness and Training Program"
- SP 800-40, "Creating a Patch and Vulnerability Management Program"SP 800-30, "Risk Management Guide for Information Technology Systems"
- SP 800-12, "An Introduction to Computer Security: The NIST Handbook"

Department of Homeland Security

The **Department of Homeland Security (DHS)** is responsible for protecting the United States from threats and emergencies. Its primary goal is to keep America safe, and it focuses on protecting the United States from terrorist attacks. DHS is also responsible for responding to natural disasters, such as hurricanes and earthquakes.

Congress passed the Homeland Security Act of 2002 in November 2002. This act established the DHS. The Homeland Security Act of 2002 and the DHS were created in response to the terrorist bombings of September 11, 2001.

The DHS includes many agencies. Some of them are:

- United States Secret Service
- United States Coast Guard
- U.S. Immigration and Customs Enforcement
- U.S. Customs and Border Protection
- Federal Emergency Management Agency

National Cyber Security Division

The **National Cyber Security Division (NCSD)** is a division of the Department of Homeland Security. It works together with private, public, and international parties to secure cyberspace and America's cyberassets.

NCSD oversees the National Cyberspace Response System. This includes the following programs:

> **NOTE**
>
> Cyber generally refers to any computer assets, but usually refers to assets on the Internet. The global network of computers on the Internet is commonly referred to as "cyberspace." Cyberwarfare, or cyberwar, refers to the attacks and counterattacks carried out against other countries or other companies.

- **Cybersecurity Preparedness and the National Cyber Alert System**—This is an e-mail alert system that allows you to subscribe to different types of e-mails.
- **United States Computer Emergency Readiness Team (US-CERT) Operations**— This division is tasked with analyzing and reducing cyberthreats and vulnerabilities. As issues become known, US-CERT disseminates information and can coordinate incident response activities. See below for more information about US-CERT.
- **National Cyber Response Coordination Group**—This group includes 13 federal agencies. Their goal is to be able to respond to nationally significant cyberattacks. They will help coordinate the federal response to an incident, including any responses by law enforcement and the intelligence community.
- **Cyber Cop Portal**—This division within NCSD coordinates with law enforcement agencies. The goal is to share information to help capture and convict attackers. More than 5,000 investigators worldwide share data from the Cyber Cop Portal.

US Computer Emergency Readiness Team

The **United States Computer Emergency Readiness Team (US-CERT)** is a part of the National Cyber Security Division. US-CERT's primary mission is to provide response support and defense against cyber attacks. Its focus is on providing support for the federal civil executive branch of government, or any sites with a .gov domain name. However, US-CERT also collaborates and shares information with several other entities, including:

- State and local governments
- International partners
- Other federal agencies
- Other public and private sectors

Information gathered by US-CERT is shared with the public through several methods. These include their Web site, mailing lists, and Really Simple Syndication (RSS) channels.

You can sign up to receive e-mails and alerts from US-CERT from this link: *https://forms.us-cert.gov/maillists*. You can sign up for any or all of the following mailing lists:

- **Technical Cyber Security Alerts**—These alerts include timely information about current security issues, vulnerabilities, and exploits. Alerts are released as needed. They are written for system administrators and experienced users. You can view past alerts at: *http://www.us-cert.gov/cas/techalerts*

- **Cyber Security Bulletins**—These provide summaries of security issues and vulnerabilities from the previous week. They are published weekly and are written for system administrators and experienced users. You can view past bulletins at: *http://www.us-cert.gov/cas/bulletins*

- **Cyber Security Alerts**—These alerts are written for home, corporate, and new users. They are published as needed and include security issues that affect the general public. You can view past security alerts at: *http://www.us-cert.gov/cas/alerts*

- **Cyber Security Tips**—These tips are targeted to home, corporate, and new users. They are published every two weeks and provide tips on many security topics. You can view past security tips at: *http://www.us-cert.gov/cas/tips*

- **Current Activity Updates**—These provide information about high-impact types of security activity. Depending on current threats, these e-mails can be sent several times a day or several times a week. You can view past updates at: *http://www.us-cert.gov/current*

> **NOTE**
>
> One of the great benefits of the National Cyber Alert System is that the e-mails don't include advertisements. Also, because they are from the U.S. government, the information is not slanted to sell or promote specific products.

> **NOTE**
>
> MITRE is an acronym, but the initials are not relevant. Many of the original employees came from the Massachusetts Institute of Technology (MIT). These employees work on research and engineering (RE). However, MITRE is not a part of MIT.

The MITRE Corporation and the CVE List

The MITRE Corporation manages four Federally Funded Research and Development Centers (FFRDCs). These FFRDCs conduct research for several major departments of the U.S. government.

The MITRE Corporation maintains the CVE list. MITRE is the editor of the list and is responsible for assigning numbers. The National Cyber Security Division of the U.S. Department of Homeland Security sponsors the CVE.

Common Vulnerabilities and Exposures (CVE) List

The CVE is an extensive list of known vulnerabilities and exposures. As new discoveries are made, they are submitted as candidates for the list. The primary benefit of the list is standardized naming and descriptions.

Before the CVE, one company may have addressed a problem as Exploit234a. The same problem could have been addressed by another company as X42A. Both companies may have published papers regarding the same problem, but it was difficult to determine if one problem was different from the other.

The CVE provides one name for any single vulnerability or exposure. Additionally, each named issue receives one standardized description. CVE entries also provide references to additional information.

The following example shows how a CVE is formatted:

- **Name**—CVE-2001-1240
- **Description**—The default configuration of sudo in Engarde Secure Linux 1.0.1 allows any user in the admin group to run certain commands that could be leveraged to gain full root access.
- **Statu**s—Entry
- **Reference**—ENGARDE:ESA-20010711-02
- **Reference**—URL:*http://www.linuxsecurity.com/advisories/other_advisory-1493.html*
- **Reference**—URL:*http://www.osvdb.org/5440*

When an entry is initially added to the CVE list, the entry has a status of "candidate." After the entry has been reviewed and accepted, its status is changed to "entry." The CVE Editorial Board, composed of representatives from multiple security-related organizations, reviews all entries.

> **NOTE**
> MITRE maintains the list at: *http://cve.mitre.org*

Standard for Information Security Vulnerability Names

The CVE is considered the standard for information security vulnerability names. MITRE launched the CVE in 1999, and it was quickly embraced. Some of the relevant milestones are:

- **Year 2000**—Over 40 products declared compatible with CVE. CVE is used by 29 organizations.
- **Year 2001**—Over 300 products and services declared compatible. CVE is used by more than 150 companies.
- **Year 2002**—NIST recommends use of CVE by U.S. agencies. NIST SP 800-51, Use of the Common Vulnerabilities and Exposures (CVE) Vulnerability Naming Scheme, is released.
- **Year 2003**—CVE Compatibility process started. This allows products and services to achieve official compatibility status.
- **Year 2004**—U.S. Defense Information Systems Agency (DISA) requires use of products that use CVE identifiers.

The FBI/SANS Top 20 List of the Most Critical Internet Security Vulnerabilities also references the CVE list.

2

Managing Risk

CHAPTER SUMMARY

Threats are always present and can't be eliminated. You reduce the potential for a threat to do harm, or you reduce the impact of a threat, but not the threat itself. However, you can take many steps to reduce vulnerabilities. The most important vulnerabilities are those that are likely to match up as a threat/vulnerability pair. Once you identify likely threat/vulnerability pairs, you can implement mitigation techniques.

The U.S. federal government has many resources that organizations can use to manage risk. The National Institute of Standards and Technology (NIST) has published several Special Publications. The SP 800 series includes many publications targeted for IT security. The Department of Homeland Security also has many divisions focused on IT security. Their resources are freely available to IT and security professionals.

KEY CONCEPTS AND TERMS

Attack surface
Buffer overflow
Configuration management
Continuous monitoring
Demilitarized zone (DMZ)
Denial of service (DoS)
Department of Homeland
  Security (DHS)
Distributed denial of service
  (DDos)
Exploit
Exploit Wednesday

Hardening a server
Intentional threats
Intrusion detection system (IDS)
National Cyber Security Division
  (NCSD)
National Institute of Standards
  and Technology (NIST)
Patch management
Patch Tuesday
Physical controls
Principle of least privilege
Principle of need to know

Script kiddie
Security policy
Separation of duties
SQL injection attack
SYN flood attack
Technical controls
Threat/vulnerability pair
Unintentional threats
United States Computer
  Emergency Readiness Team
  (US-CERT)
Version control

CHAPTER 2 ASSESSMENT

1. What is a security policy?

A. A rigid set of rules that must be followed explicitly to be effective

B. A technical control used to enforce security

C. A physical control used to enforce security

D. A document created by senior management that identifies the role of security in the organization

2. You want to ensure that users are granted only the rights to perform actions required for their jobs. What should you use?

A. Principle of least privilege

B. Principle of need to know

C. Principle of limited rights

D. Separation of duties

3. You want to ensure that users are granted only the permissions needed to access data required to perform their jobs. What should you use?

A. Principle of least privilege

B. Principle of need to know

C. Principle of limited rights

D. Principle of limited permissions

4. Which of the following security principles divides job responsibilities to reduce fraud?

A. Need to know

B. Least privilege

C. Separation of duties

D. Mandatory vacations

5. What can you use to ensure that unauthorized changes are not made to systems?

A. Input validation

B. Patch management

C. Version control

D. Configuration management

6. What are two types of intrusion detection systems?

A. Intentional and unintentional

B. Natural and manmade

C. Host-based and network-based

D. Technical and physical

7. A technical control prevents unauthorized personnel from having physical access to a secure area or secure system.

A. True

B. False

8. What allows an attacker to gain additional privileges on a system by sending unexpected code to the system?

A. Buffer overflow

B. MAC flood

C. Input validation

D. Spiders

9. What is hardening a server?

A. Securing it from the default configuration

B. Ensuring it cannot be powered down

C. Locking it in a room that is hard to access

D. Enabling necessary protocols and services

10. Which of the following steps could be taken to harden a server?

A. Removing unnecessary services and protocols

B. Keeping the server up to date

C. Changing defaults

D. Enabling local firewalls

E. All of the above

11. Which government agency includes the Information Technology Laboratory and publishes SP 800-30?

A. NIST

B. DHS

C. NCSD

D. US-CERT

12. ITL and ITIL are different names for the same thing.

A. True

B. False

2

Managing Risk

13. Which U.S. government agency regularly
publishes alerts and bulletins related to security
threats?

A. NIST
B. FBI
C. US-CERT
D. The MITRE Corporation

14. The CVE list is maintained by _____.

15. What is the standard used to create Information
Security Vulnerability names?

A. CVE
B. MITRE
C. DISA
D. CSI

Maintaining Compliance

MANY LAWS AND REGULATIONS ARE IN PLACE regarding the protection of IT systems. Companies have a requirement to comply with the laws that apply to them. The first step is to understand the laws. You're not expected to be a lawyer, but you should understand the basics of relevant laws.

Once you have an idea of which laws and regulations apply, you can then dig in deeper to ensure your organization is in compliance. The cost of not complying can sometimes be expensive. Fines can be in the hundreds of thousands of dollars. Some offenses can result in jail time.

Chapter 3 Topics

This chapter covers the following topics and concepts:

- What compliance is
- What U.S.-based laws related to compliance exist
- What some relevant regulations related to compliance are
- What organizational policies for compliance should be considered
- What standards and guidelines for compliance exist

Chapter 3 Goals

When you complete this chapter, you will be able to:

- Define compliance
- Describe the purpose of FISMA
- Identify the purpose and scope of HIPAA
- Describe GLBA and SOX, and the impact for IT
- Describe the purpose of FERPA
- Identify the purpose and scope of CIPA
- List some federal entities that control regulations related to IT
- Describe the purpose of PCI DSS
- Describe the contents of SP 800-30
- Describe the purpose of COBIT
- Describe the purpose of ISO and identify some relevant security standards
- Identify the purpose of ITIL
- Identify the purpose of CMMI

Compliance

Many laws exist in the United States related to information technology (IT). Companies affected by the laws are expected to comply with the laws. This is commonly referred to as **compliance**.

Many organizations have internal programs in place to ensure they remain in compliance with relevant laws and regulations. These programs commonly use internal audits. They can also use certification and accreditation programs. When compliance is mandated by law, external audits are often done. These external audits provide third-party verification that the requirements are being met.

An old legal saying is "ignorance is no excuse." In other words, you can't break the law and then say "I didn't know." The same goes for laws that apply to any organization. It's important for any organization to know what the relevant laws and regulations are.

You aren't expected to be an expert on any of these laws. However, as a manager or executive, you should be aware of them. You can roll any of the relevant laws and regulations into a compliance program for more detailed checks.

This section covers the following U.S. laws:

- Federal Information Security Management Act (FISMA) 2002
- Health Insurance Portability and Accountability Act (HIPAA) 1996
- Gramm-Leach-Bliley Act (GLBA) 1999
- Sarbanes-Oxley Act (SOX) 2002
- Family Educational Rights and Privacy Act (FERPA) 1974
- Children's Internet Protection Act (CIPA) 2000

Federal Information Security Management Act

The **Federal Information Security Management Act (FISMA)** was passed in 2002.
Its purpose is to ensure that federal agencies protect their data. It assigns specific
responsibilities for federal agencies.

Agencies are responsible for:

- **Protecting systems and data**—Agency heads are responsible for all the systems
  and data in their agencies.

- **Complying with all elements of FISMA**—FISMA includes details on how to protect
  systems and data. You must inventory systems. You must also do risk assessments
  to categorize systems and data. You can use different security controls based on
  risk levels. Systems must go through a certification and accreditation process.

- **Integrating security in all processes**—Use security throughout the agency.
  Do continuous monitoring to ensure the systems stay secure.

FISMA requires annual inspections. Each year, agencies must have an independent
evaluation of their program. The goal is to determine the effectiveness of the program.
These evaluations are to include:

- **Testing for effectiveness**—Policies, procedures, and practices are to be tested.
  This evaluation doesn't test every policy, procedure, and practice. Instead,
  a representative sample is tested. What is tested should be a realistic sample.

- **An assessment or report**—This report identifies the
  agency's compliance. It lists compliance with FISMA. It
  also lists compliance with other standards and guidelines.

Health Insurance Portability and Accountability Act

The **Health Insurance Portability and Accountability Act (HIPAA)**
was passed in 1996. It ensures that health information data
is protected. Before HIPAA, personal medical information was
often available to anyone. Security to protect the data was lax,
and the data was often misused.

> ▶ **NOTE**
>
> HIPAA may sound as if it applies
> only to the health care industry,
> but that's not true. Some employers
> offer health insurance, whose
> applications may include health
> information. Health plan entities
> such as Medicaid that help pay
> for medical coverage must also be
> compliant. So must medical records
> that insurance agents must check.

Chapter 2 addressed the CSI Computer Crime and Security Survey of 2009. It identifies many of the trends in IT security. Some of this data helps to show the impact of HIPAA. The following data was gathered from survey respondents:

- Only 7.7 percent were in the health services industry.
- More than 57 percent had to comply with HIPAA.
- HIPAA applies more than any other single law or regulation.

If your organization handles health information, HIPAA applies. This makes the definition of health information very important. HIPAA defines health information as any data that:

▶ NOTE

Title I of HIPAA relates to insurance portability. It identifies rules for insurance plans. For example, when an employee changes jobs, HIPAA helps employees retain insurance. Title I rules aren't related to IT compliance. Only Title II of HIPAA covers the protection of data.

- Is created or received by:
  - Health care providers
  - Health plans
  - Public health authorities
  - Employers
  - Life insurers
  - Schools or universities
  - Health care clearinghouses
- And relates to the health of an individual, including:
  - Past, present, or future health
  - Physical health, mental health, or condition of an individual
  - Past, present, or future payments for health care

Title II of HIPAA includes a section titled "Administrative Simplification." This section includes the requirements and standards of HIPAA for IT. It includes:

- **Security standards**—Every organization that handles health information must protect it. Companies must also protect systems that handle the information. This includes any health data the organization creates, receives, or sends. Specific standards are to be used for:
  - Storage of data
  - Use of data
  - Transmission of data
- **Privacy standards**—Data must not be shared with anyone without the express consent of the patient. If you've ever gone to a doctor's office or hospital, you've probably signed a consent form. It also informs you of practices used to keep your health information private.
- **Penalties**—Penalties can be levied if the rules aren't followed:
  - *Mistakes*—Fines can be $100 per violation and up to $25,000 per year for mistakes.

FIGURE 3-1
HIPAA compliance.

- *Knowingly obtaining or releasing data*—Penalties can be as high as $50,000 and one year in prison.
- *Obtaining or disclosing data under false pretenses*—Penalties can be as high as $100,000 and five years in prison.
- *Obtaining or disclosing data for personal gain or malicious harm*— Penalties can be as high as $250,000 and 10 years in prison.

If your organization includes data covered by HIPAA, it's important to have a plan. Figure 3-1 shows the process of creating a HIPAA compliance plan.

- **Assessment**—An assessment helps you identify if your organization is covered by HIPAA. If it is, you then identify what data you need to protect.
- **Risk analysis**—A risk analysis helps to identify the risks. In this phase, you analyze how your organization handles data. For example, do you only store data or do you also transfer it electronically?
- **Plan creation**—After you identify the risks, you create a plan. This plan includes methods to reduce the risk.
- **Plan implementation**—You put the plan into place.
- **Continuous monitoring**—Security in depth requires continuous monitoring. Monitor regulations for changes. Monitor risks for changes. Monitor the plan to ensure it is still used.
- **Assessment**—Conduct regular reviews. These ensure the organization remains in compliance.

Gramm-Leach-Bliley Act

The **Gramm-Leach-Bliley Act (GLBA)** was passed in 1999. It is also known as the Financial Services Modernization Act. GLBA is broad in scope. Most of it relates to how banking and insurance institutions can merge.

However, two parts of GLBA are relevant to IT security. They apply to financial institutions in the United States. They are:

- **Financial Privacy Rule**—This rule requires companies to notify customers about their privacy practices. You've probably received a notification from your bank. If you have a credit card, you received one from the credit card company. It explains how the bank or company collects and shares data.

- **Safeguards Rule**—Companies must have a security plan to protect customer information. This plan should ensure data isn't released without authorization. It should also ensure data integrity. Companies are responsible to ensure risk management plans are used. All employees must be trained on security issues.

Sarbanes-Oxley Act

The **Sarbanes-Oxley Act (SOX)** was passed in 2002. This law applies to any company that is publicly traded. It is designed to hold executives and board members personally responsible for financial data. If the data is not accurate, they can be fined and go to jail.

The goal is to reduce fraud. Because individuals can be held liable, there is more pressure to ensure the reported data is accurate. Chief executive officers (CEOs) and chief financial officers (CFOs) must be able to:

> **NOTE**
>
> SOX was passed in response to several large scandals. In these scandals, executives deliberately misled the public. Investors lost billions of dollars. For example, Enron was reportedly worth over $100 billion in 2000. It went bankrupt in 2001. It was later determined that the failure was due to fraud and corruption. Many senior officers and board members were directly involved.

- Verify accuracy of financial statements.
- Prove the statements are accurate.

Most of SOX is outside the direct scope of IT. However, Section 404 has some elements that are directly related. Section 404 pertains to the accuracy of data. It requires that a company use internal controls to protect the data.

Section 404 also requires reports from both internal and external auditors to verify compliance. For many companies, the cost of the audits represents the biggest impact of this law.

Family Educational Rights and Privacy Act

The **Family Educational Rights and Privacy Act (FERPA)** was passed in 1974. It has been amended at least nine times since then. The goal is to protect the privacy of student records. This includes education data and health data.

FERPA applies to all schools that receive any funding from the U.S. Department of Education. This includes:

- Any state or local educational agency
- Any institution of higher education
- Any community college
- Any school or agency offering a preschool program
- Any other education institution

FERPA grants rights to parents of students under 18. The parent can inspect records and request corrections. When the student reaches 18, these rights pass to the student.

All personally identifiable information (PII) about the student must be protected. Schools usually need permission from either the parent or the student to release PII.

There are a few exceptions to when PII can be accessed or released:

- Some school officials may view records.
- Data can be transferred to a new school if the student is transferred.
- Data can be transferred when some types of financial aid are used.
- Accrediting organizations can access data.
- Data can be accessed when required by a court.
- Data can be accessed for health and safety emergencies.

> **NOTE**
>
> PII is a common term used with information security. PII is any data that can be used to identify a person. PII can be a name, a Social Security number, biometric data, or any data used to identify a person. Several laws and regulations specify that PII must be protected.

Children's Internet Protection Act

The **Children's Internet Protection Act (CIPA)** was passed in 2000. It is designed to limit access to offensive content from school and library computers. Any school or library that receives funding from the E-Rate program is covered under CIPA.

CIPA requires that schools and libraries:

- Block or filter Internet access to pictures that are:
  - Obscene
  - Child pornography
  - Harmful to minors (if the computers are accessed by minors)
- Adopt and enforce a policy to monitor online activity of minors
- Implement an Internet safety policy addressing:
  - Access by minors to inappropriate content
  - Safety and security of minors when using e-mail and chat rooms
  - Unauthorized access
  - Unlawful activities by minors online
  - Unauthorized use of minors' personal information
  - Measures restricting minors' access to harmful materials

> **NOTE**
>
> The E-Rate program is a program under the Federal Communications Commission. It provides discounts to most schools and libraries for Internet access. Discounts range from 20 percent to 90 percent of the actual costs.

Using Proxy Servers to Limit Content

Most organizations use proxy servers as gateways to access the Internet. An organization configures its computers to use the proxy server. The proxy receives the request, retrieves the Web page from the Internet, and then serves the page to the client.

Proxy servers improve the level of service to clients. You can also use them to filter content. If an organization doesn't want employees to access certain content, the proxy server can block the requests to specific Web sites.

Third-party companies maintain lists of Web sites based on their content. They then sell subscriptions to these lists to any organization that wants them. For example, a company may want to restrict access to gambling sites from a work computer. The gambling list can be purchased and installed on the proxy server. The company can then block any attempts to access these sites.

Proxy servers also have the ability to log attempts by users to access unapproved sites. When a site is blocked, the user will often see a message like: "Warning. Access to this site is restricted by the acceptable use policy. Your activity is being monitored."

Similarly, schools or libraries can use proxy servers to filter content. The technology is widely available.

Some of these terms are difficult to determine, such as what is obscene or harmful to minors. CIPA includes a definitions section that identifies other specific sections of U.S. code where some of these terms are defined.

CIPA was challenged based on freedom of speech. The U.S. Supreme Court upheld the law in June 2003. All libraries were given until early 2004 to comply. At this point, it's expected that any school or library accepting E-Rate funds is complying with CIPA.

Regulations Related to Compliance

In addition to laws, there are several regulations that have created different U.S. entities. Most of these entities operate at the federal level.

Some of these entities have a direct impact on information technology (IT) initiatives for most companies. Others are related only to companies engaged in specific activities. Organizations covered in this section are:

- Securities and Exchange Commission (SEC)
- Federal Deposit Insurance Corporation (FDIC)
- Department of Homeland Security (DHS)
- Federal Trade Commission (FTC)
- State Attorney General (AG)
- U.S. Attorney General (U.S. AG)

Securities and Exchange Commission

The **Securities and Exchange Commission (SEC)** is a federal agency. It is charged
with regulating the securities industry. This includes any sales or trades of securities.
Securities include stocks, bonds, and options.

If your company is involved with the sale or trade of securities, you should be aware
of some laws. They are:

- Securities Act of 1933
- Securities Exchange Act of 1934
- Trust Indenture Act of 1939
- Investment Company Act of 1940
- Investment Advisors Act of 1940
- Sarbanes-Oxley Act of 2002

Many of these laws also apply if your company is a publicly traded company.
A "publicly traded company" is any company that has stock that outside investors
can buy and sell.

Federal Deposit Insurance Corporation

The **Federal Deposit Insurance Corporation (FDIC)** is a federal agency. It was created in
1933. The primary goal is to promote confidence in U.S. banks. The FDIC was created
as a direct result of the bank failures that occurred in the 1920s and early 1930s.
These failures led to the Great Depression.

Funds in any bank insured by the FDIC are guaranteed. Depositors will not lose
their money even if the bank goes bankrupt. The purpose is to prevent a run on a bank.
A "run on a bank" occurs when many depositors rush to withdraw their money.

Currently, funds for any individual depositor are insured to $250,000. This was
increased from $100,000 in 2007. It will return to $100,000 on January 1, 2014.

Department of Homeland Security

The Department of Homeland Security (DHS) is a federal agency. The DHS was discussed
in Chapter 2. It is responsible for protecting the United States from terrorist attacks.
It is also charged with responding to natural disasters.

The DHS was formed in 2002 as a direct response to the terrorist attacks of
September 11, 2001. It includes several divisions that are related to IT. These include:

- Office of Cyber Security and Communications
- National Cyber Security Division
- United States Computer Emergency Readiness Team (US-CERT)

Federal Trade Commission

The **Federal Trade Commission (FTC)** is a federal agency. It was created in 1914. The primary
goal is to promote consumer protection, but this has changed over the years.

3

Maintaining
Compliance

When the FTC was first created, the primary goal was to prevent unfair methods of competition. At that time, there were many special trusts in existence. These trusts were often engaged in anticompetitive practices, such as:

- Business monopolies
- Restraining trade
- Fixing prices

The creation of the FTC was one of many steps taken to "bust the trusts." Over the years, Congress has passed several consumer protection laws that the FTC enforces. These laws grant the FTC authority to address consumer protection and unfair competition issues.

At this point, the original trusts are gone. However, the FTC is still in existence and the focus has shifted to promote consumer protection.

Figure 3-2 shows the hierarchy of the FTC. As indicated in the figure, the FTC has three primary bureaus. These bureaus perform the following actions:

- **Bureau of Consumer Protection**—This bureau tries to protect consumers against unfair, deceptive, or fraudulent practices. The bureau enforces many consumer protection laws and trade regulation rules.

- **Bureau of Competition**—This bureau is the FTC's antitrust arm. It seeks to prevent anticompetitive actions. These actions include anticompetitive mergers and anticompetitive business practices.

- **Bureau of Economics**—This bureau helps the FTC evaluate the economic impact of FTC actions. It provides economic analysis for different investigations. It also evaluates the economic impact of government regulations.

The FTC also has several supporting offices that perform additional work in support of the FTC.

FIGURE 3-2

The Federal Trade Commission.

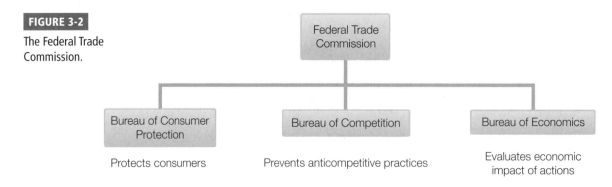

> **Power of Attorney**
>
> A power of attorney can be given to any individual to grant certain rights. For example, you can give a friend a power of attorney to sell your car in your absence. She can then legally act for you in the sale of the car.
>
> It's also possible to grant a general power of attorney. A general power of attorney allows one person to act for another for any legal issues. A general power of attorney is sometimes used if someone becomes mentally incapacitated.
>
> A state AG is a person who is granted the authority to represent the state in all legal matters. This is similar to how a general power of attorney is used. You can think of a state AG as a person granted a general power of attorney for the state.

State Attorney General

Every state has a state **Attorney General (AG)**. The AG is the primary legal advisor for the state. For many states, the AG is also the chief law enforcement officer. Although all states have an AG, the specific responsibilities can vary from state to state. For example, in some states the AG is tasked with specific IT issues, such as preventing identity theft.

The following are some of the responsibilities that can be assigned to an AG:

- Represents the state in all legal matters
- Defends the laws of the state
- Provides legal advice to all state entities
- Performs criminal investigations and prosecutes crimes as the chief law enforcement officer
- Reviews all deeds, leases, and contracts for the state
- Protects consumers by fighting ID theft and online scams
- Proposes legislation

Some AGs are elected. Others are appointed by the governor or other state officials.

U.S. Attorney General

The **U.S. Attorney General (U.S. AG)** is the head of the United States Department of Justice (DOJ). The President of the United States nominates the U.S. AG.

Specific responsibilities of the DOJ include:

- Enforcing the law
- Defending the interests of the United States according to the law
- Ensuring public safety against threats
- Providing federal leadership in preventing and controlling crime
- Seeking just punishment for those guilty of unlawful behavior
- Ensuring fair and impartial justice for all Americans

3

Maintaining Compliance

> **NOTE**
>
> "Intellectual property" is any intangible property that is the result of creativity and is produced by a person or company. Specific rights are granted to the owner of the creation. This includes music, programs, books, movies, trademarks, trade secrets, and more. The creator and owner should be able to reap the profits from the creation. However, when intellectual property rights are ignored, others benefit at the expense of the creator.

Many actions that the U.S. AG takes fall into the arena of IT. For example, the U.S. AG announced an intellectual property task force in February 2010. Companies, organizations, and governments often transfer data using intellectual property systems and networks. The goal is to address intellectual property crimes on the national and international level. Many government leaders agree that the theft of intellectual property does significant harm to the economy.

Organizational Policies for Compliance

Organizations often implement policies to ensure they remain compliant with different laws and regulations. These policies can contain multiple elements. However, in the context of this chapter, the most important element is **fiduciary responsibility**.

"Fiduciary" refers to a relationship of trust. A fiduciary could be a person who is trusted to hold someone else's assets. The trusted person has the responsibility to act in the other person's best interests. He or she should avoid conflicts of interest.

Once someone trusts a fiduciary, a fiduciary relationship exists. Notice that this requires two separate entities. The fiduciary responsibility can take many forms. Some examples of fiduciary responsibilities are:

- **An attorney and a client**—The client trusts the attorney to act in the best interests of the client.
- **A CEO and a board of directors**—The board trusts the CEO to act in the best interests of the company.
- **Shareholders and a board of directors**—Shareholders trust the board to act in the best interests of the shareholders.

A great deal of trust is granted in a fiduciary relationship. Because of this, the fiduciary is expected to take extra steps to uphold this trust. Two steps that can be taken are **due care** and **due diligence**:

- **Due diligence**—The fiduciary takes a reasonable amount of time and effort to identify risks. They investigate risks so they are understood. Failure to exercise due diligence can be considered negligence.
- **Due care**—If a risk is known, the fiduciary needs to take reasonable steps to protect against the risks. Failure to take due care to protect assets can also be considered negligence.

Exercising due care and due diligence doesn't mean that all risks should be eliminated. You may remember residual risk from Chapter 1. Residual risk is the amount of risk that remains after controls have been applied. It's also referred to as acceptable risk.

A fiduciary is expected to understand and weigh the risks. By exercising due care and due diligence, the fiduciary is less likely to be accused of acting recklessly or being negligent.

Other elements of an organizational policy could include:

- **Mandatory vacations**—Employees may be required to take an annual vacation of at least five consecutive days. The purpose of a **mandatory vacation** is to reduce fraud or embezzlement. If an employee is required to be out of the office, someone else must perform the duties. This increases the likelihood of discovering the illegal activities.

- **Job rotation**—Employees may be rotated through different jobs. When an employee is transferred into a new job, past transactions are often reviewed and examined. This oversight can uncover suspicious activity. **Job rotation** helps prevent or reduce fraudulent activity. Job rotation is also done for cross-training to expand the skills of employees.

- **Separation of duties**—This was mentioned in Chapter 2. It ensures that no single person controls an entire process. It helps prevent fraud, theft, and errors. It also prevents conflicts of interest.

- **Acceptable use**—An **acceptable use policy (AUP)** defines acceptable use for IT systems and data. Companies often inform employees of acceptable use when they are hired. Companies also sometimes use banners and logon screens to remind personnel of the policy.

Standards and Guidelines for Compliance

Several standards and guidelines exist that can be used to assess and improve security. Most of these standards are optional. However, some are mandatory for certain sectors. For example, the PCI DSS is required for merchants using specific credit cards.

The standards and guidelines covered in this section include:

- Payment Card Industry Data Security Standard (PCI DSS)
- National Institute of Standards and Technology (NIST)
- Generally Accepted Information Security Principles (GAISP)
- Control Objectives for Information and related Technology (COBIT)
- International Organization for Standardization (ISO)
- International Electrotechnical Commission (IEC)
- Information Technology Infrastructure Library (ITIL)
- Capability Maturity Model Integration (CMMI)
- Department of Defense (DoD) Information Assurance Certification and Accreditation Process (DIACAP)

Payment Card Industry Data Security Standard

The **Payment Card Industry Data Security Standard (PCI DSS)** is an international security standard. The purpose is to enhance security of credit card data. It was created by the PCI Security Standards Council with input from several major credit card companies. These companies include:

- American Express
- Discover Financial Services
- JCB International
- MasterCard Worldwide
- Visa Inc. International

The goal is to thwart theft of credit card data. Fraud can occur if a thief gets certain data. The key pieces of data are:

- Name
- Credit card number
- Expiration date
- Security code

Theft becomes easy if a thief has all of this information.

This data is often transmitted to and from the merchant. It can travel wirelessly from point-of-sale machines. It travels from the merchant's computer to an approval authority. It can be intercepted any time it's transmitted. It can be easily read if it is not encrypted.

For example, data from as many as 100 million credit cards was intercepted from a large retail chain between July 2005 and December 2006. Losses on Visa cards alone were close to $83 million. Millions of customers sued the retailer. The banks that issued the cards also sued the retailer. All of these problems could have been prevented with some basic security.

The PCI DSS is built around six principles. Each of these principles has one or two requirements. The principles and requirements are:

- **Build and Maintain a Secure Network**
  Requirement 1: Install and maintain a firewall.
  Requirement 2: Do not use defaults, such as default passwords.
- **Protect Cardholder Data**
  Requirement 3: Protect stored data.
  Requirement 4: Encrypt transmissions.
- **Maintain a Vulnerability Management Program**
  Requirement 5: Use and update antivirus software.
  Requirement 6: Develop and maintain secure systems.
- **Implement Strong Access Control Measures**
  Requirement 7: Restrict access to data.
  Requirement 8: Use unique logons for each user. Don't share user names and passwords.
  Requirement 9: Restrict physical access.

Credit Card Data Risky Behavior

The PCI Security Standards Council reports that many organizations take needless risks with credit card data. When an organization stores credit card data, it can be stolen. However, the data often does not need to be stored.

Consider a credit card transaction at a retailer. The retailer needs the name, card number, and expiration date. It sends these for approval. The retailer only needs to keep the amount of the charge and an approval number. It can discard the other data. However, if it keeps all the data this becomes a risk.

In 2007, Forrester Consulting was commissioned by RSA to conduct a PCI compliance survey of businesses in the United States and Europe. The survey found:

- 81 percent store credit card numbers.
- 73 percent store card expiration dates.
- 71 percent store card verification codes.
- 57 percent store data from the card's magnetic stripe.
- 16 percent store other personal data.

According to the Privacy Rights Clearinghouse, more than 234 million records have been breached since 2005. This sensitive data can be used to steal identities. It can also be used to fraudulently use credit cards.

On the other hand, if this data is not stored, the business is not at risk. Many merchants don't need to store the information. They can capture the data for a single transaction. When the transaction is complete, they can destroy the data.

- **Regularly Monitor and Test Networks**
  Requirement 10: Track and monitor all access to systems and data.
  Requirement 11: Regularly test security.

- **Maintain an Information Security Policy**
  Requirement 12: Maintain a security policy.

Merchants using credit cards are required to comply with PCI DSS. Compliance is monitored by the acquirer. This is the company that authenticates the transactions.

Compliance with PCI DSS is a three-step continuous process. This process is shown in Figure 3-3.

- **Assess**—The merchant inventories IT assets and processes used for credit card data. It identifies existing cardholder data. It then analyzes data and processes for vulnerabilities.

- **Remediate**—The merchant corrects vulnerabilities. It stores data only when necessary.

- **Report**—The merchant submits compliance reports to the acquiring banks.

This process is repeated at different times.

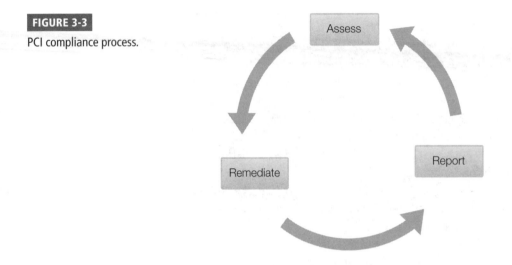

FIGURE 3-3

PCI compliance process.

National Institute of Standards and Technology

The National Institute of Standards and Technology (NIST) was mentioned in Chapter 2. It is a division of the U.S. Department of Commerce. The mission of NIST is to promote U.S. innovation and competiveness.

NIST hosts the Information Technology Laboratory (ITL). The ITL develops standards and guidelines related to IT. They are published as special publications whose titles have a prefix of SP. SP 800-30, "Risk Management Guide for Information Technology Systems," is valuable when studying risk management. It is subtitled "Recommendations of the National Institute of Standards and Technology." SP 800-30 was mentioned in both Chapters 1 and 2.

SP 800-30 includes five chapters:

- **Introduction**—This short chapter identifies the objectives and gives some references.
- **Risk Management Overview**—This chapter discusses the importance of risk management. It also mentions the system development life cycle (SDLC).
- **Risk Assessment**—This is the longest chapter. It gives ITL's definition of risk. It identifies nine steps that can be taken for risk assessment. These steps are:
  - Step 1: System characterization
  - Step 2: Threat identification
  - Step 3: Vulnerability identification
  - Step 4: Control analysis
  - Step 5: Likelihood determination
  - Step 6: Impact analysis
  - Step 7: Risk determination
  - Step 8: Control recommendations
  - Step 9: Results documentation

- **Risk Mitigation**—This chapter includes details on risk mitigation options and strategies. It talks about the types of controls you can take to reduce risks. It also has information on cost-benefit analysis and residual risk.

- **Evaluation and Assessment**—This short chapter talks about the need to repeat risk assessments. ITL recommends repeating them at least every three years. It also mentions some keys for the success of any risk management program.

Generally Accepted Information Security Principles

The Generally Accepted Information Security Principles (GAISP) is an older standard. It evolved from Generally Accepted System Security Principles (GASSP). GASSP was created in 1992. GAISP was an update to GASSP.

GAISP version 3 was released in August 2003. It was adopted by the Information Systems Security Association (ISSA). However, GAISP is no longer mentioned on the ISSA Web site. Additionally, the gaisp.org Web site is no longer maintained.

GAISP includes two major sections.

> **NOTE**
> GASSP and GAISP are no longer active. You may still see them mentioned in some documentation.

- **Pervasive principles**—These principles provide general guidance. The goal is to establish and maintain information security.

- **Broad functional principles**—These principles are derived from the pervasive principles. They represent broad goals of information security (IS).

Control Objectives for Information and Related Technology

Control Objectives for Information and related Technology (COBIT) is a set of good practices for IT management. It is designed to provide a framework for control of IT functions.

COBIT was written by the IT Governance Institute (ITGI) with ISACA. ISACA used to be known as the Information Systems Audit and Control Association. However, it now uses only the acronym. You can access many of the free COBIT resources from ISACAs Web site at: *http://www.isaca.org*.

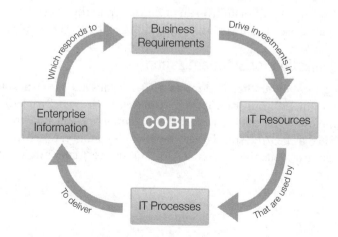

FIGURE 3-4

Basic COBIT principle.

The current version of COBIT is 4.1. It is a well-respected standard and is often referenced by other standards. For example, ITIL, which is covered later in this chapter, recommends the use of COBIT as a possible framework.

Figure 3-4 shows the basic COBIT principle. This principle helps reinforce that IT is in place to support business requirements. It's just as important to manage IT resources as it is to manage any other resources. The company needs information stored and delivered through IT resources to achieve its objectives.

- Business requirements drive investments in IT resources.
- IT resources are used by IT processes.
- IT processes deliver enterprise information.
- Enterprise information responds to business requirements.

The COBIT framework is organized in four IT domains and 34 IT processes. These domains are process oriented. In other words, they are focused on activities in the organization. Each of the four domains interacts with each other. The four domains are:

- **Plan and Organize**—This domain covers strategy and tactics. The organization compares IT resources against the strategic vision of the enterprise.
- **Acquire and Implement**—The organization purchases IT solutions and puts them into place. It compares changes against business objectives.
- **Deliver and Support**—The organization uses IT resources to deliver data and services. It compares services and business priorities. This helps ensure IT costs are acceptable. It also ensures that IT services are supporting business requirements as expected.
- **Monitor and Evaluate**—The organization uses metrics to detect problems early. It uses controls to ensure IT use is effective and efficient.

COBIT is extensive. The principles can't be implemented overnight and they require ongoing activities. However, COBIT can help an organization in the long term. It ensures that IT is being used to support the organization in the best possible manner.

International Organization for Standardization

The **International Organization for Standardization (ISO)** develops and publishes standards. It includes members from 159 countries. The main office is in Geneva, Switzerland.

ISO works with the International Electrotechnical Commission (IEC). Many of the standards are published as ISO/IEC standards. However, it's common to see the standards abbreviated as ISO. For example, the ISO/IEC 27002 standard is frequently shortened to ISO 27002.

ISO has published many standards that are relevant to risk and IT. Three important standards are:

- ISO 27002 Security Techniques
- ISO 31000 Principles and Guidelines on Implementation
- ISO 73 Risk Management—Vocabulary

You can purchase documentation for these standards from the *http://www.iso.org* Web site.

ISO 27002 Information Technology Security Techniques

ISO 27002 is a set of guidelines and principles. These are used for security management. The current version is ISO 27002:2005. It was derived from the British Standard (BS) 7799. It is a well-respected standard.

The ISO number has been changing over the years. The following list shows the history.

- **ISO/IEC 17799:2000**—The first ISO version of this document.
- **ISO/IEC 17799:2005**—An update to ISO/IEC 17799:2000.
- **ISO/IEC 17799:2005/Cor 1: 2007**—This is a one-correction document.
- **ISO/IEC 27002:2005**—This includes ISO/IEC 17799:2005 and ISO/IEC 17799:2005/Cor 1: 2007. The content is identical to 17799 but the number is changed to 27002.

> **NOTE**
>
> ISO/IEC 27002 is also commonly known as ISO 17799. The subtitle is "Code of Practice for Information Security Management." The reference number was formally changed in 2007 by ISO/IEC 17799:2005/Cor.1:2007.

> **NOTE**
>
> ISO standards can include the date of release in the ISO number. You can omit the date when citing the standard. For example, "ISO/IEC 27002:2005" indicates this standard was released in 2005. You can cite the same standard as "ISO/IEC 27002."

You can identify an organization as ISO 27002 certified. Certification requires a two-step process. First, the organization must implement certain best practices. Second, an outside source must evaluate the practices.

These best practices are related to:

- Security policy
- Organization of information security
- Asset management
- Human resources security
- Physical and environmental security
- Access control
- Incident management
- Business continuity
- Compliance

ISO 27002:2005 includes two parts labeled as Part I and Part II.

- Part I includes objectives and controls that an organization can use.
- Part II is used by an outside third party to evaluate an organization. If the organization meets Part II elements, the third party can certify it with ISO 27002. The third party can certify an organization using all of Part II or just a portion of Part II.

3

Maintaining
Compliance

ISO 31000 Risk Management Principles and Guidelines

ISO 31000:2009 provides generic guidance on risk management. It is not specific to any specific industry or sector. In other words, it doesn't apply only to IT.

An organization can use the principles and guidelines throughout its life. It can apply them to any type of risk.

There is no certification process for ISO 31000. For comparison, an organization can become ISO 27002 certified. There's no such thing as ISO 31000 certified.

Two supplementary documents associated with ISO 31000 are:

- ISO 73 Risk Management—Vocabulary
- IEC 31010 Risk Management—Risk Assessment Techniques

ISO 73 Risk Management—Vocabulary

ISO 73:2009 is a list of terms. These terms are related to risk management. The goal is to provide a common definition for terms used in risk management.

Definitions can be used by:

- Anyone managing risks
- Anyone involved in ISO and IEC activities
- Developers of other risk management standards and guides

ISO 73 refers to ISO 31000:2009 for principles and guidelines on risk management. Both ISO 73:2009 and ISO 31000:2009 were released at the same time.

International Electrotechnical Commission

The **International Electrotechnical Commission (IEC)** is an international standards organization. It prepares and publishes standards for electrical, electronic, and related technologies.

The overall objectives of the IEC are to:

- Meet the requirements of the global market.
- Ensure maximum use of its standards.
- Assess and improve products and services covered by its standards.
- Aid in interoperability of systems.
- Increase the efficiency of processes.
- Aid in improvement of human health and safety.
- Aid in protection of the environment.

The IEC has published "IEC 31010 Risk Management—Risk Assessment Techniques. This is a supporting standard for ISO 31000.

Information Technology Infrastructure Library

The **Information Technology Infrastructure Library (ITIL)** is a group of books developed by the United Kingdom's Office of Government Commerce (OGC). ITIL has been around since the 1980s and has improved and matured since then. The most recent version is known as ITIL v3 and was released in May 2007.

The UK recognized that some companies that were using IT were succeeding. Other companies using similar technologies were failing. One of the goals of ITIL was to document the differences. Early versions of ITIL identified best practices. These were proven activities or processes that were successful in many organizations.

In ITILv3 "best practice" was replaced with "good practice." A good practice is a proven, generally accepted practice. It isn't required in every organization. However, good practices are implemented whenever possible. ITIL recommends the use of several frameworks as good practices. Two of the frameworks recommend by ITIL are:

> **NOTE**
>
> ITIL is centered on services. A service is a means of delivering value to customers. It gives customers what they want. It doesn't require the customer to take ownership of the costs and risks. For example, e-mail is a service. Customers want to be able to send and receive e-mail. Most customers don't want to own and manage the e-mail servers. In this context, e-mail can be provided to employees from the IT department. The employees are the customers. The IT department is the service provider.

- Control Objectives for IT (COBIT), mentioned earlier in this section
- Capability Maturity Model Integration (CMMI), mentioned later in this section

ITILv3 Core is a collection of five books published by the United Kingdom's Office of Government Commerce (OGC). The books focus on the ITIL Core, or the ITIL life cycle.

The five books are:

- **Service Strategy**—The Service Strategy book helps an organization identify the services it should provide.

- **Service Design**—The Service Design book details how identified services can be implemented.

- **Service Transition**—Service Transition focuses on introducing the services. This also includes modifying or changing services. Most companies have learned the hard way that if changes aren't managed, changes can take systems down. Change management has become very important for many companies.

> **NOTE**
>
> One of the drawbacks to ITIL is the availability of materials. The five ITIL books have a retail cost of about $800.

- **Service Operation**—The Service Operation book focuses on day-to-day operations.

- **Continual Service Improvement**—The Continual Service Improvement book focuses on methodologies used to improve the services.

Figure 3-5 shows the relationships between the five phases of the ITIL life cycle. Any service implemented and managed within an IT organization will go through several phases. There are different concerns and requirements at each phase.

For example, consider e-mail as a provided service. Imagine that your company was moving from outsourced e-mail to an internal e-mail server. The company could use the ITIL Core for each phase of the implementation.

- **Service Strategy phase**—You evaluate services to determine if they have value to the organization. E-mail could provide value with improved sales. It could provide improved productivity due to better communication. If you determine that internal e-mail will provide value, the process continues to the next phase.

- **Service Design phase**—IT designs services for use within the organization. In this phase, you'd design your e-mail solution. For example, your IT network may be a Microsoft Windows domain, so you would design a Microsoft Exchange solution. You would identify how many servers to add and any changes needed in the network to support them.

- **Service Transition phase**—This phase includes adding and modifying services. It also includes removing obsolete services. A primary goal of this phase is to ensure the transition does not cause an outage. Adding a Microsoft Exchange e-mail solution, for example, would include several elements. You would need to modify the Active Directory schema. You may need to add global catalog servers. You would build Microsoft Exchange servers. You would install applications on user computers. You would provide training to everyone from end-users to technicians maintaining the new servers.

FIGURE 3-5

ITIL life cycle.

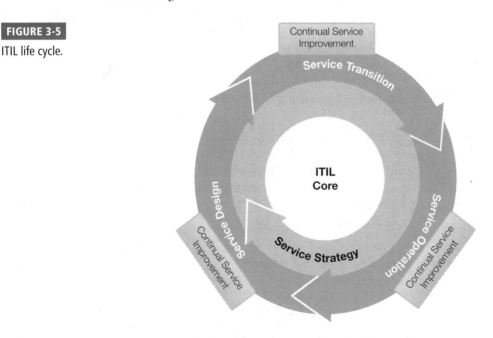

ITIL Certifications

More and more organizations are recognizing the value of ITIL. They are requiring IT personnel to learn and adopt ITIL practices. Just as you would want certified health care professionals to treat you, many organizations want to ensure a certain percentage of IT employees are certified in ITIL.

ITIL certifications validate knowledge at different levels. The first level is ITIL v3 Foundation for Service Management. This is often shortened to ITIL v3 Foundation. IT administrators and IT managers often pursue this.

From there, you can specialize in different areas of ITIL. You can then go on to become an ITIL Expert and an ITIL Master. Individuals who manage ITIL programs pursue the ITIL Expert and ITIL Master certifications, or "certs."

Global Knowledge did a salary survey in 2010. ITIL certs were listed in the top salary ranges. In 2008, the average salary reported for ITIL v3 Master was $86,600. In 2010, the average salary reported for ITIL v3 Foundation was $101,185.

It should be noted that most people with ITIL certs have other skills. ITIL practitioners start with a solid foundation in IT. That path may lead them to be IT administrators or managers for IT teams. The ITIL knowledge helps them ensure the IT network works as smoothly as possible.

- **Service Operation phase**—Daily operations and support of any service is handled here. For e-mail, this can include regular maintenance and handling any incidents that impact the service. It would also include performing backups and test restores. The goal here is to ensure the end users have access to their e-mail when they expect to have it.

- **Continual Service Improvement phase**—This phase focuses on measuring and monitoring services and processes. The goal is to determine areas where services can be improved. This can include regular monitoring and performance tuning of the e-mail servers. You can use analysis to identify problem areas before they become actual problems. This can provide insight into areas that can be improved.

You can access ITRIL resources at: *http://www.itil.co.uk*.

Capability Maturity Model Integration

The **Capability Maturity Model Integration (CMMI)** is a process improvement approach to management. It uses different levels to determine the maturity of a process.

CMMI can be used in three primary areas of interest:

- **Product and service development**—CMMI is often used with software development. It helps ensure the final product meets the original goals. It also helps ensure the product is completed within budget and time constraints.

FIGURE 3-6

CMMI characteristics.

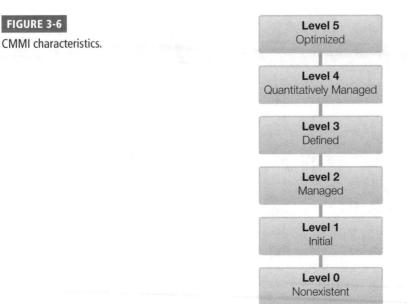

- **Service establishment, management, and delivery**—CMMI can be used to measure the effectiveness of services. Security can be considered a service. Security helps ensure confidentiality, integrity and availability of data and systems.
- **Product and service acquisition**—This can be used to ensure you consistently buy what you need. It also helps to ensure you get what you pay for.

Figure 3-6 shows the six levels of the CMMI. These are also referred to as CMMI characteristics.

You can use these levels to determine the effectiveness of security within an organization. The following list identifies the levels and how they can be used to evaluate security. Although Level 0 is listed here, it is sometimes omitted:

- **Level 0: Nonexistent**—Security controls are not in place. There is no recognition of a need for security.
- **Level 1: Initial**—This is sometimes referred to as ad hoc, or as needed. Risks are considered after a threat exploits vulnerability.
- **Level 2: Managed**—The organization recognizes risks. The organization recognizes a need for security. However, it performs controls out of intuition rather than from detailed plans. Responses are reactive.
- **Level 3: Defined**—The organization has security policies in place. It has some security awareness. Action is proactive.

- **Level 4: Quantitatively Managed**—The organization measures and controls security processes. It has formal policies and standards in place. It performs regular risk assessments and vulnerability assessments.
- **Level 5: Optimized**—The organization has formal security processes in place throughout the organization. It monitors security on a continuous basis. Its focus is on process improvement.

Level 5 shows the highest level of maturity.

Department of Defense Information Assurance Certification and Accreditation Process

The **Department of Defense (DoD) Information Assurance Certification and Accreditation Process (DIACAP)** is a risk management process. DIACAP is used for IT systems used by the U.S. DoD. It is fully documented in DoD instruction 8510.1.

> **NOTE**
> DIACAP replaced DITSCAP in 2007. DITSCAP was an acronym for DoD Information Assurance Certification and Accreditation Process.

DIACAP details specific phases that IT systems must go through. The core goal is to ensure systems are in compliance with requirements. These phases are:

- **Phase 1: Initiate and Plan**—Register the system with DIACAP. Assign information assurance (IA) controls. Create a DIACAP team. Develop a DIACAP strategy. Begin the IA plan.
- **Phase 2: Implement and Validate**—Implement the IA plan. Update the IA plan if needed. Validation activities verify compliance of the system. Document validation results.
- **Phase 3: Make Certification and Accreditation Decisions**—Analyze residual risk. Review documentation to verify certification. A decision is made to accredit the system. Once the system is accredited, it receives an authorization to operate (ATO).
- **Phase 4: Maintain ATO/Review**—Maintain the system. The goal is to ensure it stays in compliance with the requirements of the ATO. Periodically review the system for compliance.
- **Phase 5: Decommission**—Decommission the system. Dispose of DIACAP data.

> **NOTE**
> (ISC)² sponsors several certifications. The Systems Security Certified Practitioner (SSCP) is one security certification. The Certified Information Systems Security Professional (CISSP) is a higher level certification.

(ISC)² offers a civilian-based certification that you can use for DoD 8570.1. It is called Certification and Accreditation Professional (CAP). It requires two years' experience in the certification and accreditation field. You must also pass an exam with a score of at least 700.

CHAPTER SUMMARY

IT systems and data need to be protected. For the organizations that won't do this on their own, there are now many laws in place. Many of these laws are designed to ensure that the IT systems and data are protected.

Beyond the laws, there are also many regulations that apply to specific sectors. Additionally, there is a wide assortment of standards and guidelines related to IT. Many of these can be used by any organization to help it assess and improve its own security.

KEY CONCEPTS AND TERMS

Acceptable use policy (AUP)

Attorney General (AG)

Capability Maturity Model Integration (CMMI)

Children's Internet Protection Act (CIPA)

Compliance

Control Objectives for Information and related Technology (COBIT)

Department of Defense (DoD) Information Assurance Certification and Accreditation Process (DIACAP)

Due care

Due diligence

Federal Deposit Insurance Corporation (FDIC)

Family Educational Rights and Privacy Act (FERPA)

Federal Information Security Management Act (FISMA)

Federal Trade Commission (FTC)

Fiduciary responsibility

Gramm-Leach-Bliley Act (GLBA)

Health Insurance Portability and Accountability Act (HIPAA)

Information Technology Infrastructure Library (ITIL)

International Electrotechnical Commission (IEC)

International Organization for Standardization (ISO)

Job rotation

Mandatory vacation

Payment Card Industry Data Security Standard (PCI DSS)

Sarbanes-Oxley Act (SOX)

Securities and Exchange Commission (SEC)

U.S. Attorney General (U.S. AG)

CHAPTER 3 ASSESSMENT

1. FISMA requires federal agencies to protect IT systems and data. How often should compliance be audited by an external organization?

   A. Never
   B. Quarterly
   C. Annually
   D. Every three years

2. What law applies to organizations handling health care information?

   A. SOX
   B. GLBA
   C. FISMA
   D. HIPAA

3. CEOs and CFOs can go to jail if financial statements are inaccurate. What law is this from?

   A. SOX
   B. GLBA
   C. FISMA
   D. HIPAA

4. What law requires schools and libraries to limit offensive content on their computers?

   A. FERPA
   B. HIPAA
   C. CIPA
   D. SSCP

5. Employees in some companies are often required to take an annual vacation of at least five days. The purpose is to reduce fraud and embezzlement. What is this called?

   A. Job rotation
   B. Mandatory vacation
   C. Separation of duties
   D. Due diligence

6. Fiduciary refers to a relationship of trust.

   A. True
   B. False

7. Merchants that handle credit cards are expected to implement data security. What standard should they follow?

   A. GAISP
   B. CMMI
   C. COBIT
   D. PCI DSS

8. The National Institute of Standards and Technology published Special Publication 800-30. What does this cover?

   A. Risk management
   B. Maturity levels
   C. A framework of good practices
   D. Certification and accreditation

9. The COBIT framework is organized into four IT domains and 34 IT processes. Which one covers strategy and tactics?

   A. Plan and Organize
   B. Acquire and Implement
   C. Deliver and Support
   D. Monitor and Evaluate

10. A basic principle of this standard is summarized with four sentences: Business requirements drive investments in IT resources. IT resources are used by IT processes. IT processes deliver enterprise information. Enterprise information responds to business requirements. What is this standard?

    A. COBIT
    B. ITIL
    C. GAISP
    D. CMMI

11. Which of the following ISO standards can be used to verify that an organization meets certain requirements? Part I identifies objectives and controls. Part II is used for certification.

    A. ISO 73 Risk Management—Vocabulary
    B. ISO 27002 Information Technology Security Techniques
    C. ISO 31000 Risk Management Principles and Guidelines
    D. IEC 31010 Risk Management— Risk Assessment Techniques

12. Which of the following ISO documents provides generic guidance on risk management?

A. ISO 73 Risk Management—Vocabulary
B. ISO 27002 Information Technology Security Techniques
C. ISO 31000 Risk Management Principles and Guidelines
D. IEC 31010 Risk Management—Risk Assessment Techniques

13. ITIL is a group of five books developed by the United Kingdom's Office of Government Commerce.

A. True
B. False

14. In the CMMI, level _____ indicates the highest level of maturity.

15. The DIACAP is a risk management process applied to IT systems. What happens after a system is accredited?

A. It is certified.
B. It is decommissioned.
C. It is validated.
D. It receives authority to operate.

Developing a Risk Management Plan

A RISK MANAGEMENT PLAN is a specialized type of project management. You apply many of the same techniques to risk management that you would when managing any project. At the core is the need to plan. As the old saying goes, if you fail to plan, you plan to fail. Without a risk management plan, failure is much more likely than success.

A well-documented risk management plan helps ensure you are able to reach your desired goal. Primarily, you create a risk management plan to mitigate risks. This plan helps you identify the risks and choose the best solutions. It also helps you track the solutions to ensure they are implemented on budget and on schedule. A fully implemented plan will include a plan of action and milestones (POAM). You can then use the POAM to track the project.

Chapter 4 Topics

This chapter covers the following topics and concepts:

- What the objectives of a risk management plan are
- What the scope of a risk management plan is
- How to assign responsibilities in a risk management plan
- How procedures and schedules are described in the risk management plan
- What the reporting requirements are
- What a plan of action and milestones is
- How to chart the progress of a risk management plan

When you complete this chapter, you will be able to:

- Describe the objectives of a risk management plan
- Describe the purpose of a plan's scope
- Identify the importance of assigning responsibilities
- Describe the purpose of the procedures list in a risk management plan
- List reporting requirements of a risk management plan
- Document findings of a risk management plan
- Create a plan of action and milestones
- Identify a milestone plan chart
- Identify a Gantt chart and define a critical path chart

Objectives of a Risk Management Plan

One of the important first steps for a risk management plan is to establish the objectives. The objectives become the road map for your plan. They help you identify where you're going and, just as important, they help you know when you've arrived. You should establish objectives for the plan as early as possible.

The objectives identify the goals of the project. These objectives outline what you should include in the plan. Some common objectives for a risk management plan are:

- A list of threats
- A list of vulnerabilities
- Costs associated with risks
- A list of recommendations to reduce the risks
- Costs associated with recommendations
- A cost-benefit analysis
- One or more reports

While the reports document the above items, the risk management plan doesn't end there. Once top managers receive a report, they will be able to make decisions based on the data. They will accept some recommendations. They may modify some. And they may defer some.

The next phase of the risk management plan covers implementation of the plan. Implementation involves the following tasks:

- Document management decisions.
- Document and track implementation of accepted recommendations.
- Include a POAM.

Throughout this chapter, two examples are used. These examples show how you can create a risk management plan for actual projects. The two examples are:

- **Web site**—Your company, Acme Widgets, hosts a Web site used to sell widgets on the Internet. The Web site is hosted on a Web server owned and controlled by your company. The Web site was recently attacked and went down for two days. The company lost a large amount of money. Additionally, the company lost the goodwill of many customers. This was the second major outage for this Web site in the past two months. There have been many outages in the past three years.

- **Health Insurance Portability and Accountability Act (HIPAA) compliance**—Your company recently purchased Mini Acme. Mini Acme has not complied with HIPAA. Management wants to identify the risks associated with this noncompliance. Managers also want to ensure that issues are corrected as soon as possible.

> **NOTE**
>
> The Health Insurance Portability and Accountability Act (HIPAA) was presented in Chapter 3. Title II of HIPAA covers the protection of health data.

After the chapter covers a topic, these examples are sometimes used to show how you could create a portion of the plan. The examples aren't intended to show the only possible way to create a plan. An actual plan could vary based on the needs of your company.

Objectives Example: Web Site

The Acme Widgets Web site has suffered outages. These outages have resulted in unacceptable losses. These losses could have been prevented by managing risks with the Web site. You can use the risk management plan to identify these risks. The objectives of the plan are to:

- **Identify threats**—This means any threats that directly affect the Web site. These may include:
  - Attacks from the Internet
  - Hardware or software failures
  - Loss of Internet connectivity
- **Identify vulnerabilities**—These are weaknesses and may include:
  - Lack of protection from a firewall
  - Lack of protection from an intrusion detection system
  - Lack of antivirus software
  - Lack of updates for the server
  - Lack of updates for the antivirus software

> **NOTE**
>
> A **firewall** filters traffic. Firewall rules are configured to specifically allow certain traffic. Most firewalls block all traffic that is not specifically allowed. You can use both network and host-based firewalls. A network firewall usually consists of both hardware and software and filters traffic for the network. Individual systems can have a software firewall that filters traffic for a single system.

(handwritten margin notes: "Most Import c" and "why")

(handwritten numbers 3, 4, 5, 6, 7, 8, 9, 10 circled beside each bullet)

- **Assign responsibilities**—Assign responsibility to specific departments for collecting data. This data will be used to create recommendations. Later in the plan, you will assign responsibilities to departments to implement and track the plan.

- **Identify the costs of an outage**—Include both direct and indirect costs. The direct costs are the lost sales during the outage. The amount of revenue lost if the server is down for 15 minutes or longer will come from sales data. Indirect costs include the loss of customer goodwill and the cost to recover the goodwill.

- **Provide recommendations**—Include a list of recommendations to mitigate the risks. The recommendations may reduce the weaknesses. They may also reduce the impact of the threats. For example, you could address a hardware failure threat by recommending hardware redundancy. You could address a lack of updates by implementing an update plan.

- **Identify the costs of recommendations**—Identify and list the cost of each recommendation.

- **Provide a cost-benefit analysis (CBA)**—Include a CBA for each recommendation. The CBA compares the cost of the recommendation against the benefit to the company of implementing the recommendation. You can express the benefit in terms of income gained or the cost of the outage reduced.

- **Document accepted recommendations**—Management will choose which recommendations to implement. They can accept, defer, or modify recommendations. You can then document these choices in the plan.

- **Track implementation**—Track the choices and their implementation.

- **Create POAM**—Include a POAM. The POAM will assign responsibilities. Management will use the POAM to track and follow up on the project.

Objectives Example: HIPAA Compliance

Your company recently acquired Mini Acme. An inspection of some records indicates that health information isn't protected. Your company is therefore not in compliance with HIPAA. Noncompliance can result in fines and jail time.

The purpose of this plan is to ensure compliance with HIPAA. The objectives of the plan are to:

- **Identify threats**—These could be both internal and external threats.

- **Identify the vulnerabilities**—These are the weaknesses. They may include:
  - Lack of policies preventing information sharing
  - Lack of protection when the data is stored
  - Lack of protection when the data is transmitted

- **Assign responsibilities**—Assign responsibility to specific departments to identity threats and vulnerabilities. You will use the threats and vulnerabilities data to identify corrective actions. Later, you can assign responsibilities to departments to implement and track the plan.

- **Identify the costs of noncompliance**—Costs include the legal fines associated with noncompliance. Additional costs may result from lawsuits or the loss of customer confidence.

- **Provide recommendations**—Create a list of recommendations. This list may include a change of procedures. It could include protecting the data with access controls. It could also include encrypting the data when it is transmitted.

- **Identify the costs of recommendations**—Identify and list the cost of each recommendation.

- **Provide CBA**—Complete a CBA for each recommendation. It will compare the cost of the recommendation against the cost of the outage.

- **Document accepted recommendations**—Management will choose which recommendations to implement. Managers can accept, defer, or modify recommendations. These choices will be documented in the plan.

- **Track implementation**—The plan will track the choices.

- **Create a plan of action and milestones**—Include a POAM. The POAM will assign responsibilities. It will also be used by management to track and follow up on the project.

Scope of a Risk Management Plan

In addition to the objectives, it's also important to identify the **scope** of a risk management plan. The scope identifies the boundaries of the plan. The boundaries could include the entire organization or a single system. Without defined boundaries, the plan can get out of control.

A common problem with many projects is **scope creep**. Scope creep comes from uncontrolled changes. As the changes creep in, the scope of the project grows. Changes bring in additional requirements. Uncontrolled changes result in cost overruns and missed deadlines.

For example, consider the HIPAA compliance example mentioned earlier. The objective of this project is to bring Mini Acme into compliance with HIPAA. Suppose you find other unprotected data that is not health data. It could be financial data, research data, or user data.

If you roll this data into the project, it would expand the project. You would have to identify threats and vulnerabilities. You would have to calculate the costs of the data loss. You would need to identify additional recommendations and their costs. All of this will take more time and more money.

This is not to say that the scope of a project should never change. The key is to control the changes. A risk management project manager should work with stakeholders to identify what changes are acceptable.

Scope Creep in Application Development

Scope creep is a common problem in application development. Programmers often see how a program can be improved by tweaking it a little here or there. Although the programmers are well intentioned, these changes can sometimes have far-reaching effects.

In one project, a programmer added an additional capability to a program. This change allowed the user to search through data. This was clearly outside the scope of the project. However, it didn't take much time to program it and the change was added without much notice to anyone. The application was then shipped to the customer with the new capability.

The customer used the program successfully for a few months. Later, the format of the data was changed. The change of the format didn't affect the primary purpose of the program. It still worked as required. However, the additional search feature no longer worked.

Who's responsible for fixing the problem? The application developer was responsible.

A change that originally looked like added value actually became added liability. Even though the search capability was outside the scope of the project, it became part of the application. This added capability would have to be maintained just as any other part of the application needs to be maintained. The developer didn't have much choice. If he refused to fix the problem, it would affect the perceived usability of the program.

At this point, it wasn't easy to remove the added capability. It looked and behaved like a feature. While it would not have been missed if it was never added, it would now be missed if it was removed.

▶ **NOTE**

Companies typically have high-level executives identified as CEO, CIO, CFO, and so on. CCO is short for chief compliance officer. CEO is short for chief executive officer. CFO is short for chief financial officer. CIO is short for chief information officer. CSO is short for chief security officer. CTO is short for chief technology officer.

A **stakeholder** is an individual or group that has a stake, or interest, in the success of a project. A key stakeholder is a stakeholder who has authority to make decisions about the project, including the ability to grant additional resources. Examples of a key stakeholder could be a company executive such as a CIO or CFO. It could be a vice president who will "own" the project upon completion.

It's good to involve stakeholders in drafting a scope statement. This involvement can be anything from drafting the statement to approving it. This involvement helps the stakeholder have ownership of the project. Ownership is also referred to as "buy in" for the project.

A true stakeholder has a vested interest in the project and wants to see it succeed. On the other hand, a stakeholder named as a figurehead without a stake in the project sees it as a nuisance. A project without a true stakeholder will often die due to lack of support. Resources aren't allocated. Decisions aren't made. Team members realize it's not supported and stop contributing.

Consider the unprotected data from the HIPAA example. If a risk management team discovered unprotected financial data, they could present their concerns to the project manager (PM). The PM can evaluate the data and determine that none of it is HIPAA related but realize it is important. The PM can pass the information on to a stakeholder as an issue of concern. A stakeholder may direct the PM to include the data in the plan. At that point, it is a controlled change.

Example scope statements for the Web site and HIPAA compliance projects are provided in the following sections.

Scope Example: Web Site

The purpose of the risk management plan is to secure the Acme Widgets Web site. The scope of the plan includes:

- Security of the server hosting the Web site
- Security of the Web site itself
- Availability of the Web site
- Integrity of the Web site's data

Stakeholders for this project include:

- Vice president of sales
- IT support department head

Written approval is required for any activities outside the scope of this plan.

Scope Example: HIPAA Compliance

The purpose of the risk management plan is to ensure compliance with HIPAA for Mini Acme's data. The scope of the plan includes:

- Identification of all health data
- Storage of health data
- Usage of health data
- Transmission of health data

Stakeholders for this project include:

- CIO
- Human resources department head

Written approval is required for any activities outside the scope of this plan.

Assigning Responsibilities

The risk management plan specifies responsibilities. This provides accountability. If you don't assign responsibilities, tasks can easily be missed. You can assign responsibilities to:

- Risk management PM
- Stakeholders
- Departments or department heads
- Executive officers such as CIO or CFO

It's important to ensure that any entity that is assigned a responsibility has the authority to complete the task. This is especially important for the PM.

For example, team members may not work directly for the PM. Their tasking can compete with the goals of the project. If the PM doesn't have the authority to resolve these problems, they can affect the success of the project. At the very least, the PM should have access to stakeholders to resolve problems.

The PM is responsible for the overall success of the plan. Some of the common tasks of a PM are:

- Ensuring costs are controlled
- Ensuring quality is maintained
- Ensuring the project stays on schedule
- Ensuring the project stays within scope
- Tracking and managing all project issues
- Ensuring information is available to all stakeholders
- Raising issues and problems as they become known
- Ensuring others are aware of their responsibilities and deadlines

Individual responsibilities could be assigned for the following activities:

- **Risk identification**—This includes threats and vulnerabilities. The resulting lists of potential risks can be extensive.

- **Risk assessment**—This means identifying the likelihood and impact of each risk. A threat matrix is a common method used to assess risks.

- **Risk mitigation steps**—These are steps that can reduce weaknesses. This can also include steps to reduce the impact of the risk.

- **Reporting**—Report the documentation created by the plan to management. The PM is often responsible for compiling reports.

Examples of responsibility statements for the Web site and HIPAA compliance scenarios are presented in the following two sections.

Responsibilities Example: Web Site

The CFO will provide funding to the IT department to hire a security consultant. This security consultant will assist the IT department.

The IT department is responsible for providing:

- A list of threats
- A list of vulnerabilities
- A list of recommended solutions
- Costs for each of the recommended solutions

The sales department is responsible for providing:

- Direct costs of any outage for 15 minutes or longer
- Indirect costs of any outage for 15 minutes or longer

The CFO will validate the data provided by the IT and sales departments. The CFO will then complete a cost-benefit analysis.

Responsibilities Example: HIPAA Compliance

The human resources (HR) department is responsible for identifying all health information held by Mini Acme. The HR department is responsible for providing:

- A list of all health information sources
- Inspection results for all data sources regarding their compliance with HIPAA:
  - How the data is stored
  - How the data is protected
  - How the data is transmitted
- A list of existing HIPAA policies used by Mini Acme
- A list of needed HIPAA policies
- A list of recommended solutions to ensure compliance with HIPAA
- Costs for each of the recommended solutions
- Costs associated with noncompliance

The IT department is responsible for providing:

- Identification of access controls used for data
- A list of recommended solutions to ensure compliance with HIPAA
- Costs for each of the recommended solutions

The CFO will validate the data provided by the IT and sales departments. The CFO will then complete a cost-benefit analysis.

Using Affinity Diagrams

While it's easy to assign responsibility, it may not be so easy to accomplish the tasks. One of the challenging tasks is to generate lists of realistic threats, vulnerabilities, and recommendations. An affinity diagram can help with these tasks.

An **affinity diagram** is created in four basis steps. These are:

- **Identify the problem**—Create a basic problem statement. For example, consider the Web site problem. It could be stated as: "Web site outages result in lost sales."
- **Generate ideas**—The more the better. The ideas can be about any elements of the problem. They can include threats and vulnerabilities. They can also include recommended solutions. **Brainstorming** is one method that can be used. In a brainstorming session, participants are encouraged to mention anything that comes to mind. All ideas are written down without any judgment. The creative process can often bring out a wealth of ideas.
- **Gather ideas into related groups**—After the ideas are generated, group them together. For a risk management plan, the groups will usually fit into categories of threats, vulnerabilities, and recommendations. Some of these categories may include sub-categories. For example, you could divide vulnerabilities into network and server weaknesses.
- **Create an affinity diagram**—Figure 4-1 shows an example of an affinity diagram. It groups all of the ideas together.

In an actual scenario, the affinity diagram is likely to be much larger. You could divide threats into external and internal threats. There can be an almost endless list of vulnerabilities.

Describing Procedures and Schedules for Accomplishment

You create this part of the risk management plan after the project has started. You include a recommended solution for any threat or vulnerability, with a goal of mitigating the associated risk. While you can summarize a solution in a short phrase, the solution itself will often include multiple steps.

For example, an existing firewall may expose a server to multiple vulnerabilities. The solution could be to upgrade the firewall. This upgrade can be broken down into several steps, such as:

- Determine what traffic should be allowed.
- Create a firewall policy.
- Purchase a firewall.
- Install the firewall.
- Configure the firewall.
- Test the firewall.
- Implement the firewall.

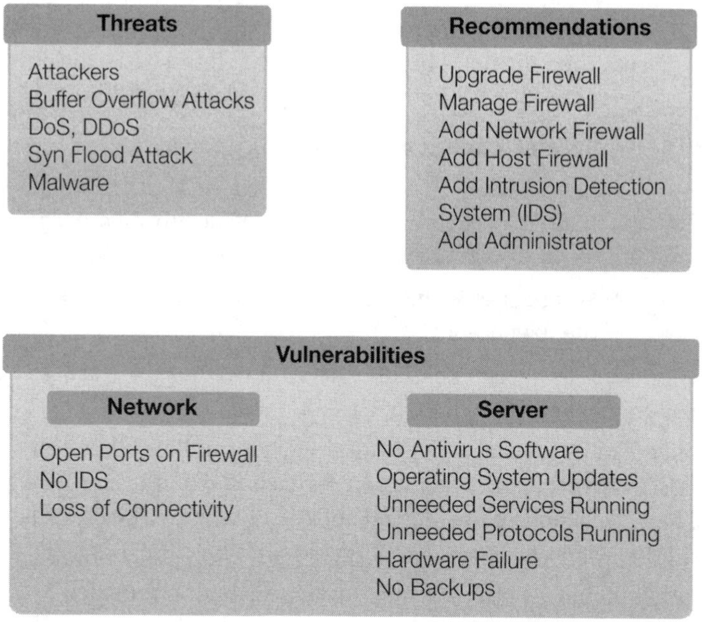

Threats

Attackers
Buffer Overflow Attacks
DoS, DDoS
Syn Flood Attack
Malware

Recommendations

Upgrade Firewall
Manage Firewall
Add Network Firewall
Add Host Firewall
Add Intrusion Detection
System (IDS)
Add Administrator

Vulnerabilities

Network

Open Ports on Firewall
No IDS
Loss of Connectivity

Server

No Antivirus Software
Operating System Updates
Unneeded Services Running
Unneeded Protocols Running
Hardware Failure
No Backups

> **NOTE**
>
> MITRE includes a risk management toolkit area on its Web site at *http://www.mitre.org/work/ sepo/toolkits/risk/index.html*. This site includes information on creating affinity diagrams.

FIGURE 4-1

Affinity diagram.

You can describe each of these steps in further detail. In addition, you can include a timeline for completion of each of the steps.

There are a couple of things to remember at this point:

- Management is responsible for choosing the controls to implement.
- Management is responsible for residual risk.

Because management has not reviewed the recommendations yet, this schedule will usually not include dates. Instead, the schedule will list how long it may take to complete any of the recommendations.

For example, a single recommendation may include five tasks. You can list the time required for each of these tasks. You can add start and end dates later.

Partial listings of procedures for the Web site and HIPAA examples are given in the following sections.

▶ **NOTE**

DoS attacks were mentioned in Chapter 2. A DoS attack is any attack designed to prevent a system from providing a service. A distributed DoS (DDoS) attack is an attack launched from multiple systems at the same time. DDoS attacks often include zombie computers controlled in a botnet.

Procedures Example: Web Site

The Web site is vulnerable to denial of service (DoS) attacks from the Internet. This risk cannot be eliminated. However, several tasks can be completed to mitigate the risk:

- **Recommendation**—Upgrade the firewall.
- **Justification**—The current firewall is a basic router. It filters packets but does not provide any advanced firewall capabilities.
- **Procedures**—The following steps can be used to upgrade the new firewall:

1. Start firewall logging. This log can be used to determine what ports are currently being used. Logs should be collected for at least one week.

2. Create a firewall policy. A **firewall policy** identifies what traffic to allow past the firewall. This is a written document. It is created based on the content of the firewall logs. You can use the firewall policy to configure the firewall.

3. Purchase a firewall appliance. A **firewall appliance** provides a self-contained firewall solution. It includes both hardware and software that provides protection for a network. Firewall appliances range from $200 to more than $10,000. The SS75 model is recommended at a cost of $4,000. It can be purchased within 30 days of receiving funds.

4. Install the firewall. The firewall could be installed in the server room. Existing space and power could be available there.

5. Configure the firewall. Configuration would be done using the firewall policy.

6. Test the firewall. Do this before going live. It will ensure normal operations are not impacted. You can complete testing in one week.

7. Bring the firewall online. This can be done within a week after testing is completed.

FYI

Firewalls labeled as appliances are intended to be easy to use. The implication is that you can plug them in and they work. You don't have to be an expert in how they work. It's like a toaster. You put bread in and toast comes out. You don't have to know how the toaster works to make toast. Similarly, you don't have to be an expert on firewalls to use a firewall appliance.

Procedures Example: HIPAA Compliance

Employees of Mini Acme are not aware of HIPAA. They don't understand the requirements of the law. They don't understand the consequences of noncompliance. You can complete the following tasks to mitigate the risk of noncompliance:

- **Recommendation**—Increase awareness of HIPAA.
- **Justification**—Make clear that noncompliance can result in fines totaling $25,000 a year for mistakes.
- **Procedures**—Use the following steps to increase awareness.
    1. Require all employees to read and comply with HIPAA policies. Don't create new policies. Require Mini Acme employees to read and acknowledge HIPAA policies currently in place. This can be accomplished in 30 days.
    2. Provide training to all employees on HIPAA compliance. Training will include what data is covered by HIPAA. It will also include consequences of noncompliance. Training can be completed in 30 days.

Reporting Requirements

After you collect data on the risks and recommendations, you need to include it in a report. You will then present this report to management. The primary purpose of the report is to allow management to decide on what recommendations to use.

There are four major categories of reporting requirements. They are:

- **Present recommendations**—These are the risk response recommendations.
- **Document management response to recommendations**—Management can accept, modify, or defer any of the recommendations.
- **Document and track implementation of accepted recommendations**—This becomes the actual risk response plan.
- **Plan of action and milestones (POAM)**—The POAM tracks the risk response actions.

Present Recommendations

You compile the collected data into a report. It will include the lists of threats, vulnerabilities, and recommendations. You then present this report to management. Management will use this data to decide what steps to take.

It's important to remember the overall goal of the risk management plan at this stage. The goal is to identify the risks and recommend strategies to reduce them. Most of the risks won't be eliminated, but instead they will be reduced to an acceptable level. For every risk identified, there will be an accompanying recommendation to reduce the risk.

This report should include the following information:

- Findings
- Recommendation cost and time frame
- Cost-benefit analysis

Findings

The findings list the facts. Remember, losses from risks occur when a threat exposes a vulnerability. Risk management findings need to include threats, vulnerabilities, and potential losses. These are described as cause, criteria, and effect.

- **Cause**—The cause is the threat. For example, an attacker may try to launch a DoS attack. In this case, the threat is the attacker. When you list the cause, it's important to identify the root cause. A successful attack is dependent on an attacker having access and the system being vulnerable. Risk management attempts to reduce the impact of the cause, or reduce the vulnerabilities.

- **Criteria**—This identifies the criteria that will allow the threat to succeed. These are the vulnerabilities. For example, a server will be susceptible to a DoS attack if the following criteria are met:

  - *Inadequate manpower*—If manpower isn't adequate to perform security steps, the site is vulnerable.

  - *Unmanaged firewall*—Each open port represents a vulnerability. If ports are not managed on a firewall, unwanted traffic can be allowed in.

  - *No intrusion detection system (IDS)*—Depending on the type of IDS, it can not only detect intrusions but also respond to intrusions and change the environment.

  - *Operating system not updated*—Apply patches to the system as they are released and tested. If you don't apply updates, the system is vulnerable to new exploits.

  - *Antivirus software not installed and updated*—Antivirus software can detect malware. You should update it with definitions to ensure it will detect new malware.

- **Effect**—The effect is often an outage of some type. For example, the effect on a Web site could be that the Web site is not reachable any more.

An important consideration as you document findings is resource availability. It could be that all the discovered issues were previously known. However, money may not have been allocated to purchase the solutions in the past. It's also possible that manpower wasn't adequate to implement the solutions.

When adequate manpower isn't available, security is often sacrificed for ease of use. Consider the Web site example. The first goal may be to ensure the Web site is operational. Once it's up, resources may be used for other jobs. The Web site may still not be secure, backups may not be made, or other security issues may still exist.

A **cause and effect diagram** can be used to discover and document the findings. Figure 4-2 shows a sample cause and effect diagram for the Web site scenario. In this diagram, the primary cause is an attack. The remaining items are contributing factors that allow the attack to succeed. The effect is an outage.

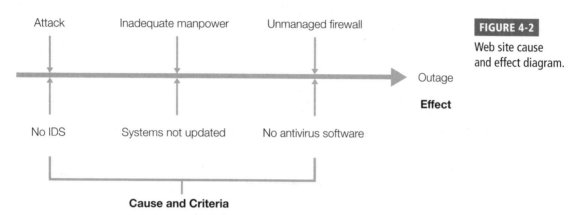

FIGURE 4-2

Web site cause
and effect diagram.

There are several advantages to using a cause and effect diagram. It can help guide discussions during the discovery process. It can also help visualize the relationships between causes and effects in documentation. Cause and effect diagrams can be used for any problem.

A cause and effect diagram starts by creating the line and the ultimate effect. In Figure 4-2, the effect is the outage. Then you add additional items (the causes), making the diagram look similar to a fishbone. You can expand the diagram for any of the elements. For example, you could expand "attack" to include specific types of attacks. Attacks may include malware, DoS, buffer overflow, or other types of attacks.

When creating a cause and effect diagram, you can run out of ideas or focus on a single topic. To balance the diagram, consider the following five elements. You're not required to include all the elements. However, you can use any of them to help identify causes.

> **NOTE**
> The cause and effect diagram is also called an Ishikawa diagram, or a fishbone diagram. It is used to link problems with causes.

- **Methods**—What methods could contribute to an outage?
- **Machinery**—What machinery issues could contribute to an outage?
- **Manpower**—What manpower issues could contribute to an outage?
- **Materials**—What material issues could contribute to an outage?
- **Environment**—What environmental issues could contribute to an outage?

Figure 4-3 shows another example of a cause and effect diagram. In this example, the cause is loss of confidentiality. The remaining items show the criteria that can allow the loss of data. For HIPAA, the effect can be substantial fines.

Recommendation Cost and Time Frame

In addition to the findings, the report will include a list of recommendations. These recommendations will address the potential causes and criteria that can result in the negative effect.

Each item should include the cost required to implement it. Also include the timeline to implement the solution. Management will use this data to decide if the solution should be applied.

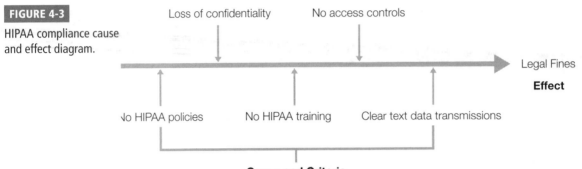

FIGURE 4-3

HIPAA compliance cause and effect diagram.

For example, the following partial list of recommendations could be included in the Web site risk management plan.

- **Upgrade firewall**—Initial cost: $4,000. Ongoing costs: $1,000 annually. The initial cost will cover the purchase of the firewall. The ongoing costs are related to training and maintenance.
  Purchase and install the firewall within 30 days of approval.
- **Purchase and install IDS**—Initial cost: $800. Ongoing costs: negligible.
  Purchase and install the IDS within 30 days of approval.
- **Create plan to keep system updated**—Initial cost: manpower.
  Ongoing costs: manpower.
  Purchase and install the system within 30 days of approval.
- **Install antivirus software on server**—Initial cost: $75. Ongoing costs: negligible.
  Purchase and install the software within 30 days of approval.

Cost Estimate Accuracy

Because a CBA is only as valuable as its cost estimates, it's important to get accurate data. However, this can be difficult. It helps to understand how data can be skewed.

Costs for solutions are often underestimated. For example, ongoing costs may not be included in the initial cost estimates. A product that looks easy to manage may require expensive training.

The success of a solution can be overestimated. A solution may be expected to reduce incidents by 90 percent. In practice, the reduction may be closer to 50 percent.

There are times when personnel don't have a vested interest in providing accurate information. For example, sales personnel interested in an initial sale may sometimes gloss over ongoing costs. You can also expect them to stress the most positive aspects of their products.

- **Update antivirus software**—Initial cost: negligible. Ongoing costs: negligible.
  Configure antivirus software for automatic updates after installation.
- **Add one IT administrator**—Cost: negotiated salary. Due to the ongoing maintenance requirements of these recommendations, an additional administrator is required.

> **NOTE**
>
> The individual ongoing costs may be small, but the cumulative requirements may be more. In this example, the time required to maintain these solutions may justify an additional administrator.

Cost-Benefit Analysis

The CBA was presented in Chapter 1. It is a process used to determine how to manage a risk. If the benefits of a control outweigh the costs, the control can be implemented to reduce the risk. If the costs are greater than the benefits, the risk can be accepted.

In this context, the CBA should include two items:

- **Cost of the recommendation**—The recommendation is the control intended to manage the risk. If you anticipate that there will be ongoing costs, you should include them in the calculation.
- **Projected benefits**—Calculate benefits in terms of dollars. Benefits can be expressed as money earned or losses reduced.

Management is responsible for making the decisions on how to manage the risks. An accurate CBA allows management to make intelligent decisions.

Here is an example CBA for a Web site recommendation.

- **Recommendation**—Install antivirus (AV) software on the Web server.
- **Cost of the recommendation**—$75.
- **Background**—AV software was not installed on the Web server in the past because of performance concerns. The Web server was infected with malware at least once this year. The malware resulted in outage of the Web server of approximately five hours. The Web server generates approximately $500 per 15 minutes of up time, or $2,000 per hour. AV software is expected to prevent 90 percent of infections.
- **Loss before AV software**—$30,000. A single instance resulted in $10,000 of direct loss of revenue ($2,000 × 5 hours). Indirect losses are estimated to be $20,000. This includes the advertising costs to bring back lost customers.
- **Expected loss with AV software**—$3,000. The AV software is expected to reduce the losses by 90 percent ($30,000 − ($30,000 × .9) = $3,000).
- **Benefit of AV software**—$27,000 ($30,000 × .9 = $27,000).
- **CBA**—$26,925. The CBA is calculated as:
  - Loss before AV software − loss after AV software − cost of AV software
  - $30,000 − $3,000 − $75 = $26,925

You can't overestimate the importance of accurate data. The key to completing an accurate CBA is starting with accurate data. Again, this is sometimes difficult to get. It often requires digging below the surface to determine costs.

Probing questions can often uncover flaws in the data. Consider the following scenarios and questions.

- If a control is said to reduce losses by 90 percent, you can ask,
  "How did you arrive at 90 percent?"
- If the cost of a control is given, you can ask,
  "Does this include any ongoing costs?"

Probing questions don't need to be accusatory. The goal isn't to create a conflict. Instead, the goal is to validate the data. Questions should be asked with a tone of "help me understand." If the data is flawed, the presenter can easily get defensive. On the other hand, if the data is valid, the presenter can answer questions with facts to support the claims.

Risk Statements

Reports are often summarized in **risk statements**. You use risk statements to communicate a risk and the resulting impact. They are often written using "if/then" statements. The "if" part of the statement identifies the elements of the risk. The "then" portion of the statement identifies the effect.

For example, the following risk statement could be used for the Web site.

- If AV software is not installed on the Web server, then the likelihood that the server will become infected is high. The Web server has a constant connection to the Internet.
- If the server is infected, then an outage is likely to occur. Any outage will result in $500 of lost sales for every 15 minutes of downtime.

You should be able to match the risk statements to the scope and objectives of the project. If the statement isn't within the scope or objectives, the risk assessment may be off track. You'll then need to go back and focus the findings or the recommendation.

Document Management Response to Recommendations

After you present your managers with the recommendations, they will decide what to do. They can accept, defer or modify recommendations.

- **Accept**—Management approves the recommendation. Approved recommendations are funded and implemented. They will then be added to a POAM for tracking.
- **Defer**—Management can also defer a recommendation. It may still be implemented at a later time. However, do not include it in the list of accepted recommendations.

- **Modify**—Management can also decide to modify a recommendation. For example, you may recommend a firewall. Management may decide on two firewalls to implement a demilitarized zone (DMZ). On the other hand, you may recommend a $4,000 firewall. Management may decide to purchase an $800 firewall instead.

> **NOTE**
>
> A demilitarized zone (DMZ) is commonly used to protect Internet-facing servers. It usually consists of two firewalls. One firewall filters traffic from the Internet to the DMZ. The other firewall filters traffic from the internal network to the DMZ.

Document and Track Implementation of Accepted Recommendations

It's important to document the decisions made by management. As time passes, the decisions can become distorted if you don't document them. This is especially true if the recommendations are deferred or modified.

Imagine you managed the risk management plan for the Web site. The plan recommended purchase of AV software, but this recommendation was deferred. Three months later the system is infected with malware. A four-hour outage results in losses exceeding $8,000. You may be asked why the software wasn't purchased.

If you documented the decisions, this is a simple matter to address. Without documentation, the result may be uncomfortable finger-pointing.

The documentation doesn't need to be extensive. It could be a simple document listing the recommendation and the decision. It could look similar to this:

- **Recommendation to purchase AV software**—Accepted
  Software is to be purchased as soon as possible.

- **Recommendation to hire an IT administrator**—Deferred
  IT department needs to provide clearer justification for this. In the interim, the IT department is authorized to use overtime to ensure security requirements are met.

- **Recommendation to purchase SS75 firewall**—Modified
  Two SS75 firewalls are to be purchased as soon as possible. These two firewalls will be configured as a DMZ.

Plan of Action and Milestones

A **plan of action and milestones (POAM)** is a document used to track progress. POAMs are used in many types of project management. A POAM is used to assign responsibility and to allow management follow-up.

> **NOTE**
>
> A POAM is sometimes abbreviated as POA&M.

- **Assignment of responsibility**—The POAM makes it clear who is responsible for each task. When a task is not completed on schedule, it also makes clear whom to hold accountable.

- **Management follow-up**—PMs and upper level management can use the POAM to follow up on a project. The POAM allows managers to quickly determine the status of any project. When project management tools are used, the source of the problem is often easy to identify.

POAMs are also useful for any audited projects. For example, HIPAA requires regular reviews. The POAM can show the progress the company has made to become compliant. If a company is not 100 percent compliant but can show it has made significant progress, fines may be waived or reduced. If a company doesn't have any documentation indicating progress, maximum fines could be assessed.

There are no specific formats required for a POAM. One company may create a POAM in a Microsoft Excel spreadsheet with 15 columns for every item. Another company may create a POAM in a Microsoft Word document.

The POAM is a living document. It is not a report that is created once and is complete. Instead, you should update the POAM throughout the life cycle of a project. Additionally, the POAM may look different depending on the phase of the project. Early in the project, the POAM may be generic. Later in the project, it could be more specific.

For example, consider the Web site risk management plan. The Web site has been attacked. It has suffered two major outages in the last two months. The cause of these two incidents is probably well known. However, all the threats and vulnerabilities are probably not known. The initial POAM might have the following generic items:

- **Approve risk management plan:** Assigned to _____ Due by _____
- **Identify threats:** Assigned to _____ Due by _____
- **Identify vulnerabilities:** Assigned to _____ Due by _____
- **Identify potential solutions:** Assigned to _____ Due by _____
- **Prepare risk management plan report:** Assigned to _____ Due by _____
- **Approve risk response plan:** Assigned to _____ Due by _____
- **Begin implementation of plan:** Assigned to _____ Due by _____
- **Complete implantation of plan:** Assigned to _____ Due by _____

> **NOTE**
>
> A **milestone** is a scheduled event. It indicates the completion of a major task or group of tasks. Milestones are commonly used in project management to verify how the project is doing. When milestone dates are missed, the project is behind schedule.

Later, when management approves the specific recommendations, you can create a POAM for the approved and modified recommendations. Each recommendation within the POAM could have multiple line items. For example, the task to upgrade the firewall could be the major milestone. When all of the tasks are completed, the milestone is met.

- **Log current firewall activity:** Assigned to _____ Due by _____
- **Purchase two SS75 firewalls:** Assigned to _____ Due by _____
- **Create firewall policy:** Assigned to _____ Due by _____
- **Test firewalls:** Assigned to _____ Due by _____
- **Implement external firewall:** Assigned to _____ Due by _____
- **Implement internal firewall:** Assigned to _____ Due by _____
- **Move Web server to DMZ:** Assigned to _____ Due by _____

> ## Project Management Software
>
> There are many different versions of project management software available. One example is Microsoft Office Project. It includes different versions such as Microsoft Office Project Standard and Project Professional.
>
> Project software includes additional tools that can be used to create charts. Charting tools provide a graphical representation of the project. They can also automatically detect the status of a project.
>
> Some software will indicate the status of a project with colors such as green, yellow, or red. Green could indicate on schedule and on budget. Yellow could indicate a danger of going over schedule or over budget. Red could indicate over schedule or over budget.
>
> A PM can enter data as the risk management project progresses. These charts will automatically be updated. It's also possible to use a server to host data on multiple projects. Managers can access reports on any of the projects via a Web browser.

Each line item could include the following details:

- Task name
- Associated threat or vulnerability
- Risk level (low, medium, or high)
- Step or milestone name
- Assignment of responsibility
- Point of contact
- Estimated cost
- Actual cost
- Estimated person hours to complete task
- Actual person hours to complete task
- Scheduled start date
- Actual start date
- Milestone due date
- Current status
- Scheduled completion date
- Actual date of completion
- Comments

You can use different tools to assist in tracking the POAM. These tools don't replace the POAM but instead provide graphical representations of the POAM and its progress. These tools include:

- Milestone plan chart
- Gantt chart
- Critical path chart

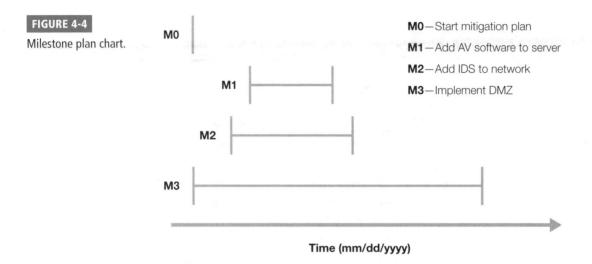

FIGURE 4-4

Milestone plan chart.

M0—Start mitigation plan

M1—Add AV software to server

M2—Add IDS to network

M3—Implement DMZ

Time (mm/dd/yyyy)

Charting the Progress of a Risk Management Plan

Milestone Plan Chart

A **milestone plan chart** is a simple graphical representation of major milestones. It shows the major milestones laid out in a graphical format. If there are any dependencies between the milestones, this chart will show them. In other words, if milestone 2 can't begin until milestone 1 has been completed, this chart will show this dependency.

It's also common to include actual start and end dates in the chart. Figure 4-4 shows an example of a milestone plan chart.

The milestone plan chart can also help allocate resources. For example, the tasks in Figure 4-4 aren't dependent on one another. However, you can see that the tasks are staggered. It's possible for each task to start at the same. However, if the same person or same department will perform all of the tasks it may not be possible to start each one at the same time.

In this case, start the longest task milestone first. In the figure, the M3 milestone will implement a DMZ and is the longest. Once you order the firewalls, you can start another task while waiting for the firewall to arrive. M2 can start at that point. Once you order the IDS software, you can start milestone M1.

This chart can also help management change the priority of any of the milestones. The installation of AV software may be considered the most important first step. The figure shows that the M1 is being delayed so that M3 can start first. This can be changed so M1 starts first with an accepted delay in the implementation of the DMZ.

Gantt Chart

A **Gantt chart** is a chart that that shows a project schedule. Gantt charts are commonly used in project management. The primary difference between the milestone plan chart and the Gantt chart is that the Gantt chart shows more detail.

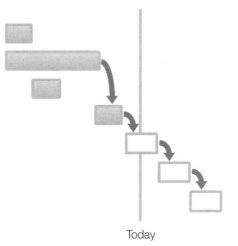

Log Firewall Activity

Purchase Two Firewalls

Create Firewall Policy

Install Firewalls

Configure Firewalls

Test Firewalls

Move Server to DMZ

Today

FIGURE 4-5

Gantt chart.

Figure 4-5 shows an example of a Gantt chart. The shaded items show the tasks that have been completed. Notice that the Gantt chart is showing the detailed steps for the implementation of the DMZ.

The Gantt chart allows any manager to quickly view the progression and status of the project. In the figure, all of the tasks that were supposed to be completed before today are complete. The PM needs only to focus on the task in progress or future tasks.

On the other hand, if previous tasks weren't completed, the PM can quickly identify where to focus attention. For example, if the firewalls weren't installed yet, the Install Firewalls task would not be shaded. The PM could see this element is past due and address the issue.

Most project management software automates the creation of Gantt charts. Additionally, as the tasks in the project are completed, it will automatically indicate completion in the chart. Before computers were so popular, these charts would be filled in by hand.

> **NOTE**
>
> The Gantt chart was developed by Henry Gantt. He worked with the Army Bureau of Ordnance during World War I. He realized that processes could be controlled easier if they were broken down into smaller elements. As the often repeated saying goes: "How do you eat an elephant? One bite at a time."

4

Developing a Risk
Management Plan

Critical Path Chart

Some tasks within a project can be delayed without impacting the project finish date. Other tasks must be completed on time. A **critical path chart** shows a list of project tasks that must be completed on time. If any task in the path is delayed, the overall project will be delayed.

Critical path chart.

Purchase Two Firewalls

Install Firewalls

Configure Firewalls

Test Firewalls

Move Server to DMZ

Today

For example, you cannot install a firewall until the firewall is purchased. If the purchase is delayed, the installation will be delayed. These two items would be in the critical path. On the other hand, you can delay creating a log of current firewall activity. As long as the delay isn't too long, it won't impact the overall schedule.

Figure 4-6 shows an example of a critical path chart. This is the critical path for the firewall project.

Notice that two tasks are missing. Log firewall activity and create firewall policy are two tasks that are not in the critical path. If these two tasks are delayed, they will not delay the entire project.

CHAPTER SUMMARY

A risk management plan is a specific type of project plan. The project is to identify and mitigate risks. You start by creating objectives and a project scope. You then identify risks. Finally, you create a response plan as recommendations to mitigate the risks. Management can then choose to accept, defer, or modify the risks.

You then implement the recommendations. A primary tool used to track the recommendations is a plan of action and milestones (POAM). This POAM is a living document that is updated throughout the project. You can supplement it with different charting tools to ease project management tasks.

KEY CONCEPTS AND TERMS

Affinity diagram	Firewall policy	Risk statement
Brainstorming	Gantt chart	Scope
Cause and effect diagram	Milestone	Scope creep
Critical path chart	Milestone plan chart	Stakeholder
Firewall	Plan of action and milestones	
Firewall appliance	(POAM)	

CHAPTER 4 ASSESSMENT

1. What are valid contents of a risk management plan?

A. Objectives
B. Scope
C. Recommendations
D. POAM
E. All of the above

2. What should be included in the objectives of a risk management plan?

A. A list of threats
B. A list of vulnerabilities
C. Costs associated with risks
D. Cost-benefit analysis
E. All of the above

3. What will the scope of a risk management plan define?

A. Objectives
B. POAM
C. Recommendations
D. Boundaries

4. What problem can occur if the scope of a risk management plan is not defined?

A. Excess boundaries
B. Stakeholder loss
C. Scope creep
D. SSCP

5. What is a stakeholder?

   A. A mark that identifies critical steps

   B. An individual or group that has an interest in the project

   C. A critical process or procedure

   D. Another name for the risk management plan project manager

6. A key stakeholder should have authority to make decisions about a project. This includes authority to provide additional resources.

   A. True

   B. False

7. A risk management plan project manager oversees the entire plan. What is the project manager responsible for? (Select two.)

   A. Ensuring costs are controlled

   B. Ensuring the project stays on schedule

   C. Ensuring stakeholders have adequate funds

   D. Ensuring recommendations are adopted

8. A risk management plan includes steps to mitigate risks. Who is responsible for choosing what steps to implement?

   A. The project manager

   B. Management

   C. Risk management team

   D. The POAM manager

9. A risk management plan includes a list of findings in a report. The findings identify threats and vulnerabilities. What type of diagram can document some of the findings?

   A. Gantt chart

   B. Critical path chart

   C. POAM diagram

   D. Cause and effect diagram

10. What three elements should be included in the findings of the risk management report?

   A. Causes, criteria, and effects

   B. Threats, causes, and effects

   C. Criteria, vulnerabilities, and effects

   D. Causes, criteria, and milestones

11. What is a primary tool used to identify the financial significance of a mitigation tool?

   A. Ishikawa diagram

   B. Fishbone diagram

   C. CBA

   D. POAM

12. A fishbone diagram can link causes with effects.

   A. True

   B. False

13. You present management with recommendations from a risk management plan. What can management choose to do?

   A. Accept or reject the recommendations.

   B. Adjust, defer, or modify the recommendations.

   C. Accept, defer, or modify the recommendations.

   D. Allow or deny the recommendations.

14. What is a POAM?

   A. Project objectives and milestones

   B. Planned objectives and milestones

   C. Project of action milestones

   D. Plan of action and milestones

15. A POAM is used to track the progress of a project. What type of chart is commonly used to assist with tracking?

   A. Fishbone chart

   B. Cause and effect chart

   C. GANTT chart

   D. POAM chart

PART TWO

Mitigating Risk

Defining Risk Assessment Approaches

A RISK ASSESSMENT IS PERFORMED to identify the most serious risks. Earlier chapters in this book presented risk management techniques. These included avoid, transfer, mitigate, or accept. The risk assessment allows you to prioritize the risks. You manage the high-priority risks and accept the low-priority risks. The risk assessment also helps you identify the best methods to control the risks. This helps ensure the controls you purchase provide the best benefits.

There are two primary methods used to create a risk assessment, quantitative and qualitative. You can use a quantitative method with predefined formulas. For example, you can calculate annual loss expectancy (ALE) by multiplying annual rate of occurrence (ARO) times single loss expectancy (SLE). This is expressed as $ALE = ARO \times SLE$. The qualitative method can also be used. It uses values or words assigned to the probability of a risk occurring and the impact of a risk if it occurs. It's important to understand both methods so you can apply them in different scenarios.

Chapter 5 Topics

This chapter covers the following topics and concepts:

- What risk assessment is
- What the critical components of a risk assessment are
- What types of risk assessments are available
- Which risk assessment challenges you should address
- What best practices for risk assessment are

Understanding Risk Assessment

A **risk assessment (RA)**, also referred to as "risk analysis," is a process used to identify and evaluate risks. Risks are then quantified based on their importance or impact severity. These risks are then prioritized.

Risk assessments are a major part of an overall risk management program. They help identify which risks are most important. A major difference between a risk assessment and a risk management program is that the risk assessment is created at a moment in time, while a risk management program is a continuous process.

An RA is used to help identify which safeguards to implement. **Safeguards** are also known as controls. They are used to control or reduce risk. A control may reduce a vulnerability or it may reduce the impact from a threat. Either way, the risk is reduced.

Any company has a finite amount of money. While a security expert may continuously want more money spent on security, there is a limit. If you spend too much money on security, you affect the profit and health of the company. How much is too much? Where is the line? An RA can help you determine where to draw the line.

> **NOTE**
>
> Chapter1 discussed profitability and survivability. A risk assessment helps a company maintain a proper balance between these two goals.

Consider a company that has data that was created after years of research. The same company has data that indicates what food will be served in the cafeteria next week. If you are prioritizing security funds, which data will get more money? The research data, of course. It's easy to identify the priority in this example, but it isn't always so easy.

Now consider the same company that holds data covered by both the Health Insurance Portability and Accountability Act (HIPAA) and Sarbanes-Oxley (SOX) laws and regulations. Which data is more important? Which data should have a higher priority of protection? What controls should be implemented to protect the data? These questions aren't so easy to answer. A risk assessment could be completed for both the HIPAA and the SOX data to help answer these questions.

> **NOTE**
>
> HIPAA governs the control of health-related data. SOX governs the accuracy of financial data. Both laws were covered in Chapter 3.

Importance of Risk Assessments

Risk assessments are an important part of the risk management process. Without an RA, it becomes difficult to determine which systems should be protected. It also remains unclear how to protect them. However, an RA will help you identify the most important systems to protect. It will also give you insight into what controls will provide the most value.

An RA should be completed:

- **When evaluating risk**—Risk assessments are a part of the overall risk management process. Risk assessments are useful any time risk management is being used. This is especially true if the risks need to be prioritized.

- **When evaluating a control**—You can use an RA to evaluate the usefulness of a control. Management can't approve all controls. They will approve some controls and not others. An RA helps management decide which controls to adopt.

- **Periodically after a control has been implemented**—An RA is a point-in-time document. However, risks don't stand still. Attackers are constantly upgrading their techniques and tactics. You should schedule RAs on a regular basis after a control has been implemented. The goal is to determine if the control is still useful.

Purpose of a Risk Assessment

Risk assessments are important tools to assist management. They help management quantify risks. They also help management identify controls and evaluate the effectiveness of these controls. Risk assessments tend to:

- **Support decision making**—The RA prioritizes risks. This helps decision makers determine which risks should be reduced. As a reminder, not all risks have to be reduced. Risks can be avoided, transferred, mitigated, or accepted. High-priority risks should be mitigated. Lower priority risks may be accepted.

- **Evaluate control effectiveness**—You implement controls to reduce a risk. The RA gives insight into how effective specific controls will be for specific risks.

An RA involves many steps. It isn't a task that you can complete in a single sitting, a single day, or even a single week. When done properly, it involves the input of several key players. Steps involved in the RA include:

- **Identify threats and vulnerabilities**—When a threat exploits a vulnerability, a risk occurs. Threats and vulnerabilities are identified as risks.
- **Identify the likelihood that a risk will occur**—This can be based on historical data or opinions. For example, imagine a risk occurred an average of four times in the past three years. If no steps are taken to reduce the risk, it will probably occur four times next year. If historical data isn't available, experts can provide opinions on the likelihood of the risk occurring.
- **Identify asset values**—The value of assets helps to determine the impact of a risk. The assets can be hardware assets, software assets, or data. Some risks can affect all three.
- **Determine the impact of a risk**—This can also be based on historical data or opinions. Imagine a risk resulted in losses averaging $20,000 a year in the past three years. If no steps are taken to reduce the risk, it will probably result in a loss of about $20,000 next year. If historical data isn't available, experts can provide opinions on the impact of the risk occurring.
- **Determine the usefulness of a safeguard or control**—Safeguards or controls are used to reduce the risk or reduce the impact. Some controls will be more effective than others. The RA helps determine which ones to implement.

The RA identifies threats and vulnerabilities against the current system. It assumes current controls are working as expected. Another way of saying this is that an RA is performed at a moment in time based on current conditions. This is unlike risk management as a whole. Risk management is a continuous process. RAs are not continuous.

Critical Components of a Risk Assessment

There are several components that you should consider when tasking and performing an RA. You should complete three critical steps early. These identify major components of the RA and will directly impact its success. These steps are:

- Identify scope.
- Identify critical areas.
- Identify team.

The following sections explore each of these steps in depth.

Identify Scope

The scope identifies the boundary of the RA. You learned about risk management plans in Chapter 4. It's important to identify the scope of a risk management plan to eliminate scope creep. It helps to keep the project on track. Similarly, the scope of the RA helps to keep the RA on track.

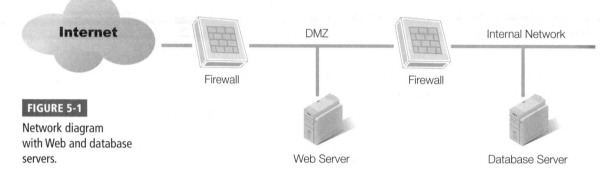

FIGURE 5-1

Network diagram with Web and database servers.

For example, consider Figure 5-1. The figure shows a Web server configured in a network. The server hosts a Web site that is accessible from the Internet. Customers can access the Web site and make purchases. The Web server hosts the Web site application. However, all the data is hosted on the back-end database server.

> **TIP**
>
> It is common to focus the scope on system ownership. This makes it easier to implement the recommendations. For example, imagine an RA that includes three servers. Each of the three servers is owned by a different department. The departments may have conflicting goals and interests that prevent the recommendations from being easily implemented. In this case, a separate RA should be created for each department.

You could set the scope to focus only on the Web server. Alternatively, the scope could include the Web server and the database server. It's also possible to include both of the firewalls in the demilitarized zone (DMZ).

Imagine that the Web server was attacked several times in the past year. Some of these attacks resulted in the Web site crashing or the Web server failing. However, existing controls protected the data on the database server. Data was not accessed inappropriately or lost. In this example, you may choose not to include the database server. It's also possible to include the database server just to ensure the existing controls will protect against current risks.

There's no right or wrong choice for what's included in the scope. Management can decide to include or exclude anything. The most important point is to make a choice.

Identify Critical Areas

The RA also identifies critical areas that should be included. This helps the RA team focus only on what's important. For example, a scope could include a Web server, a database server, and a firewall. The RA could identify the following critical areas:

- **Web server**—Address all elements of the Web server. This includes hardware, the operating system, and the Web site application. For hardware, focus on any single point of failure. A **single point of failure (SPOF)** is any single piece of hardware whose failure can take down the Web site. You should consider a process that regularly updates the operating system, in addition to applying best practices to prevent attacks on the Web site application. This includes buffer overflow and SQL injection attacks.

- **Database server**—The database server hosts about 20 databases. You should include in the RA only the databases accessed by the Web server through the firewall. You should definitely consider SQL injection attacks. However, you will implement the primary protection from SQL injection attacks in the Web site application.

- **Internal firewall**—The internal firewall controls all traffic to and from the internal network. You do not need to include all traffic in the RA. Address only the rules affecting communication between the Web server and database server.

> **NOTE**
> Buffer overflow and SQL injection attacks are common attacks for Internet-facing Web servers. These were both presented in Chapter 2.

When you identify critical areas, you should focus on areas that are most critical to the business. Profitability and survivability were mentioned previously in this chapter. It is good to keep these concepts in mind.

Some data is critical, such as financial data and customer data. Other data, such as public data, doesn't need the same level of protection. Similarly, some servers or IT services are critical. Other servers and services are less critical.

Although it certainly makes sense to include only critical areas, the RA team may not understand what is critical to management. The team should stay focused on what management considers important.

Identify Team

Risk assessment team personnel should not be the same people who are responsible for correcting deficiencies. This helps avoid a conflict of interest.

For example, imagine that an administrator is responsible for implementing controls on a Web server. His input may be slanted by his desire to implement the control. If disinterested parties provide the input, there is a better chance of getting accurate, objective data.

This is not to say that you shouldn't get input from the responsible department. Its staff probably has excellent insight into the problems and how to fix them. However, when prioritizing risks and determining the usefulness of controls, input from the people who correct deficiencies should not be the deciding factor.

Types of Risk Assessments

When considering an RA, you first need to identify what method to use. The two primary methods used in the IT field are:

- **Quantitative**—This is an objective method. It uses numbers such as actual dollar values. A quantitative RA requires a significant amount of data. Gathering this data often takes time. If the data is available, this type of RA becomes a simple math problem with the use of formulas.

▶**TIP**

It's important to understand types of risk assessments for the (ISC)[2] Systems Security Certified Practitioner (SSCP) and Certified Information Systems Security Professional (CISSP) exams. You should have a good understanding of quantitative and qualitative methods. This includes all the associated terms of quantitative methods.

- **Qualitative**—This is a subjective method. It uses relative values based on opinions from experts. Experts provide their input on the probability and impact of a risk. A qualitative RA can be completed rather quickly.

Both of these methods are explored in greater depth in the following section.

As you learn about these two methods in the next few sections, it's important to realize that neither method is superior to the other. They both have benefits and limitations. However, one method sometimes works better than the other in specific situations. When you're aware of the different options, it becomes easier to choose the right method for the right situation.

Quantitative Risk Assessments

A **quantitative risk assessment** uses numbers such as dollar values. You gather data and then enter it into standard formulas. The results can help you identify the priority of risks. You can also use the results to determine the effectiveness of controls.

Some of the key terms associated with quantitative risk assessments are:

- **Single loss expectancy (SLE)**—The total loss expected from a single incident. An incident occurs when a threat exploits a vulnerability. The loss is expressed as a dollar value such as $5,000. It includes the value of hardware, software, and data.

- **Annual rate of occurrence (ARO)**—The number of times an incident is expected to occur in a year. If an incident occurred once a month in the past year, the ARO is 12. Assuming nothing changes, it's likely that it will occur 12 times next year.

- **Annual loss expectancy (ALE)**—The expected loss for a year. ALE is calculated by multiplying SLE X ARO. Because SLE is a given in a dollar value, ALE is given as a dollar value. For example, if the SLE is $5,000 and the ARO is 12, the ALE is $60,000.

- **Safeguard value**—This is the cost of a control. Controls are used to mitigate risk. For example, antivirus software could have an average cost of $50 for each computer. If you have 100 computers, the safeguard value is $5,000.

Consider this scenario: A company issues laptop computers to employees. The value of each laptop is $2,000. This includes the hardware, software, and data. About 100 laptops are being used at any time. In the past two years, the company has lost an average of one laptop per quarter. These laptops were stolen when systems were left unattended. With this information, can you answer these questions?

- What's the SLE?
- What's the ARO?
- What's the ALE?

Because the value of each laptop is $2,000, the SLE is $2,000. One laptop is lost each quarter resulting in an ARO of 4. The ALE is calculated as $2,000 × 4, or $8,000.

You can then use the ALE to determine the usefulness of a control. For example, the company could purchase hardware locks for the laptops in bulk at a cost of $10 each. The safeguard value is $10 × 100 laptops, or $1,000. It's estimated that if the locks are purchased, the ARO will decrease from 4 to 1. Should the company purchase these locks?

You can determine the effectiveness of the control using the following calculations:

- Current ALE = $8,000 (ARO of 4 × $2,000)
- ARO with control = 1
- ALE with control = $2,000 (ARO of 1 × $2,000)
- Savings with control = $6,000 (Current ALE of $8,000 − ALE with control of $2,000)
- Safeguard value (cost of control) = $1,000 ($10 × 100)
- Realized savings = $5,000 (Savings with control of $6,000 − safeguard value of $1,000)

In this example, the savings in the first year is $5,000. This provides a cost-benefit analysis (CBA) and clearly indicates the locks should be purchased. If nothing is done, the company will likely lose $8,000. However, if the locks are purchased at a cost of $1,000, the company will only lose $2,000. In other words, the company is spending $1,000 to save $6,000.

> **NOTE**
> These formulas typically look at a single year. The calculations can become quite complex if you include other costs. Depreciation costs, maintenance costs, and replacement costs for follow-on years are usually not included in the calculations.

Benefits

One of the primary benefits of a quantitative RA is that it becomes a simple math problem. This is especially true if you use tools that automate the assessment. For example, applications are available that allow you to plug in values for SLE, ARO, and safeguard value. The application then calculates the results and provides a recommendation. Because the application performs the calculations, the data is often more accurate.

> **NOTE**
>
> Cost-benefit analysis was covered in Chapter 1. If the benefits of a control outweigh the costs, you can implement the control to reduce the risk. If the costs are greater than the benefits, you can accept the risk.

Another big benefit of a quantitative RA is that it provides a CBA. When you have accurate values for the SLE, ARO, and safeguard value, you can also calculate the CBA. You saw this in the previous section.

Management is often familiar with quantitative assessment terminology. For example, a quantitative assessment uses dollar terms to express losses. Because of this, it becomes easy for management to grasp the details of the assessment and its recommendations.

Last, the formulas use verifiable and objective measurements. If a Web site makes $2,000 in revenue an hour, it will lose that revenue if it is down for one hour. This isn't a debatable opinion; it's a verifiable fact.

Limitations

There are some limitations to using a quantitative analysis. One of the biggest limitations is that accurate data isn't always available. This is especially true when identifying ARO reductions. The accuracy of these estimates can be difficult to verify.

For example, an earlier example stated that if hardware locks were purchased, the ARO would decrease from 4 to 1. In other words, instead of four laptops being stolen each year, only one laptop would be stolen. It sounds good, but how do you know it's true? The accuracy of this estimate is difficult to verify. This difficulty is also a vulnerability when reporting to skeptical or unsupportive managers.

Another limitation is ensuring that people use the control as expected. Hardware locks were mentioned in the example to protect the laptops. As long as everyone uses the hardware locks, they will work. However, users may consider them inconvenient. Just because the locks are purchased doesn't mean they will be used.

You may need to take additional steps to ensure users are aware of the importance of the control. Even though laptop computers are stolen all the time, users are still very surprised when it happens to them. You may need to create policies requiring the use of the control. Additionally, you may need to include training to reinforce the importance of the control.

Qualitative Risk Assessments

A **qualitative risk assessment** doesn't assign dollar values. Instead, it determines the level of risk based on the **probability** and **impact** of a risk. You determine these values by gathering the opinions of experts.

Probability and impact are defined as:

- **Probability**—The likelihood that a threat will exploit a vulnerability. The risk occurs when a threat exploits a vulnerability. You can use a scale to define the probability that a risk will occur. The scale can be based on word values such as Low, Medium, or High. You can then assign percentage values to these words. For example, you could assign a value of 10 percent to a low probability. You could assign 100 percent to a high probability.

- **Impact**—The negative result if a risk occurs. Impact is used to identify the magnitude of a risk. The risk results in some type of loss. However, instead of quantifying the loss as a dollar amount, an impact assessment could use words such as Low, Medium, or High. You may also use these categories to identify probabilities. However, where a probability is expressed as a percentage, impact is expressed as a relative value. For example, Low could be 10. Medium could be 50. High could be 100.

> **NOTE**
>
> An important point to realize about the qualitative RA is that you must define the scale. However, there is no single standard. One company may use three values of Low, Medium, and High. Another company may use five values of Slight, Slightly Moderate, Moderate, Moderately Severe, and Severe. As long as you define the scale in the RA, any scale can be used.

You can calculate the risk level with the following formula:

Risk level = Probability × Impact

Tables 5-1 and 5-2 show one way you could define the scales in an RA. You would assign the values for each of these scales based on current known threats and vulnerabilities, as well as current controls.

TABLE 5-1	Probability scale.
PROBABILITY	**DESCRIPTION**
Low	It is unlikely the risk will occur. Threats are not active. Vulnerabilities are either not known or have been mitigated. Low equates to a value of 10 percent.
Medium	There is a moderate chance the risk will occur. It has occurred in the past, but mitigation controls have reduced recent occurrences. Medium equates to a value of 50 percent.
High	There is a high probability the risk will occur. It has occurred in the past and will occur again if not mitigated. High equates to a value of 100 percent.

TABLE 5-2	Impact scale.
IMPACT	**DESCRIPTION**
Low	If the risk occurs, it will have minimal impact on the company. The attack will not impact any critical data or systems.
Medium	If the risk occurs, it will have a moderate impact on the company. It may affect critical data or systems, but not to a large extent.
High	If the risk occurs, it will have a high impact on the company. It will affect critical data or systems and cause substantial losses.

A qualitative analysis can be divided into two sections:

- The first section attempts to prioritize the risk.
- The second section evaluates the effectiveness of controls.

It is possible to perform both sections at the same time. However, for clarity, they are presented as two separate actions in this chapter.

Prioritizing the Risk

The goal of this part of the RA is to identify which risks are most important. You do this by assigning probability and impact values to known risks.

For example, your company Web site sells company products. Due to some recent outages, you are trying to identify the most important risks to the Web site. Based on feedback from several experts, you have come up with a list. You now want to prioritize these risks.

The risk categories are:

- **DoS attack**—Any denial of service (DoS) or distributed DoS (DDoS) attack that results in an outage
- **Web defacing**—Modification of the Web site by unauthorized parties
- **Loss of data from unauthorized access**—Any loss of confidentiality. This could be from an attacker accessing customer data. It could also be from an attacker accessing any internal private data. It does not include the loss of public data that is freely available.
- **Loss of Web site data due to hardware failure**—This indicates the loss of any Web site data. This can include any data used to show the Web pages to customers. It can also include the Web site application used to retrieve and format the data into Web pages.

The Web site is protected in a demilitarized zone (DMZ). It also has antivirus (AV) software installed. You could distribute the survey on the next page to key experts to determine risks.

You can conduct these surveys in several ways: via surveys that are filled out independently, by interviewing experts, or within a meeting but without discussion. Consider what can happen if there is discussion: If the boss says "Clearly, loss of data will have a high impact," the statement may influence subordinates. Some may have thought the value is Low, but may instead enter it as High or Medium.

After you gather data from the experts, you compile and summarize it. If you assign numerical values to Low, Medium, and High, such as 10, 50, and 100, you can calculate the averages.

Table 5-3 shows how the results could look. The average probabilities and impacts have been summarized and entered into each box. For example, for the DoS attack, the average probability was determined to be 100 and the impact was also determined to be 100. This was calculated by averaging each of the inputs by the different experts. You determine the risk level by multiplying the Probability × the Impact.

Survey for Determining Risks

We are attempting to identify the most serious risks to our Web site. Please fill in each block of the following table with a level of Low, Medium, or High. Your decisions should be based on current controls and safeguards. For example, the Web site is currently placed on the Internet and is protected with a host-based firewall. Assume this firewall will remain.

Qualitative analysis survey.		
CATEGORY	PROBABILITY THE RISK WILL OCCUR (Low, Medium, High)	IMPACT IF THE RISK OCCURS (Low, Medium, High)
DoS attack		
Web defacing		
Loss of data from unauthorized access		
Loss of Web site data due to hardware failure		

TABLE 5-3	Qualitative analysis survey results.		
CATEGORY	PROBABILITY	IMPACT	RISK LEVEL (1 to 100)
DoS attack	100	100	100 (1.0 × 100)
Web defacing	50	90	45 (0.5 × 90)
Loss of data from unauthorized access	30	10	3 (0.3 × 10)
Loss of Web site data due to hardware failure	30	27	27 (0.3 × 90)

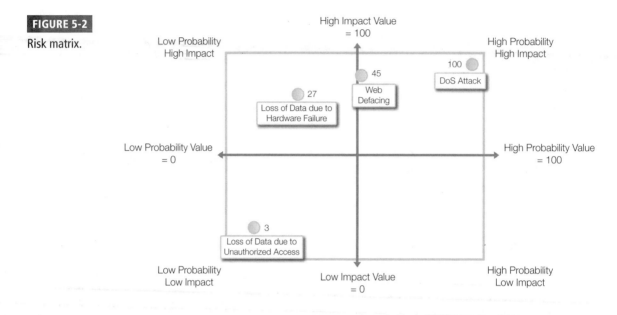

FIGURE 5-2

Risk matrix.

You can present this data graphically in many ways. The risk matrix in Figure 5-2 shows one method.

At this point, it's clear that the highest risk is from a DoS attack. It has a risk level of 100. The lowest risk level is 3 for the loss of data from unauthorized access.

Loss of data sounds as if it would be very important. However, if existing controls and practices have removed most of the risk, the impact is reduced. For example, all non-public data could already have been removed from the Web site. While someone may try to hack into the Web site to get the data, the impact is Low since the site holds only public data.

On the other hand, the risk of a DoS attack clearly rises to the top as the biggest risk. Based on the current controls, the experts agree that the system will be attacked. When it is attacked, they also agree that the impact will be high.

The list of risks from most important to least important is:

- **Priority 1**—DoS attack, with a value of 100
- **Priority 2**—Web defacing, with a value of 45
- **Priority 3**—Loss of Web site data due to hardware failure, with a value of 27
- **Priority 4**—Loss of data from unauthorized access, with a value of 3

Evaluating the Effectiveness of Controls

A this point, you could determine which safeguards or controls to apply for high-impact risks. A survey could help here also. For example, you could use the following survey.

Notice that "Loss of data from unauthorized access" is not included in the survey table. Because the experts have agreed that it doesn't present a risk, there is no need to mitigate it. Said another way, management in this case has decided to accept the risk.

Survey for Determining Safeguards or Controls

The following table lists controls in the left column. Across the top it lists risks. Please enter a value of Low, Medium, or High in each box. The value you enter should indicate the value of the control to mitigate the risk. For example, if you think placing the Web server in a DMZ will have a high success rate in preventing DoS attacks, enter High in this box. If you think it will have a low success rate, enter Low.

Mitigation choices survey.			
CONTROL	**DOS ATTACK** (Low, Medium, High)	**WEB DEFACING** (Low, Medium, High)	**LOSS OF WEB SITE DATA DUE TO HARDWARE FAILURE** (Low, Medium, High)
Place Web server in DMZ			
Add IDS			
Add RAID for data			
Create backup plan			

Just as you can summarize the risks, you can also summarize the effectiveness of the controls. Table 5-4 shows the presumed results of the survey. As in other surveys, high has a value of 100. Medium has a value of 50. Low has a value of 10.

FYI

RAID is an acronym for **redundant array of independent disks**. It is also called "redundant array of inexpensive disks." Different RAID configurations allow a system to continue to run even if a disk drive fails. Sophisticated RAIDs allow a system to operate even if more than one disk drive fails. RAID provides fault tolerance. A fault can occur and the disk subsystem can tolerate it. It will continue to operate. "IDS" stands for intrusion detection system.

TABLE 5-4	Mitigation choices survey results.		
CONTROL	**DOS ATTACK**	**WEB DEFACING**	**LOSS OF WEB SITE DATA DUE TO HARDWARE FAILURE**
Place Web server in DMZ	100	75	10
Add IDS	75	25	10
Add RAID for data	10	10	100
Create backup plan	10	50	100

From Table 5-4 you can see that placing the server in the DMZ will provide the best protection from a DoS attack. Additionally, an IDS will also provide a high level of protection. The table helps to match up the best controls for the individual risks as follows:

- **DoS attack**—Protect with DMZ and/or IDS.
- **Web defacing**—Protect with DMZ.
- **Loss of Web site data due to hardware failure**—
  Protect with RAID and backup plan.

Benefits

A qualitative assessment has several primary benefits:

- Uses the opinions of the experts
- Is easy to complete
- Uses words that are easy to express and understand

Data is gathered from the experts. These people know the systems the best. Their combined system knowledge and experience allows them to identify the source of problems quickly. As long as you have access to the experts, the RA is easy to complete. You don't even need to have them meet together. You can interview them separately. You can provide the experts with surveys and have them complete the surveys at their own pace.

The qualitative risk assessment uses scales. These scales can easily be adapted to the culture of the organization. They allow individuals to understand what the values are, and they can be expressed in words they use every day. This also makes it easier to involve people who may be expert in their field, but not an expert on security or computers.

For example, a human relations (HR) expert may have significant knowledge about the requirements for HIPAA. He or she know the dangers if data is not protected— the actual fines that can be assessed or the jail time awarded. HR experts can provide substantial input into the risk assessment.

Performing an Assessment with the Delphi Method

One way that is commonly used to perform a qualitative assessment is the Delphi Method. This can be used to gather data and help create or identify a consensus.

A primary benefit of the Delphi Method is that it allows individuals to freely share their opinions without pressure. Instead of all the participants talking through an issue in a meeting, responses are gathered independently.

The Delphi Method can be accomplished in several ways. One way is to work through the following steps:

1. **Identify a problem.** This can be a single IT system or a group of servers. The problem should be within the knowledge of experts you'll add to the team. For example, the problem could be related to the Web site failures. It could be stated as: WebServer1 has suffered four failures in the past year resulting in losses.

2. **Gather input from experts.** Send the problem to the group of experts and ask them to respond. For the Web server failure, you could ask them to identify primary risks. If you have an idea of the causes, you can then ask them to identify the probability and risk. If you know the highest risks, you can repeat the process to identify the best solutions.

3. **Collate the responses.** The responses will be in different forms for different phases. For example, the responses could just be a list of risks. They could be a prioritized list of risks. Or they could be a list of controls to mitigate the risk.

4. **Share the results.** This will also look different depending on the phase you're in. If you've just collated a list of risks, you can now ask the team to identify the probability and impact of each risk. When you start working on the controls, you can repeat the process. Ask for a list of controls to mitigate the risk. You can then ask the team to identify the effectiveness of the different controls for specific risks.

5. **Repeat as necessary.** Repeat the process until all the data is gathered.

You have a lot of flexibility with the process. Today, this can often be done via e-mail. Many e-mail programs actually allow you to send surveys so users only need to click a button. You could also have them fill out surveys created on an internal Web server. This may take a little time to develop, but you can quickly collate the results.

In is important that the data be gathered independently. If you gather the data in a meeting, participant responses may be slanted based on the opinions of others in the room. A strong participant can sway others and prevent full participation from the team.

Limitations

A qualitative assessment has several limitations. These include:

- **Subjective**—The analysis and results are based on opinions more than facts. A different perspective on these opinions could provide a completely different result. If the opinions are gathered in a group, a strong participant could shape the ideas of the entire group.
- **Based on expertise of the experts**—The value of the assessment is only as valuable as the expertise of the experts. If the experts have a solid foundation of knowledge and wide breadth of experience, the results can be valuable. On the other hand, if you don't have access to real experts, the results may have very limited value.
- **No CBA**—It does not include a cost-benefit analysis. The usefulness of the controls isn't as clear as with a quantitative analysis. Although the opinions of the experts are still valuable, the results may not be as clear to management. Management may have a more difficult time deciding which safeguards to use.
- **No real standards**—A company needs to define the scales used in the process. For example, the scale can be as simple as Low, Medium, and High. However, the scale needs to be developed and defined for the participants. This requires the expertise of someone that understands risk assessments and how the data will be used.

Comparing Quantitative and Qualitative Risk Assessments

As a reminder, neither method is considered superior to the other. They both have benefits and limitations. As a summary, here are a few comparisons between both quantitative and qualitative risk assessments.

Quantitative analysis:

- Objective
- Uses numeric values such as dollar amounts
- More time consuming
- Requires access to a significant amount of historical data
- Data not always easy to obtain
- Based on SLE, ARO, and ALE formulas
- Shows clear losses and savings with dollar values
- Data can easily be used in a CBA

Qualitative analysis:

- Subjective
- Based on opinions of experts
- Can be done quicker at a lower cost than quantitative analysis
- Uses word values such as Low, Medium, and High
- Requires a definition of scales used in the RA

Sample Risk Assessment Outline

A risk assessment ends with a report. This report can then be used by management to decide what controls to implement. The following is a list of topics that are commonly included in a risk assessment report:

- **Introduction**—The introduction provides the purpose and scope of the risk assessment. It includes descriptions about the components, users, and locations for the system considered in the RA.

- **Risk assessment approach**—This section identifies the approach used to complete the RA. It includes details on how the data was collected and who was involved. If a qualitative approach is used it will describe the risk scale.

- **System characterization**—This section provides more details on the system. It could include details on the hardware, software, or network connections. It may include diagrams to graphically show the assessed system.

- **Threat statement**—This section lists potential threats, threat sources, and threat actions. For example, one threat may be an attacker launching a denial of service (DoS) attack on an Internet facing server.

- **Risk assessment results**—Results can be listed as vulnerability/threat pairs representing a risk. The risk is described with existing security controls. The likelihood of the risk occurring with current controls is listed. How the risks are described depends on which analysis is used. A quantitative method uses terms such as SLE, ARO, and ALE. A qualitative method identifies probability and impact based on a defined scale. All of this data is supported with discussions identifying how the result was obtained.

- **Control recommendations**—A list of recommended safeguards or controls is provided. This list can include comments on the effectiveness of the controls. A quantitative method will often be accompanied by a CBA for each control. qualitative method will often rank the effectiveness of the control.

- **Summary**—The summary can be in one or more tables that summarize the results. This format makes it easy for management to see the highest risks based on the risk rating. It also makes it easy to approve any of the recommendations.

Risk Assessment Challenges

When completing any risk assessment, you have several challenges to address and overcome. Many of these are dependent on the type of assessment you choose. Both the quantitative and qualitative assessments have their own challenges. These were listed in the previous section as limitations.

There are several additional challenges. These include:

- Using a static process to evaluate a moving target
- Availability of data and resources
- Data consistency
- Estimating impact effects
- Providing results that support resource allocation and risk acceptance

These challenges are explored in the following sections.

Using a Static Process to Evaluate a Moving Target

As mentioned previously, the RA is a point-in-time assessment. It evaluates the system against known risks at a specific time. It considers the risks based on current controls. In other words, the RA is a static process. However, security is not static. Risks can and do change. Attackers and attacks are constantly changing. Security does not stand still.

As attackers become successful at any attack, security experts implement controls. At some point, these attacks are less successful. Attackers then learn new methods of attack. Security experts modify the controls, or implement new controls. The battle continues daily.

Some threats and vulnerabilities look as if they've been mitigated successfully and no longer present a risk. Then, they appear suddenly as another threat. Domain Name Server (DNS) cache poisoning is a good example. DNS cache poisoning can cause a system to resolve a Web site name to a bogus Internet Protocol (IP) address. For example, users may try to access Acme.com with a Web browser. However, they are instead redirected to Malware4u.com. DNS cache poisoning was identified years ago as a significant threat. It was successfully mitigated and fell into disuse. From an IT security perspective, it almost became a historical footnote.

Then in the summer of 2008, a flaw was discovered and published by Dan Kaminsky. Quick as a flash, DNS cache poisoning was once again an issue. Once the results were published, attackers quickly learned how to exploit the vulnerability. DNS cache poisoning was once again raised as a serious concern.

If your RA was completed in March, but a vulnerability is announced in June that affects your system, the validity of the assessment is affected. For this reason, you'll need to be aware of new risks as they become known.

FYI

One way to stay informed of vulnerabilities is to subscribe to alerts from the US-Computer Emergency Readiness Team (US-CERT). If you do so, you'll see that new vulnerabilities are discovered every week. Some of these represent very serious risks. You can sign up to receive e-mails and alerts from the US-CERT team at *https://forms.us-cert.gov/maillists*.

Availability

Availability challenges are present in two primary areas. One relates to the availability of resources. The other relates to the availability of data. Both are important to address early in the process of the RA. If not addressed, they can seriously affect the quality.

First, resources: Personnel involved in the assessment should be knowledgeable about the system they are assessing. With a higher level of expertise, you can expect a higher quality assessment. If the RA team does not have the high level of knowledge and experience they need, they may have to resort to guessing.

The RA needs support from upper management. This support will help ensure that management dedicates adequate resources to the team. If you're leading an RA and have problems getting support from a specific department, upper management can help. On the other hand, if you don't have upper level support, you're likely to get less and less support for the project.

As far as data goes, its availability is also important. Data availability will drive the type of assessment you perform. For example, if you have a lot of internal historical data related to actual performance and outages, you can use it to perform a quantitative RA. You can use this historical data to identify values for SLE and ARO. If this data isn't available, you will probably do a qualitative RA instead.

> **TIP**
>
> If you have access to historical data, you may still decide to perform a qualitative risk assessment. One of the reasons you may choose to do a qualitative RA instead of a quantitative RA is time. You can usually complete a qualitative RA more quickly than a quantitative RA.

Without the availability of the right personnel and the right data, the RA becomes much more difficult to complete. If you address the issues early, you'll have a better chance of success.

Data Consistency

Another challenge with risk assessments is data consistency. Data consistency refers to the accuracy of data. Several issues can affect data consistency. These include:

- Differences in data format
- Changes in data collection
- Changes in the business

Each of these concerns can directly affect the accuracy of the data. However, even if the data isn't 100 percent accurate, it doesn't mean that you can't use it.

Some risk assessments address the accuracy of data with an **uncertainty level**. An uncertainty level indicates how valid the data is. If all conditions were ideal the data would be 100 percent accurate, and you would be 100 percent sure that it is accurate. In this case, you would have a zero percent uncertainty level. In the real world, however, a zero percent uncertainty level is unlikely.

For example, historical data could indicate that a Web site generates approximately $2,000 per revenue per hour. Current data could indicate this trend is continuing with slight growth. You could be 80 percent certain that the data is accurate, or have a 20 percent uncertainty level. When using this sales data to calculate SLE, you could also provide the uncertainty level.

Differences in Data Format

Data format can affect how data is used, manipulated, and interpreted. In general, a database is more efficient to query and manipulate large amounts of data. However, data could have been originally created in a word processing document or a spreadsheet. If data was migrated from one format to another, you can choose to weigh the accuracy of the data differently.

For example, say image data was previously stored in a Microsoft Excel worksheet but is now stored in a Microsoft SQL Server database. When it was stored in the worksheet, it met the needs of the user. However, it wasn't easy to view data from different perspectives or query it to show different totals and subtotals. In the database, it is now easy to use queries to view the data with multiple perspectives. The data may be very similar, but the database allows you to gain a deeper perspective on the data.

With this in mind, the users who worked with the Excel worksheets may have drawn accurate conclusions. However, the conclusions may not be as substantial as conclusions drawn from data stored in a database.

If the data is from different sources, you should recognize that it may have been interpreted differently. With this in mind, you may notice some inconsistencies when comparing the data. All of this can affect the uncertainty level of the data.

Changes in Data Collection

Changes in data collection can also affect the accuracy of data. The primary change you'll likely see is a change from manual data collection to automated data collection.

There are many wonderful things to say about humans, but the truth is humans aren't the best at mundane repetitive tasks. Computers are. When people collect and enter data manually, you should have checks in place. In other words, is the data entered by one user double-checked by another user? Manual data entry can negatively affect your uncertainty level. Failing to double-check the data for accuracy can also affect the uncertainty level.

On the other hand, if data is collected using automated methods, the predictability of data is much higher. If data is collected, stored, and manipulated using automated methods, your uncertainty level will be much lower.

Changes in the Business

The amount of business a company does this year is usually different from last year. This is often due to growth. For some businesses, however, it could be due to loss of market share or some other business reason. The fact is, sales are rarely stagnant. In fact, stagnant sales are perceived negatively.

It is important to understand what happened in the past so you can predict what will happen in the future. However, the future is never exactly the same as the past. For example, a Web site may have had an average of $2,000 per hour in revenue last year. However, the sales over the Christmas season may have doubled over the previous year and current predictions are that this year's sales may also double. All this put together may require that you modify the average sales per hour to $4,000 instead of $2,000.

Similarly, the company could have lost market share in a certain sales market. There may be less money for research and development, less money for marketing, or any of a dozen other reasons for this change. So, if sales are decreasing, you should take this into consideration.

Then again, while sales data may show that sales data are decreasing, a new manager may be instituting changes to increase sales. There may be preliminary signs of increased sales. All of this could lead you to change the uncertainty level of numbers used.

Estimating Impact Effects

The potential impact of any risk is difficult to estimate. The most important thing to realize is that this is an estimate. If you could accurately predict exactly what will happen in the future, you probably wouldn't be working in the IT field.

When estimating the impact effects, several factors come into play. This is true even if you have accurate historical data. For example, a Web site could have been attacked resulting in an outage of several hours. While troubleshooting the outage the technicians learn quite a bit. Yes, the primary focus is to resolve this current outage. However, the knowledge and experience is tucked away. The next time the server suffers an outage, the recovery time may be much quicker.

Even this example is dependent on different variables. A company with a high turnover rate of IT professionals doesn't build up the same experience level. If a system is down for the same reason it was down six months ago, but it's the first time a new technician has seen it, the outage will likely be just as long.

On the other hand, previous attacks may have been successful due to vulnerabilities in the system. If these vulnerabilities were discovered, they were likely corrected. However, even if they were corrected, it doesn't mean you'll know about the corrections. The changes may have been made without any documentation.

You may think that everything is the same today as it was during the previous attack. Instead, several changes may have been implemented that reduce the likelihood of the attack, or the impact of the attack. In this example, the uncertainty level may be dependent on change management practices in the organization.

> **NOTE**
>
> Change management is a process that ensures that changes are made only after a review process. Additionally, change management ensures that changes are documented. Chapter 3 mentioned the Information Technology Infrastructure Library (ITIL). Change management is an important process covered by ITIL. Other companies use change management processes even if they aren't following ITIL practices directly.

Providing Results That Support Resource Allocation and Risk Acceptance

The results of an RA need to be useful. That probably doesn't come as any surprise. However, it is possible for security professionals to fall into the trap of thinking security must be pursued at all costs. This isn't true. A proper balance between profitability and survivability must constantly be considered.

Two important points to consider are:

- Resource allocation
- Risk acceptance

Resource Allocation

Security teams don't have an unlimited amount of funds, or an unlimited number of personnel. Instead, security will be allocated a finite percentage of resources. This is important to keep in mind when performing the risk assessment.

Any recommendations need to be realistic. They need to consider the culture of the business and the actual potential for the recommendations to be accepted.

Risk Acceptance

Some organizations are willing to accept more risks than others. This isn't right or wrong, it's just the way a business operates. When creating a risk assessment you need to be aware of the business culture.

There are two sides to accepting more risk:

1. The greater the risk, the greater the rewards.
2. Bigger risks present larger potential losses.

> **NOTE**
>
> Residual risk was presented in Chapter 1. Any risk that remains after management has decided to implement controls is referred to as residual risk. Senior management is responsible for making these decisions. Additionally, senior management is responsible for any losses that occur as a result of residual risk.

Consider the stock market. There are many companies in existence today that had stock for sale for less than a dollar at one point. If you bought $10,000 of their stock, you'd be a millionaire today. However, few actually bought that $10,000 of stock. The reason is that when the stock was at a low price it wasn't clear the company would survive. Some people took the risk and have great rewards. However, others took similar risks on other companies that have since gone bankrupt. Their risky investment turned out to be a huge loss.

It's important to remember who makes the big decisions in a company—senior management. They are responsible for identifying what risks to mitigate, transfer, avoid, or accept. When making your recommendations to senior management, you should consider what residual risk you expect them to accept. Your recommendations should be consistent with what you expect to be accepted.

This is not to say that data should be hidden. You still have a responsibility to present all of the data. If some of the recommendations clearly don't look as if they will be accepted, you can include them in the report. You just don't need to include them in the list of actual recommendations.

Best Practices for Risk Assessment

Risk assessments can proceed differently in different organizations. A risk assessment of a Web server may look substantially different from an assessment that evaluates HIPAA data. However, you can include several things to help ensure success.

The following list identifies several best practices for risk assessment approaches:

- **Start with clear goals and a defined scope**—Ensure that you know what you want to achieve with the assessment. A risk assessment should include a scope statement. The scope statement helps keep the assessment on track and prevents scope creep.

- **Ensure senior management support**—Senior management needs to be committed to the RA. Without support, the RA loses value. When RA teams realize the RA isn't valued, they put less time and effort into it. An assessment without senior management support is almost doomed from the outset.

- **Build a strong RA team**—The value of the RA is based on the competence and expertise of the RA team. Team members should have expertise in the system. For example, imagine that you are using a qualitative analysis. If you are gathering data from personnel who aren't experts, their opinions aren't as valuable. Team members should also understand the methodology used for the RA.

- **Repeat the RA regularly**—Threats, risks, and vulnerabilities are constantly evolving. An RA should be repeated on a regular basis. Some federal agencies require RAs to be repeated at least every three years. Many organizations create a risk assessment policy. The policy identifies what the organization is expected to do on a recurring basis. It can also be used to define generic goals for any risk assessments.

- **Define a methodology to use**—If you consistently use the same methodology, people become better at it. For example, your company could decide to use qualitative risk assessments on a regular basis. If this is the case, you should also define scales that should be used. When assessments are done the same way, they are easier to accomplish and tend to provide higher quality results.

- **Provide a report of clear risks and clear recommendations**—Every risk assessment should end with a report that identifies the findings. These findings should be clearly stated. It's important to ensure that the risks are clearly defined. It's even more important to ensure that recommendations are clear. The whole purpose of the RA is ultimately to mitigate risks with recommended controls. If the recommendations aren't clear, the report loses a significant amount of value.

CHAPTER SUMMARY

Risk assessments are used to identify and quantify risks. They do so by identifying threats and vulnerabilities and then applying an assessment methodology to prioritize the risks. Once the risks are quantified, controls and safeguards can be identified. A risk assessment can also be used to identify the best controls to implement.

The two primary risk assessment methods are quantitative and qualitative. You use a quantitative risk assessment when historical data is readily available. This data can be used to derive the ALE from SLE and ARO: ARO = SLE × ARO. A qualitative risk assessment uses the opinions of experts. It doesn't have predefined formulas but instead requires you to create your own scale, such as Low, Medium, and High. The quantitative RA provides a cost-benefit analysis. The qualitative RA, on the other hand, can be accomplished in a shorter period of time.

KEY CONCEPTS AND TERMS

Annual loss expectancy (ALE)
Annualized rate of occurrence (ARO)
Impact
Probability

Qualitative risk assessment
Quantitative risk assessment
RAID (redundant array of independent disks)
Risk assessment (RA)

Safeguard
Safeguard value
Single loss expectancy (SLE)
Single point of failure (SPOF)
Uncertainty level

CHAPTER 5 ASSESSMENT

1. What can you use to help quantify risks?

    A. SLE

    B. ARO

    C. Risk assessment

    D. Risk mitigation plan

    E. All of the above

2. A risk _____ is a major component of a risk management plan.

3. Risk assessments are a continuous process.

    A. True

    B. False

4. A _____ uses SLE.

5. What elements are included in a qualitative analysis?

    A. SLE, ALE, ARO

    B. ALE, ARO, ARP

    C. Probability and impact

    D. Threats and vulnerabilities

6. What elements are included in a quantitative analysis?

    A. SLE, ALE, ARO

    B. ALE, ARO, ARP

    C. Probability and impact

    D. Threats and vulnerabilities

7. Qualitative analysis is more time consuming than quantitative analysis.

    A. True

    B. False

8. You are trying to decide what type of risk assessment methodology to use. A primary benefit of a _____ risk assessment is that it can be completed quicker than other methods.

9. You are trying to decide what type of risk assessment methodology to use. A primary benefit of a _____ risk assessment is that it includes details for a cost-benefit analysis.

10. What must you define when performing a qualitative risk assessment?

    A. Formulas used for ALE

    B. Scales used to define probability and impact

    C. Scales used to define SLE and ALE

    D. Acceptable levels of risk

11. A _____ risk assessment is objective. It uses data that can be verified.

12. A _____ risk assessment is subjective. It relies on the opinions of experts.

13. One of the challenges facing risk assessments is getting accurate data. What can be included in the risk assessment report to give an indication of the reliability of the data?

    A. Probability statement

    B. Accuracy scale

    C. Validity level

    D. Uncertainty level

14. You are working on a qualitative risk assessment for your company. You are thinking about the final report. What should you consider when providing the results and recommendations? (Select two.)

    A. Resource allocation

    B. Risk acceptance

    C. SLE and ARO

    D. SLE and ALE

15. Of the following, what would be considered a best practice when performing risk assessments?

    A. Start with clear goals and a defined support

    B. Ensure support of senior management

    C. Repeat the risk assessment regularly

    D. Provide clear recommendations

    E. All of the above

Performing a Risk Assessment

T HERE ARE SEVERAL STEPS TO TAKE when performing a risk assessment. You start by clearly defining what you will assess. This involves describing the system. You then collect data to identify threats and vulnerabilities. These threats and vulnerabilities help you identify the risks.

Then identify countermeasures or controls that can mitigate the risks. Evaluate in-place and planned controls. Finally, evaluate and recommend additional controls. You can support these recommendations with a cost-benefit analysis.

Chapter 6 Topics

This chapter covers the following topics and concepts:

- What to consider when selecting a risk assessment methodology
- How to identify the management structure
- How to identify assets and activities
- How to identify and evaluate relevant threats
- How to identify and evaluate relevant vulnerabilities
- How to identify and evaluate countermeasures
- How to select a methodology based on the assessment needs
- How to develop mitigating recommendations

Chapter 6 Goals

When you complete this chapter, you will be able to:

- Select an appropriate risk assessment methodology
- Define the operational characteristics and mission of the system to be assessed
- State the importance of reviewing previous findings and status
- Describe the relevance of a management structure to a risk assessment
- Identify the types of assets to include in a risk assessment
- List steps to identify and evaluate threats
- List actions to identify and evaluate vulnerabilities
- List actions to identify and evaluate countermeasures
- Describe the difference between in-place and planned countermeasures
- Describe the process used to assess threats, vulnerabilities, and exploits
- Describe the process used to develop mitigation recommendations
- Describe the results of a risk assessment
- List best practices for performing risk assessments

Selecting a Risk Assessment Methodology

Once you decide to perform a risk assessment (RA), you'll need to outline how you'll proceed. In other words, you'll need to decide what specific steps to take. An RA isn't a project that you can decide to do one day and complete it the next. It takes time and planning.

Chapter 5 covered RA approaches with a focus on types of RAs. The two primary types are quantitative and qualitative. This chapter helps to paint the overall picture of an RA. Later chapters will provide details of each step in the process. In general, a risk assessment involves the following steps:

1. Identify assets and activities to address.
2. Identify and evaluate relevant threats.
3. Identify and evaluate relevant vulnerabilities.
4. Identify and evaluate relevant countermeasures.
5. Assess threats, vulnerabilities, and exploits.
6. Evaluate risks.
7. Develop recommendations to mitigate risks.
8. Present recommendations to management.

Before progressing with the RA, you need to complete two preliminary actions. These are:

- Define the assessment.
- Review previous findings.

Defining the Assessment

You need to clearly define what you'll assess. If it's a system, you need to describe the system. If it's a process, you need to describe the process.

It's also important to describe the system or process as it is right now. Chapter 5 stressed that an RA is a point-in-time assessment. This is unlike overall risk management, which is a continuous process.

When describing the system or process, you will often focus on two primary areas:

- Operational characteristics
- Mission of the system

Another point from Chapter 5 was the importance of defining the scope of the risk assessment. When you define the assessment, you are defining the scope and boundaries. This helps prevent scope creep.

Operational Characteristics

Operational characteristics define how the system operates in your environment. It's not enough to just name the system, such as "E-mail server." Instead, you need to identify how the system is currently configured and operating.

Consider Figure 6-1. This shows a single e-mail server in a network. The e-mail server handles all e-mail to and from the Internet. It provides e-mail services for all clients in the internal network. Now, let's say this illustration is old and doesn't reflect the organization's current configuration.

FIGURE 6-1

E-mail server in a network.

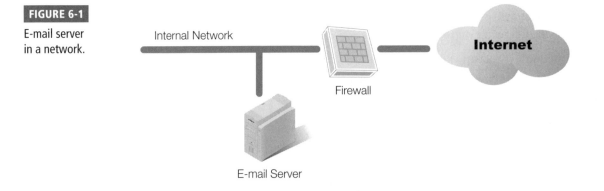

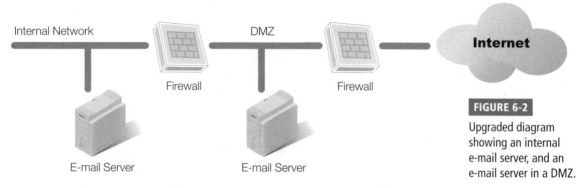

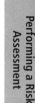

FIGURE 6-2

Upgraded diagram
showing an internal
e-mail server, and an
e-mail server in a DMZ.

Now look at Figure 6-2. Figure 6-2 shows the organization's current network diagram, which has a demilitarized zone (DMZ). The DMZ includes one e-mail server used to send and receive e-mail from the Internet. The internal e-mail server sends and receives e-mail from the DMZ server but does not interact with the Internet.

The differences between Figures 6-1 and 6-2 help show the importance of documenting operational characteristics. What would happen if you began an RA by evaluating the threats against the system in Figure 6-1? Your information would be outdated, and you would spend valuable time on the wrong effort.

You need to perform the RA against the current system. However, the current configuration isn't always apparent or readily available. It sometimes takes some digging. Some simple questions you can ask include:

- Do you have current diagrams that show all of the current systems?
- Do you have documentation of the current configuration?

Mission of the System

The mission of the system defines what the system does. Compared to the operational characteristics of the system, the mission is easy to define. The mission definition for any single system can be as short as a paragraph. It can also consist of simple bullet statements.

For example, an e-mail system could have the following mission:

The e-mail server provides all e-mail services for the network. This includes the following functions:

- Routing e-mail between internal clients
- Accepting e-mail from external e-mail servers and routing to internal client
- Accepting e-mail from internal clients and routing to external e-mail servers
- Scanning all e-mail attachments and removing malware
- Scanning all e-mail for spam and stripping out confirmed spam

Managing Configuration and Change

Configuration management and change management are two important risk management processes. They also have a direct impact on risk assessments. These two processes are sometimes mentioned together, but they are different.

Configuration management ensures that similar systems have the same, or at least similar, configurations. When systems are very similar, you can use techniques such as baselines, scripting, and automation to configure them more efficiently. Systems that share the same configuration are easier to maintain collectively. They are also easier to evaluate for risks.

Change management prevents unapproved changes to systems. All changes are formally requested using a change management process. Technical experts review the requests and then either approve or disapprove them. The goal is to reduce unintended outages from changes.

When you don't use change management, a change to one system can easily cause an outage in another system. For example, a technician in a large organization was troubleshooting a problem with a printer. The printer wasn't automatically receiving an Internet Protocol (IP) address, which prevented print jobs from reaching the printer. The technician manually assigned an IP address and verified the printer worked. This may sound harmless, and even helpful. It wasn't.

The IP address assigned to the printer was also assigned to a server that was being worked on at the time. After the server was repaired and brought online, it no longer worked. Its IP address was being used by the printer, causing an IP address conflict. Technicians had to spend extra time troubleshooting the issue and correcting both problems.

These problems could have been avoided with a change management process. The printer technician would have submitted the change request for the printer. The administrator that assigns IP addresses would easily have seen the conflict and denied the request. The server wouldn't have had an extended outage.

Additionally, the change management process ensures the correct documentation for changes.

When an organization has mature processes in place for configuration and change management, risk assessments are easier to perform. It's easier to identify the current status of a system. Available documentation is more up to date.

Chapter 9 covers configuration and change management in more depth.

Review Previous Findings

If previous audits or risk assessments are available, you should review them. These reports can contain a lot of valuable information to make your job easier.

These reports list assets, threats, and vulnerabilities. They should also list controls currently in place. They may provide recommendations for additional controls. Three items especially worth investigating are:

- **Recommendations**—Previous recommendations give insight into several issues. They address threats and vulnerabilities considered relevant at the time. They also include controls considered valuable at the time. Even though many issues may have changed, some may be the same or similar.

- **Current status of accepted recommendations**—Ideally, all accepted previous recommendations are in place. You can then measure the effectiveness of approved and implemented recommendations. However, if an approved recommendation isn't in place, the previous report may help you determine the reason why. Perhaps the hardware or software is still in the purchasing pipeline. Maybe the approved recommendation was simply ignored.

- **Unapproved recommendations**—The recommendations that were not approved can also give some insight into the business. They may indicate that the organization is willing to accept a higher level of residual risk. The organization could have suffered losses that would have been mitigated by an unapproved control. If that's true, management may be more receptive to the control at this time.

Identifying the Management Structure

The management structure refers to how responsibilities are assigned. When you define the scope of the RA, it's helpful to keep the scope within the ownership of a single entity. This allows for easier implementation of recommendations.

A small organization may have a single IT section. This single section is responsible for all IT systems and processes. Because this section controls all IT systems, the section can implement recommendations for any of the systems.

However, a larger organization may have multiple IT sections or divisions. In this case, various managers or management teams oversee different IT systems. Each manager has different responsibilities. For example, an organization may have the following sections for IT management:

- **Network infrastructure**—This section is responsible for all the routers and switches in the network. It may include all the firewalls.

- **User and computer management**—This section performs the day-to-day management of the network and accounts. It may also include basic security measures. For example, the **Group Policy** tool can manage accounts in a Microsoft domain. Administrators who manage the Microsoft domain would manage Group Policy.

> **NOTE**
> Group Policy is an automated management tool. You can set a policy once and allow it to apply to all users and computers in the domain. For example, you can set a password policy that applies to all users. This can ensure that end users use strong passwords and regularly change their passwords.

- **E-mail servers**—Some larger organizations have 10 or more e-mail servers to manage e-mail. Trained personnel are dedicated to primarily managing these servers. Personnel ensure e-mail delivery. They also manage spam filtering and malicious attachments.

- **Web servers**—An organization can have dozens of Web servers configured in one or more Web farms. A Web farm can generate a significant amount of revenue and have dedicated personnel to manage it.

- **Database servers**—Many organizations have a large amount of data stored in databases. Large databases are stored on dedicated servers. The knowledge needed to manage these servers is specialized, so some organizations have dedicated database administrators to manage them.

- **Configuration and change management**—This section oversees configuration and changes to either all servers or all systems. The team may be responsible for building new servers. They also coordinate and document all change requests.

A small organization may perform a risk assessment for many systems at the same time. However, a larger organization will likely separate the risk assessments.

For example, a larger organization that performs a risk assessment on Web servers, database servers, and firewalls at the same time can face problems. Three separate sections with three separate managers would need to implement the recommendations. The goals and schedules could compete with internal priorities.

However, if the organization assesses a single section at a time, the results are easier to implement. For example, you could perform three separate RAs. You could assess the Web servers, database servers, and firewalls separately. Each assessment would have specific recommendations targeted for the owners of the system.

Identifying Assets and Activities Within Risk Assessment Boundaries

Asset valuation is the process of determining the fair market value of an asset. This is one of the first priorities of risk management. You can determine the value from the replacement value of the asset. You can determine the value based on either what the asset provides to the organization, or the cost to recover the asset. It's also possible to determine the value using a combination of both values.

> **NOTE**
>
> This section introduces assets and activities related to risk assessment. Chapter 7 covers these topics in greater depth.

Once you know the value of your assets, you can then prioritize their importance. If an asset is worth $1,000, it needs one level of protection. If another asset is worth $1 million, it needs another level of protection.

It is important that you evaluate only assets that are within the boundary of the RA. Scope creep occurs when you start evaluating assets outside the scope of the RA. This results in wasted time and wasted resources.

When considering the value of an asset, you can look at it from different perspectives:

- **Replacement value**—This is the cost to purchase a new asset in its place. For example, if a laptop fails or is stolen, the price to purchase a new laptop with similar hardware and software may be $1,500.

- **Recovery value**—This is the cost to get the asset operational after a failure. For example, if the hard drive on a server fails, you wouldn't replace the entire server. Instead, you'd replace the hard drive and take steps to recover the system. This may require you to reinstall the operating system and restore data from a backup. You would also consider the time needed to perform the repair. For example, if a repair requires two hours, the system is not available for two hours. If it's a Web server generating $10,000 an hour in revenue, you would include $20,000 as part of the recovery value.

There are several elements to consider when determining the value of different assets. These include:

- System access and system availability
- System functions
- Hardware assets
- Software assets
- Personnel assets
- Data and information assets
- Facilities and supplies

System Access and System Availability

Access and availability refers to how and when the asset needs to be available. Some assets need to be available 24 hours a day, 7 days a week. Other assets only need to be available Monday through Friday during business hours. The more available the asset needs to be, the more risks you have related to outages.

For example, consider a Web server used to sell products over the Internet. Customers may access the Web site at any time. If the Web site is not operational when the customer tries to access it, you have lost a sale. More, you may have lost a customer.

With this in mind, the risk assessment needs to consider the risks associated with this Web site going down at any given time. Additionally, you need to consider how to perform maintenance on the system without taking the Web site down. This includes performing backups of the data. It also includes keeping the system up to date.

The Web server may be one of many servers in a Web farm. It may be one of multiple Web servers in a failover cluster. Both configurations allow a single server to go down while the Web site continues to function. If you run a single server, an outage can be catastrophic.

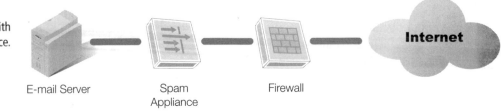

FIGURE 6-3

E-mail server with a spam appliance.

E-mail Server   Spam Appliance   Firewall   **Internet**

On the other hand, you could have a file server that is only used internally. Internal employees access it when they are at work. For example, employees may have standard works hours between 8:00 a.m. to 5:00 p.m., Monday through Friday. This schedule gives you extensive time to perform backups or other maintenance when employees are not at work.

System Functions

If a system provides a service, you should consider the functions of the system when determining the asset's value. Of particular importance is how the functions are performed: manually or through automation.

For example, imagine you're evaluating the value of e-mail in your organization. Your e-mail system could have multiple elements, including a spam filter. Studies report that as much as 90 percent of the e-mail sent through the Internet is spam. Spam filters will eliminate some of this spam with a goal of not eliminating any valid e-mails.

A spam filter that filters out as much as 30 percent of the spam provides a significant reduction in unwanted e-mail with a high assurance that valid e-mail isn't filtered. Figure 6-3 shows an e-mail server with a spam appliance added to filter spam.

In the figure, all e-mail is routed from the Internet through the spam appliance. The appliance filters some of the spam and sends the rest of the e-mail to the e-mail server.

With this in mind, what is the value of the spam filter? It uses an automated process so the value is simply the value of the appliance. If it breaks or malfunctions, you can replace it.

However, some spam filters require much more interaction. You could have dedicated technicians that are constantly viewing the filtered spam to ensure it doesn't include any valid e-mails. These technicians could be adding valid e-mail source addresses to whitelists. They could also be adding known spammers to blacklists.

> **FYI**
>
> An e-mail **whitelist** is a list of approved e-mail addresses or e-mail domains. For example, you can add *ProfJohnson@xyz.edu* to the whitelist to ensure any e-mail from this address is never marked as spam. You could also add the *xyz.edu* domain to ensure e-mail from anyone in the *xyz.edu* domain is not marked as spam. Addresses added to a **blacklist** are automatically marked as spam.

IT Appliances

Many IT appliances exist to help make the IT jobs a little easier. Technicians don't have to know how an appliance works. They just plug it in and it works.

Compare this to a toaster. You don't have to know the technical details of how the toaster works. You put in bread. Hot toast pops out. Of course, even a toaster has some knobs and controls. It does require a little user interaction.

A spam appliance works similarly. You give it power, connect the input to receive external e-mail, and send the output to your e-mail server. It automatically filters out some of the spam. Administrators can still interact with the spam filter. They may want to view the filtered spam. They may want to adjust the sensitivity of the spam filter. Many spam filters also allow you to add addresses. They let you always block some or always allow others.

A firewall appliance is another example. It needs little configuration after you plug it in. Administrators can still tweak it here and there for special needs. However, it will do most of what is needed right out of the box.

When calculating the value of the manually managed spam appliance, you also need to consider the work done by the administrators. The value may be higher if it takes additional man hours and expertise to initially configure it as well as manage it.

Hardware and Software Assets

Hardware assets are any assets that you can physically touch. This includes computers such as laptops, workstations, and servers. It also includes network devices such as routers, switches, and firewalls.

There is a wide range of values among the devices. A simple desktop PC can cost less than $500. However, a high-end server can cost tens of thousands of dollars.

Software assets include both the operating systems and the applications. The operating system is what allows the computer to operate. This could be a Microsoft operating system such as Windows 7 or Windows Server 2008. It could also be a UNIX or Macintosh operating system.

Applications allow you to perform tasks. For example, Microsoft Word is an application that allows you to create and edit documents. Similarly, Oracle is a server-level application used to manage databases.

Operating systems and applications can also have a wide range of costs. For example, the operating system and applications for a desktop PC can range in the hundreds of dollars. However, the operating system and applications for a server can easily range in the thousands of dollars.

Personnel Assets

Personnel assets are also very important to value. An organization that is able to retain personnel often has fewer problems than an organization with a high turnover rate. There are specific things an organization can do to retain valued personnel.

For example, organizations have different levels of benefit packages. These include different types of insurance such as health, dental, and life. They also include retirement plans such as matching 401K contributions. Many organizations also take additional steps to increase the morale and working environment.

The steps you take to retain employees are often dependent on how much you value them. When IT administrators have the high level of knowledge required to keep your network running in good order, they have a high value.

Data and Information Assets

Data and information assets can have different levels of value depending on the data. Most organizations will take steps to identify the classification of data. For example, your organization could identify the following data classifications:

* **Public data**—This data is freely available to anyone. It may be available via public sources such as news releases or other publications. It could also be freely available via an organization's Web site.
* **Private data**—This is internal data. It includes data on employees and customers. Due to its delicate nature, personal data should be protected for fear that the information may be abused, for example, for purposes of identify theft. It may also include data on internal processes.
* **Proprietary data**—This is highly valuable data. It deserves a lot of protection. If this data is lost, it could seriously affect the company's profitability. For example, a company could spend millions of dollars on research and development. The goal is to create a product they will sell. If a competitor gets this data, they could beat the company to market and sell the product themselves. The research and development funds would be lost.

Facilities and Supplies

Other items to consider when valuing your assets are the facilities and supplies needed to run your business. You'll need this information when calculating your insurance needs.

Insurance is one of those items you always want to have but never want to use. It provides a layer of protection if you suffer a loss. However, the loss is rarely painless. Even if the insurance company covers the loss, the process is difficult.

Some organizations may realize that one of its facilities is so important it needs redundancy. In this case, "redundancy" is another site that can perform the same functions. The three types of alternate sites are:

- **Hot site**—A location that can take over the operations of another location within a short period. A hot site has all the hardware, software, and data needed to perform the critical functions of the original site. A hot site is the most expensive of the three types of alternate sites.

- **Cold site**—A building with electricity and running water but little else. You can bring your computers and data to this location and set up operations. A cold site is the least expensive of the three sites. However, it takes the longest time to set up and is the hardest to test.

- **Warm site**—A compromise between a hot site and a cold site. It may include all the hardware but the data may not be up to date. It may take as long one or more days to implement.

The type of alternate site you choose depends on the value of the primary location. You'll also need to consider the supplies that will be stored there to ensure the alternate location can perform the same type of work. Of course, it's also possible you don't need an alternate location at all.

Identifying and Evaluating Relevant Threats

A threat is any potential danger. The danger can be to the data, the hardware, or the systems. A threat assessment is the process of identifying threats.

It's important to understand how threats interact with risks as a whole. Consider Figure 6-4. This shows the relationship between threats, attacks, vulnerabilities, and loss. A threat creates an attack. The attack exploits a vulnerability. When the threat/vulnerability pair occurs, it results in a loss.

> **NOTE**
>
> This section introduces threats and activities related to risk assessment. Chapter 8 will cover threats and threat assessments in greater depth.

In the diagram, an attacker is presented as a threat. However, a threat can be anything that can compromise confidentiality, integrity, or availability. You learned about threats in Chapter 1. As a reminder, threats can be external or internal, natural or man-made, or intentional or accidental.

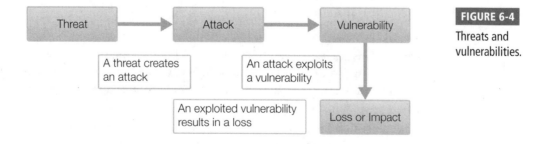

FIGURE 6-4

Threats and vulnerabilities.

You can use one of two primary methods to identify threats. They are:

- Review historical data
- Modeling

Reviewing Historical Data

History often repeats itself. This is true in so many areas of life. It's also true with IT systems. You can save yourself a lot of time by reviewing historical data to identify realistic threats.

When reviewing historical data, you can look for the following events:

- **Attacks**—If your Web site was attacked before, it's likely to be attacked again. The success of the next attack depends on the level of protection you implemented since then. The same is true for any type of event.

- **Natural events**—If hurricanes have hit your location before, they likely will do so in the future. Most organizations that are in risk zones for natural disasters have disaster recovery and business continuity plans in place. This includes disasters such as hurricanes, tornadoes, and earthquakes. These plans should be reviewed, if not tested, on a regular basis, such as once a year.

- **Accidents**—Accidents can be any accidental event that affects confidentiality, integrity, or availability. This includes users accidentally deleting data. It can also include user errors or mishaps in the workplace.

- **Equipment failures**—Equipment failures result in outages. Some systems are more prone to failure than others. Additionally, some failures have a much greater impact on the mission of the business. By analyzing past failures, you can often predict future failures. You can identify the systems that will benefit from additional redundant hardware.

Modeling

Threat modeling is a process used to identify possible threats on a system. It attempts to look at a system from the attacker's perspective. The result of threat modeling is a document called a threat model.

The threat model provides information on:

- **The system**—This includes background information on the system.
- **Threat profile**—This is a list of threats. It identifies what the attacker may try to do to the system, including possible goals of the attack. For example, one attack may attempt to take the system down. Another attack may attempt to access data in the system.
- **Threat analysis**—Each threat in the threat profile is analyzed to determine if an asset is vulnerable. Threat analysis includes review existing controls to determine their effectiveness against the threat.

Threat modeling allows you to prioritize attacks based on their probability of occurring and the potential harm.

Identifying and Evaluating Relevant Vulnerabilities

Chapter 1 introduced vulnerabilities. As a reminder, a vulnerability is a weakness. It can be a weakness in physical security, technical security, or operational security. It can be procedural, technical, or administrative.

Two things are certainly related to vulnerabilities:

- **All systems have vulnerabilities**—You can't eliminate all vulnerabilities any more than you can eliminate all risks. Your goal is to identify the relevant vulnerabilities. You can then choose to implement controls to reduce the weakness.

- **Not all vulnerabilities result in a loss**—It's only when the threat and vulnerability come together as a threat/vulnerability pair that a loss occurs. You only need to identify and evaluate the relevant vulnerabilities.

> ▶ **NOTE**
>
> This section introduces the identification and evaluation of vulnerabilities process. Chapter 8 covers the process in greater depth.

One of the ways to identify and evaluate vulnerabilities is by using assessments. The two primary assessments are:

- Vulnerability assessments
- Exploit assessments

Vulnerability Assessments

A **vulnerability assessment** is a process used to discover weaknesses in a system. The assessment will then prioritize the vulnerabilities to determine which weaknesses are relevant.

You can perform vulnerability assessments internally or externally. An internal assessment attempts to discover weaknesses from within the network. An external assessment attempts to discover what attackers outside the company may see.

A vulnerability assessment often starts by gathering information. Vulnerability scanners perform network reconnaissance. This is similar to an enemy scouting out a target to evaluate it and identify the best method of attack. A vulnerability assessment may have multiple goals, such as:

- **Identify IP addresses**—Ping scanner tools identify which IP addresses are in use. If the system responds to a ping, you know it is operational with this IP address.

- **Identify names**—You can use "whois" tools to identify the name of a computer from the IP address. This works for computers on the Internet.

- **Identify operating systems**—A fingerprinting tool can tell you what operating system is running on an IP address. The tool sends traffic to and receives traffic from the system. It then analyzes the traffic to determine which operating system is running. For example, a Microsoft operating system includes unique bits in some Internet Control Message Protocol (ICMP) traffic. These bits verify that it is a Microsoft product. Similarly, some UNIX and Linux operating systems also package packets with some unique bits.

- **Identify open ports**—A port scan identifies open ports. This tells you which protocols are running and what services are running. For example, if port 80 is open, the Hypertext Transfer Protocol (HTTP) protocol is running on the system. This indicates it is a Web server.
- **Identify weak passwords**—A password cracker determines the password for one or more accounts. The success of the password cracker largely depends on the strength of the password. In other words, a password cracker can discover weak passwords.

- **Capture data**—Data transferred over the network can be captured and analyzed. You can then read any data that has been transferred in clear text, or unencrypted.

> **NOTE**
>
> You perform a vulnerability assessment to discover weaknesses. However, it's important to realize that attackers can perform the same steps.

If you need to perform vulnerability assessments, you can choose from many different tools. Some tools perform only a specific function, such as only translating an IP address to a name. Other tools include multiple functions. This is similar to Microsoft Office, which includes a full suite of applications.

Some of the commonly used vulnerability assessments tools are:

- **Nmap**—Nmap is a network mapping tool. It combines a ping scanner to discover IP addresses with a port scanner to determine open ports. It then uses other techniques to discover the operating system and other details of the remote system. Nmap is free.
- **Nessus**—Nessus is a commercial product that provides a full suite of additional tools. As an example, it can run Nmap, or one of several other port scanners. It can detect common vulnerabilities in the configuration of a system. It also includes password crackers. Tenable Network Security sells Nessus. The company regularly improves Nessus by publishing new tools in the form of snap-ins.
- **SATAN**—SATAN is an acronym for Security Administrator Tool for Analyzing Networks. It was very popular in the 1990s but is no longer updated with additional snap-ins like Nessus. Although SATAN is still used, it isn't as popular as some other tools.
- **SAINT**—SAINT is an acronym for System Administrator's Integrated Network Tool. Just as Nessus is a full suite of tools, SAINT is also a full suite of vulnerability tools. Saint Corporation sells SAINT and other security tools.

Exploit Assessments

An **exploit assessment** attempts to discover what vulnerabilities an attacker can exploit. Exploit assessments are also referred to as "penetration tests." You usually start an exploit assessment with a vulnerability assessment. After you discover weaknesses, you attempt the exploit.

There is a significant difference between the exploit assessment and the vulnerability assessment. Specifically, an exploit assessment is intrusive. The goal is to test the exploit. If the exploit assessment is successful, it can disrupt operations. With this in mind, you should be cautious when performing exploit assessments.

Many of the popular vulnerability assessment suites include tools you can use to perform exploit assessments.

Identifying and Evaluating Countermeasures

A **countermeasure** is a security control or a safeguard. You implement a countermeasure to reduce a risk. You can reduce a risk by reducing vulnerabilities or by reducing the impact of the threat.

> **NOTE**
>
> This section introduces the identification and evaluation of countermeasures. Chapter 9 covers this subject in greater depth.

When identifying and evaluating the countermeasures, you should consider:

- **In-place controls**—These are controls that are currently installed in the operational system.

- **Planned controls**—These are controls that have a specified implementation date.

- **Control categories**—Controls fall into three primary categories: administrative controls, technical controls, and physical controls. When reviewing all of the controls, you should consider the purpose.

In-Place and Planned Countermeasures

Countermeasures cost money. Prior to purchasing a countermeasure, an organization will evaluate their options. During their evaluation of alternative countermeasures, the organization will gather relevant documentation. When performing a risk assessment, you should retrieve the documentation for these controls and review it. This documentation can reveal several things to you.

If the control is in place, you can measure its effectiveness. Ideally, countermeasures are as effective as you expect them to be. Some aren't as effective. You may have added an intrusion detection system and found that due to the high level of false alarms, administrators ignore it. You may have added a spam appliance and found that it marks valid e-mails as spam.

If an **in-place countermeasure** is not effective, you'll want to know why. The risk assessment can include an evaluation of this control to determine what to do differently. If the control is effective, that's also important to know.

You probably won't change **planned countermeasures**. However, it is still valuable to review the documentation that recommended them. You can evaluate the current systems to ensure the original threats and vulnerabilities still exist. Additional tools or techniques may also exist that will allow you to enhance the original recommendations.

CONTROL CLASS	CONTROL FAMILIES
Management	Security and assessment and authorization
	Planning
	Risk assessment
	System and services acquisition
	Program management
Technical	Access control
	Audit and accountability
	Identification and authentication
	System and communications protection
Operational	Awareness and training
	Configuration management
	Contingency planning
	Incident response
	Maintenance
	Media protection
	Physical and environment protection
	Personnel security
	System and information integrity

TABLE 6-1 NIST control classes and families.

Control Categories

There are several ways that controls are organized or classified. One of the popular methods is to define them based on these three categories:

- Administrative security controls
- Technical security controls
- Physical security controls

The following sections explain these three categories. However, you may also see different categories. For example, NIST SP 800-53 identifies controls in three classes and 18 families, as listed in Table 6-1. Chapter 9 explores these 18 families in more detail.

Chapter 2 presented information on the National Institute of Standards and Technology (NIST). They have published many documents related to information security. SP 800-53 Revision 3, titled "Recommended Security Controls for Federal Information Systems and Organizations," was released in August 2009.

No matter how the controls are listed, the goals are the same. These controls protect the confidentiality, integrity, and availability of systems and data.

Administrative Security Controls

Administrative security controls are the controls in place in response to the rules and guidelines directed by upper-level management. These include several specific controls. However, one important point about administrative controls is that they are implemented with a written document.

Some examples of administrative controls are:

- **Policies and procedures**—This may be an organization's security policy. It can also be the specific procedures used to back up a server, for example.

- **Security plans**—These are comprehensive plans to help an organization deal with different events. For example, a disaster recovery plan helps an organization plan for a disaster, such as a hurricane or earthquake.

- **Insurance**—Insurance can reduce the impact of a risk. Common examples include fire insurance and flood insurance.

- **Personnel checks**—An organization may have polices in place to perform different types of checks on personnel. This could include background checks or financial checks.

- **Awareness and training**—Many organizations regularly take steps to raise the security awareness of personnel. This can be done through formal training, posters, and e-mails, for example.

- **Rules of behavior**—Many organizations use acceptable use policies (AUPs) to let people know what they can do with computers and systems. This is often a document that users read and sign when they are hired. It's common to require employees to review the documents on a regular basis, such as once a year.

Technical Security Control

A **technical security control** uses computers or software to protect systems. The benefit is that the control is automated. You can set it once and it will consistently enforce the control.

Some examples of technical controls are:

- **Login identifier**—Users are required to provide credentials before you grant access to the system. This is also referred to as authentication. Three primary factors of authentication exist:
  - Something you know, such as a user name and password
  - Something you have, such as a smart card
  - Something you are, as captured by biometrics

- **Session timeout**—Many systems automatically time out after a period of inactivity. For example, a password-protected screen saver locks a computer after a specific number of minutes. When the time has passed, the screen saver starts and the user must enter credentials before accessing the system again.

- **System logs**—System logs log activity performed by systems, users, or attackers. For example, a system log can identify when a server is shut down, or when specific services are stopped or started. Application logs can log specific application activity.

- **Audit trails**—You can use many types of audit logs to create an audit trail. A security log can log all access to specific files. A firewall log can log all traffic entering or leaving a network.

- **Input validation**—Applications can use data range and reasonableness checks to validate data before using it. As a simple example, it is not possible to divide by zero. A program that accepts values used in a divide operation can ensure the value is not zero before using it.

- **Firewalls**—Network firewalls can control traffic coming in and out of a network. Host-based firewalls can restrict traffic for individual systems.

- **Encryption**—You can encrypt data when it is stored on a drive or when it is transmitted over a network. This provides confidentiality of the data.

Physical Security Controls

A **physical security control** controls the physical environment. This includes controls such as locks and guards to restrict physical access. It also includes elements to control the environment, such as heating and cooling systems.

Some examples of physical controls are:

- **Locked doors**—You can lock server rooms to protect your servers. You can lock wiring closets that host routers and switches. You can also protect proprietary data, such as employee files or research data, by locking doors and filing cabinets.

- **Guards and access logs**—You can have guards control access to sensitive areas. This can be at the front entrance of a building or in internal areas. You can use an access log to list individuals who are authorized access. The guard then only allows access to personnel on this list. You can also use access logs to record individuals who have accessed a room.

- **Video cameras**—Cameras can monitor areas on a continuous basis. Many closed circuit television (CCTV) systems can record data from multiple cameras. CCTV systems work very well as a deterrent.

- **Fire detection and suppression**—A fire can destroy a significant amount of data and hardware in a very short period. Effective detection and suppression systems detect the fire before it gets too big. They then quickly extinguish it.

- **Water detection**—Some areas are prone to flooding. When water is detected, pumps can be turned on automatically to remove the water. If the flooding can't be controlled, the detection system can turn off electrical systems to reduce possible damage.

- **Temperature and humidity detection**—Systems need to operate within certain temperature ranges. If they get too hot, electrical components overheat and fail. High humidity can cause condensation on the systems that can also cause failures. Heating, ventilation, and air conditioning (HVAC) systems control the temperature and humidity.

- **Electrical grounding and circuit breakers**—Proper grounding ensures that dangerous voltage is routed to ground when electronic systems fail. This protects equipment and personnel. Circuit breakers protect systems and wiring. When a failure results in excess current, the circuit breaker will pop before the excess current can start a fire or damage the equipment.

Selecting a Methodology Based on Assessment Needs

Once you have identified and evaluated the elements individually, you need to calculate the associated risk. Chapter 5 explored the two primary methodologies that you can use. These are:

- Quantitative
- Qualitative

Quantitative

The quantitative method uses predefined formulas. You need to use the data you collected to identify the following values:

- **Single loss expectancy (SLE)**—This is the expected loss for any single incident. You express this in monetary terms, such as $1,000.

- **Annual rate of occurrence (ARO)**—This is the number of times you expect the loss to occur each year. For example, the risk may have occurred four times last year, so the ARO is four.

- **Annual loss expectancy (ALE)**—You can calculate ALE as SLE $\times$ ARO. For example, it could be $1,000 $\times$ 4 or $4,000.

- **Safeguard or control value**—This is the cost of the countermeasure or the control. You express this in monetary terms.

You implement a control to reduce the risk. More directly, the control will reduce the ARO. If the ARO was four before the control, the ARO should be less than four after the control. You then compare the cost of the control with the savings.

For example, consider the following scenario. A Web site generates revenue of $5,000 an hour. In the past two years, it has suffered two hard drive failures. Each year, one of the several hard drives in the system has failed. Each failure has resulted in about three hours down time. The hard drive cost was about $300. What is the SLE, ARO, and ALE?

- The SLE is $15,300. You calculate this as $5,000 × 3 for the outage.
  You then add $300 for the new hard drive.
- The ARO is 1. Historically, the outage has occurred once a year.
  If you don't take steps to reduce the risk, it will likely occur once each year.
- The ALE is $15,300. You calculate this as $15,300 × 1.

This example doesn't include intangible costs. For example, a customer who visited the Web site when it was down may never come back. The cost to get this customer back, or to get another customer, is an intangible cost.

You may decide that a hardware redundant array of independent disks (RAID) can eliminate this risk. You've identified a hardware RAID that costs $3,000. It includes several disk drives. If any single drive fails, the RAID can detect the failure and automatically recover. In other words, the failure of a drive will not cause the system to fail. It will change the ARO from 1 to 0.

Should this RAID be implemented? You determine this by comparing three pieces of information:

- **ALE before control**—This is $15,300.
- **Cost of control**—The hardware RAID costs $3,000.
- **ALE after control**—This is zero, resulting in a savings of $15,300

If the cost of the control is less than the ALE after the control, the cost is justified. In other words, you are spending $3,000 to save $15,300. This results in a realized savings of $12,300.

On the other hand, if the cost of the control was $50,000, the cost is not justified based on the data you have. You would spend $50,000 to save $15,300, which puts you in the hole. If the cost of the control is close to the ALE after the control, you can also calculate the return on investment over several years.

Qualitative

You often don't have access to the actual costs, or the costs aren't easy to calculate. You can instead use a qualitative methodology. A qualitative methodology uses the opinions of experts to determine two primary data points:

- **Probability**—This is the likelihood that the risk will occur. You can express it in words, such as Low, Medium, or High. You can also express it in a percentage, such as 10 percent, 50 percent, or 100 percent.
- **Impact**—This identifies the magnitude of the loss if the risk occurs. You can express it in words, such as Low, Medium, or High. You can also express it as a number in a range, such as 1 to 10 or 1 to 100.

The probability and impact allows you to rank the risks. This ranking allows you to prioritize the most important and least important risks. For example, imagine you are evaluating buffer overflow attacks, SQL injection attacks, and Web defacing for a Web server.

TABLE 6-2	Qualitative analysis survey with existing controls.	
RISK	**PROBABILITY**	**IMPACT**
Buffer overflow	10	50
SQL injection	75	90
Web defacing	25	25

Experts have provided you with the data shown in Table 6-2. They provided this input based on the current controls protecting the server.

You can now prioritize each of these risks.

- **Buffer overflow**—Risk score of 5. You calculate this as $.10 \times 50$.
- **SQL injection attacks**—Risk score of 67.5. You calculate this as $.75 \times 90$.
- **Web defacing**—Risk score of 6.25. You calculate this as $.25 \times 25$.

This shows you clearly that the highest risk based on current controls is from SQL injection attacks. You can now identify controls to mitigate this risk.

You can then query the experts to identify the controls that will provide the best gain. You can use a similar survey that identifies the probability and impact of a risk after implementation of a control.

Develop Mitigating Recommendations

After performing the analysis, you can provide specific recommendations. These recommendations should mitigate the risks. You can include the data you've collected to support the recommendations.

Supporting data may include:

- Threat/vulnerability pairs
- Estimate of cost and time to implement
- Estimate of operational impact
- Cost-benefit analysis

Threat/Vulnerability Pairs

The recommended controls should address specific risks. As a reminder, a risk occurs when a threat exploits a vulnerability. If a threat doesn't exist to exploit a vulnerability, a risk doesn't exist. Similarly, if a vulnerability doesn't exist that a threat can exploit, a risk doesn't exist.

For example, malicious software is a very real threat. However, if you create an isolated system that will never connect to the Internet or accept data from other sources, it is not vulnerable. In this example, a threat/vulnerability pair doesn't exist. The threat can't be matched to a vulnerability. In contrast, consider a typical computer system.

It has access to the Internet, accepts e-mail, and allows users to connect universal serial bus (USB) devices. It is highly vulnerable.

A control needs to address specific threat/vulnerability pairs. Each recommendation will address one or more threat/vulnerability pairs. If you can't associate a control with a threat/vulnerability pair, you don't need the control. This becomes an easy check for the validity of the control.

Many controls will address several threat/vulnerability pairs. If the control will mitigate several pairs, you should list each of them.

Estimate of Cost and Time to Implement

You should include the cost of the control in the recommendation. This will be included in the cost- benefit analysis. It's important to accurately identify this cost by including both direct and indirect costs.

The direct cost is the purchase of the control. However, indirect costs aren't always easy to identify. For example, the indirect costs could include the man hours needed to learn the control. They could also include the cost of training.

A common mistake is underestimating the costs needed to implement a control. For example, a sophisticated firewall may require a trained administrator. If you acquire a firewall but your administrators don't have the knowledge to use it, it will sit idle. Administrators will then need to master it on their own or attend a formal class. In the interim, the firewall sits in the box.

You should also include a schedule or time to implement the control. For simple controls, the time can be negligible. For other controls, the time can be extensive. For example, imagine you decide to increase security when users log on. Instead of using user names and passwords, you decide to use smart cards. This will require a phased approach. You'll add a public key infrastructure (PKI) to issue certificates. You'll need to add card readers to all systems. You can then issue smart cards to users.

Estimate of Operational Impact

Countermeasures can sometimes consume so many system resources that the system is unable to perform its primary job. If a control has any effect on the system's normal operations, it has an operational impact. You can identify the **operational impact** of a control as negligible, low, medium, high, or overwhelming. Ideally, a control will have very little impact on normal operations. If the impact is too high, you may not be able to use the control. It's important to consider the operational impact while developing recommendations.

Any computer system has four primary resources. If a control has an operational impact, it will usually show up in one of these resources. These are:

- **Processor**—The processor performs the majority of the computing work. Desktop PCs usually have a single processor. Servers often have multiple processors. Countermeasures can often consume a significant amount of processing power. If the server's processor usage peaks close to 100 percent, the system slows to a crawl.

Overwhelming Countermeasures

One organization spent over $10,000 to implement a security control they weren't able to use. A little planning could have prevented this loss.

As background, you can use a **host-based intrusion detection system (HIDS)** as a security control. It's installed on individual systems. HIDS is used in addition to antivirus (AV) software. The AV software detects and prevents malware attacks. HIDS will detect intrusion attacks on the system.

This organization had AV software installed on the systems. They then purchased and installed the HIDS. The combination of the AV and HIDS software overwhelmed the resources of the systems. The processor usage started peaking close to 100 percent. Even simple tasks such as launching a word processor took a long time.

The company removed the HIDS from all the systems. Over time, the systems were upgraded and the HIDS was added onto the newer systems. However, this proved embarrassing for the manager who approved the purchase of the HIDS.

- **Memory**—The processor can only work with data that is in memory. The amount of memory in a system is often a limiting factor. If the system is low on memory, it swaps data back and forth between memory and the disk drive. This swapping slows down the system considerably.
- **Disk**—The capacity and speed of the disk subsystem is important to consider. Countermeasures often require a minimum amount of disk space. Additionally, data is stored on the disk until needed by the processor. When the processor needs the data, it swaps it into the memory. If the speed of the disk is slow, it may slow down the system.
- **Network interface card (NIC)**—A computer uses a NIC to access resources on the network. If the control you're considering will transfer data on the network, you should consider the current bandwidth of the NIC.

Prepare Cost-Benefit Analysis

You should include a cost-benefit analysis (CBA) to support your recommendations. A CBA shows that the cost is justified. Ideally, the CBA will show that you can spend a small amount of money up front to save a lot of money in the long term. The CBA is an important tool needed by management to justify the cost.

As demonstrated earlier, a quantitative RA includes dollar figures. You can use the dollar figures in the CBA. A qualitative RA doesn't include direct dollar figures. When using the qualitative RA, you need to take additional steps to create the CBA.

Present Risk Assessment Results

After you complete the RA, you create a report documenting the results. This report should include two phases.

In the first phase, you present the recommendations to management. As a reminder, management decides which recommendations to implement. It's possible that management won't approve every recommendation.

Management may determine that the CBA for a recommendation doesn't justify the cost. For another recommendation, they may decide they want to accept the risk. Any risk that remains after controls are implemented is a residual risk. Because management decides which controls to implement, management is also responsible for the residual risks.

> **NOTE**
>
> Chapter 4 covered the POAM in more detail.

In the second phase, you document the decisions made by management. You then create a plan of actions and milestones (POAM). You can use the POAM to track and monitor the controls. The POAM helps ensure the controls are implemented. It also helps track the actual costs.

Best Practices for Performing Risk Assessments

There are several steps you can take to ensure success when performing RAs. The following list identifies some best practices for performing RAs:

- **Ensure systems are fully described**—This includes both the operational characteristics and the mission of the system. It's also important to ensure that you have current data. IT systems change as they are upgraded and improved. If current documentation isn't used, resources are wasted.

- **Review past audits**—If audits have been performed, ensure you review the results. Audits identify vulnerabilities and often include specific recommendations. These recommendations either should be in place or planned.

- **Review past risk assessments**—If a previous RA was performed, you should review it. Some systems are assessed on a regular basis, such as every year or every three years. You can review this information and compare it to recent activity. For example, new threats or vulnerabilities may have resulted in outages that weren't previously addressed.

- **Match the RA to the management structure**—Perform the RA based on the ownership or responsibility of the system. When the RA crosses management lines, it becomes harder to implement the controls.

- **Identify assets within the RA boundaries**—When identifying assets, ensure that only assets within the scope of the RA are included. This will help eliminate scope creep.

- **Identify and evaluate relevant threats**—Ensure that only relevant threats are evaluated. You can review historical data to determine what threats have caused problems in the past. You can also use threat modeling to identify threats.

- **Identify and evaluate relevant vulnerabilities**—Many weaknesses exist. You won't include them all. You want to include only the vulnerabilities that are relevant to the RA.

- **Identify and evaluate countermeasures**—Ensure that all countermeasures are directly related to at least one threat/vulnerability pair. Additionally, ensure that the CBA justifies the cost of the control.

- **Track the results**—Document the results of the RA. Document the approved recommendations. Create a POAM to track the implementation of the recommendations.

CHAPTER SUMMARY

The performance of the risk assessment takes several specific steps. It's important to start with a clear definition of the system to be assessed. Whenever possible you should also consider the management structure to ensure easy implementation of the recommendations.

Identify threats and vulnerabilities. Relevant threat/vulnerability pairs identify actual risks. Then evaluate controls to mitigate these risks. Present these recommendations to management for a decision with a CBA. Finally, use a POAM to track the approved recommendations.

KEY CONCEPTS AND TERMS

Administrative security control	In-place countermeasure	Threat modeling
Blacklist	Operational impact	Vulnerability assessment
Countermeasure	Physical security control	Whitelist
Exploit assessment	Planned countermeasure	
Group Policy	Technical security control	

CHAPTER 6 ASSESSMENT

1. You are beginning an RA for a system. You should define both the operational characteristics and the mission of the system in the early stages of the RA.

   A. True
   B. False

2. Which of the following should you identify during a risk assessment?

   A. Assets
   B. Threats
   C. Vulnerabilities
   D. Countermeasures
   E. All of the above

3. Of the following choices, what would be considered an asset?

   A. Hardware
   B. Software
   C. Personnel
   D. Data and information
   E. All of the above

4. When defining the system for the risk assessment, what should you ensure is included?

   A. Only the title of the system
   B. The current configuration of the system
   C. A list of possible attacks
   D. A list of previous risk assessments

5. What can you use to identify relevant vulnerabilities?

   A. Historical data
   B. Threat modeling
   C. CBA
   D. A and B only
   E. None of the above

6. Which type of assessment can you perform to identify weaknesses in a system without exploiting the weaknesses?

   A. Vulnerability assessment
   B. Risk assessment
   C. Exploit assessment
   D. Penetration test

7. An acceptable use policy is an example of an _____ security control.

8. Your organization requires users to log on with smart cards. This is an example of a _____ security control.

9. You use video cameras to monitor the entrance of secure areas of your building. This is an example of a _____ security control.

10. Which of the following should you match
with a control to mitigate a relevant risk?

 A. Threats
 B. Vulnerabilities
 C. Threat/vulnerability pair
 D. Residual risk

11. What does a qualitative RA use to prioritize
a risk?

 A. Probability and impact
 B. SLE, ARO, and ALE
 C. Safeguard value
 D. Cost-benefit analysis

12. What does a quantitative RA use to prioritize
a risk?

 A. Probability and impact
 B. SLE, ARO, and ALE
 C. Safeguard value
 D. Cost-benefit analysis

13. Your organization purchased a control and
installed it on several servers. This control is
consuming too many server resources, and the
servers can no longer function. What was not
evaluated before the control was purchased?

 A. The cost and time to implement the control
 B. The operational impact of the control
 C. The in-place and planned controls
 D. The impact of the risk

14. What is included in an RA that helps justify
the cost of a control?

 A. Probability and impact
 B. ALE
 C. CBA
 D. POAM

15. What is created with a risk assessment
to track the implementation of the controls?

 A. CBA
 B. POAM
 C. ALE
 D. SLE

Identifying Assets and Activities to Be Protected

I T'S DIFFICULT TO KNOW HOW TO PROTECT SOMETHING before you know what you're protecting. An important first step in risk management is identifying valuable assets in your organization. Any organization has a wide variety of assets that need to be protected. This includes obvious assets such as hardware and software. It includes data and personnel. It also includes system functions and system processes.

After you've identified the important assets, you can then take steps to protect them. A business impact analysis helps you to identify the impact if a service fails. A disaster recovery plan can help you identify the steps needed to restore a failed system. On a larger scale, you can use a business continuity plan to help ensure that mission-critical systems continue to operate even after a disaster.

Chapter 7 Topics

This chapter covers the following topics and concepts:

- What system access and availability are
- What manual and automated system functions are
- What hardware, software, and personnel assets are
- What data and information assets are
- How asset and inventory management are related to the seven domains of a typical IT infrastructure
- How to identify facilities and supplies needed to maintain business operations

Chapter 7 Goals

When you complete this chapter, you will be able to:

- Identify the importance of system access and availability
- Differentiate between manual and automated system functions
- Identify hardware assets that need to be protected
- Identify software assets that need to be protected
- Identify personnel assets that need to be protected
- Identify organizational data and information assets
- Identify customer data and information assets
- Identify intellectual property data and information assets
- Identify data warehouse and data mining assets
- Identify asset management and inventory management steps that can be taken for each of the seven domains of an IT infrastructure
- Describe the purpose of identifying mission-critical systems and applications identification
- Describe the purpose of business impact analysis planning
- Describe the purpose of business continuity planning
- Describe the purpose of disaster recovery planning
- Describe the purpose of business liability insurance planning
- Describe the purpose of asset replacement insurance planning

System Access and Availability

System access and availability refers to when users or customers need a system or service. This is an important consideration. Some systems need to be operational 99.999 percent of the time. Other systems need to be operational only during limited business hours, such as between 8 a.m. to 6 p.m. Monday through Friday.

It is possible to achieve five nines. Consider Figure 7-1. This shows a database server service protected with a two-node **failover cluster**. A failover cluster provides fault tolerance for a server. It ensures that a service provided by a server will continue to run even if a server fails. It includes at least two servers, called "nodes."

> ▶ **NOTE**
>
> Five nines, or 99.999 percent up time, is sometimes needed for certain services. This equates to about 5.25 minutes of downtime a year. You can calculate it as 60 minutes × 24 hours × 365 days × .00001.

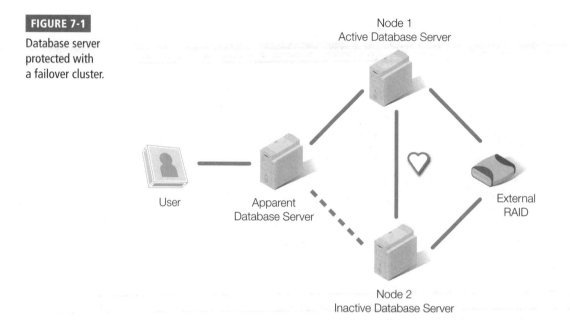

FIGURE 7-1

Database server
protected with
a failover cluster.

Node 1
Active Database Server

User

Apparent
Database Server

External
RAID

Node 2
Inactive Database Server

In a failover cluster, a user appears to connect to a single database server. Figure 7-1 shows this server as the apparent database server. Nodes 1 and 2 are physical servers that you can actually touch. The apparent database server is just the logical view of the active node.

While node 1 is active, node 2 is inactive. Node 1 will serve all data requests. It accesses the data on an external drive. Node 2's only job is to query node 1 and check its heartbeat as often as every 30 seconds. As long as node 1 is up, node 2 doesn't do anything.

However, if node 1's heartbeat stops, indicating that node 1 has failed, node 2 will go into action. It will take over the services of node 2. Because node 2 has access to the same data on the external drive, data isn't lost. The user is still connected to the apparent database server, but data is now served from node 2. To the end user, the switchover is not seen, but it should provide uninterrupted service.

The external drive can be a single point of failure. A **single point of failure** is any part of a system that can cause an entire system to fail, if it fails. A hardware redundant array of independent disks (RAID) is often used to ensure that data isn't lost, even if a drive fails.

> **NOTE**
>
> Failover clusters can have more than two nodes. For example, you can protect multiple services in an eight-node failover cluster. In an eight-node cluster, two nodes are often inactive, with six active.

The failover cluster also allows you to perform maintenance without any downtime. You can perform maintenance on the inactive node without affecting users. If the active node needs servicing, you can switch nodes, making the other node active. You can then perform maintenance on the newly inactive node.

Although this can help achieve 99.999-percent uptime, it comes at a high cost. At a minimum, you'll need two powerful servers. Additionally, you'll never use both servers at the same time. One will always be idle, just checking to see if the other one is up. However, if maximum uptime is required, the cost is justified.

What systems require 99.999-percent access and availability? You can determine this by identifying the value of the service provided. The highly valued systems require greater protection. You can measure value by measuring revenue or productivity.

- **Direct and indirect revenue**—A Web server is an example of a service that can provide direct revenue. If the Web server sells products, you can determine how much revenue it earns per hour. You can use this figure to determine the direct costs of the outage. Remember, there are also indirect costs to calculate. These include, for example, the cost to bring back customers that are lost during the outage.

- **Productivity**—Some services are needed by employees to perform their job. For example, consider a warehouse application used to manage inventory. Employees may use it accept products coming in and locate products they are shipping out. Management can use it to determine the value of the current inventory at any time. If this application fails, all shipments may stop. If the failure isn't restored quickly, it may result in delayed shipments, an inaccurate inventory, and other problems. Similarly, many companies consider e-mail a critical service today. If it fails, productivity drops quickly.

Interestingly, the value of system access and availability is sometimes underestimated. That is, until it fails. Proactive risk managers will include system access and availability when identifying assets.

How Much Downtime Can You Accept?

Ask a non-technical manager "How much down time can you accept?" and the answer is often "none." That answer is not always accurate, though.

Although 99.999-percent uptime is achievable, it is expensive. It requires multiple servers configured in failover cluster configurations. It requires hardware RAID. It may even require labor to watch the system 24 hours a day, 7 days a week, 365 days a year.

The cost of all of these pieces can be very high. Although you may not want a system to suffer any downtime, most systems can accept some. If you're investigating how much downtime is acceptable, try to determine the associated cost. You'll probably end up with answers that are more accurate.

System Functions: Manual and Automated

Services are usually provided by combining multiple functions. These functions can be manual, automated, or a mixture of the two. When identifying your system assets, it's important to understand the difference.

Chapter 6 introduced system functions. It used an example of an automated spam appliance to filter spam. You could also consider the spam appliance as one of many functions used to provide e-mail service. Other functions for e-mail could include the ability to scan for malware. You can also add the ability to sign and encrypt messages.

Manual Methods

For example, consider a hotel using manual methods. Manual methods can be used to track everything from the initial reservation to checkout. Although it seems hard to believe, that's how it was done about 20 years ago. If the process is manual, there are two primary asset values:

- **Written records**—The guest log is a handwritten log that records when guests check in and when they check out. Managers use this log to bill the customer.
- **Knowledge of process**—Employees would know how to create the bill from the available records. Once the payment is received, there would be a separate process to deposit the money. If this is a small mom-and-pop hotel, it's possible that only the owners and one or two employees know the entire process.

With this example, the value is the written records and the personnel with the knowledge of the process. Although you're unlikely to visit a hotel that uses only manual methods today, you may work at a company that uses manual internal company processes.

Automated Methods

A hotel may be able to automate many of the processes. Because it is part of a service industry, the hotel may still include some human interaction. The following example shows how a hotel could automate the majority of the processes:

Customers could register online. Many hotels prefer this and sometimes give discounts for users that do register online. Customers would be able to see what days are available, and what the costs are for each day. They can pick their days and make deposits or payments. Online registration reduces the cost of labor for the hotel.

The reservation would then be in the system when the customers arrive. They would check in with a friendly receptionist who would check the details via the automated system. The receptionist would confirm the details and the customers would soon be on their way to the room, perhaps with the bell staff towing their luggage.

Some hotels offer convenience bars that include snacks and refreshments. These are often automated. When the customer picks anything up, the convenience bar senses the change in weight, and the front desk is alerted upon checkout that the customer may owe something. The charge for this convenience is often very high. For example, a candy bar purchased for $.75 elsewhere may cost $5.00.

Many hotels often include a TV channel showing the customer's bill. This bill is updated automatically when a customer charges a bill at a restaurant or retrieves a cold bottle of water from the convenience bar. When the customer is ready to check out, he or she accesses the TV channel to pay the bill. Soon the customer is heading to the airport and home sweet home.

When evaluating this type of automated method, there are several other things to consider, such as the following:

- **Value to the customers**—These automated methods are often considered valuable to the customers. If the registration process is clear and streamlined, customers are more likely to use it. If the checkout process is error-free, it takes the chaos out of checking out. The benefits may be difficult to quantify, but these types of services may result in more return visits or word-of-mouth advertising.

- **Value to the company**—Any process that can be automated requires less labor to use. Less labor results in a lower cost and higher profit. You need to balance the reduced labor with the cost to implement and maintain the system. You may replace 10 lower-paid service people with one higher-paid IT professional, still saving plenty of salary.

- **Ensuring process stays up**—You need to ensure the process is available when the customer wants to access it. This includes the reservation system available on the Internet. It also includes the automated customer checkout system.

- **Protection of data**—Instead of just protecting a guest book to check people in and out, you'll be maintaining large databases. These databases include personally identifiable information (PII) such as customer names, credit card data, addresses, and phone numbers. If this data is compromised, the company may be liable for customer losses due to identity theft.

> **NOTE**
> Many laws mandate the protection of personally identifiable information (PII). PII is any data that can be used to identify an individual. PII can also be medical, financial, or criminal data. The National Institute of Standards and Technology (NIST) published SP 800-122. This is a guideline used to help government entities and public companies protect PII.

The important point to remember is that assets are more than just things. They can be the processes that provide the services.

Hardware Assets

Hardware assets are the assets you can touch with your hands. These include any types of computers, such as servers or desktop PCs. They include networking devices, such as routers and switches. They also include network appliances, such as firewalls and spam appliances. Not all organizations have the same hardware assets, but you should be aware of the assets you have.

> **NOTE**
> Most organizations use databases to track hardware assets.

However, you need to know much more than just the number of devices you own. Some of the other information you need to know includes:

- Location
- Manufacturer
- Model number
- Hardware components such as processor and random access memory (RAM)
- Hardware peripherals such as add-on network interface cards (NICs)
- Basic Input/Output System (BIOS) version

This list may seem like overkill, but it's not. You need to know all the details of the hardware for successful security and configuration management. Consider these few examples where this information is useful.

Microsoft released some patches to their operating systems that put systems into an endless reboot cycle. The systems start to boot, crash into a blue screen, recover to start to boot again, and crash again. When this occurs, the problem is often with a specific manufacturer and model number. Sometimes it's because of a specific driver. Other times it's because of the way the systems were prepared before being shipped. If your inventory includes the manufacturer and model numbers, you'll easily be able to see if a Microsoft update will affect operations.

Similarly, imagine a serious exploit is discovered that affects specific routers. If your hardware inventory includes the manufacturer and model numbers of routers, you'll easily know if you're vulnerable. Without an inventory, you may not know you're vulnerable until after a successful attack.

Hardware inventories can also help you identify unneeded components. For example, some systems may include modems. Modems can present a significant risk. If users dial in to an Internet service provider (ISP) to access the Internet, the connection isn't controlled. Users could visit sites normally blocked by your proxy server. They could

---

Controlling Hardware Purchases

Many organizations have policies to control hardware purchases. Only hardware on the approved hardware list can be purchased. Although this is often inconvenient for the users, it provides an added layer of security.

First, you can verify that the hardware on the approved list has only the necessary components for your environment. If a component hasn't been added, there are no risks for that component. However, if an unnecessary component is added, it needs to be managed to reduce any potential risks.

Second, you can control the number of configurations introduced in your environment. This improves availability. Consider this: If all the users have identical desktop PCs, desktop support personnel need to learn the specifics of only one system. Once they master the one system, they can easily troubleshoot all the systems. On the other hand, if your environment has 30 different types of desktop PC, they can be harder to troubleshoot.

download malware that would normally be filtered by your firewall. The dial-up modem allows the system to bypass all controls providing access to the Internet. Removing the modem removes the risk.

Software Assets

Software assets include the operating system and applications. The operating system (OS) is used to start the computer. Examples of operating systems are Microsoft Windows, Mac OS, and Red Hat Linux. The applications perform specific functions or tasks. Examples of applications are Microsoft Word or Adobe Reader.

Most organizations use a database to track hardware assets. It's common to use the same database to track software assets.

When identifying software assets, it's important to be specific. It's not enough to list an OS as just Windows or Linux. There are many versions of Windows and many Linux distributions (aka "distros"). Similarly, it's not enough to list an application as just Word.

OS specifics should include:

- Hardware system where it's installed
- Name of the operating system, such as Microsoft Windows 7
- Latest service pack installed

An accurate listing of OSs can help you quickly identify if you are vulnerable to new threats. For example, imagine a new exploit is discovered for Microsoft Windows XP. If you know how many Windows XP systems you have and where they are, you can quickly address the exploit.

On the other hand, if you don't have an accurate listing, your job will be much harder. You'll have to check them all. Even if you have to check as few as 50 systems, this will take time. If you have 5,000 systems, the task becomes impossible to complete manually. Automated asset management becomes necessary.

However, if you have an accurate inventory your job becomes much easier. A simple look at the inventory will identify how many systems are running Windows XP. Additionally, the inventory will link the operating system to the hardware, and you'll know exactly where the Windows XP systems are located.

FYI

A **service pack (SP)** is a group of updates, patches, and fixes that apply to a specific operating system. SPs occasionally include extra capabilities for the operating system. SPs are usually cumulative. For example, Microsoft Windows Vista SP1 includes all the updates, patches, and fixes released since the operating system was released. Windows Vista SP2 also includes all the updates, patches, and fixes since the operating system was released.

Automated Asset Management

You can use many enterprise tools to automate asset management. These tools can identify all the hardware in your networks. This includes the desktop PCs, servers, and network devices, such as switches and routers.

For example, Microsoft sells the System Center Configuration Manager (SCCM). SCCM can identify all the systems in the network using tools in a Microsoft domain. Once SCCM identifies the systems, it methodically queries each system to identify the installed software.

Most systems will reveal their actual model number and serial numbers when queried correctly. Administrators can print out lists of these systems with the software installed on each. Administrators then use these lists to match the supposed inventory against the actual inventory.

Administrators also use these lists to discover software that has been installed without authorization.

This helps administrators discover two important types of unauthorized software. The first is malware, which can be damaging to the system or the network. The second is unlicensed software. If a company purchases 100 copies of an application but 200 copies are installed, the company may have unnecessary legal liabilities.

Similarly, the specifics of installed applications should include:

- Name of the application, such as Microsoft Windows Office Professional
- Version number
- Service pack or update information if it is available

All this information is almost impossible to gather if you're doing so manually. However, you can automate the process. Many tools are available that can identify all the hardware and software assets in your organization.

Personnel Assets

Personnel assets are the people you have working for you. The success of any organization is due in large part to its personnel. However, things sometimes work best when you have several key personnel trained for any key function, instead of a single person.

When any function or process depends on a single person, that person becomes a single point of failure. Although it's good to have talented and skilled personnel, it's not good to have too much reliance on a single person.

Many things can take an employee out of your environment. These include illness, accident, family emergency, winning the lottery, or a better job or more money elsewhere.

You can't control most of these. As an employer or manager, you can control the job conditions and the pay. However, you can't control many other events.

Earlier in this chapter, you learned about single point of failure. A hard drive can be a single point of failure. You can protect the hard drive with a redundant array of independent disks (RAID). A server can also be a single point of failure. You can use a failover cluster to protect against the failure of a server.

Similarly, a person can be a single point of failure, as mentioned above. If only one person knows how to maintain a system, that system is at risk. You can reduce this risk by taking different measures, such as:

- **Hire additional personnel**—If you have a critical system maintained by only one person, you can hire additional personnel to help.

- **Cross training**—Ensure that personnel are cross trained in different systems. Personnel will still perform a primary job function, but they will occasionally spend time learning about other job functions. Cross training helps broaden personnel's understanding of overall operations. They will then be able to step in for short term emergencies when necessary.

- **Job rotation**—You can rotate personnel into different jobs on a regular basis, such as once a year. Rotating people into different jobs helps them build skills in different technologies. It also helps ensure that more than one person knows how to maintain any IT system. **Job rotation** also helps an organization discover dangerous shortcuts or fraudulent activities. When you rotate personnel in and out of jobs, you gain more internal oversight into job practices. This ensures that personnel are following rules and policies. It also reduces the possibility of collusion. Collusion occurs when two or more people engage in secret activity for fraudulent purposes.

Data and Information Assets

Another important asset to consider is data and information held by the company. The value of data can't be overstated. If an organization loses data, it can have a tragic result.

Data is protected in two ways:

- **Access controls**—These protect data from unauthorized disclosure. Chapter 1 presented the security triad of confidentiality, integrity, and availability. Access controls help protect the confidentiality of data.

- **Backups**—These protect the data when it becomes corrupted or accidentally deleted. At least two copies of backups should exist. One copy is kept locally. Another copy is kept in a separate geographical location. The second copy protects against disasters, such as fire or flood. If the only backup of the data is kept above the server, you'll have no backups if the server room burns.

There are endless stories about different companies that failed due to a data loss. The story often goes like this: The company has been steadily growing. Data is stored on a single computer. This includes billing data, such as accounts payable and receivable data.

Classification of Data

Most organizations take the time to classify their data. Different classifications warrant different levels of protection.

The government uses classifications such as Confidential, Secret, and Top Secret. Each classification has a formal definition. For example, Top Secret data includes information whose unauthorized disclosure would pose the gravest threat to national security. Data classified at different levels receives different levels of protection. For example, Top Secret data would receive the highest level of protection.

Figure 7-2 shows how an organization can classify its data. In the figure, three classifications are used. They are Public, Private, and Proprietary.

An organization can define the data in any way that fits. Public data could be defined as any data that is accessible from public sources, such as Web sites. Private data could be customer or employee data. Proprietary data could be financial data or data created from research and development.

Organizations can use any classification labels desired. The labels aren't as important as using some method of data classification. In other words, the classifications could be Unclassified, Sensitive, and Privileged instead of Public, Private, and Proprietary. Additionally, an organization can use as many data classifications as it needs to protect its data. You are not limited to only three labels. However, an organization must consider how easily and readily employees will classify new data as they create it.

FIGURE 7-2

Classification of data.

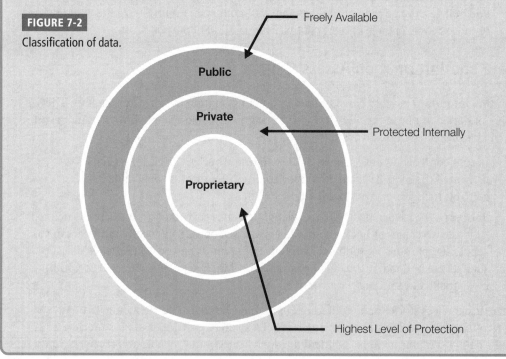

It includes customer data. It includes all the critical data for the company. One day, the hard drive on the computer crashes. None of the data is accessible and no backups exist. With customer and billing data lost, the company soon fails.

This might seem like fiction, but it's not. The same story repeats for small businesses across the country. Many organizations simply don't recognize the value of their data until it is lost. However, once the data is lost, it's too late to recover it.

It's important to recognize the value of your data. After you identify your valuable data, you'll need to ensure that steps are taken to protect it. This includes taking steps to back up the data regularly. It also includes taking steps to protect it from unauthorized disclosure.

Data and information assets include the following categories:

- Organization
- Customer
- Intellectual property
- Data warehousing
- Data mining

Organization

Organization data includes any internally used data. Most of it would remain private. However, if it's a publicly held company, some of the financial data may be published. It can include:

- **Employee data**—This includes any information held about employees. Most companies have internal human resources (HR) departments that maintain records on employees. This can include personal data, employee reviews, health care choices, and more.
- **Billing and financial data**—This includes accounts payable and accounts receivable data. It also includes any data related to the financial health of the company. This could include loan data. It could also include profit-loss statements.
- **System configuration data**—The configuration of each system is often documented in a database. This includes the basic system configuration. It also includes any changes.
- **System process data**—Process data includes documents that show how systems function. It can include network layout diagrams identifying how servers are connected. It can also include data flow diagrams. For example, a diagram could show the flow of e-mail.
- **Vendor data**—Vendor data includes any information on companies that supply products or services to your company.

Many laws mandate the protection of different types of data. The Health Insurance Portability and Accountability Act (HIPAA) mandates the protection of health-related data. Most employee files include HIPAA data even if the organization isn't involved in health care. The Sarbanes-Oxley Act (SOX) addresses the accuracy of financial data for publicly traded companies. Organizations must protect certain financial data to remain in compliance with SOX.

Customer

Customer data includes the data you hold on customers. Depending on how you choose to collect and use the customer data, you may have only minimal data, or a full-blown database.

For example, your company may want to send out a monthly newsletter via e-mail to customers. You'll only need the e-mail address. If desired, you could also collect customer names to personalize the e-mail.

On the other hand, your company may do extensive sales via a Web site. In this case, you may want to collect as much information as possible. When customers come to your site, you'll know what they purchased in the past. You can automate advertisements or recommendations for sales based on their past purchases. When customers are ready to purchase, they won't need to reenter credit card data because it's already stored.

Customer data could include:

- Name
- Address
- Phone numbers
- E-mail address
- Historical purchases
- Accounts receivable data
- Credit card or banking data
- Account name and password
- Demographic data, such as age and gender

It's important to realize that the more data you store, the more valuable that collection of data becomes. For example, imagine you collect only e-mail addresses. If someone hacks into your system and views this data, it isn't necessarily critical. However, if you collect personally identifiable information (PII), several laws mandate that you protect it. Additionally, if you collect credit card data and an attacker gains access to it, you may be liable for financial losses.

Intellectual Property

Intellectual property (IP) data is data created by a person or an organization. It can include inventions, literary and artistic works, symbols, names, and images. The World Intellectual Property Organization (WIPO) divides IP into two categories:

- **Industrial property**—This includes industrial designs, trademarks, inventions, and patents.

- **Copyright**—This includes literary and artistic works, such as books, films, and music. It also includes artistic works, such as paintings and drawings.

Organizations can have either or both categories of IP. It depends on the function of a company. For example, a recording company may focus on copyright IP. However, a medical research company may focus only on industrial property.

Both national and international laws protect IP. However, thieves still steal it. The money invested in the creation of the property can be lost if the data is not protected. For example, consider a television company. It could spend several years and millions of dollars developing a new screen that provides a 3D view with vivid colors. About six months before the company is ready to go to market, a competitor accesses all the research data. The competitor then creates a similar product. Because the competitor doesn't have to recoup the research and development costs, it can actually sell the TV cheaper than the company that created it.

If your organization has IP, you need to protect it. The level of protection depends on the value of the IP.

Data Warehousing and Data Mining

Data warehousing and **data mining** techniques combine to retrieve meaningful data from very large databases (VLDBs). Although a database can host huge amounts of data, that data isn't readily useful. The goal is to convert the raw data into useful intelligence. This can be done with data warehousing and data mining:

- **Data warehousing**—The process of gathering data from different databases. The data is retrieved from the source databases and placed in a central database. New relationships between the source databases are created in the central database. This central database is the data warehouse. Data in a warehouse is not modified. Instead, data is modified in the source databases. Periodically, the data in the data warehouse is refreshed. This brings the data warehouse current with the source data. Refreshing the data warehouse can be very resource-intensive.

- **Data mining**—A group of techniques used to retrieve relevant data from a data warehouse. Decision makers are able to view the data from different perspectives. This allows them to make predictions about future events. For example, a manager can predict how many specific products will sell in December.

Most databases are optimized as online transactional processing (OLTP) databases. In other words, they can quickly record transactions. A "transaction" is any type of addition, deletion, or modification of data. For example, an OLTP database is very effective at recording sales. However, OLTP databases aren't very effective for data analysis. Instead, the OLTP database is reorganized in a data warehouse. It can be combined with one or more other OLTP databases. Once the databases are reorganized, data mining can retrieve relevant data.

Data mining is a part of an overall business intelligence (BI) solution. BI solutions attempt to bring actionable intelligence to the decision maker when the decision maker needs it. A BI solution is also referred to as a decision support system. The idea is that the database holds the answers to any questions a decision maker may have. By creating a data warehouse and using data mining techniques, the answers are readily available.

For example, here are some possible questions a manager may have:

- How many widgets has the organization sold this year?
- What was the peak month for widget sales?
- Who is the top performing sales person this quarter?
- Who is the bottom performing sales person this quarter?
- What were the sales figures for each of the regions this quarter?
- How does this compare to sales figures for the same quarter last year?

If your organization uses data warehouses, you need to include methods to protect the source databases and the data warehouse. The most important element is to have effective backup strategies. Additionally, ETL processes often require a lot of time to develop. Developers create the ETL processes using scripts or tools to identify the steps. You should include the ETL processes in the backup strategy.

Extract, Transform, and Load (ETL)

Data is moved from a database to a data warehouse using extract, transform, and load (ETL) techniques. The ETL process is an important element of a BI solution. Database developers identify the data to retrieve, how to modify it for the target database, and how to load it. The three steps are:

- **Extract**—The process of retrieving data from existing databases. Not all the data is extracted. Instead, only the data that is relevant to the decision makers is retrieved. For example, some customer sales data can be extracted for analysis. However, other customer data, such as credit card data, may not be needed, so it isn't extracted.

- **Transform**—The process of converting the data into a common format needed for the data warehouse. For example, one database may identify the male gender as "M" while another database uses "Male." Neither "M" nor "Male" is incorrect. However, the designation needs to be consistent in the target database. The transform process will change the data so it is consistent in the data warehouse.

- **Load**—The process of loading the data into the data warehouse. Data is loaded after it has been transformed to a standard format. Depending on how the data warehouse is configured, it's possible to load the same data in different locations. Although this isn't efficient for an OLTP database, it is efficient for data mining.

The ETL process is automated using scripts or other techniques. If necessary, you can perform the ETL process regularly on new data. This enables you to keep the data warehouse up to date with the actual source data.

Asset and Inventory Management Within the Seven Domains of a Typical IT Infrastructure

Chapter 1 presented the seven domains of a typical IT infrastructure. It can often be useful to approach an IT management problem from the perspective of these seven domains. This includes **asset management** and **inventory management**.

As a reminder, the seven domains of a typical IT infrastructure are:

- User Domain
- Workstation Domain
- LAN Domain
- LAN-to-WAN Domain
- WAN Domain
- Remote Access Domain
- System/Application Domain

Figure 7-3 shows the seven domains of a typical IT infrastructure.

In this context, there is a difference between inventory management and asset management. Basic definitions of the two are:

- **Inventory management**—This is used to manage hardware inventories. It includes only the basic data, such as model and serial numbers. It shows what assets are on hand, where they're located, and who owns them. Inventory management is valuable to ensure that the inventory isn't easily lost or stolen.

- **Asset management**—This is used to manage all types of assets. It includes much more detailed data than an inventory management system includes. For example, asset management would cover installed components, hardware peripherals, installed software, update versions, and more.

An organization may decide to use either or both types of management for different areas. For example, an organization may use inventory management for desktop PCs. This ensures the PCs are tracked and the investment is not lost. However, the same organization can also use automated asset management techniques. Asset management ensures the systems are patched correctly.

For each of the seven domains, consider the assets you have and ask yourself some basic questions:

- Are the assets valuable to the organization?
- Are they included in any type of inventory or asset management system?

If they're valuable, they should be included in either an inventory or an asset management system.

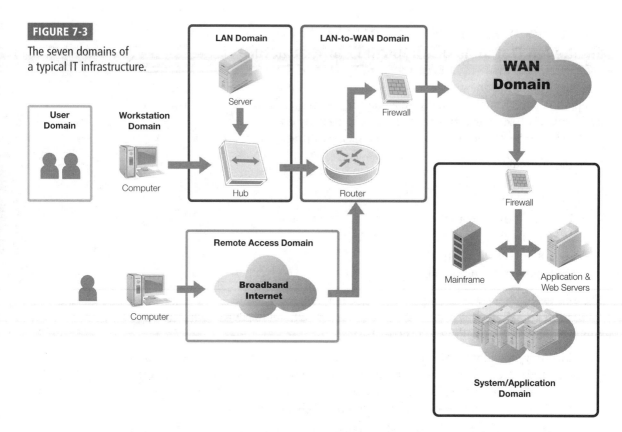

FIGURE 7-3

The seven domains of a typical IT infrastructure.

User Domain

The User Domain includes people or employees. An HR department maintains records on employees. These can be manual records, such as folders held in filing cabinets, or files held on servers.

Data on users includes:

- Personal and contact data
- Employee reviews
- Salary and bonus data
- Health care choices

A significant concern with asset management in the User Domain is confidentiality. Data must be protected against unauthorized disclosure. At the very least, the data includes PII that must be protected by law. If any health care data is included, HIPAA mandates its protection. If salary and bonus data is leaked, it often results in morale problems.

Workstation Domain

The Workstation Domain includes the PCs used by employees. It could include typical desktop PCs. It could also include mobile computers or laptops. Assets in the Workstation Domain have two risks to address:

- **Theft**—An organization has a significant investment in these systems. It can't afford to allow them to disappear. Inventory management systems include processes where each item is manually located on a periodic basis. This verifies the system is still in the organization's control.
- **Updates**—As updates, fixes, and patches are released, they need to be applied to the systems. If the systems are not updated, they become vulnerable to new exploits. Use automated asset management systems to keep systems up to date. An automated system will often perform three steps: 1) inspect systems for current updates, 2) apply updates, and 3) verify the updates.

LAN Domain

The LAN Domain includes all the elements used to connect systems and servers together. The local area network (LAN) is internal to the organization. The primary hardware components are hubs, switches, and routers.

It's important to have a basic inventory of these devices. This includes the basics such as model, serial number, and location. Although any network device includes firmware, the more functional network devices such as routers and switches have a built-in operating system (OS). The version of the OS determines its capabilities, so it's often useful to include the version in the inventory.

> **NOTE**
>
> Switches have replaced hubs in most organizations today. A switch is more efficient. More, a switch provides an added layer of security. An attacker using a protocol analyzer will be able to capture only a limited amount of data when a switch is used in place of a hub.

You should also include configuration data for these devices in an asset management system. For example, you can run scripts to configure routers and switches. These scripts configure the devices to pass or block specific traffic. If a device loses its configuration, you run the script again. This assumes, of course, that the script is available. If the script isn't available, you'll need to type in the configuration data line by line. If you don't even have a record of the previous configuration data, you'll have to troubleshoot until you get it back to the original configuration.

LAN-to-WAN Domain

The LAN-to-WAN Domain is the area where your internal LAN connects to the wide area network (WAN). In this context, the WAN is often the Internet. The primary devices you're concerned with here are the firewalls. You can have a single firewall separating the LAN from the WAN. You can also have multiple firewalls to create a demilitarized zone (DMZ) or a buffer area.

Firewalls in the LAN-to-WAN Domain are hardware firewalls. You can program them to allow and block specific traffic. You'll want to include the following information in an asset management system:

- **Hardware information**—This includes basics, such as the model and serial number. If the model supports different add-ins, such as additional memory, or additional network interface cards, you'll want to include these.

- **Configuration data**—A significant amount of time goes into creating a firewall policy. You then create firewall rules and exceptions to implement the policy. At the very least, all these rules and exceptions need to be documented. Whenever possible, you should create scripts to automate the process. You should then back up these scripts.

> **NOTE**
>
> Internal computers have access to the Internet, but not directly. Most organizations direct client traffic through a proxy server to give clients indirect access to the Internet. The proxy server has connectivity to the WAN with a public IP address. It also has connectivity to internal clients with a private IP address.

> **NOTE**
>
> Hardening a server makes it more secure from the default installation. You start by removing unneeded services and protocols. You enable the local firewall. Additionally, you keep the server up to date by regularly applying updates after testing them.

WAN Domain

The WAN Domain includes any servers that have direct access to the Internet. This includes any server that has a public Internet Protocol (IP) address. It also includes any public-facing server in the DMZ.

Most organizations won't have many servers in the WAN Domain. However, any servers in the WAN have significantly higher risks. It's very important to take extra precautions to ensure these servers are hardened as much as possible.

Inventory and asset management information for WAN-based servers include:

- **Hardware information**—This information includes basics, such as the model and serial number. Documentation is similar to how you'd document servers in the LAN-to-WAN Domain.

- **Update information**—Servers in the WAN need to be kept up to date. This is an important step to ensure the server stays secure. As patches, fixes, and updates are released, you need to evaluate them. If the update is needed and testing shows it doesn't have negative effects, you should apply it. Updating of servers can be manual or automated. Either way, it's important to have an accurate record of updates installed on the server.

Remote Access Domain

Remote access technologies give users access to an internal network via an external location. This can be done via direct dial-up or virtual private network (VPN).

When dial-up is used, clients and servers have modems and access to phone lines. When a VPN is used, the VPN server has a public IP address available on the Internet. Clients access the Internet, and then use tunneling protocols to access the VPN server.

> **NOTE**
> A VPN provides access to a private network over a public network, such as the Internet.

Inventory and asset management information needed for servers in the Remote Access Domain are similar to those in the WAN Domain. However, for dial-up remote access servers, you'll also need to include the dial-up equipment. This includes both modems and phone branch exchange (PBX) equipment.

- **Modems**—Modems for a remote access server are more sophisticated than a simple modem for a client. They are often configured in banks of multiple modems and can be programmed to answer calls from more than one line.

- **PBX equipment**—Phone systems are managed using a PBX. PBXs often come as mini-servers with full operating systems.

System/Application Domain

The System/Application Domain includes servers used to host server applications. Some examples of different types of application servers include:

- **E-mail servers**—This can be a single e-mail server. It can also be a larger e-mail solution, including both front-end and back-end server configurations.

- **Database servers**—This can be an Oracle or Microsoft SQL server. It can be a single server or a group of servers.

- **Web servers**—Web servers host Web sites and serve them to Web clients. A single Web server can host a single Web site or hundreds of Web sites.

- **Networking service servers**—This includes Domain Name System (DNS) servers and Dynamic Host Configuration Protocol (DHCP) servers.

Inventory and asset management systems should include the following information on any servers in the System/Application Domain:

- **Hardware information**—This includes basics such as the model and serial number, just as you'd inventory a workstation. It should also include an inventory of the hardware components.

- **Update information**—Servers need to be kept up to date. This is especially true if any of these servers are public-facing servers, such as Web servers and some e-mail servers.

Identifying Facilities and Supplies Needed to Maintain Business Operations

Accidents and disasters happen. Some can be so catastrophic that a business can stop functioning. If you want to ensure your business can continue to function even after a catastrophe, you have to plan beforehand.

You can take several steps in the planning process. These include:

- Mission-critical systems and applications identification
- Business impact analysis planning
- Business continuity planning
- Disaster recovery planning
- Business liability insurance planning
- Asset replacement insurance planning

Mission-Critical Systems and Applications Identification

A primary step in any planning is to identify what systems and applications are mission-critical. A mission-critical system is any system that must continue to run to ensure your business continues to run. Similarly, a mission-critical application must also continue to run to ensure your business continues to run.

It's impossible to determine what is mission-critical before first understanding how an organization operates. For example, imagine that sales people within your company sell products directly to customers. Customers submit orders over the phone or in person. Sales people then enter the order into an application connected to a back-end database. In this example, the mission-critical systems are the phone, the application, and the back-end database.

On the other hand, imagine that your company sells the same products as in the example above. However, customers are able to place their orders directly through a Web site. In addition, they can send orders to sales people via e-mail, and the sales people then enter the orders into an application. This application is connected to the same database that the Web site uses. It's also possible for customers to phone orders in, but this occurs less than 10 percent of the time. In this example, the organization has more mission-critical systems. The phone, the application, and the back-end database are still mission-critical. However, the Web site application and e-mail would also be mission-critical.

The point to remember here is that the importance of a system is determined by how it's used. One organization may consider a specific system mission-critical. Another organization may consider the same system disposable.

Business Impact Analysis Planning

A **business impact analysis (BIA)** identifies the impact of a sudden loss of business functions. The impact is often quantified in a cost. You use both direct costs and indirect costs to calculate the impact. Direct costs are the immediate loss of sales, or expenses related to recovering from the loss. Indirect costs are related loss of customer confidence.

NOTE

Chapter 12 covers business impact analysis in greater depth. The BIA is part of a business continuity plan.

The BIA provides an analysis of the effect of a loss of specific IS services. For example, a BIA can be used to determine the impact of a loss of e-mail, or loss of a specific database. The BIA also helps an organization determine the minimum set of services required for the company to continue to operate.

For example, consider remote access. Remote users may use VPN technologies to connect into the private network from remote locations. If VPN services stopped, would the mission of the business stop? You could complete a BIA to make that determination.

It's possible that other methods are available for remote users to connect into the company. For example, remote users may still have access to e-mail using a Web page. Remote sales people may still be able to place orders using the phone. The BIA could determine that although the VPN services are valuable, their loss would have minimal impact on the overall mission of the company.

NOTE

The BIA is an important part of a business continuity plan. It can also be part of a disaster recovery plan (DRP).

On the other hand, a BIA for e-mail services may determine that the loss of e-mail would have a significant impact on the company. E-mail may be used for customer contact, project tasking, tracking, and other important communications.

When completing a BIA, you would take the following steps:

- **Define the scope**—The scope of a BIA is limited to specific IT systems. For example, the BIA could examine the impact of loss of e-mail, or loss of a Web site. If the scope is limited to loss of e-mail, loss of additional IT services should not be included. You reduce the possibility of scope creep by defining the scope early in the project.

  It is possible to perform a BIA for a total loss of services for a specific location. For example, a company could have multiple locations. One location could be in an earthquake or hurricane zone. The BIA could determine the impact if a disaster caused a total loss of services from this latter location.

- **Identify objectives**—BIA objectives are related to the scope of the BIA. The objectives identify specifically what the BIA should achieve. For example, a BIA task may include the following objectives:

  - Determine the direct impact of the loss of e-mail services for one business day.
  - Determine the indirect impact of the loss of e-mail services for one business day.
  - Calculate the impact of the loss of e-mail services for three business days.
  - Calculate the impact of the loss of e-mail services for five business days.

- **Identify mission-critical business functions and processes**—Not all business functions and processes are mission-critical. Some are convenient and help productivity, but the mission can still survive without them. The BIA separates the critical functions from the non-critical functions.

- **Map business functions and processes to IT systems**—This step can be easy or complex. For example, if the BIA analyzes e-mail services served by one e-mail server, the IT system is the e-mail server. On the other hand, if an organization uses Microsoft SharePoint Portal Servers to increase collaboration among employees, multiple IT systems are being used. A SharePoint solution can include Web servers, file servers, and database servers. Documentation on the IT systems will help you complete this step.

The result of the BIA is a BIA report. This report documents the findings of the analysis. It often includes direct and indirect costs, maximum acceptable outage, and materials or resources needed for recovery.

Business Continuity Planning

> **NOTE**
>
> Chapter 13 covers business continuity planning in greater depth.

A **business continuity plan (BCP)** is a document used to help a company plan for a disaster or an emergency. The goal is to ensure that the critical operations of an organization continue to function. The BCP includes procedures and instructions used to restore operations in the event of disaster.

When completing a BCP, you would take the following steps:

1. Identify scope.
2. Identify key business areas.
3. Identify critical functions.
4. Identify dependencies between different business areas and functions.
5. Determine acceptable downtime.
6. Create plan to maintain operations.

Details from a BIA report helps in the creation of the BCP. You commonly complete the BIA and BCP in conjunction with each other.

The BCP includes specific steps that you can take for different phases. The content of the phases is dependent on the disaster. For example, a hurricane gives plenty of warning. One phase might be 72 hours prior. Another phase might be 36 hours prior. However, an earthquake or a fire wouldn't include these same phases.

BCP phases include the following:

- **Notification/activation phase**—Assessment teams are activated to respond to the emergency. You can activate these teams before the emergency in some situations, such as with a hurricane. For more immediate emergencies such as a fire, the notification is done when the emergency occurs. The goal of this phase is to take steps to continue operations.

- **Recovery phase**—During this phase, you assess the damage. If there are any losses, you can take immediate steps to recover the systems. The focus in this phase is on the mission-critical systems.

- **Reconstitution phase**—During this phase, the organization returns to normal operations. If any mission-critical systems were kept operational using recovery operations, they can be normalized. For example, operations moved to an alternate server during the recovery phase can be returned to their original location. You can return non-mission-critical systems to operation in this phase.

Disaster Recovery Planning

A **disaster recovery plan (DRP)** includes the details needed to recover a system from a disaster. It provides the details necessary to respond immediately to a disaster. A DRP is included as part of a BCP.

> **NOTE**
>
> Chapter 14 covers a disaster recovery plan (DRP) in greater depth.

BCP Versus DRP

Some documentation indicates that a BCP and a DRP are the same thing. Some organizations treat the two topics as though they are the same thing.

However, when you are studying for the (ISC)[2] Certified Information Systems Security Professional (CISSP) and Systems Security Certified Practitioner (SSCP) exams, it's important to realize that a BCP and DRP are not the same. Domain 6 of the CISSP exam is Business Continuity and Disaster Recovery Planning. It includes both topics, and you're expected to know the differences. The SSCP exam has this specific objective: "6.4 Differentiate between a Business Continuity Plan (BCP) and a Disaster Recovery Plan (DRP)."

The National Institute of Standards and Technology (NIST) published Special Publication (SP) 800-34, titled Contingency Planning Guide for Information Technology Systems. SP 800-34 provides the following definitions:

- **Business continuity plan (BCP)**—"The documentation of a predetermined set of instructions or procedures that describe how an organization's business functions will be sustained during and after a significant disruption."

- **Disaster recovery plan (DRP)**—"A written plan for processing critical applications in the event of a major hardware or software failure or destruction of facilities."

In these definitions, you can see that a BCP has a wider scope than the DRP. The BCP helps an organization continue to operate. The DRP is used to restore a system to operation after a major failure.

Note that it's possible to restore a system but still not be able to perform mission-critical operations. For example, imagine that a fire destroyed a building. You may be able to restore a single database server, including restoring the data from off-site backups. However, this server won't necessarily restore all the critical operations.

The terms BCP and DRP are sometimes used interchangeably. However, they are separate. It's worthwhile noting the differences:

- **BCP**—The BCP is an overall plan used for emergency response. It identifies the critical systems for an organization, including acceptable downtimes. The BCP includes BIAs and DRPs for individual IT systems.

- **DRP**—The DRP is a key component of a BCP. It includes the details needed to recover one or more systems after a disaster. For example, a fire may have destroyed several servers in the server room. The DRP identifies the steps needed to recover the servers, including restoring data from backups.

Business Liability Insurance Planning

Chapter 1 mentioned the four risk management techniques. They are avoid, transfer, mitigate, and accept. You can transfer risk by outsourcing, but you can also do it by purchasing insurance. Business liability insurance is used to protect an organization from lawsuits. It covers the company for damages from a lawsuit along with legal costs.

Three primary types of business liability insurance exist. The type of insurance needed depends on the function of the business. The types of liability insurance are:

- **General**—Almost any organization will purchase this. It provides protection against injury claims and property damages. This provides an overall umbrella of insurance covering most lawsuits. It may be all that an organization needs.

- **Professional**—This protects the company if an employee provides faulty or inaccurate advice. It includes protection against malpractice, errors, and negligence. A company providing IT services to other companies may need this.

- **Product**—This protects the company if a customer becomes injured because of using the product. For example, batteries in mobile computers sometimes cause risks. This insurance would provide protection if a faulty battery caused a fire.

Asset Replacement Insurance Planning

Another type of insurance you can purchase is asset replacement insurance. This is intended to replace any assets damaged from a disaster. This is usually purchased in conjunction with other steps to prevent a disaster.

For example, an organization may want to protect itself from fire damage. It can install fire suppression equipment throughout the building. It can also place portable fire extinguishers throughout the building. However, despite best efforts, fires still occur.

Fire insurance can help a company replace assets if a fire causes damage. Other types of insurance that provide protection for assets include:

- Flood insurance
- Hurricane, wind, tornado, or other weather insurance
- Life insurance for certain people, such as for key officers

The insurance you purchase depends on many factors. This includes the value of the assets for your organization. For inexpensive assets, the cost of the insurance isn't justified. It could cost more for the insurance over several years than it would cost to replace the product. The insurance you purchase also depends on the relevant risks. Hurricane insurance is relevant for coastal states like Florida, Louisiana, and Texas. It is not relevant for landlocked states like Iowa or Ohio.

CHAPTER SUMMARY

This chapter provided information on identifying assets. Asset identification is an important first step in any risk identification process. An organization's assets include the hardware and software. They include data and information assets. They also include personnel. You can use the seven domains of a typical IT infrastructure to ensure you identify all the assets.

Once you identify the assets, you can use different tools to help protect them. A business impact analysis helps you to identify the impact to the business if a service fails. This helps you prioritize the most important assets. A disaster recovery plan documents the steps you would need to take to restore a failed system. A business continuity plan is broader and is used to help ensure that mission-critical systems continue to operate even after a disaster.

KEY CONCEPTS AND TERMS

Asset management

Business continuity plan (BCP)

Business impact analysis (BIA)

Data mining

Data warehousing

Disaster recovery plan (DRP)

Failover cluster

Intellectual property (IP)

Inventory management

Job rotation

Service pack (SP)

Single point of failure

CHAPTER 7 ASSESSMENT

1. It is possible to ensure a service is operational 99.999 percent of the time even if a server needs to be regularly rebooted.

   A. True
   B. False

2. What is a single point of failure?

   A. Any single part of a system that can fail
   B. Any single part of a system that can cause the entire system to fail, if it fails
   C. Any single part of system that has been protected with redundancy
   D. Any single part of a system

3. When identifying the assets you have in your organization, what would you include?

   A. Hardware
   B. Software
   C. Personnel
   D. Only A and B
   E. A, B, and C

4. When identifying hardware assets in your organization, what information should you include?

   A. Model and manufacturer
   B. Serial number
   C. Location
   D. Only A and C
   E. A, B, and C

5. An organization may use a _____ rotation policy to help discover dangerous shortcuts or fraudulent activity.

6. What type of data should be included when identifying an organization's data or information assets?

   A. Organizational data
   B. Customer data
   C. Intellectual property
   D. A and B only
   E. A, B, and C

7. What is a data warehouse?

   A. A database used in a warehouse
   B. A database used to identify the location of products in a warehouse
   C. A database created by combining multiple databases into a central database
   D. One of several databases used to create a central database for data mining.

8. What is data mining?

   A. The process of retrieving relevant data from a data warehouse
   B. A database used in metal mining operations
   C. A database created by combining multiple databases into a central database
   D. A process used to extract, load, and transform a data warehouse.

9. You are reviewing your organization's asset management data. You want to ensure that all elements of the organization are included. What can you compare the asset management system against to ensure the entire organization is covered?

   A. Hardware and software assets
   B. Software assets
   C. Personnel and data assets
   D. The seven domains of a typical IT infrastructure

10. You are tasked with updating your organization's business continuity plans. When completing this process, you should only include _____ systems.

11. What can you use to transfer risk associated with potential disasters?

   A. Business impact analysis
   B. Business continuity plan
   C. Disaster recovery plan
   D. Insurance

12. An organization wants to determine what the impact will be if a specific IT server fails. What should they use?

   A. BIA
   B. BCP
   C. DRP
   D. BCC

13. An organization wants to ensure they can continue mission-critical operations in the event of a disaster. What should they use?

   A. BIA
   B. BCP
   C. DRP
   D. BCC

14. An organization wants to ensure they can recover a system in the event of a disaster. What should they use?

   A. BIA
   B. BCP
   C. DRP
   D. BCC

15. A BCP and DRP are the same thing.

   A. True
   B. False

7

Assets and Activities to Be Protected

Identifying and Analyzing Threats, Vulnerabilities, and Exploits

R ISKS OCCUR when threats are able to exploit vulnerabilities. With this in mind, it becomes very important to be able to identify and analyze threats, vulnerabilities, and exploits. You can do so with threat assessments, vulnerability assessments, and exploit assessments.

A threat assessment attempts to identify as many threats as possible. It cannot identify all possible threats. Instead, it attempts to identify as many likely threats as possible. You can identify threats by reviewing historical data and using different threat modeling techniques.

A vulnerability assessment can help you identify weaknesses in your network. You can discover these weaknesses through several means. Some are manual, such as reviewing documentation, performing audits, or interviewing personnel. Others are automated by using vulnerability scanners.

An exploit assessment attempts to identify vulnerabilities that can actually be exploited.

Chapter 8 Topics

This chapter covers the following topics and concepts:

- What threat assessments are
- What vulnerability assessments are
- What exploit assessments are

Chapter 8 Goals

When you complete this chapter, you will be able to:

- Describe techniques used to identify threats
- List best practices for threat assessments within the seven domains of a typical IT infrastructure

- Describe the value of reviewing documentation for a vulnerability assessment
- Describe the value of reviewing system logs, audit trails, and intrusion detection system outputs for a vulnerability assessment
- Identify tools used to perform vulnerability scans
- Describe the value of performing audits and personnel interviews for a vulnerability assessment
- Describe and contrast process analysis and output analysis within the context of a vulnerability assessment
- Describe the different types of system testing used with vulnerability assessments
- List best practices for vulnerabilities assessments within the seven domains of a typical IT infrastructure
- Identify exploits throughout the seven domains of a typical IT infrastructure
- Describe how to mitigate exploits using a gap analysis and remediation plan
- Explain the value of configuration management and change management to mitigate identified exploits
- Describe how to verify and validate that an exploit has been mitigated
- List best practices for exploit assessments within a typical IT infrastructure

Threat Assessments

A **threat assessment** identifies and evaluates potential threats. The goal is to identify as many potential threats as possible. You then evaluate the threats. One important element is an estimate of a threat's frequency.

Chapter 6 covered risk assessments. As a reminder, a risk assessment is performed for a specific time. Risks that exist today may not exist in a year. Similarly, a threat assessment is performed at a specific time. The threat assessment evaluates current threats in the existing environment.

Threats were presented in Chapters 1 and 2. A threat is any activity that represents a possible danger. This includes any circumstances or events with the potential to adversely cause an:

> **NOTE**
>
> Threat assessments will not always be complete. A listing of all potential threats will take too much time and effort. Instead, the goal is to identify the most likely threats. With this in mind, there is no single "right result" for a threat assessment.

- **Impact on confidentiality**—Any unauthorized disclosure of data. You can apply access controls to ensure only specific users have access to data. Encryption techniques also help to protect confidentiality.

- **Impact on integrity**—The modification or destruction of data. Access controls protect data from malicious attackers who want to modify or destroy data. Hashing techniques verify integrity by detecting if the data has been modified.

- **Impact on availability**—The availability of any service or system. Different fault-tolerance strategies ensure that systems and services continue to operate even if an outage occurs. Data is backed up to ensure it can be restored even if data is lost or becomes corrupt.

When a threat is matched with a vulnerability, a risk occurs. The following equation shows the relationship between risk, vulnerabilities, and threats:

$$\text{Risk} = \text{Vulnerability} \times \text{Threat}$$

Figure 8-1 shows the different threats to an organization. They are generically categorized as either human or natural. Human threats can be internal or external. They can also be intentional or unintentional. Internal threats are by far the biggest threats to a company. Natural threats occur from weather or other non-manmade events.

External attackers can be hackers launching denial of service (DoS) attacks on your network. They can be malware writers trying to access, modify, or corrupt your organization's data. They can even be terrorists launching attacks on buildings or entire cities.

Internal users can also cause damage. A disgruntled employee may be able to access, modify, or corrupt the organization's data. If proper access controls aren't used, other employees may also access, modify, or corrupt data. Although the disgruntled employee's actions will be purposeful, regular employees' actions are accidental.

Natural threats include weather events such as floods, earthquakes, tornados, and electrical storms. Fires can also be a natural threat.

The goal of a threat assessment is to identify threats. You can identify threats by reviewing historical data. You can also identify threats using threat modeling.

After you've identified threats, you'll try to determine the likelihood of the threat. Some threats are more likely to occur, while others are less likely. Next, you prioritize the threats. There are times when you'll be able to match threats with vulnerabilities to determine costs. However, other times you won't be able to identify costs without also completing a vulnerability assessment.

The last step in a threat assessment is to provide a report. This report lists the findings. It includes the threats, the likelihood, and any identified costs.

This section on threat assessments includes:

- Techniques for identifying threats
- Best practices for threat assessments within the seven domains of a typical IT infrastructure

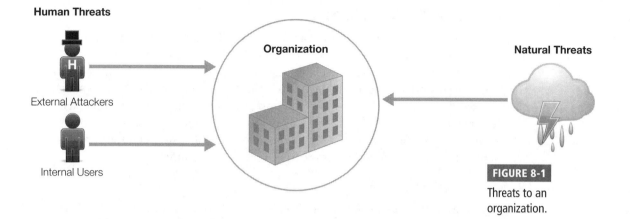

Human Threats

External Attackers

Internal Users

Organization

Natural Threats

Threats to an organization.

8

Threats, Vulnerabilities, and Exploits

The Top Threats Are Internal

It's not always apparent, but the top threats are internal. Some are accidental, and some are malicious. However, if you can train employees and control their actions, you'll reduce a significant number of threats.

Some of the common threats from internal sources are:

- **Unintentional access**—Access controls take a lot of effort to implement and maintain. This includes ensuring authentication processes are secure. It also includes enforcement of least-privilege and need-to-know policies. When users have access to data they don't need, the data is at risk. Users can accidentally delete the data. They can also share the data with someone else who shouldn't have access to it.

- **Disgruntled ex-employees**—When an employee is terminated, the user account should be either deleted or disabled. If not, the ex-employee may be able to access the same data or systems. The ex-employee could also pass on his or her credentials to someone else in-house to act as a proxy. The unauthorized access could result in data corruption or system sabotage.

- **Responding to phishing attempts**—Many users don't understand the risks with computers. More sophisticated phishing attempts target specific companies and fool the users. **Spear-phishing** is a targeted phishing attempt that looks as if it's coming from someone in the company.

- **Forwarding viruses**—Users can open infected e-mails and forward them to coworkers without realizing the danger. Users can bring viruses from home on universal serial bus (USB) flash drives.

- **Lack of laptop control**—Laptops are easily stolen. When users don't exercise physical control over laptops, the computers often disappear. The organization loses the hardware and software. What's more, data on the laptop is compromised.

Techniques for Identifying Threats

There are two primary techniques you can use to identify threats. You can review historical data. You can also perform threat modeling. The techniques you choose depend largely on your environment and available materials. It's possible to use both techniques.

If you have historical data available, this is often the easier approach. Historical data provide specific information on past threats. However, there is no guarantee that past threats will repeat. Additionally, there is no guarantee that a new threat won't appear. Threat modeling is more complex. It requires you to examine systems and services from a broader perspective. The process can be very time consuming.

Review Historical Data

One of the best ways to determine what threats exist is to analyze past incidents. This includes past incidents at the organization, at similar organizations, and in the local area:

- **Organization**—A review of past incidents will reveal threats that have resulted in losses.
- **Similar organizations**—Incidents with organizations in the same business will reveal possible threats in your organization.
- **Local area**—Natural and weather events are likely to repeat in the same area.

You can gather this data by compiling records and conducting interviews. Data can be compiled from any existing records. These can be security records. They can be insurance claims. You can also review troubleshooting records to determine outages and their causes. You can conduct interviews with management and other employees. Employees often know exactly what the problems are and where the threats exist. Management knows the particular threats that have resulted in significant losses.

Organization Historical Data. You can review an organization's historical data to identify past incidents from threats. Past incidents can take many forms. They can result from users accidentally or maliciously causing problems. They can come from external attackers. They can come from natural events.

Here are a few possible examples:

> **TIP**
>
> The principles of **need to know** and **least privilege** specify that users are granted access to only what they need to perform their job. The need-to-know principle specifies users only have access to the data they need. The least-privilege principle specifies that users have only the rights they need to perform their job.

- **Internal users**—Users were granted access to data they didn't need. They stumbled upon it and shared it with coworkers. This resulted in unauthorized disclosure of confidential data.
- **Disgruntled employee**—An employee was terminated for cause on a Monday. His account was not disabled or deleted. The employee accessed his account on Wednesday and deleted a significant amount of data. Some of the data was not backed up and was lost permanently.

- **Equipment failure**—A server crashed after a power spike. The server remained down for several hours until a power supply was replaced.

- **Software failure**—An ordering database application crashed on a database server. The server had to be rebuilt from scratch. Administrators reinstalled the operating system. They reinstalled the database application. They then restored the data from backups. This process took over 10 hours and customers could not place online orders during this time.

- **Data loss**—All users are required to store their data on a central file server. The data is backed up once a week on Sunday. The file server crashed on a Wednesday and many users lost over two days of work.

- **Attacks**—An e-mail server became infected with a virus. This virus spread to all the e-mail users' mailboxes. It took approximately two days to clean the system and return e-mail services to users.

Note that each of these examples shows only the threat. You could implement different countermeasures to prevent the threat. For example, if users have access to data they don't need, the principles of least privilege and need to know could be implemented. However, the goal at this stage is only to identify the threat.

Similar Organization's Historical Data.   Many threats are common to similar organizations. By identifying the threats against similar organizations, you can identify possible threats against your organization.

For example, attackers get a kick out of defacing any law enforcement Web site. Years ago, there were many instances of such Web sites being defaced. However, most law enforcement agencies recognize the threat today. They take additional steps to protect their Web sites. This is not to say they are immune to the threat. They have simply taken extra steps to protect themselves.

Any organization with public-facing servers faces similar threats. Apache is a popular Web server product that can run on UNIX, Linux, and Microsoft platforms. It serves Web pages over the Internet. Any company that hosts Apache faces the same threats.

> **NOTE**
>
> An attacker defaces a Web site by changing the contents. For example, instead of seeing the home page for the Web site, a user might see the home page for a porn site. In addition, attackers often leave a calling card of sorts. Somewhere on the page, an attacker may include text similar to "hacked by xxx." Another variation is "p'wned by xxx." Pwn and p'wned are slang for own or owned. In other words, conquered.

Local Area Data.   Primary considerations for the local area are weather conditions and natural disasters. If a location is on the coast, and the coast has had hurricanes in the past, it will likely have hurricanes in the future. If a location is in a flood zone, it will likely flood in the future.

Anyone who has lived in the area knows what the natural threats are. If you're new to the area, you can interview employees or other locals. When identifying natural threats, it's important to get more than one perspective. One person's disaster may be another person's minor inconvenience. You want to ensure you don't take steps to resolve problems based on anecdotal evidence.

For example, some local employees may live in a flood zone. They may relay horrific stories of how flood waters flowed into their homes and destroyed everything on the first floor. While this is horrific for them, it doesn't mean your organization will flood. You should balance this information against other sources. Flood zone maps show exactly what areas are likely to flood. If your organization is on high ground and not in a flood zone, you don't need to take steps to protect it from a flood.

Threat Modeling

Threat modeling is more complex than just researching historical data for threats. It is a process used to assess and document an application or system's security risks.

Ideally, you perform threat modeling before writing an application or deploying a system. This is done when security is considered throughout the full life cycle of a product or service. In other words, if security is only considered at the end of the project, it frequently falls short.

When threat modeling is used, you first need to identify the assets you want to evaluate. Chapter 7 covered the importance of asset management. Asset management helps you to identify the assets that are important to an organization, including their value. You can then take steps to identify the threats against the valuable assets.

A key part of threat modeling is to change your perspective. Instead of thinking like an administrator, you try to think like an adversary. In this context, the adversary can be an external attacker or an internal user. The internal user doesn't have to be malicious to be a threat. However, if the internal user has the potential to accidentally cause harm, the result is the same.

An excellent starting point when performing threat modeling is to use the seven domains of a typical IT infrastructure. As a reminder, the seven domains were covered in Chapter 1. They are presented later in this section with some best practices.

Some of the key questions you can ask yourself when performing threat modeling are:

- What system are you trying to protect?
- Is the system susceptible to attacks?
- Who are the potential adversaries?
- How might a potential adversary attack?
- Is the system susceptible to hardware or software failure?
- Who are the users?
- How might an internal user misuse the system?

Threat modeling for complex systems can become quite extensive. Depending on the system you're evaluating, you may need to define specific objectives to limit the scope of the evaluation.

Wireless and WEP

Wired Equivalent Privacy (WEP) is an example of how security can fall short if not considered throughout the development cycle. In the early days of wireless network development, the primary goal was to ensure that devices could easily connect. This was a huge success.

Toward the end of the development cycle, the developers started looking at security of wireless networks. They came up with WEP as a way to provide the same level of security in wireless networks as was available in wired networks. WEP fell well short of its goal.

WEP had several vulnerabilities, and tools became available to hack into it. Eventually, the group that designed wireless had to go back to the drawing board to redesign security. They came up with Wi-Fi Protected Access (WPA) as an interim fix and then WPA2 as a permanent fix.

You can create secure wireless networks today. However, if threat modeling techniques were used during the beginning stages of the wireless life cycle, it's possible the problems with WEP would never have occurred. Developers may have identified and fixed the vulnerabilities before WEP was released.

When performing threat assessments, it's important to ensure you understand the system or application you're evaluating. This includes what systems are involved. It also includes an understanding of how data flows in and out of systems. Without a full understanding of a system, it's difficult to shift your perspective to an attacker. Understanding a system often requires you to interview the experts and review the documentation on the system.

Analogy and Comparison with Similar Situations and Activities

Law enforcement personnel commonly use threat assessments. This includes local law enforcement, the FBI, and Secret Service personnel.

For example, every time local police answer calls to crime scenes, they quickly evaluate the situation. Consider a domestic dispute. A wife calls to complain that her husband is abusing her. Police know that this can be a violent and explosive scene. The husband could have a weapon. Additionally, if the wife realizes her husband is being arrested, she may turn on the police.

Similarly, every time the president of the United States travels somewhere, Secret Service teams go there first and perform threat assessments. The teams evaluate every path the president will take and look for potential threats. They visit the ultimate destinations and evaluate them. They consider the possibility of snipers and bombs. They evaluate employees with a focus on new employees. They investigate any tips.

Best Practices for Threat Assessments Within the Seven Domains of a Typical IT Infrastructure

One method of ensuring that you have addressed all threats is to use the seven domains of a typical IT infrastructure. As a reminder, the seven domains are the User Domain, Workstation Domain, LAN Domain, LAN-to-WAN Domain, WAN Domain, Remote Access Domain, and System/Application Domain. Figure 8-2 shows the seven domains.

You can methodically go through each of these domains and evaluate the threats. This allows you to evaluate the potential threats from different perspectives. Some best practices you can use when evaluating these threats include:

- Assume nothing, recognizing that things change.
- Verify that systems operate and are controlled as expected.
- Limit the scope of the assessment to a single domain at a time.
- Use documentation and flow diagrams to understand the system you're evaluating.
- Identify all possible entry points for the domain you're evaluating.
- Consider threats to confidentiality, integrity, and availability.
- Consider internal and external human threats.
- Consider natural threats.

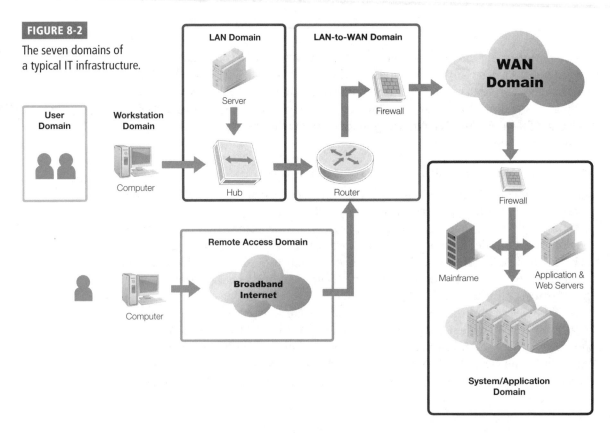

FIGURE 8-2

The seven domains of a typical IT infrastructure.

Vulnerability Assessments

A vulnerability assessment (VA) is performed to identify vulnerabilities within an organization. Vulnerabilities are any weaknesses in your IT infrastructure. They can exist for a specific server. They can exist for entire networks. They can also exist with personnel.

For example, a single Web server could be vulnerable to a buffer overflow attack. Imagine that a buffer overflow bug has been discovered in May. If it's not patched until July, it remains vulnerable between May and July.

> **NOTE**
>
> Buffer overflow vulnerabilities were presented in Chapter 2. A buffer overflow occurs when an attacker sends more data or different data than a system or application expects. Buffer overflow vulnerabilities are fixed with updates or patches. If servers aren't patched, the vulnerability remains.

Entire networks can be vulnerable if access controls aren't implemented. For example, if all users are granted the same rights and permissions for a network, there is no access control. All data on the network could be vulnerable to unauthorized disclosure. However, administrative models can be used to implement access controls. The principles of least privilege and need to know ensure that users have the access they need, but no more.

Vulnerabilities exist with personnel if they don't understand the value of security. Social engineering tactics trick people into revealing sensitive information or taking unsafe actions. If users don't understand the value of security practices, they are less likely to take specific actions. For example, an employee may receive a phone call that goes like this:

> "Hi. This is Joe in IT. We're doing a system upgrade and discovered a problem with your user account. In order to fix it and ensure you don't lose any data, we'll need to log onto your account from the server. Can you give me your user name and password?"

Of course, Joe doesn't work in the IT shop, but instead is trying to get a user to reveal a user name and password. If users frequently give out their password to administrators, this will easily succeed. If users are told to *never* give out their passwords, it may not succeed.

You perform vulnerability assessments to check for any of these types of vulnerabilities. You will perform some assessments more often than others.

Automated vulnerability scans of systems are usually performed more frequently. You can do them with assessment tools on a weekly basis. You can perform audits on an annual basis to see if security controls are being used as expected. For example, an annual audit can detect if access controls are still being used as expected. Additionally, you can do tests to see if personnel respond to social engineering tactics on annual basis.

An added benefit of a vulnerability assessment is the resulting documentation. You can use this documentation to show compliance with various laws and guidelines. Chapter 3 covered several laws that govern IT. These include laws such as the Sarbanes-Oxley Act (SOX), the Gramm-Leach-Bliley Act (GLBA), and the Health Insurance Portability and Accountability Act (HIPAA).

8

Threats, Vulnerabilities, and Exploits

▶ **TIP**

If possible, personnel who own the system or are responsible for its security should not perform the assessment. It's harder to have an objective view if you have a stake in making the system look good. It's also hard to be objective if you are so immersed in the details of the system that you may not be able to assess the vulnerabilities with fresh eyes.

You can perform vulnerability assessment testing internally or externally:

- **Internal assessments**—Security professionals try to exploit the internal system to see what they can learn about vulnerabilities. Some large companies have dedicated staff that regularly perform assessments. A smaller company could assign this as an extra task for an IT administrator.

- **External assessments**—Personnel outside the company try to exploit the system to see what they can learn. These are consultants hired to assess the security. Outside consultants provide a fresh look at your system. They are usually very good at quickly identifying weaknesses.

It's always important to gain permission when performing any vulnerability assessment. While most VAs are non-intrusive and won't affect operations, some VA methods can take a system down or simulate a DoS attack.

This section on vulnerability assessments includes the following topics:

- Documentation review
- Review of system logs, audit trails, and intrusion detection system outputs
- Vulnerability scans and other assessment tools
- Audits and personnel interviews
- Process analysis and output analysis
- System testing
- Best practices for performing vulnerability assessments within the seven domains of a typical IT infrastructure

Documentation Review

One of the steps you can take when performing a VA is to review the available documentation. The documentation can be from multiple sources, including:

- **Incidents**—If any security incidents have occurred, you should review the documentation from the incident. Often, the cause of an incident is directly related to a vulnerability. For example, a successful buffer overflow attack on an Internet facing server may have resulted in a malware infection. This may indicate that the system is not being updated often enough.

- **Outage reports**—You can investigate any outage that has affected the mission of the business. If the outage affected the bottom line, you can probably identify a vulnerability.

- **Assessment reports**—Past assessment reports should be reviewed. This helps identify common problems. It also helps identify problems that have not been corrected.

Review of System Logs, Audit Trails, and Intrusion Detection System Outputs

In addition to reviewing past assessment reports, there is a lot of additional information you can review to determine vulnerabilities. The three common sources of information are system logs, audit trails, and intrusion detection systems.

There is no particular order you should review these in. However, if your network has the data available, you should review all of it.

System Logs

Any computer system has some type of system logs. These logs have different names for different operating systems, but overall have the same purpose. They log data based on what the system is doing.

For example, Microsoft Windows systems have a log called System. You view this log using the Windows Event Viewer. The System log records system events such as when systems and services start or stop. The log records errors, warning, and information events.

You can determine what is happening to a system by reviewing the system logs. Some events such as warnings and errors will jump right out, indicating obvious problems. Others need a little more analysis to identify trends.

Audit Trails

An **audit trail** is a series of events recorded in one or more logs. These logs are referred to as audit logs, but an audit trail can be recorded in many types of logs. For example, Microsoft Windows includes a Security log that records auditable events. Additionally, security applications like firewalls record auditable events.

Any type of audit log attempts to log at least who, what, when, and where. If a user is logged on, the credentials are used to identify who accessed the data. For some logs such as firewall logs, the "who" may be the source's Internet Protocol (IP) address instead of a user name.

Auditable events are any events that you want to track. For example, you may want to know if anyone accessed a folder. You could enable auditing on the folder, and each time someone accessed any files within the folder, the access would be recorded. The event would include the user name, what file was accessed, when it was accessed, and the server or computer where it was accessed.

Many organizations have automated systems that can review audit trails. An automated system has the capability of examining logs from multiple sources. These are sometimes combined with intrusion detection systems that can review the events to detect intrusions.

> **NOTE**
> Attackers often attempt to erase the audit trail after an attack. The goal is often to get in, take some action, erase the audited events, and get out.

Intrusion Detection System Outputs

Chapter 2 presented intrusion detection systems. As a reminder, an intrusion detection system (IDS) is able to monitor a network or system and send an alert when an intrusion is detected. A host-based IDS is installed on a single system. A network-based IDS has several monitoring agents installed throughout the network that report to a central server.

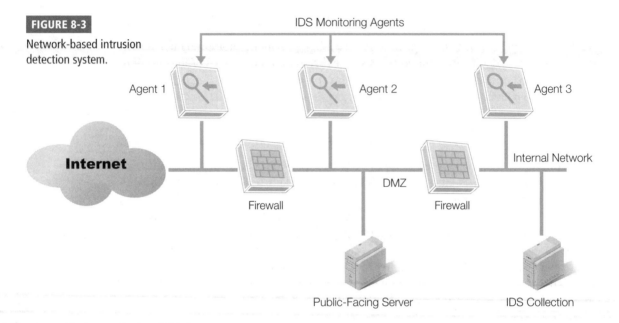

FIGURE 8-3

Network-based intrusion
detection system.

Figure 8-3 shows an example of a network-based IDS with three monitoring agents
installed on the network. Notice the location of the three monitoring agents. One is on
the Internet side. One is in the demilitarized zone (DMZ). One is on the internal network.
If you examine the output of the IDS, it will reveal several key points.

These three agents work together to identify what type of attacks are launched against
the network. They also give you insight into the success of different mitigation techniques.

Events from agent 1 show how many attacks are launched against your network from
the Internet. Events from agent 2 identify the attacks that are able to get through the
external firewall. This shows you the effectiveness of the firewall against specific types
of attacks. It also helps reveal the vulnerabilities for any public-facing servers in the DMZ.
Agent 3 shows the attacks that are able to get through the second firewall of the DMZ.
These attacks on your internal network can be very damaging if not addressed.

Although the focus of Figure 8-3 is on attacks from the Internet, it's also possible to
have internal attacks. The network agent on the internal network monitors for internal
attacks. It's common for a network to have several internal agents installed to monitor
an internal network.

Internal attacks aren't necessarily from malicious users. Instead, internal attacks
are often from malware that has infected one or more systems on the network. However,
the benefit of a network-based IDS is early detection of an infection.

Vulnerability Scans and Other Assessment Tools

Many tools are available to perform vulnerability scans within a network. Chapter 6
mentioned some of the commonly used tools. These include Nmap, Nessus, SATAN,
and SAINT.

These tools provide several benefits. Some of the benefits include:

- **Identify vulnerabilities**—They provide a fast and easy method to identify vulnerabilities. You simply run the scan and then analyze the report.

- **Scan systems and network**—Vulnerability scanners can inspect and detect problems on the network and on individual hosts. They can detect vulnerabilities based on the operating system, applications, and services installed on the host. They can detect open ports and access points on the network.

- **Provide metrics**—A key part of management is measurement. If you can measure something, you can identify progress. This is also true with vulnerabilities. If you are just starting to run regular vulnerability scans, the scans will likely discover many vulnerabilities. Six months later, if you analyze the metrics, you'll notice that the issues are significantly reduced. If not, you may have other problems. For example, if you have all of the same vulnerabilities six months after the first scan, the vulnerabilities are not getting fixed.

- **Document results**—The resulting documentation provides input for internal reports. It also provides documentation for compliance. You can use scanner reports to prove compliance with different laws and regulations.

Vulnerability scanners do have some weaknesses. First, they must be updated regularly. Threats change. Systems change. The scans must also change to ensure they are looking for both past and current vulnerabilities.

> **TIP**
>
> When shopping for a VA scanner, you should pay attention to how updates are accomplished. A scanner that isn't updated regularly may only be useful for a short period of time. A scanner that is regularly updated is worth the extra expense.

Many scanners also have a high false positive error rate. While this can be annoying, it makes sense from a security perspective. If there's a possibility for error, the scanner errs on the side of too many warnings, instead of not enough. Consider these two situations.

- Your system is vulnerable but you don't know about it. This can occur from a low false-positive error rate.

- Your system is not vulnerable, but you're notified that it may be. This can occur from a high false-positive error rate.

Most security professionals want to avoid the first scenario. You don't want your system to have unknown vulnerabilities.

Last, some scanners can generate a lot of network traffic. This network traffic could interfere with normal operations if the network is already busy.

Audits and Personnel Interviews

An **audit** is performed to check compliance with rules and guidelines. A VA audit checks compliance with internal policies. In other words, an audit will check to see if an organization is following the policies that are in place.

FYI

Employees should never reveal their passwords to anyone else. This includes responses to e-mails that may be phishing attempts. It includes requests over the phone or in person that could be social engineering attacks. When an organization begins making exceptions, such as it is OK to give a password to someone from the IT department, the user gets confused. They may think that the phishing attempt or social engineering attack is another exception.

For example, an organization may have a policy in place related to employees who leave the company. The policy may state that user accounts should be disabled if an employee leaves. Six months later, the account should be deleted.

An audit determines if the policy is being followed. The audit can be quick and automated if the auditor has some scripting skills. An auditor could write a script to check for enabled accounts that haven't been used in the past 15 days. The output is then checked with the human resources department to determine if any of these users are still employed. A similar script could be used to determine if any accounts exist that haven't been used in the past six months.

Personnel interviews are completed to gain insight into possible new issues. For example, you could ask personnel what they consider to be current vulnerabilities. Often employees know what the issues are, but aren't asked.

In addition, you can conduct personnel interviews to identify the security knowledge of personnel. For example, employees could be asked when it is acceptable to give out their password. A secure organization will have a policy in place stating that users should never give out their password to anyone.

Process Analysis and Output Analysis

Process analysis is performed in some systems to determine if vulnerabilities exist in the process. In other words, instead of just looking at the output, you evaluate the processes used to determine the output. Output analysis, on the other hand, is performed by examining the output to determine if a vulnerability exists.

Neither analysis is superior to the other. However, there are times when one will be preferable over the other.

FIGURE 8-4

Network-based intrusion detection system.

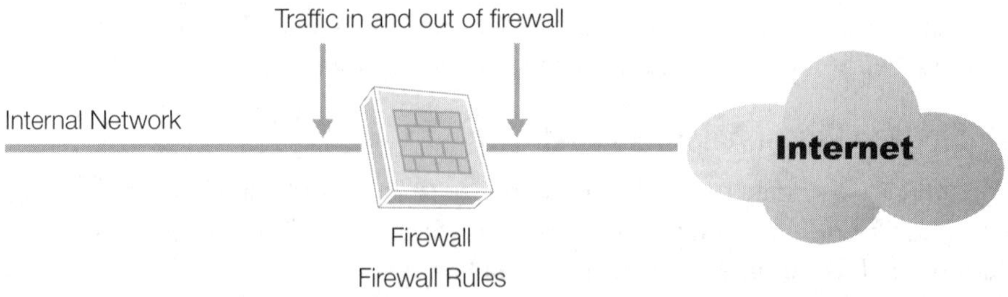

Traffic in and out of firewall

Internal Network

Firewall
Firewall Rules

Internet

For example, you may be concerned about the effectiveness of a firewall. Firewalls use rules to determine if traffic is allowed. You can use either process analysis or output analysis to determine the effectiveness of the firewall.

Consider Figure 8-4. The firewall is blocking and allowing traffic into and out of the network. Process analysis requires you to review all the rules to determine if the rules provide the desired security. Output analysis will examine the input and output of the firewall to determine if only desired traffic is allowed through the firewall.

If the firewall has only five rules, process analysis would be completed rather easily. However, if the firewall has over 100 rules, output analysis may be easier to perform.

System Testing

System testing is used to test individual systems for vulnerabilities. This includes individual servers and individual end-user systems. The primary testing performed on systems is related to patches and updates. This is because the majority of vulnerabilities occur because of bugs that are resolved by patching.

For example, you could have a bank of servers that are running Microsoft Windows Server 2008. Several patches and updates have been released for the servers since they've been installed. System testing queries the servers to determine if they are up-to-date.

You can do system testing with traditional management tools, with VA tools, or both. For example, Microsoft includes traditional tools such as Windows Server Update Services (WSUS) and System Center Configuration Manager (SCCM). Each of these server products can query systems in the network and ensure they have all the appropriate updates. If a system doesn't have an update, WSUS or SCCM can push the update to the system and double check to ensure it has been installed.

For example, Microsoft Security Bulletin MS08-067 identified a critical vulnerability in the Server service for almost any Windows systems from Windows 2000 to Windows 2008. This vulnerability allows attackers to send specially crafted requests to the systems that can then run arbitrary code. The arbitrary code can install malware. You can read about this vulnerability at *http://www.microsoft.com/technet/security/Bulletin/MS08-067.mspx.*

Microsoft has released updates for all affected systems. Any system that doesn't have the update related to MS08-067 is vulnerable. WSUS and SCCM can be used to check clients for the vulnerability and deploy the appropriate updates.

As an additional check, a VA tool can verify that systems have appropriate updates. Most VA tools can't also deploy the updates. Instead, they simply check for vulnerabilities.

Functionality Testing

Functionality testing is primarily used with software development. It helps ensure that a product meets the functional requirements or specifications defined for the product.

One of the problems that can occur with software development is scope creep. This occurs when additional capabilities are added that weren't originally planned. In other words, the add-ons are outside the scope of the original product specifications. While this looks good on the surface, it adds additional security issues.

Each additional line of code that is added to an application represents a potential bug. If additional capabilities are added, they need to be tested. If they are added without being documented, it's highly unlikely that they will be tested.

When an application is developed with the original functions, functional testing ensures that the application works as expected. Functional testing often includes attempts to develop an application.

Edge testing is one technique that can often detect potential buffer overflow errors. For example, if an input between 1 and 100 is expected, edge testing enters numbers on the edges. The numbers 0 and 1 are on the beginning edge of the range. The numbers 100 and 101 are on the outer edge of the range.

Access Controls Testing

Access controls testing verifies user rights and permissions. A "right" grants the authority to perform an action on a system, such as to restart it. A "permission" grants access to a resource, such as a file or printer.

Most organizations have administrative models in place that specify what rights and permissions regular users are granted. These models ensure that users have what they need to perform their job, but no more. They help support security principles of least privilege and need to know.

Consider Figure 8-5. A company has some resources that only sales personnel should access. It has other resources that only IT department personnel should access. Access restrictions are enforced by putting employees into the appropriate groups and assigning permissions to the group.

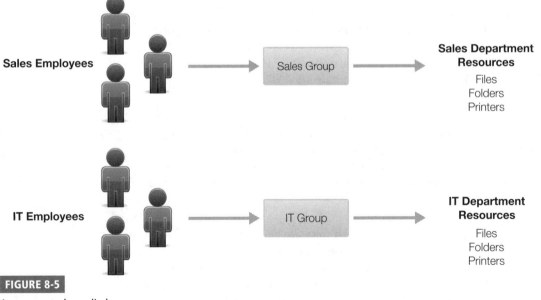

FIGURE 8-5

Access controls applied to users.

Security or Usability?

A company that had explosive growth in a short time was faced with some basic technical challenges. The company had a single administrator managing the entire network. Although this administrator managed the network well when the company was smaller, he was overwhelmed when the company grew.

He was faced with two competing goals: security or usability. Users requested changes to their rights and permissions more and more often. He understood that rights and permissions ensure that users have only what they need to perform their job. He also understood the value of the principles of least privilege and need to know. Instead of just making the changes, he tried to investigate the need. These delays resulted in complaints to his manager.

The administrator expressed a need to the manager for additional help. He also tried to explain the purpose of access controls to the manager. Unfortunately, he was unable to get any additional help. The manager also stressed that he didn't want to hear of any more complaints from users needing additional access.

In this situation, the manager was focused on usability and the administrator was focused on security. However, the manager is the boss. What the boss says goes.

Two things happened. First, the administrator added all users to administrator accounts. This ensured that all users would always have access to anything they needed. It also ensured the manager would not hear any complaints of access controls. Second, the administrator began looking for another job.

Any member of the Sales group automatically has access to the Sales resources. Any member of the IT group automatically has access to the IT resources. Members of the Sales group do not have access to IT department resources. Members of the IT group do not have access to Sales department resources.

Similarly, only certain users within an organization should have administrative rights to systems. From a usability perspective, it's easier to grant everyone administrative access. However, granting everyone administrative access sacrifices security. It violates the least privilege principle by giving all users rights to do anything. It violates the need to know principle by granting all users access to all data in the organization.

Access controls testing verifies that the users are granted the rights and permissions needed to perform their jobs, and no more. It ensures that an administrative model is used as it was designed.

▶ **NOTE**

Penetration testing is also referred to as **exploit testing**. Exploit testing is explored in more depth later in this chapter.

Penetration Testing

Penetration testing attempts to exploit vulnerabilities. In other words, you'll often complete a VA to discover vulnerabilities. You'll then perform a penetration test to see if a vulnerability can be exploited.

A penetration test can be much more invasive than VA tests. Specifically, if a penetration test is successful, it may actually take a system down. With this in mind, you need to be cautious when performing penetration tests.

Penetration testing verifies the effectiveness of countermeasures or controls. In other words, you've discovered a vulnerability and implemented a control to protect against the vulnerability. You can now perform a penetration test to see if the control works.

If the penetration test is successful, you know the controls aren't adequate. You'll need to take additional steps to protect against an attack.

Transaction and Applications Testing

Transaction and application testing ensures that an application will function correctly with a back-end database.

A **transaction** in a database is a group of statements that either succeed or fail as a whole. If any single statement fails, the entire transaction fails.

For example, imagine you are withdrawing $100 from your ATM. The ATM verifies you have the money in your account and gives you the money. However, just before it debits the $100 from your account, the ATM loses power. You have the money, but it hasn't been debited from your account. Is this acceptable? Maybe to you, but not to the bank.

Instead, the ATM will record the actions this way. It checks your account and verifies you have the money. It debits the amount from your account. It then gives you the money. Once you have the money, it views the transaction as complete and commits the transaction, making it final.

▶ **TIP**

SQL injection attacks were mentioned in Chapter 1. In a SQL injection attack, the attacker can read sections of a database, or the entire database, without authorization. SQL injection attacks can also be used to modify data in the database.

However, if the ATM loses power before giving you the money, the ATM does not commit the transaction. The debit is recognized as part of an incomplete transaction and it is rolled back.

Transaction testing ensures that transactions behave as expected.

Application testing is used to ensure that the application works with the back-end database as expected. A well-known vulnerability with front-end applications that interact with back-end databases is SQL injection. This is true for applications that are on the Web as well as non-Web applications.

Many tools are available that can automate SQL injection testing on systems.

Best Practices for Performing Vulnerability Assessments Within the Seven Domains of a Typical IT Infrastructure

When performing vulnerability testing, you should ensure that each of the seven domains of a typical IT infrastructure is considered. These seven domains were mentioned earlier and shown in Figure 8-2.

Vulnerabilities exist in each of the domains. It's possible to focus on only a single domain at a time. However, you should examine all seven domains on a regular basis.

You may have tools that are focused on the LAN Domain or the LAN-to-WAN Domain. However, if this is the only vulnerability testing you are doing, you are missing many other potential problems. For example, social engineering attacks against the user domain are often successful simply because users don't understand the risks.

The following best practices apply to most of the domains:

- **Identify assets first**—Chapter 7 covered asset management. Asset management helps you identify what resources to protect. There is no need to perform VAs on all assets. You only want to take these steps on the valuable assets.

- **Ensure scanners are kept up to date**—Vulnerability scanners need to be updated regularly. This is similar to how antivirus (AV) software needs to be updated with

---

Vulnerability Assessment Report

Although there is no standard format that must be used when completing VA reports, there is some common information you should include. You should consider including the following information in a VA report:

- **Table of contents**—If the report is lengthy, include a table of contents to make it easy for the reader to find relevant information.

- **Executive summary**—This provides a short summary of the report. Executive summaries are generally limited to no more than a single page, or 10 percent of the total document for large reports.

- **Methods**—This section identifies what tools were used to perform the assessment. It should include enough detail so that someone else is able to reproduce the results. The same person could be performing the same assessment six months later, and this section will help them ensure they are performing the same tests.

- **Results**—This section identifies the results of the assessments. It lists discovered vulnerabilities. Whenever possible, this section should also include estimates on the likelihood of the vulnerability being exploited.

- **Recommendations**—Some vulnerabilities should be mitigated while others may be ignored. The recommendations section identifies what vulnerabilities are serious and which ones are minor. If available, controls and countermeasures can also be included.

malware definitions. An AV program that isn't kept up to date is only marginally better than no AV program at all. This is the same for a vulnerability scanner. A scanner that isn't kept up date is only marginally better than no scanner at all.

- **Perform internal and external checks**—Attacks can come from internal and external sources. You should perform VAs from internal and external locations. Check within the firewall. Check from outside the firewall. If you have a DMZ, check for vulnerabilities from outside the network.
- **Document the results**—Document the results of every VA. You can use this documentation in several ways. Older results can be compared against current results to track progress. Some VAs can be used to document compliance with laws and regulations.
- **Provide reports**—Provide reports to management. These reports will summarize the important findings and provide recommendations.

Exploit Assessments

Exploit assessments attempt to exploit vulnerabilities. In other words, they simulate an attack to determine if the attack can succeed. An exploit test usually starts with a vulnerability test to determine the vulnerabilities. It follows with an attempt to exploit the vulnerability.

Many large organizations have dedicated security teams used to perform exploit assessments. Others hire outside professionals to perform exploit assessments. These personnel spend close to 100 percent of their work time learning about vulnerabilities and exploits. They learn how to identify the vulnerabilities. They learn how to exploit them. They also learn what is needed to protect an organization from the exploits.

Unless you are a security professional focused only on vulnerability and exploit assessments, you won't have the detailed knowledge of these teams. However, whether you're working as an IT professional or in IT management, you should understand some of the basics.

The following sections cover some of the basic topics related to exploit assessments:

- Identify exploits
- Mitigate exploits with a gap analysis and remediation plan
- Implement configuration or change management
- Verify and validate the exploit has been mitigated
- Best practices for performing exploit assessments within your IT infrastructure

Identify Exploits

The first step in an exploit assessment is to perform a vulnerability test. The vulnerability test will provide you with a list of potential vulnerabilities that can be exploited. However, just because you know that a vulnerability can be exploited, you won't necessarily know how to exploit it.

Some vulnerabilities are easily exploited through existing tools. Developers have already identified the exploit and written an application. Now the attacker only needs to run the application. These applications are so easy to use that kids can use them. A "script kiddie" is someone who has the application but doesn't really know what he or she is doing.

Other vulnerabilities require the expertise of talented programmers or developers. For example, the Microsoft Security Bulletin MS08-067 was mentioned earlier. Although the documentation indicates what is possible, it doesn't include code identifying what to do or how to do it.

Anyone who wants to exploit this vulnerability would need to write code to simulate the attack. This is not an easy task.

When attempting to identify exploits, you should look at all seven domains of a typical IT infrastructure. The following list shows some possible items to check in each of the seven domains:

> **TIP**
>
> A script kiddie gives the image of a bored teenager downloading and running applications. The applications are easy to use, but can also cause significant damage. It doesn't matter whether the attack is coming from a script kiddie or a dedicated criminal with IT skills. You need to protect against all attacks.

- **User Domain**—Common exploits against users are related to social engineering. If users can be easily tricked or conned, it indicates more training is needed.

- **Workstation Domain**—Two common things to check on workstations are updates and antivirus software. Common exploits occur when systems aren't patched. Additionally, systems need to have updated antivirus software installed to protect against malware.

- **LAN-to-WAN Domain**—This is the boundary between the public Internet and the private network. Attackers attempt to discover holes in the firewall and exploit them. An aggressive policy of only allowing required traffic through the firewall provides the best protection. Additionally, intrusion detection systems can detect and mitigate many of the threats.

- **WAN Domain**—This includes any Internet-facing servers. Common exploits against these systems are buffer overflow attacks. The best defense is to keep the systems updated. Additionally, these servers are commonly protected in a DMZ.

- **Remote Access Domain**—This includes dial-up remote access servers and virtual private network (VPN) servers. Common exploits attempt to break through the authentication and authorization process to access the internal network.

- **System/Application Domain**—Exploits in this domain are dependent on the system or application. Database servers have specific exploits such as SQL injection attacks. Unpatched Web servers are commonly vulnerable to buffer overflow attacks. E-mail servers are vulnerable to spam infected with malware.

Many common exploits exist. Even though they are common, they can still succeed and cause damage. The following sections include details on some of these exploits.

Social Engineering

Social engineering attacks often succeed due to the trusting nature of people. As a simple example, consider piggybacking.

▶ **TIP**

Piggybacking is also known as tailgating. Mantraps are commonly used to prevent piggybacking. A mantrap allows only a single person to pass through at a time. It can be as simple as a subway-like turnstile that allows only a single person through, or a full-sized cage that allows one person to walk through at a time.

Piggybacking occurs when one person follows another person into a secure area without using a key, badge, or cipher code. Imagine a company that has restricted access to a building. Personnel are required to use a badge and a personal identification number (PIN) to open a door. However, once the door is open, multiple people can walk through the door. The additional people that walk through the door are piggybackers or tailgaters.

A security consultant was hired to perform a security assessment for a company. She hung back waiting for someone that looked friendly. She loaded her arms up with books, boxes, and briefcases. The person in front of her not only allowed her in without a badge, he actually held the door open for her.

It's good to be courteous and kind, and slamming the door in front of someone needing assistance conflicts with courtesy. However, in this case, courtesy was a problem. The exploit assessment indicated that the vulnerability could be exploited by exploiting a person's natural courtesy.

MAC Flood Attack

Most organizations replace hubs with switches to prevent unrestricted sniffing attacks. A sniffing attack allows an attacker to connect a network interface card into an unused wall socket and capture data. If a hub is used, an attacker can capture any data traveling through the hub. If a switch is used, the attacker is not able to capture as much data.

However, an attack on the switch can cause it to work like a hub. Switches build tables matching their physical ports to Media Access Control (MAC) addresses. Most systems have only a single MAC address. In this case, the switch matches one port to one MAC address.

In a MAC flood attack, the attacker sends hundreds of packets to the same port. However, she uses spoofing to change the MAC address so that the switch sees hundreds of MAC addresses from the same port. At some point, the switch can no longer keep up. It "fails open" and works like a hub.

Imagine that an attacker or tester has access to an unprotected network jack in a conference room. After plugging in, she can launch the MAC flood attack. After a while, the switch goes to "fail open" mode. She then turns on her protocol analyzer and captures all the data going through the switch.

TCP Syn Flood Attack

The TCP Syn flood attack is a common attack against public-facing servers. It helps to understand how a Transmission Control Protocol (TCP) session works to understand this exploit.

Consider Figure 8-6. This shows the TCP three-way handshake used by TCP to establish a session between two systems. The first system sends a packet with the Synchronize (Syn) flag set. The second system responds with a packet that has the Synchronize (Syn) and Acknowledge (Ack) flags set. The original system then responds with a packet with the Ack flag set. The two systems have now started a session.

> **NOTE**
>
> A TCP Syn flood attack is a specialized type of DoS attack. Any DoS attack attempts to prevent a server or system from responding to normal requests. Hacker tools exist that allow an attacker to enter the IP address of the server to attack and click Go. The tool launches the DoS attack without any additional input needed by the attacker.

This is similar to two people starting a conversation. The first person says "Hi" and sticks his hand out. The second person says "Hi" and extends her hand. The two people shake hands and a conversation starts. Admittedly, not everyone starts a conversation by shaking hands. Even if you're not shaking hands, there is verbal or non-verbal communication between two people before the conversation starts.

In a TCP Syn flood attack, the handshake never completes. Consider Figure 8-7. The systems send the first two packets. However, the originating system never sends the third packet. It's as if one person stuck his hand out to shake, but when the other person extended her hand, the first person pulled his hand away.

If this happens once, it won't cause a problem. However, in a TCP Syn flood attack, an attacking system may send hundreds of Syn packets to start the TCP session. The attacking system never completes the handshake by sending the last Ack packet. This leaves hundreds of open sessions on the server while waiting for the Ack packet to complete the handshake. A TCP Syn flood attack consumes resources on a server and can cause the server to crash.

8

Threats, Vulnerabilities, and Exploits

FIGURE 8-6

TCP three-way handshake.

① Syn
② Syn/Ack
③ Ack

Host   Server

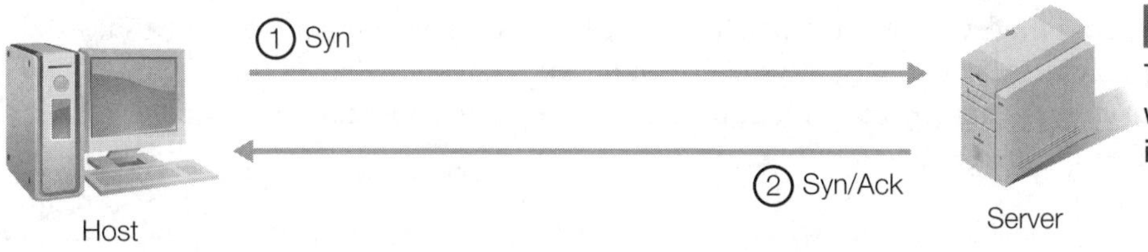

FIGURE 8-7

TCP Syn flood attack withholds third packet in three-way handshake.

① Syn
② Syn/Ack

Host   Server

A common way these attacks are mitigated is with an IDS. An IDS can detect the attack and mitigate it. For example, the IDS can close all the open sessions before they become a problem. It can also change settings so that all packets from the attacking computer are blocked.

Mitigate Exploits with a Gap Analysis and Remediation Plan

An exploit assessment will identify exploits that are mitigated. It will also identify exploits that are not mitigated. The difference between what is mitigated and what is not mitigated represents a gap in the security. A **gap analysis** report documents these differences.

> **TIP**
>
> A gap analysis and remediation plan are often done to satisfy regulatory compliance requirements. For example, if your organization is governed by HIPAA, a gap analysis can identify where the organization stands right now. The remediation plan identifies what steps need to be taken to ensure the organization is in full compliance with HIPAA when the plan is completed.

A remediation plan is often included with a gap analysis. It includes details on what you would need to do to close the gap. The goal is to ensure that all serious exploits are mitigated once the remediation plan is completed.

It's common to use both a gap analysis and a remediation plan for any company that is regulated by HIPAA or SOX. This was especially true when the laws were first introduced and companies were taking steps to ensure compliance. In other words, organizations weren't expected be 100 percent compliant with the law the day it was enacted. Instead, the organization was expected to take specific steps to become compliant.

Due to the highly technical nature of some of these laws, organizations will often bring in outside consultants to perform the gap analysis. The consultants can often perform the analysis by reviewing existing documentation and procedures combined with interviews of appropriate personnel. If desired, they can also create a remediation plan.

Implement Configuration or Change Management

Configuration management and change management can both help prevent or remediate exploits. Configuration management was presented in Chapter 2. In configuration management, you use standards to ensure that systems are configured similarly. Additionally, you perform compliance auditing to ensure that systems have not been improperly modified.

When you use configuration management techniques, you have a higher level of confidence that systems are protected against exploits. For example, imagine that a well-known exploit can target systems that haven't had an update in three years. Configuration management techniques ensure that an update is always included in any new deployment.

Change management is a process that controls changes to systems. You perform changes only after they have been reviewed and approved. Change management is an important process because many IT outages occur due to unauthorized changes. Organizations with mature change management processes reduce these outages.

A common example is a well-meaning administrator who makes a change to solve a small problem on a local system. She inadvertently creates a much larger problem on the network. For example, an application may not work with a specific update applied. The administrator removes the update, making the system vulnerable to the exploit.

Verify and Validate the Exploit Has Been Mitigated

After you have deployed countermeasures or controls to mitigate an exploit, you need to ensure that they work. In other words, you need to repeat the testing to ensure that the exploit has been mitigated.

Two possibilities exist. One, the control may not work at all. If this is the case, it needs to be replaced. Two, the configuration may need to be slightly modified to work completely. For example, certain settings may have been required when the control was first deployed, but were missed. You can go back, make these changes, and test the control again.

The easiest way to verify that an exploit has been mitigated is the same way you identified it originally. If a vulnerability scan found the problem, run it again. If an audit identified the problem, audit the specifics related to the exploit.

Best Practices for Performing Exploit Assessments Within an IT Infrastructure

The following list identifies several best practices you can follow when performing exploit assessments:

- **Get permission first**—An exploit assessment can take a system down. Ensure that management understands the risks and approves the process. Without permission, several issues can arise. If you're an outside consultant, you may be liable for damages caused by the outage. If you're an inside employee, you may have an opportunity to update your résumé while you look for another job.

- **Identify as many exploits as possible**—Use all of the tools available with vulnerability assessments to identify possible exploits. Examine all seven domains of a typical IT infrastructure.

- **Use a gap analysis for legal compliance**—If you are identifying exploits for legal compliance such as for HIPAA, use a gap analysis. The gap analysis identifies the differences between what is needed and what you have in place. This provides formal documentation to show that you are taking steps to become compliant with the law.

- **Verify that exploits have been mitigated**—After you've implemented controls to mitigate exploits, ensure that they work. Use the same techniques you originally used to discover the exploit to verify it is mitigated.

CHAPTER SUMMARY

This chapter provided information on threat assessments, vulnerability assessments, and exploit assessments. Each can be used to identify potential risk factors in your IT infrastructure. The goal is to identify as many threats, vulnerabilities, and exploits as possible. Once they are identified, you can take steps to mitigate them.

Threat assessments aren't expected to be all-encompassing or complete. Instead, they are performed to identify the likely threats that will occur. You identify these threats by reviewing historical data, and through threat modeling. Vulnerability assessments identify weaknesses in your network. You can perform some vulnerability assessments manually. Other vulnerability assessments can be performed using automated tools such as Nessus, a popular vulnerability scanner tool. Any scanning tool has to ensure that systems have no vulnerabilities, and thus must be up to date. An exploit assessment determines if weaknesses can be exploited. An exploit assessment can be performed before a control has been implemented, and afterwards to verify the effectiveness of the control.

KEY CONCEPTS AND TERMS

Audit	Gap analysis	Social engineering
Audit trail	Least-privilege principle	Spear phishing
Change management	Need-to-know principle	Threat assessment
Exploit testing	Penetration testing	Transaction

CHAPTER 8 ASSESSMENT

1. The two major categories of threats are human and _____.

2. A threat is any activity that represents a possible danger, with the potential to affect confidentiality, integrity, or availability.

A. True
B. False

3. Which of the following methods can be used to identify threats?

A. Review historical data
B. Perform threat modeling
C. Both A and B
D. Neither A nor B

4. What are some sources of internal threats? (Select all that apply.)

    A. Disgruntled employee
    B. Equipment failure
    C. Software failure
    D. Data loss

5. Which of the following choices is *not* considered a best practice when identifying threats?

    A. Verify systems operate and are controlled as expected.
    B. Limit the scope of the assessment.
    C. Consider threats to confidentiality, integrity, and availability.
    D. Assume the systems have *not* changed since the last threat assessment.

6. A _____ assessment is used to identify vulnerabilities within an organization.

7. Who should perform vulnerability assessments?

    A. Internal security professionals working as employees
    B. External security professionals hired as a consultants
    C. Either internal or external security professionals, or both
    D. Only the IT personnel that own the systems

8. What is the name of a common tool used to perform an automated vulnerability assessment scan?

    A. Wireshark
    B. Superscan
    C. Nessus
    D. VA Scanner

9. What is a common drawback or weakness of a vulnerability scanner?

    A. A high false-positive error rate
    B. A high false-negative error rate
    C. A low false-positive error rate
    D. A low false-negative error rate

10. Your organization wants to check compliance with internal rules and guidelines. They want to ensure that existing policies are being followed. What should be performed?

    A. Threat assessment
    B. Gap analysis
    C. An audit trail
    D. An audit

11. You want to know if users are granted the rights and permissions needed to do their job only, and no more. You should perform a(n) _____ test.

12. You want to identify if any of the discovered vulnerabilities can be exploited. What should you perform?

    A. Audit
    B. Transaction and applications test
    C. Functionality test
    D. Exploit assessment

13. Your organization is governed by HIPAA. You suspect that your organization is not in compliance. What would document the differences between what is required and what is currently implemented?

    A. Gap analysis
    B. Vulnerability assessment
    C. Threat assessment
    D. Penetration test

14. What management program can be implemented to ensure that the configuration of systems is not modified without a formal approval?

    A. Configuration management
    B. Change management
    C. Gap analysis
    D. Process analysis

15. Configuration management ensures that changes are not made to a system without formal approval.

    A. True
    B. False

8

Threats, Vulnerabilities, and Exploits

Identifying and Analyzing Risk Mitigation Security Controls

CONTROLS MITIGATE RISK. In other words, they reduce or neutralize threats or vulnerabilities to an acceptable level. At any point in time, you will likely have controls that are in place, controls that are planned, and controls that are needed or being considered.

There are hundreds of controls you can implement in any environment. When evaluating controls, it's best to consider controls in different categories. The National Institute of Standards and Technology published Special Publication SP 800-53. This document groups 18 families of controls into three classes: Technical, Operational, and Management. The document also categorizes controls as Administrative, Technical, and Physical.

Chapter 9 Topics

This chapter covers the following topics and concepts:

- What in-place and planned controls are
- What the different categories of controls defined by NIST are
- What administrative controls are
- What technical controls are
- What physical controls are
- What best practices for risk mitigation security controls are

In-Place Controls

When identifying and analyzing risk mitigation security controls, you need to identify what is in place. An in-place control is installed in an operational system. There should be associated documentation identifying its purpose.

This is not to say that you won't replace any of the in-place controls. You may. It just depends on whether they meet your goals. For example, there may be antivirus (AV) software installed on systems in your network. However, your systems may have been infected by malware in the past year. You may decide to replace the AV software with something considered more reliable.

With this in mind, you should evaluate any controls in place for their effectiveness. If you determine a control is not effective, you can identify an alternative control.

Controls, or countermeasures, will reduce or neutralize threats or vulnerabilities. Controls have three primary objectives:

- Prevent
- Recover
- Detect

Some controls focus on only one objective. Other controls focus on more than one. However, if a control can't meet one of these objectives adequately, it should be replaced.

Planned Controls

Planned controls are those that have been approved but not installed yet. Planning documents identify what the controls have been purchased for, with supporting documentation. A planned control will have a specified implementation date.

There are reasons a control might not be implemented yet. Perhaps the control has been purchased, but hasn't yet arrived. Perhaps the control has arrived but hasn't been installed. The reason why a control hasn't been implemented isn't as important as realizing that it will be implemented.

It's important to identify any planned controls before approving others. The vulnerabilities these controls will mitigate still exist. However, you don't want to purchase two different controls for closing the same vulnerability.

You can still evaluate the effectiveness of a planned control. This won't be as easy because you can only research the information. You can't test the planned control until it's implemented. However, if you determine that a different control will work better, you may be able to cancel the planned control and purchase a different one.

Control Categories

There are hundreds, if not thousands, of types of security controls. To make these types a little easier to comprehend, risk mitigation security controls are divided into categories. However, the categories are grouped differently depending on who does the categorizing. There's no single way you'll see them presented and no single way that is correct.

You may run across controls categorized using one of the following methods:

- **NIST SP 800-53, "Recommended Security Controls for Federal Information Systems and Organizations"**—The National Institute of Standards and Technology (NIST) SP 800-53 rev 3 identifies 18 families of controls. It groups these controls into three classes: Technical, Operational, and Management.

- **Implementation method**—Three implementation methods are used to categorize controls. The methods are administrative controls, technical controls, and physical controls. This chapter focuses on these implementation methods.

- **COBIT**—Control Objectives for Information and related Technology (COBIT) divides the categories into four domains. The domains are: Planning and Organization, Acquisition and Implementation, Delivery and Support, and Monitor. These domains include 34 high-level objectives and over 300 detailed objectives.

NIST Control Classes

NIST special publications are becoming more and more valuable for IT professionals in the United States. They document security best practices and provide a central source of knowledge for IT security professionals.

SP 800-53, "Information Security," provides guidance on controls that you can use. These controls handle a wide range of security issues. SP 800-53 identifies three classes of controls in 18 families.

> **TIP**
>
> NIST SP 800-53 rev 2 identified 17 families of controls. NIST SP 800-53 rev 3, released in August 2009, revised this identification to 18 families of controls. The extra control family is Program Management.

Functional Controls

Some controls are identified based on the function they perform. Three broad classes of controls identify the functions of a control. They are preventative, detective, and corrective.

Preventative controls attempt to prevent the risk from occurring. For example, many actions taken to harden a server are preventative. This includes disabling unneeded services and removing unneeded protocols. If the service or protocol is not on the server, it can't be attacked. Similarly, keeping a system updated with patches is preventative. If the update is installed, the attack can't succeed.

Detective controls attempt to detect when a vulnerability is being exploited. Audit logs and audit trails are examples of passive detective controls. When the logs are reviewed, the incident is discovered. An intrusion detection system (IDS) is an example of an active detective control. An IDS can review logs in real time. This allows it to detect an attack when it is occurring.

Corrective controls attempt to reverse the effects of a problem. File recovery and data correction are examples of corrective controls. For example, reliable backups allow you to restore data if it becomes corrupt. Many corrective controls are also considered recovery controls.

You can use NIST SP 800-53 to review security in any organization. For example, you may be interested in reviewing physical security. The Physical and Environmental Protection family includes 19 different controls. Organizations use these controls for better physical security. You can review these controls to determine if they are relevant to your organization. Many of the controls described include additional references that provide more details on how to implement them.

The three classes of controls are Technical, Operational, and Management. Figure 9-1 shows the three classes with all the control families listed.

Appendix F and Appendix G of NIST SP 800-53 thoroughly document these classes. SP 800-53 is a living document. In other words, the security controls documented in the catalog will change over time. Some controls will be added. Some will be removed. Others will be modified.

The Technical class of controls includes four families. These families include over 75 individual controls. Following is a list of each of the families in the Technical class, with the family identifier in parentheses:

- **Access Control (AC)**—This family of controls helps an organization implement effective access control. They ensure that users have the rights and permissions they need to perform their jobs, and no more. It includes principles such as least privilege and separation of duties. Chapter 2 presented these principles. The AC control family includes 22 items.

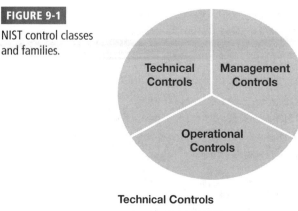

FIGURE 9-1

NIST control classes and families.

Management Controls
- Certification, Accreditation, and Security Assessment (CA)
- Planning (PL)
- Risk Assessment (RA)
- System and Services Acquisition (SA)
- Program Management (PM)

Operational Controls
- Awareness and Training (AT)
- Configuration Management (CM)
- Contingency Planning (CP)
- Incident Response (IR)
- Maintenance (MA)
- Media Protection (MP)
- Physical and Environment Protection (PE)
- Personnel Security (PS)
- System and Information Integrity (SI)

Technical Controls
- Access Control (AC)
- Audit and Accountability (AU)
- Identification and Authentication (IA)
- System and Communications Protection (SC)

> **NOTE**
>
> **Non-repudiation** techniques prevent someone from denying he or she took an action. For example, an audit log records who, what, where, and when details for events. If an audit log recorded that a user deleted a file, the user cannot believably deny it. The user logged on and the audit log recorded the action with the user's logon credentials. The only alternative is that the user has given out his or her credentials. Digital signatures also provide non-repudiation.

> **NOTE**
>
> The Technical Control Examples section is presented later in this chapter. It provides many examples of controls in the Technical class.

- **Audit and Accountability (AU)**—This family of controls helps an organization implement an effective audit program. It provides details on how to determine what to audit. It provides details on how to protect the audit logs. It also includes information on using audit logs for non-repudiation. The AU control family includes 14 items.

- **Identification and Authentication (IA)**—These controls cover different practices to identify and authenticate users. Each user should be uniquely identified. In other words, each user has one account. This account is only used by one user. Similarly, device identifiers uniquely identify devices on the network. The IA control family includes eight items.

- **System and Communications Protection (SC)**— The SC family is a large group of controls that cover many aspects of protecting systems and communication channels. Denial of service protection and boundary protection controls are included. Transmission integrity and confidentiality controls are also included. The SC control family includes 34 items.

The Management class of controls includes five families. These families include over 40 individual controls. Following is a list of each of the families in the Management class, with the family identifier in parentheses:

- **Certification, Accreditation, and Security Assessment (CA)**—This family of controls addresses steps to implement a security and assessment program. It includes controls to ensure only authorized systems are allowed on a network. It includes details on important security concepts, such as continuous monitoring and a plan of action and milestones. The CA control family includes seven items.

- **Planning (PL)**—The PL family focuses on security plans for systems. It also covers Rules of Behavior for users. Rules of Behavior are also called an acceptable use policy. The PL control family includes six items.

- **Risk Assessment (RA)**—This family of controls provides details on risk assessments and vulnerability scanning. The RA control family includes five items.

- **System and Services Acquisition (SA)**—The SA family includes many controls related to the purchase of products and services. It also includes controls related to software usage and user installed software. The SA control family includes 15 items.

- **Program Management (PM)**—This family is driven by the Federal Information Security Management Act (FISMA). It provides controls to ensure compliance with FISMA. These controls complement other controls. They don't replace them. The PM control family includes 11 items. This is the only family that is not covered in Appendix F of SP 800-53. Instead, it is covered in Appendix G.

> **NOTE**
>
> The Administrative Control Examples section is presented later in this chapter. It provides many examples of controls in the Management class.

The Operational class of controls includes nine families. These families include over 80 individual controls. The following list covers each of the families in the Operational class, with the family identifier in parentheses:

- **Awareness and Training (AT)**—This family of controls includes steps that can be implemented to raise the security awareness of all users in the organization. The AT control family includes five items. These items help an organization identify needed training, and properly document the training.

- **Configuration Management (CM)**—This family of controls addresses both configuration management and change management. Change control practices prevent unauthorized changes. They include goals such as configuring systems for least functionality as a primary method of hardening systems. The CM control family includes nine items.

- **Contingency Planning (CP)**—CP controls are used to help an organization recover from a failures or disasters. They include controls related to planning, training, and testing for failures and disasters. They also include controls related to alternate sites for storage or processing. NIST SP 800-34 is the primary reference. The CP control family includes 10 items.

- **Incident Response (IR)**—IR controls cover all aspects of security incidents. They include training, testing, handling, monitoring, and reporting. NIST SP 800-84 and SP 800-115 are the primary references. The IR control family includes eight items.

- **Maintenance (MA)**—MA controls cover security aspects related to maintenance such as tools, maintenance personnel, and timely maintenance. The MA control family includes six items.

- **Media Protection (MP)**—Media Protection includes removable digital media such as tapes, external hard drives, and USB flash drives. It also includes non-digital media such as paper and film. This family of controls covers the access, marking, storage, transport, and sanitization of media. The MP control family includes six items.

- **Physical and Environment Protection (PE)**—The PE family provides an extensive number of controls related to physical security. Many of these controls are included in the Physical Controls section later in this chapter. The PE control family includes 19 items.

- **Personnel Security (PS)**—The PS family of controls includes aspects of personnel security. It includes personnel screening, termination, and transfer. The PS control family includes eight items.

> **NOTE**
>
> The Physical Control Examples section is presented later in this chapter. It provides many examples of controls in the Operational class.

- **System and Information Integrity (SI)**—This family of controls provides information to maintain the integrity of systems and data. Flaw remediation identifies steps to keep systems updated. Malicious code protection lists steps to protect against malware. The SI control family includes 13 items.

Appendix F and Appendix G of SP 800-53 document the controls in each of these categories. These appendices are close to half the size of the entire document, which is about 140 pages as of this writing. If you're looking for specific things you can do in your organization to improve security in any of these areas, it is an excellent place to start.

Administrative Control Examples

Administrative controls refer to the written documents an organization uses for security. These are directives from senior management. They provide direction on how to address security within the organization.

> **NOTE**
>
> It's important that the administrative controls have support from senior management. If management doesn't support the guidelines, it soon becomes apparent to employees. The organization will have two sets of policies. One is the written set of policies. The other is the unwritten set of policies that everyone follows.

The following sections provide examples of some common administrative controls in these categories:

- Policies and procedures
- Security plans
- Insurance
- Background checks
- Data loss prevention program
- Awareness and training
- Rules of behavior
- Software testing

Policies and Procedures

Policies and procedures are written documents that provide guidelines and rules for an organization. An organization will typically have multiple policies and procedures

A policy is a high-level document that provides overall direction without details. A procedure provides the detailed steps needed to implement a policy.

Policies have widespread application. They identify the direction management wants to take on a specific topic. In other words, they document high-level management decisions. Personnel within the organization can then take steps to implement the policy.

Policies also provide authority. This authority can be used to purchase resources in support of a policy. Without the policy in place, it may be more difficult to justify a purchase.

Consider a backup policy. It would identify what data to back up, based on its value. It could include user data, databases, application data on servers, and more. The backup policy would also identify storage and retention requirements. It would specify that copies of backups be stored in a separate location. This provides protection against a disaster such as a fire.

A backup policy would include a retention policy. This identifies how long backups are retained. For example, it might specify that some data be retained for three years. It might say that other data should be retained for only 30 days. Again, the choices are dependent on management decisions. The policy documents the decisions.

With a backup policy in place, the department responsible for backing up the data can purchase resources to implement the policy. These include tape drives, tapes, and software. Backups can get expensive, and without a backup policy in place, managers sometimes balk at the cost.

Procedures are narrower in scope and more task-oriented than policies. They identify specific steps needed to implement a policy. Any policy could have multiple procedures.

For example, consider the backup policy. It would state backups that need to be performed, but not how to perform them. Procedures, on the other hand, state how to perform backups. You could create one procedure for backing up user data. You could create another procedure for backing up databases. A third procedure could cove how to back up other application data. A fourth procedure could identify how to transfer tapes to an off-site location.

Examples of policies might be:

- **Acceptable use policy (AUP)**—An AUP defines acceptable use of systems. It identifies what a user can and cannot do on a system. It is sometimes referred to as Rules of Behavior.
- **Vulnerability scanning policy**—A vulnerability scanning policy provides authority to perform regular scans. It identifies specific goals of the scans. It also specifies how often the scans are performed.
- **Removable media policy**—Many organizations recognize the risks associated with removable media, such as USB flash drives. By means of a policy, they restrict the use of these drives.

Examples of procedures might be:

- **AUP procedure**—This procedure identifies how users acknowledge the AUP. For example, users may be required to read and acknowledge understanding of the AUP.
- **Vulnerability scanning procedures**—Procedures would be completed for different types of scans. The procedures would specify how the scans are documented and reported.
- **Removable media enforcement**—Different procedures can enforce the restriction of removable media. You could manipulate the BIOS to prevent their use. You could purchase third-party software to prevent their use. Microsoft domains allow administrators to restrict removable media using Group Policy.

Security Plans

Organizations create different security plans to address different scenarios. Many of the security plans are common to most organizations. Part III of this book covers a number of them in more depth. This section covers the following security plans found in many organizations:

- Business continuity plan
- Disaster recovery plan
- Backup plan
- Incident response plan

> **NOTE**
>
> Chapter 7 presented business continuity plans and disaster recovery plans. Chapter 14 will cover business continuity plans in more depth. Chapter 13 will cover disaster recovery plans in more depth.

Business Continuity Plan.   A business continuity plan (BCP) is one type of security plan. It is a comprehensive plan that helps an organization prepare for different types of emergencies. It ensures that mission critical functions continue to operate even after a disaster strikes.

A BCP often starts with a business impact analysis (BIA). The BIA identifies the critical functions. The BCP then documents how to keep these functions operating during a disaster.

Disaster Recovery Plan.   A disaster recovery plan (DRP) provides the details to recover one or more systems from a disaster. DRPs and BCPs are sometimes considered the same thing. However, they are different. The BCP keeps the critical functions running during a disaster. The DRP has a narrower focus and identifies how to recover a system.

For example, a BCP might identify how an organization responds to a threatening hurricane. When a hurricane is threatening, critical functions could be moved to an alternate location. After the hurricane passes, the DRP identifies how the organization should recover its systems. For example, flooding may have destroyed several servers. The DRP identifies how these servers can be recovered. The BCP would also identify how the critical functions are returned to normal operation after the DRP recovers them.

Backup Plan. A backup plan is often included as part of a DRP. You can't recover data after a disaster unless you've backed it up. The backup plan is derived from a backup policy.

The backup policy identifies data valuable to the organization. It also specifies storage and retention requirements. The backup plan includes procedures identifying how this data can be backed up. Not all data is backed up the same way.

User data is simple to back up if the data is stored centrally. Often an organization will require users to store their data on a central server. This requirement is documented in the backup plan. It allows administrators to back up the data on the server. Backing up data on each individual user system is almost impossible.

Databases hosted on database servers require dedicated software to back them up. You can't use the same software to back up both user data and databases. Additionally, many other server applications, such as e-mail servers, require dedicated backup software.

Backup plans also identify how to perform test restores. A test restore verifies that backed-up data can be restored. Many horror stories relate how an organization regularly went through the motions to back up their data. When the data needed to be restored, they discovered that none of the backups were successful. A test restore simply restores a backup tape to ensure the backup is valid.

Incident Response Plan. An incident response plan documents how an organization should respond to a security incident. The organization could have multiple incident response plans, depending on the complexity of the organization.

A security incident is any incident that affects the confidentiality, integrity, or availability of systems or data. Security incidents occur when a threat exploits a vulnerability.

For example, say a system is infected with malware. The organization's plan could be to take the following steps in response to an infection:

- Disconnect the local area connection cable
- Leave the system power up
- Write down any messages that appear
- Report the incident

A more complicated problem may occur from a denial of service (DoS) attack on a server. This would require a response from an administrator or security professional. Once the incident is verified, the administrator could then take steps to isolate the incident, and then protect any evidence about the attack.

Insurance and Bonding

Chapter 1 presented the different ways you can manage risk. You can avoid, transfer, mitigate, or accept a risk. In cases where the likelihood of damage is very low and the impact is very high, the option to transfer the risk is often preferred. The primary way you transfer the risk is by purchasing insurance.

9

Risk Mitigation Security Controls

You can purchase many types of insurance. The goal is to protect your company from a loss. If the risk occurs, the insurance helps pay for the loss. This keeps the risk from bankrupting the company.

An organization can purchase many types of insurance. Some types of insurance, such as fire and flood insurance, are obvious. Other types of insurance deserve an explanation.

Business interruption insurance can be purchased as an add-on to some policies. For example, a company may add business interruption insurance onto a fire insurance policy. If a fire occurs and the company can't operate normally, the insurance pays for losses until the company opens up again. This usually covers operational expenses such as rental of equipment. It would also pay for profits that the company would have normally earned.

Errors and omissions insurance is also known as professional liability insurance. It is valuable if your company supplies services to other companies. For example, imagine your company performs maintenance on a customer's servers. In the process of performing the maintenance, your technician accidentally plugs in a power supply the wrong way and ruins the server. The customer may take you to court. This insurance will provide protection.

Similarly, your company may provide consultants to customers. A consultant may help a customer create a backup plan but forget to include offsite storage. Because the consultant is the expert, this is a glaring omission. If the customer suffers a fire and loses all the backups for the organization, the company may sue. Again, the errors and omissions insurance provides protection.

Bonding is a type of insurance to cover against losses by theft, fraud, or dishonesty. A person covered by bonding insurance is referred to as being bonded. Organizations purchase bonding insurance when required by law. They may also purchase it to provide a level of security to their customers.

For example, imagine your company provides IT support to customers at their homes. You could purchase bonding insurance for your technicians. If a technician in your company steals from a customer while performing the service, the bonding company would pay for the loss. Bonding insurance is often very narrow. For example, the insurance may not pay unless the employee has been tried and convicted of the theft. Instead of pursuing a conviction against the employee, the customer may just sue you.

Background Checks and Financial Checks

Many organizations perform background checks and financial checks on prospective employees. These checks are completed prior to the employee being hired.

Background checks commonly include police and FBI checks. These checks identify any criminal behavior on the part of a prospective employee. Past mistakes won't automatically stop someone from being hired. However, there are times when past convictions are very relevant.

A truck driver is unlikely to be hired if he has a reckless driving conviction on his record. Similarly, an administrator is unlikely to be hired if he's recently been convicted of theft. A shoplifting conviction is enough to prevent a company from hiring an employee in a position of trust.

Most companies also complete financial checks for prospective employees. A person with a poor credit rating may be viewed suspiciously. Employers wonder if the poor credit rating is a reflection of responsibility and accountability. If a person ignores his or her debts, does that imply irresponsibility on the job?

Internet resources are commonly included in background investigations today. This includes simple Google or Facebook searches. A person who has fanatically ranted on a topic may be viewed as problematic. More than anything, companies want employees who can work well with others. Someone who has a Facebook page filled with attacks on others may be bypassed for someone who has never had a Facebook page.

Data Loss Prevention Program

A data loss prevention program helps a company prevent data loss. Data loss can be viewed in one of two ways:

- **Loss of confidentiality**—You lose confidentiality when unauthorized entities view data. For example, if an unauthorized user views data, confidentiality is lost. Inadequate access controls may allow an unauthorized user to view data. An attacker could hack into an online site and access a back end database. A user could lose a laptop that has proprietary information stored on it.

- **Loss due to corruption**—Files can become corrupt through a variety of ways. The disk drive could crash. An application could hiccup when writing a file, corrupting the data. Other users could accidentally or purposely delete or modify data. How the data is lost isn't as important as preparing for the loss with backups.

An organization can protect against loss of confidentiality using two methods. The first method is using access controls. Authentication methods identify users. Permissions then grant authorization to access resources. The principle of least privilege ensures that users have access to only the resources they need and no more.

The second method of protection against loss of confidentiality is encryption. Data can be encrypted while it's at rest or being transferred. At-rest data is any data that is stored on media such as a hard drive or USB flash drive. You can also encrypt data when it's transferred over the network.

A data loss prevention program identifies the data that is valuable to an organization. Data can be classified as Public, Private, or Proprietary. The data loss prevention program would then specify the importance of data in each of these categories. The program would also specify if the organization wants to protect against loss of confidentiality, loss due to corruption, or both.

> **▶ NOTE**
> The actual methods used to protect against loss of data are technical controls. However, the program that identifies what data to protect is an administrative control.

Awareness and Training

An organization can have the best documented security controls on the planet. However, if the employees don't know what they are or how to implement them, the controls simply aren't effective. Awareness and training controls ensure that employees are aware of an organization's security standards. They also ensure that employees know how to implement security controls.

> **TIP**
>
> SP 800-50, "Building an Information Technology Security Awareness and Training Program," is published by NIST. It provides details on how to design, develop, and implement an awareness and security training program.

Awareness programs are generic and apply to all personnel. They use different techniques to inform and remind people about security. They try to have users personalize security. In other words, instead of security being someone else's responsibility, users recognize that security is everyone's responsibility, including theirs. Some examples of how awareness can be raised include:

- Logon or welcome banners
- E-mails
- Posters

Training is provided for different audiences. Some training is generic and for all personnel. For example, you may want to educate all users on social engineering tactics.

Other training is specialized and targeted at specific groups. For example, training on how to maintain a specific firewall is provided to the administrators who will maintain it. Specific security professionals are trained on how to run and interpret vulnerability scans.

Rules of Behavior

> **TIP**
>
> Rules of Behavior are called an acceptable use policy (AUP) in some organizations. Most private organizations use an AUP. The purpose of each is the same.

Rules of Behavior let users know what they can and cannot do with systems. Users read this document before being granted access to a system. Users are often required to sign a document indicating that they have read and understand the rules of behavior.

The Office of Management and Budget (OMB) mandates the use of Rules of Behavior for agencies under OMB. This is documented in OMB Circular A-130, Appendix III. This appendix also references the Rules of Behavior control documented in SP 800-53.

Some common elements in a Rules of Behavior document are:

- **Privacy**—Many organizations stress that users have no expectation of privacy. If they are using employer resources, they are subject to monitoring. Data can be viewed at any time. This includes a user's data files and any e-mail files. It also includes a history of a user's Internet activity. Organizations frequently scan all outgoing transmissions such as e-mails. This helps them ensure that personally identifiable information (PII) is not being released.

- **List of restricted activities**—Most systems restrict certain kinds of activities. Organizations will often explicitly restrict access to any sites with sexual or pornographic content. The list of restrictions could also include gaming, gambling, or personal business. Although these restrictions try to avoid offending employees, other restrictions intend to protect resources. For example, some companies restrict any type of audio or video streaming, such as online radio stations.

- **E-mail usage**—Users are informed of what e-mail can be used for and what restrictions exist. Most companies allow users to send and receive personal e-mail. However, users should not use email for any type of harassment, or transmission of objectionable materials.

- **Protection of credentials**—Users are told to protect their credentials, such as user name and password. Additionally, they are given information on how to create a strong password.

- **Consequences or penalties for noncompliance**—These could be reprimands or suspension of privileges. Serious offenses could result in the termination of the employee.

This list isn't all-inclusive. An organization will include the information necessary to ensure that users understand what is expected of them. Some organizations limit this information to a single page. Other organizations make this list a little longer.

Software Testing

An organization that develops software should take the time test it. This starts with a policy mandating software testing. The primary reason to test the software is to reduce the number of undiscovered bugs in the software.

NIST reported in 2002 that software bugs cost the U.S. $59.5 billion annually. They also reported that over $22 billion could be saved with more aggressive testing. The Software Engineering Institute at Carnegie Mellon University estimated in 2005 that there are 100 to 150 bugs in every 1,000 lines of programming code.

The types of software testing performed are technical controls. For example, you could perform data range and reasonableness checks. However, you start by creating a policy requiring software testing.

Technical Control Examples

Technical controls are software tools that automate protection. This is significantly different from an administrative control. The administrative control identifies what should be done. It often requires a person to intervene and ensure the administrative control is followed.

In contrast, a technical control is enforced using technology. For example, you can create a password enforcement policy on many systems. This password policy could specify that passwords must be strong. A strong password has at least eight characters and is a mixture of upper case, lower case, numbers, and special characters. The policy could also specify changing passwords every 30 days.

The system prompts users to change their password. If they choose not to, the system locks them out until they change it. When they change it, the new password must be strong. The system rejects weak passwords.

This section presents examples of other technical controls including:

- Logon identifier
- Session timeout
- System logs and audit trails
- Data range and reasonableness checks
- Firewalls and router tables
- Encryption
- Public key infrastructure

Logon Identifier

A logon identifier is another name for a user account. The account is uniquely identified and matched to the user. Every time the user logs in, this account is used. This helps enforce several other controls.

A logon identifier is needed for access control. If every user logged on with an account named "Bob," then every user would have the same access. It doesn't matter what a user's real name is. Permissions granted to "Bob" are granted to all users that log on with the Bob account.

However, if every user logs on with a different account, permissions can be assigned individually. Users who need access to resources will be granted the access. Users who don't need access aren't granted the access.

Audit logs use logon identifiers. You may remember that audit logs record who, what, where, and when. The "who" comes from the logon identifier. Users log on with their own account. Any auditable actions are recorded with this account information.

The logon identifier also provides non-repudiation. The user can't believably deny she took an action.

Session Timeout

Most systems include session timeout controls. This helps ensure that an unauthorized user doesn't have access to a session without providing credentials.

A simple session timeout example is a screen saver. You can configure a screen saver to start after 10 minutes of inactivity. You can also configure it to require users to log on again after the screen saver starts. That way, if a user walks away from a computer without locking it, the screen saver will start after 10 minutes and lock the system.

Many Web sites include session timeouts. For example, many banking sites will close the session after 20 minutes. When you log onto the banking site, you provide your credentials. As long as you are active on the site, the session remains open. This allows you to go to different pages without logging on again.

However, if you leave the Web page open but don't do anything with it for 20 minutes, the timeout control will close the Web page and clear out your session data. If you try to access the page again, you'll need to log on again.

Similarly, if you leave a session open on a public computer and walk away, it will close after 20 minutes. This helps prevent unauthorized users from accessing the site.

System Logs and Audit Trails

Operating systems and network devices include the capability to log different types of events. By logging events and regularly reviewing the logs, you can identify what is occurring. You can use logs to investigate security events. You can also use them to troubleshoot problems.

Logs typically log the following details on events:

- Who did it
- What happened
- Where it happened
- When it happened

This is often shortened to who, what, where, and when. The logon identifier identifies who took the action. The system identifies what happened and where it happened. A clock provides a time stamp to record when it happened.

There are multiple types of logs in any network. Desktop and server operating systems include logs. Firewalls include logs to track allowed and blocked traffic. Network server applications such as Domain Name System (DNS) log events. You can enable or enhance logging on just about any system.

System logging tracks different types of events on the operating system. For example, Microsoft Windows operating systems include the System log to record system events. This includes events such as when services start or stop or when the system starts or stops. These events are categorized as errors, warnings, and information events.

Security logging focuses on security events. Some security events are automatically logged. However, you can configure logging to record additional auditable events. For example, if you wanted to know whether anyone accessed a folder holding sensitive data, you could enable auditing on the folder. This auditing allows you to record details if anyone read, modified, or deleted data.

You should not log all events. Instead, you should identify what you need. When too many events are logged, it takes up extra resources. This includes processing power to capture and log the events. It also includes disk space as the log fills up.

> **TIP**
>
> The default timeout for Web sites is 20 minutes. That is a long time. If you're using a public computer, you should always log out as soon as you're done. If you just walk away, someone else could access the computer 15 minutes later. The intruder would then have access to your session, which would stay open for them as long as it was kept active.

> **TIP**
>
> NIST SP 800-53 recommends internal system clocks for time stamps. The internal clock provides a consistent time for all events.

> **TIP**
>
> Logs need to be reviewed. This seems obvious but this step is overlooked most often in the auditing process. Administrators often become overwhelmed with day-to-day tasks, and the log reviews become less important. It becomes even more difficult when too many events are logged. Many organizations use automated tools to review the logs for key events. These tools provide alerts on key events and track trends.

Data Range and Reasonableness Checks

Application developers use data range and reasonableness checks to help ensure they are receiving valid data. The developer can't ensure the data is accurate. However, the developer can ensure the data is valid.

Valid data follows a specific format. For example, imagine a text box that expects a five digit U.S. Zip Code. The only valid characters are numbers. Additionally, only five digits are valid. If the user enters anything other than five numbers, the data is not valid.

Along the same lines, imagine the user's Zip Code is 23456. If the user accidentally enters 33456, the application can't tell that the Zip Code is incorrect. Because 33456 is a valid five-digit number, it will pass the validation test.

You've probably seen validation checks on Web sites. You're prompted to enter certain data such as a name and e-mail address. If you miss something, or enter something incorrectly, the Web site complains to you. It will often show a red asterisk with an error explanation. The explanation may say something like "You must enter an e-mail address."

Data range checks ensure data is within a certain range. For example, users may be asked to enter a number between 1 and 100. The data range check ensures the number is between 1 and 100. If the entered data is outside the valid range, it is not used. Instead, the user is prompted to try again.

Similarly, a data range can verify that dates are within in a certain range. For example, a birth date could be used to ensure someone is over a certain age. It compares the current date with the birth date. If the user is too young, the Web site could redirect the user to an error page.

Reasonableness checks ensure that the entered data is reasonable. For example, how many letters would you expect in a first name? What types of characters are valid in a first name?

You could decide that a first name shouldn't have more than 25 characters. Additionally, you could decide that a first name cannot contain numbers. When a user enters data for a first name, you could check it to ensure that it is less than 26 characters and doesn't include numbers.

You can use reasonableness checks for any type of data. You just need to understand the data that you're using. For example, if you want to use a reasonableness check for a first name, you need to know what a first name could be. Five letters as a maximum for a first name isn't acceptable.

Firewalls and Routers

Firewalls and router software are used as technical controls in a network. They control the traffic by allowing some traffic and blocking other traffic.

Many firewalls and routers use an implicit deny philosophy. In other words, all traffic is blocked unless it is explicitly allowed. Firewalls use rules to identify allowed traffic. Routers use access control lists (ACLs) to identify allowed traffic.

A router provides basic filtering of traffic. A router can filter traffic based on:

> **NOTE**
> Routers use routing tables to identify how to route traffic. The routing table identifies the best path to get traffic from one point to another. The routing tables are required to route the traffic. However, the ACLs provide the security.

- Internet Protocol (IP) addresses
- Ports
- Some protocols

Consider Figure 9-2. The router can be configured to allow traffic from any hosts with IP addresses on subnet 1, subnet 2, or subnet 3. Ports are used to identify protocols. For example, HTTP uses port 80. An ACL can be configured to allow HTTP traffic to the intranet Web server on subnet 1. SMTP uses port 25. An ACL can be configured to allow SMTP traffic to the e-mail server on subnet 2.

The firewall starts with basic routing capabilities. However, most firewalls are much more advanced. Router ACLs can only evaluate a single packet at a time. However, a firewall can evaluate the entire conversation. Once a session is established between two hosts, the firewall can evaluate all of the traffic between them. This is also referred to as stateful evaluation.

Rules created on the firewall allow you to protect your network from external attacks. By allowing only specific traffic, you limit the capabilities of attackers from the Internet.

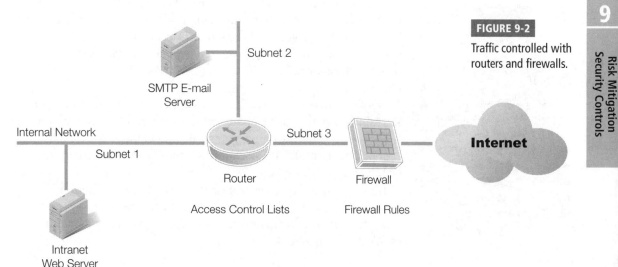

FIGURE 9-2

Traffic controlled with routers and firewalls.

Well Known Ports

Ports 0 through 1023 are Well Known Ports. Each port in this range is assigned to a protocol. When the port is used, an operating system recognizes that it is for the related protocol.

The Internet Assigned Numbers Authority (IANA) assigns Well Known Ports. You can view the full list of ports here: *http://www.iana.org/assignments/port-numbers*.

The Well Known Port for HTTP is port 80. When a system receives a packet with a destination port of 80, it knows to pass this packet to the service handling the HTTP protocol. A server running the HTTP protocol is normally a Web server.

Because port 80 is a Well Known Port, it doesn't need to be included in the URL. However, you could include it. The following is a URL with the port added: *http://www .iana.org:80/assignments/port-numbers*.

Firewalls and routers use these port numbers to identify allowed traffic. For example, if a firewall wanted to allow HTTP traffic, it would have a rule to allow traffic on port 80. Similarly, a router would allow HTTP traffic with an entry in the ACL.

> **TIP**
>
> Encryption provides confidentiality for data. It helps prevent unauthorized disclosure. Only users with access to decryption keys can decrypt the data.

> **NOTE**
>
> A packet analyzer that can capture traffic is commonly called a **sniffer**. Capturing packets over the network is called sniffing. A patient attacker can sniff network traffic and capture a significant amount of data.

Encryption

Encryption changes plain text data into ciphered data. For example, the word "password" is in plain text, but encrypted it may look like this: $MFIGs3x/\$6oOD$.

Data can be encrypted at rest, or when transferred. At rest data is any data stored on media such as a hard drive or a USB flash drive. If a user stores sensitive data on a laptop computer, the data can be encrypted to protect it. If the laptop is lost or stolen, there is less chance the data will be compromised. Similarly, if data is stored on a USB flash drive, it can be encrypted. If it's lost, data can't be read easily.

Data sent over the network can be captured and read. For example, Wireshark is a free packet analyzer that can capture data sent over the network. Once the data is captured, individual packets can be opened and analyzed. If the data was sent over the network in clear text, it can easily be read.

It's not impossible to decrypt encrypted data. Given enough resources and enough time, encrypted data can be decrypted. However, encryption algorithms are designed to make it too hard or take too long to make it worthwhile.

Consider the Rivest, Shamir, Adelman (RSA) encryption used on the Internet. Years ago, it was common to use 40-bit keys. In their time, they were very secure. However, in 1997 a student at UC Berkeley cracked a 40-bit RSA key in three and half hours. Today, it takes minutes. Currently it's common to use 1,024- or 2,048-bit keys with RSA. Some estimates indicate it will take over 100 years to crack RSA with 2,048-bit keys.

Encryption is classified as either:

- **Symmetric**—This uses one key. For example, the key of 53 could be used to encrypt data. Data is decrypted with the same key of 53. Keys are much more complex than just a two-digit number. Strong symmetric algorithms use 256 bits.
- **Asymmetric**—Asymmetric encryption uses two keys. One key is called the public key. The other key is called the private key. These two keys are matched to each other. Any data encrypted with the public key can be decrypted only with the matching private key. Any data encrypted with the private key can be decrypted only with the public key.

Advanced Encryption Standard (AES) is the primary symmetric encryption protocol used today. In the 1990s, NIST asked for developers to submit cryptographic algorithms for evaluation. After a lengthy evaluation, NIST selected and ratified AES in 2000 as a standard.

AES is fast and efficient. It's quick even when encrypting small amounts of data, such as on USB flash drives. It doesn't need as much processing power as some older encryption algorithms.

Public Key Infrastructure (PKI)

A public key infrastructure (PKI) is created to provide support for certificates. The PKI has several elements. However, the purpose of all the elements is centered on certificates. Some of the elements of a PKI are:

- Certification authority
- Certificates
- Public and private keys

A **certification authority (CA)** issues and manages certificates. A CA can be public such as VeriSign. VeriSign is a well-known public CA. A CA can also be private. A private CA is created within a company and issues certificates internally.

Systems have a listing of CAs that they trust. If a system trusts a CA, it automatically trusts any certificates issued by the CA. This is similar to driver's licenses issued by a department of motor vehicles (DMV). If you present a driver's license as identification, it is trusted. This is because the DMV is trusted. All driver's licenses issued by the DMV are automatically trusted. Similarly, all certificates issued by a trusted CA are automatically trusted.

> **TIP**
>
> A private CA is simply a server running the certification authority software. When referring to a public CA, you usually refer to the company. However, when referring to a private CA, you usually refer to the server hosting the software.

Certificates are used for identification and to aid in encryption. Certificates include details on the entity that received the certificate. For example, if the certificate was issued to a server, the certificate would include details on the server, such as its name. The server is able to present the certificate as proof of its identity.

Public and private keys are used with a PKI. As a reminder, these are matched keys. Data encrypted with one of the keys can be decrypted only with the matching key. A public key is embedded in the certificate and passed to others. The private key always stays private.

For example, imagine a certificate issued to a Web server. When a user connects to the Web server and starts a secure session, the server sends the certificate to the user. The certificate includes a public key. The user can encrypt data with the public key and send it to the server. Because the server holds the private key, it can decrypt the data. Because no other entity has the private key, no one else can decrypt the data.

Certificates are also used with **digital signatures**, a method used for the identification of documents.

For example, you can sign an e-mail with a digital signature. The receiver has verification that it was sent by you, and not someone trying to impersonate you. You create a digital signature in two steps:

- Create a message hash
- Encrypt the hash with the sender's private key

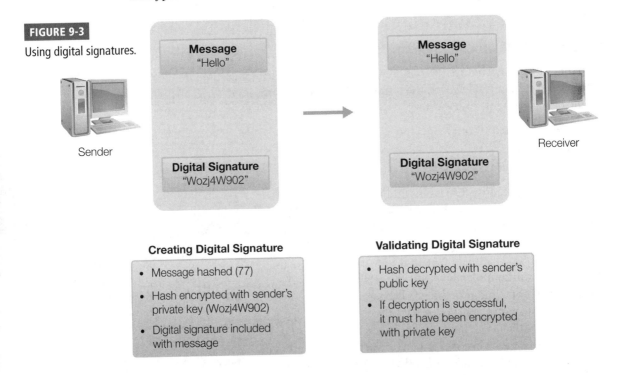

FIGURE 9-3

Using digital signatures.

Message "Hello"

Digital Signature "Wozj4W902"

Sender

Message "Hello"

Digital Signature "Wozj4W902"

Receiver

Creating Digital Signature

- Message hashed (77)
- Hash encrypted with sender's private key (Wozj4W902)
- Digital signature included with message

Validating Digital Signature

- Hash decrypted with sender's public key
- If decryption is successful, it must have been encrypted with private key

Consider Figure 9-3. A hash is simply a number created by running an algorithm. For example, a simple hash for a message could be 77. No matter how many times you run the algorithm, the hash would always be 77. The hash is then encrypted with the sender's private key. The result may be Wozj4W902.

The encrypted hash is sent with the message. The receiver has the public key. The public key is then used to decrypt the hash. If it can decrypt the hash, it must have been encrypted with the private key.

A digital signature is not possible without a PKI. You must have matching public and private keys. You must be able to package the public key into a certificate. You need a CA to issue the certificates.

Physical Control Examples

Physical controls protect the physical environment. They include basics such as locks to protect access to secure areas. They also include environmental controls. This section presents the following examples of physical controls:

- Locked doors, guards, access logs, and closed-circuit television
- Fire detection and suppression
- Water detection
- Temperature and humidity detection
- Electrical grounding and circuit breakers

Locked Doors, Guards, Access Logs, and Closed-Circuit Television (CCTV)

Any organization has some areas that are more secure than others. These areas are protected with physical security.

For example, a server room holds servers that shouldn't be accessible to just anyone. Servers need to be protected. You can use different types of physical security to protect the servers.

The simplest method is simply using locked doors. The locks could be simple locks with keys. They could be cipher locks where users need to enter a combination of numbers to gain access. They could require proximity cards issued to employees. Some proximity cards also require users to enter a PIN.

FYI

A proximity card is a small credit-card sized device. It includes electronics that will activate when it is close to a proximity reader. The card sends a signal to the reader identifying it. If the card is authorized, the door will open.

Some credit cards also use this technology. All you do is wave the card in front of the credit card reader and it registers. Unfortunately, proximity card readers are portable. An attacker can put one in a small box or bag. He can then gather credit card data just by riding up and down on an elevator for a day.

Three-Barrier Protection

Many organizations utilize three barriers of protection. These include a main entrance, a more secure employee area, and a more secure computer area. Each of these barriers is layered. In other words, the secure computer area is within the employee area. The employee area is within the main entrance.

The main entrance is often open, allowing anyone to come and go. However, it's common to monitor main entrances with video cameras.

Employee areas are a little more secure. Guards may be in place to ensure that only employees or authorized visitors can enter the employee area. Cipher locks could be used requiring employees to tap in codes to gain access. Some organizations issue access cards to employees. The card must be used to gain access.

Computer centers are the third barrier. They can be a server room, a wiring closet, or anywhere else that stores secure hardware or data. Only select groups of employees, such as administrators, are allowed access.

Guards can also be used to protect secure areas. Guards will often be given a list of authorized personnel. As long as someone is on the access list, access is granted.

Access logs provide an audit trail of who has entered and exited a building. Access logs can be manually created or automatically created. For example, guards can keep a log of all personnel who enter or exit the building. Additionally, some proximity readers or badge readers can be automated. Each time a user enters or exits the building, it's recorded.

Closed-circuit television (CCTV) uses video cameras to monitor areas. Cameras can be stationary. They can also be pan, tilt, and zoom (PTZ) cameras. PTZ cameras can be controlled by security personnel to focus on any area covered by the camera.

The level of protection for any area is dependent on the importance of the hardware or data stored there. One organization may have a limited number of physical controls while another organization may have extensive physical controls. Neither choice is right or wrong. If the systems or data are valuable, you spend a lot of money to protect them.

Fire Detection and Suppression

Fire detection and suppression systems provide protection against fires. Fires can start and spread rapidly, so the goal is to have a system that can detect them as quickly as possible. Once the fire is detected, the suppression system attempts to put the fire out.

Detection systems detect changes in the environment that indicate a fire is burning. This includes significant changes in heat, smoke, and gases.

Fire suppression systems vary depending on the type of fire. There are four classes of fires:

- **Class A**—Ordinary combustibles, such as wood and paper
- **Class B**—Flammable liquids such as gasoline
- **Class C**—Electrical fires
- **Class D**—Combustible metals such as magnesium

You fight different classes of fires differently. For example, you can extinguish a Class A fire with water. However, you can't put water on an electrical fire. It will damage the equipment. Additionally, if the electricity is still on, it could travel up the stream of water and electrocute the fire fighter.

> **TIP**
>
> Personnel safety should always be the top priority. If an electrical fire has started, turn off the power first.

Server rooms are at most risk of Class C fires. A primary way to fight Class C fires is with gas systems such as carbon dioxide (CO_2). Gas systems flood an area with a gas to displace oxygen and disrupt the chemical reaction causing the fire.

Gas systems can be dangerous to personnel. For example, technicians may be working in a server room when a fire is detected. If the gas is released without warning, it will remove the oxygen. Most gas displacement systems provide a warning to personnel, giving them time to leave the room.

Fire detection systems and prevention systems are physical controls. However, they work in conjunction with the administrative control of insurance. The insurance provides an added layer of protection by paying for any damage that occurs. Most insurance companies will not provide insurance unless you have adequate detection and suppression systems.

Water Detection

Some locations are susceptible to flooding. Water damage can be very expensive, but there are ways to protect an area. For example, water can be pumped out with water pumps before it rises to a dangerous level.

Water detection systems will detect when water is seeping into an area. The detection system will automatically start the pumps. The pumps will continue until the water is no longer detected.

Temperature and Humidity Detection

High temperatures and humidity levels can damage electrical equipment. When the temperature rises, electrical components can overheat and burn up. If the humidity is too high, moisture can condense on the equipment. This water causes electrical shorts, damaging the equipment.

> **TIP**
>
> Heating, ventilation, and air conditioning (HVAC) systems control both the temperature and humidity.

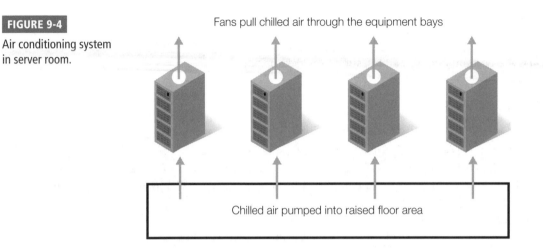

FIGURE 9-4

Air conditioning system
in server room.

Most server rooms are kept very cool to prevent heat damage. Sophisticated server rooms use raised flooring to cool the room. Consider Figure 9-4.

Chilled air is pumped into the area under the raised floor. Equipment is installed in equipment bays. These bays have hollow bases and are installed over holes in the raised floor. They also have strong fans at the top of the bays to pull the air from the raised floor through the equipment and out the top of the bays.

If the air conditioning fails, the equipment is at risk. Temperatures inside electrical equipment are often 10 degrees warmer than the room temperature. Many organizations have policies in place to turn off equipment if the AC fails and the area reaches a certain temperature. The short-term loss of the mission is better than the long-term loss of the equipment.

Electrical Grounding and Circuit Breakers

Electrical grounding and circuit breakers protect equipment from electrical damage if a failure occurs.

If a short occurs in an electrical system, it's possible for a dangerous voltage to exist on the case of the system. If someone touches the case, they could be shocked. This is unacceptable. To prevent this, systems are grounded.

An electrical ground is a wire driven into the ground, often with a stake. Access to this ground wire is available throughout a building. Any electrical systems are wired so they can connect to this ground. If a failure occurs, dangerous voltages are sent to the electrical ground. This helps ensure that dangerous voltages don't present a risk to personnel.

Circuit breakers detect changes in heat. If the circuit breaker detects excessive heat, it opens and breaks the circuit. This prevents dangerous conditions that can cause fires.

Here's how a circuit breaker works: Electricity travels down wires. Each wire is rated to carry a certain load rated as current. Current is measured in amperes, or amps. If a wire has excessive current, it can overheat and cause a fire. Instead of allowing this, a circuit breaker is installed on the same line that carries the current. Circuit breakers are rated for certain loads measured as amps. If the load exceeds the rated amps, the circuit breaker opens and the current flow stops. This protects the system.

> **NOTE**
> Fuses also function like circuit breakers. If excessive current flows through the fuse, the connection in the fuse will overheat and burn up. This breaks the connection. One important difference between fuses and circuit breakers is that fuses must be replaced. Circuit breakers can simply be reset.

Best Practices for Risk Mitigation Security Controls

The following list identifies several best practices you can follow when identifying risk mitigation security controls:

- **Ensure the control is effective**—It should be able to reduce or eliminate a threat or vulnerability. It does so by preventing, recovering, and/or detecting events.

- **Review controls in all areas**—Review administrative, technical, and physical controls. It's easy to focus on controls in one area and neglect controls in other areas.

- **Review NIST SP 800-53 classes**—These classes provide an excellent check to determine if controls are implemented throughout the IT infrastructure.

- **Redo a risk assessment if a control is changed**—Remember that a risk assessment is performed at a point in time. If the control is changed, you need to redo the risk assessment using the new control.

CHAPTER SUMMARY

This chapter provided information on different types of controls. Effective controls will reduce or neutralize threats or vulnerabilities to an acceptable level. In-place controls are operating. Planned controls have a planned implementation date.

When considering additional controls, you can evaluate them in specific categories. NIST SP 800-53 provides detailed guidance on controls. It includes information on 18 families of controls in three classes: Technical, Operational, and Management. You can also consider controls as Administrative, Technical, and Physical. It's important to evaluate controls in all classes or categories. For example, technical controls alone cannot address all risks.

KEY CONCEPTS AND TERMS

Advanced Encryption Standard (AES)
Certificates
Certification authority (CA)
Corrective control
Detective control
Digital signature
Non-repudiation
Preventative control
Rules of Behavior
Sniffer

CHAPTER 9 ASSESSMENT

1. A _____ will reduce or eliminate a threat or vulnerability.

2. Controls can be identified based on their function. The functions are preventative, detective, and corrective.

   A. True
   B. False

3. What are the primary objectives of a control?

   A. Prevent, control, attack
   B. Prevent, respond, log
   C. Prevent, recover, detect
   D. Detect, recover, attack

4. What type of control is an intrusion detection system (IDS)?

   A. Preventative
   B. Detective
   C. Corrective
   D. Recovery

5. NIST SP 800-53 identifies controls in three primary classes. What are they?

   A. Preventative, Detective, Corrective
   B. Administrative, Technical, Operational
   C. Technical, Administrative, Environmental
   D. Technical, Operational, and Management

6. A(n) _____ control is used to ensure that users have the rights and permissions they need to perform their jobs, and no more.

7. Logon identifiers help ensure that users cannot deny taking a specific action such as deleting a file. What is this called?

   A. Digital signature
   B. Encryption
   C. Non-repudiation
   D. PKI

8. What should you use to ensure that users understand what they can and cannot do on systems within the network?

   A. Acceptable use banner
   B. Data range checks
   C. Rules of behavior
   D. Audit trails

9. What can be used to ensure confidentiality of sensitive data?

   A. Encryption
   B. Hashing
   C. Digital signature
   D. Non-repudiation

10. What should be logged in an audit log?

   A. All system events
   B. All security related events
   C. The details of what happened for an event
   D. Who, what, when, and where details of an event

11. Your organization wants to issue certificates for internal systems such as in internal Web server. You'll need to install a _____ to issue and manage certificates.

12. Which of the following is an administrative control?

   A. Session timeout
   B. Reasonableness check
   C. Water detection
   D. DRP

13. Which of the following is a technical control?

   A. PKI
   B. Awareness and training
   C. Guards
   D. Electrical grounding

14. Which of the following is a physical control?

   A. Logon identifiers
   B. CCTV
   C. Encryption
   D. BCP

15. A PTZ camera is used within a CCTV system. It can pan, tilt, and zoom.

   A. True
   B. False

9

Risk Mitigation Security Controls

Planning Risk Mitigation Throughout Your Organization

AFTER COMPLETING THE BASICS of identifying assets, threats, and vulnerabilities, you can begin identifying controls. Controls mitigate risk throughout an organization. One of the ways to evaluate controls is to identify critical business operations and critical business functions. Controls should be in place to protect against risks for these critical areas of your business.

Compliance is an important topic in IT today. If any laws or guidelines govern your organization, you need to ensure you're compliant. Noncompliance can be quite expensive. The first step is identifying the relevant laws and guidelines to see if they apply to your organization. If they do apply, you need to assess the regulations to identify the impact on your organization.

Chapter 10 Topics

This chapter covers the following topics and concepts:

- Where your organization should start with risk mitigation
- What the scope of risk management for your organization is
- How to understand and assess the impact of legal and compliance issues on your organization
- How to translate legal and compliance implications for your organization
- How to assess the impact of legal and compliance implications on the seven domains of a typical IT infrastructure
- How to assess how security countermeasures and safeguards can assist with risk mitigation
- What the operational impacts of legal and compliance requirements are
- How to identify risk mitigation and risk reduction elements for an entire organization
- What a cost-benefit analysis is
- What best practices for planning risk mitigation throughout an organization are

Chapter 10 Goals

When you complete this chapter, you will be able to:

- Describe how an organization should start with risk mitigation
- Identify the scope of risk management within an organization
- Apply risk management scope concepts to critical business operations
- Apply risk management scope concepts to customer service delivery
- Apply risk management scope concepts to mission-critical business systems, applications, and data access
- Apply risk management scope concepts to the seven domains of a typical IT infrastructure
- Apply risk management scope concepts to systems security gaps
- Assess the impact of legal and compliance issues within an organization
- List compliance laws, regulations, and mandates that apply to an organization
- Describe legal and compliance implications within an organization
- Describe the impact of legal and compliance implications on the seven domains of a typical IT infrastructure
- Evaluate security countermeasures and safeguards that can assist with risk mitigation
- Describe operational impacts of legal and compliance requirements
- List risk mitigation and risk reduction elements
- Describe a cost-benefit analysis
- List best practices for planning risk mitigation throughout an organization

Where Should Your Organization Start with Risk Mitigation?

Your organization should start by identifying assets. An asset inventory helps you determine the value of your systems, services, and data. The value of the assets can be monetary, or it can be relative. For example, you may decide to assign values such as High, Medium, and Low for assets. These values do not necessarily equate to the cost of equipment. Rather, the value relates to the possible business impact if the assets are damaged or lost.

> **NOTE**

This list isn't intended to be a complete list of all assets. Instead, it provides a sample of how an organization may prioritize its assets. Chapter 7 covered identifying assets and activities in much more depth.

As an example, your asset inventory could have resulted in the following priorities:

* Database servers—High
* File servers—High
* E-mail servers—High
* Network infrastructure—High
* Web server—Medium
* User desktop systems—Medium
* User laptops—Low

Next, you identify and analyze threats and vulnerabilities. Chapter 8 covered how to perform threat assessments, vulnerability assessments, and exploit assessments. You can perform a threat and vulnerability assessment on each asset.

For example, you can begin an assessment on the database servers. You can start several ways. One way is to consider the basics and ask yourself some questions:

* **Loss of confidentiality**—Is the data sensitive? Are access controls in place? Should at-rest data be encrypted? Should data be encrypted when it's transferred?

* **Loss of integrity**—Can the database recover from power loss? Are data versions required? Is configuration of the database documented? Are change management practices followed?

* **Loss of availability**—Are reliable backups performed regularly? Are copies of backups stored offsite? What are the required hours for data availability? Are redundant drives used? Are failover clusters required?

The questions you ask will be different for different assets. For example, if you are examining the network infrastructure, you'll have different concerns than if you are examining another asset. The point here isn't the specific questions you're asking. Instead, the point is that you are asking questions to identify areas of concern.

Chapter 9 presented the National Institute of Standards and Technology (NIST) Special Publication 800-53. SP 800-53 includes extensive documentation on controls. A good way of ensuring you ask yourself the right questions is by using SP 800-53. Go through the control families one by one. If they apply, ensure your plan considers them.

You then evaluate the controls to determine what controls to implement. A significant part of this step is the cost-benefit analysis (CBA). CBAs are covered later in this chapter.

What Is the Scope of Risk Management for Your Organization?

The scope of risk management indicates your area of concern. You can also think of it as your area of control. There are some things you can control and some things you can't control.

For example, you can't control hurricanes or earthquakes. You can reduce the impact of these events by planning how your organization will respond. However, you can't stop them from occurring.

When considering risk management scope within your organization, consider the following items:

- Critical business operations
- Customer service delivery
- Mission-critical business systems, applications, and data access
- Seven domains of a typical IT infrastructure
- Information systems security gap

The following sections cover these topics.

Critical Business Operations

An early step in risk management is identifying what business operations are critical. In other words, you want to identify what business operations must be functional to ensure the organization stays afloat.

> **TIP**
>
> It's essential that risk management be driven by business needs. In other words, the risks you manage are those that have the potential to affect your business. Costs to manage risks outside this scope are not justified.

A business impact analysis (BIA) is the key tool you'll use for this step. It helps an organization identify the effect if different risks occur.

One of the key elements of the BIA is the identification of costs. You identify both direct and indirect costs. The direct costs reflect the immediate cost of an outage. For example, if a Web server fails and cannot process sales, the sales lost during this period are direct costs. Indirect costs include the loss of customer goodwill and the cost to restore the goodwill.

These costs help identify the priority of the service or function. If the costs of an outage are high, you are justified to spend more money to prevent the outage.

BIAs identify the **maximum acceptable outage (MAO)**. The MAO is the maximum amount of time a system or service can be down before affecting the mission. The MAO is sometimes referred to as maximum tolerable outage (MTO) or maximum tolerable period of disruption (MTPOD).

The MAO directly affects the required recovery time. In other words, imagine that the MAO is 30 minutes. Recovery plans must be able to restore a failed system within 30 minutes.

A big part of the BIA is data collection. You can collect data by going through available reports. You can also collect data by interviewing personnel.

When completing a BIA of a specific service or function, you'll try to answer different questions. Some of the key questions you'll try to answer are:

> **NOTE**
>
> Chapter 12 covers business impact analysis (BIA) in more detail.

- How does this service affect the organization's profitability?
- How does this service affect the organization's survivability?
- How does this service affect the organization's image?
- How will an outage affect employees?
- How will an outage affect customers?
- When does this service need to be available?
- What is the MAO of the service?

Customer Service Delivery

Risk management includes an evaluation of services you provide to customers. In this context, a customer is any entity that receives a service.

> **NOTE**
>
> Entities within the same organization often have agreements similar to an SLA. For example, a remote office may have an agreement with the main office that VPN services will be provided during business hours. This isn't as formal as an SLA. Additionally, it wouldn't have monetary penalties. However, this agreement does specify expectations of service.

Obvious customers are those that purchase your services. For example, if your organization provides e-mail services to small businesses, these small businesses are your customers. Instead of managing their own e-mail servers, they outsource the service to you.

These customers have an expectation of the service. They could expect that e-mail is available 24 hours a day, seven days a week. Alternatively, they may expect access to the e-mail only during their business hours. Either way, it's important to identify the expectations.

A **service level agreement (SLA)** is a document that identifies an expected level of performance. It identifies the minimum uptime or the maximum downtime. Organizations use SLAs as a contract between a service provider and a customer. An SLA can identify monetary penalties if the terms aren't met.

If your organization has SLAs with other organizations, these should be included in the risk management review. You should pay special attention to monetary penalties.

For example, an SLA could specify a maximum downtime of four hours. After four hours, hourly penalties will start to accrue. You can relate this to the MAO.

Of course, SLAs that promise low levels of downtimes cost more. This extra cost is imposed to pay for the extra controls that are used. These extra controls provide a higher level of service.

A less obvious customer is the internal customer. Any employee or department that receives a service is a customer. Some common services provided to internal employees include:

- E-mail services
- Access to the Internet
- Network access
- Server applications, such as database servers
- Access to internal servers, such as file servers
- Desktop computer support

Employees won't have SLAs with an IT department. However, there are expectations of a specific level of service. If any of these services fails for too long, it will begin to affect the mission. This also refers to the MAO.

Just because a service doesn't have an external customer doesn't mean it should be ignored. Many services are required for internal customers.

Mission-Critical Business Systems, Applications, and Data Access

Many organizations have mission-critical systems, applications, and data. When these are not available, the mission is affected. It's important to identify and review these when reviewing risk management and risk mitigation plans.

Mission-critical business systems are any systems or processes integral to the organization. You really need to understand the business to identify these. You can help identify these by first identifying **critical business functions (CBFs)** and **critical success factors (CSFs)**.

A CBF is any function considered vital to an organization. If the CBF fails, the organization will lose the ability to perform essential operations, such as sales to customers. If the organization cannot perform the function, it will lose money. The loss could be due to lost revenue or indirect losses.

A CSF is any element necessary to perform the mission of an organization. An organization will have a few elements that must succeed in order for the organization to succeed. For example, a reliable network infrastructure may be considered a CSF for many companies today. If the network infrastructure fails, communication can stop.

Critical business functions are supported by multiple elements. For example, consider an organization that sells products on the Internet. Figures 10-1 through 10-3 show the different supporting elements in a complete transaction. By analyzing these elements, you can identify the critical business functions.

In Figure 10-1, the customer makes the purchase. In this example, the customer is purchasing the product from an Internet Web server. Additionally, a back-end database server records the transaction.

FIGURE 10-1

Critical business functions—making the purchase.

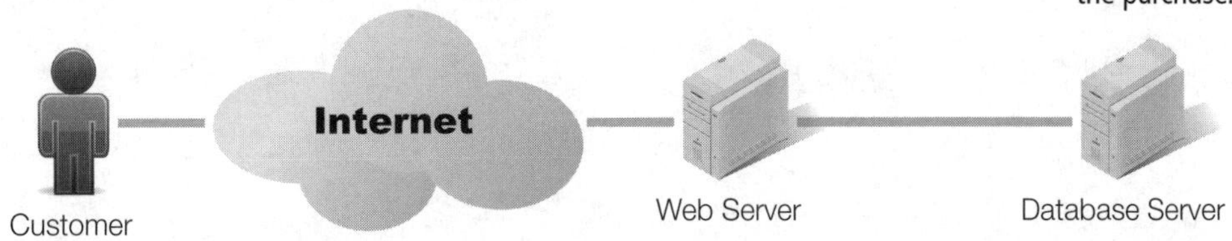

Customer   **Internet**   Web Server   Database Server

Critical business functions here are:

- **Internet access**—The Web server must have reliable Internet access. If Internet access fails, the customer can't access the Web server.
- **Web server availability**—The Web server must be operational. This includes the Web server and the Web application. If the Web server fails, the customer can't complete the purchase.
- **Database server availability**—A database server records the transaction. This includes details on the customer, the product purchased, and payment information. If the database server fails, the Web application cannot complete the transaction.

Figure 10-2 shows how payment is received. Although payment processing will often occur as part of the transaction, it's separated here for clarity. Credit card transactions are common on the Internet. The organization must comply with the Payment Card Industry Data Security Standard (PCI DSS) to process credit card payments. The Web application uses data in the database to identify details for the credit card payment. It then sends a request to the appropriate bank for payment.

> **NOTE**
>
> Chapter 3 presented PCI DSS. It is also discussed later in this chapter in the "Legal Requirements, Compliance Laws, Regulations, and Mandates" section.

This step requires the same critical business functions as the purchase step. However, one additional element is needed. PCI DSS compliance is required. This ensures the organization is meeting minimum security standards for credit card data. If the organization is not compliant with PCI DSS, it can lose the ability to process credit cards. Noncompliance can also result in fines.

FIGURE 10-2

Critical business functions— receiving funds.

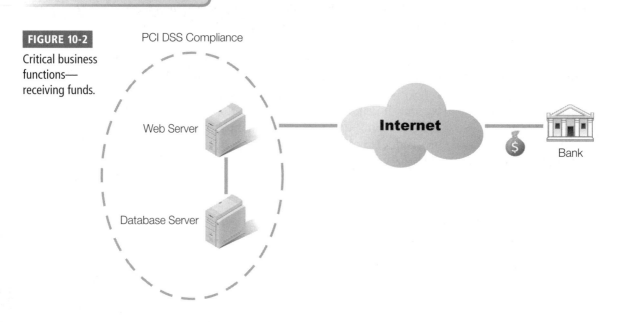

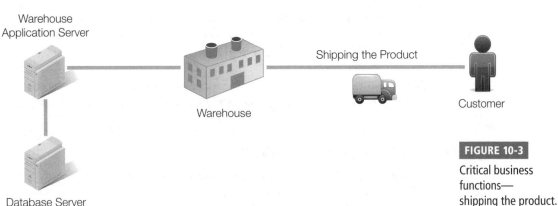

Warehouse
Application Server

Shipping the Product

Warehouse

Customer

Database Server

FIGURE 10-3

Critical business
functions—
shipping the product.

Figure 10-3 shows the last step in the process. In this step, workers use a warehouse application to identify products to ship. This application interacts with a database server. The database server has details on purchased products, customers, and product locations. The warehouse workers then ship the product to the customer.

This step has several additional critical functions:

- **Warehouse application server**—This application must be available to the workers. It must also be able to interact with the database server. If the application is not available, the workers won't be able to identify products to ship. Shipping will stop.

- **Database server**—The database server is needed to identify what products to ship. It also identifies details on where to ship them. If the data from this server is not available, shipping will stop.

- **Workers**—The workers pack and ship the purchased products. They use the warehouse application to identify the materials. If the workers aren't available, shipping stops. Even if an organization has been able to automate some of the functions, such as retrieving products, workers would finalize the process. Additionally, human interaction is valuable for quality control.

> **TIP**
>
> The warehouse database server holds a lot of the same data as the Web database server. However, it will probably be a different server. The servers have different availability needs. The Web application needs to be operational all the time. The warehouse application needs to be available only when workers are shipping goods. Automation techniques would regularly move data from the Web database server to the Warehouse database server.

- **Warehouse**—The products are stored and shipped from the warehouse. If the warehouse is damaged, two things are affected. First, the inventory may be lost. For example, a fire could destroy some or all of the inventory in the warehouse. Second, shipping may stop or be slowed. If the shipping area is damaged, shipping may stop completely. If products are damaged, shipping will be delayed for these products.

With the critical business functions identified, you can now focus on risk management. Each of these functions can be reviewed to ensure that adequate steps are taken to protect them.

Notice that some of the functions will require different levels of protection. For example, the Web server and the Web database server need to be operational all the time. The MAO is very short. The servers may require failover clusters to ensure the services continue to run even if a server fails.

However, shipping may only occur six days a week during the daytime. The warehouse servers won't need the same level of protection. The MAO for these servers is significantly longer.

Seven Domains of a Typical IT Infrastructure

You can also review the seven domains of a typical IT infrastructure. By looking at each of these domains, you can identify the scope of risk management needed for your organization. Figure 10-4 shows the seven domains of a typical IT infrastructure.

User Domain

Every organization has users. Computers by themselves do a lot, but they can't yet do everything. Instead, the computers are here to support the users.

With this in mind, let's look at risks associated with users. The primary risks associated with the User Domain are related to social engineering. Users can be conned and tricked.

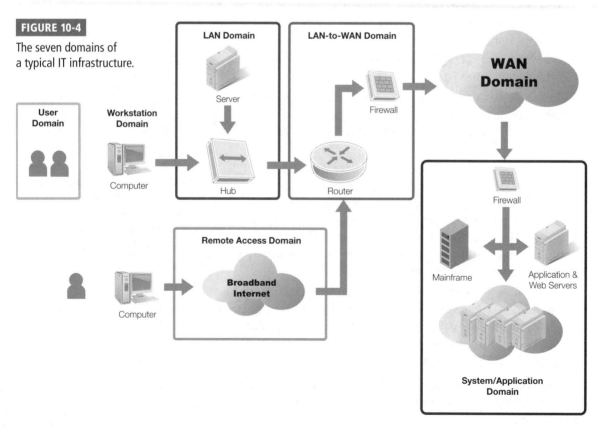

FIGURE 10-4

The seven domains of a typical IT infrastructure.

A social engineer tries to trick a user into giving up information or performing an unsafe action.

You combat these risks by raising user awareness. Implement acceptable use policies (AUPs) to ensure users know what they should and shouldn't be doing. Use logon banners to remind users of the AUP. Send out occasional e-mails with security tidbits to keep security in their minds. Use posters in employee areas.

Workstation Domain

The Workstation Domain is the computers that users will use. In some organizations, all employees have computers on their desks. In other organizations, desktop computers may be limited. For example, not every user in a warehouse needs a computer.

However, when users do have computers, they face risks. Some of the primary risks associated with workstations are related to malware. Users can bring malware from home on universal serial bus (USB) flash disks. They can accidentally download malware from Web sites. They can also install malware from malicious e-mails.

The primary protection is to ensure that you install antivirus (AV) software. Additionally, you need to update AV signatures regularly. You can't depend on the users to keep their signatures up to date. Instead, you must take control of the process. Many AV vendors provide tools to automatically install and update AV software on workstations.

You must also be sure to keep operating systems up to date. When security patches become available, they should be evaluated and deployed when needed. Many of these security patches remove vulnerabilities. Without the patch, the systems remain vulnerable.

Just as you can use tools to ensure AV software remains updated, you can also use tools to keep systems patched. The same concepts apply. You can't depend on users to keep their systems updated. Instead, you must take control of the process.

LAN Domain

The LAN Domain includes the networking components that connect systems on a local area network (LAN). This includes hardware components such as routers and switches. It also includes the wiring, and wiring closets used to connect the users.

Computers are connected with server operating systems. For example, in a Microsoft environment clients are connected in a Microsoft domain. This includes at least one server acting as a domain controller. In a Microsoft domain, every user must have an account to log onto the domain. Additionally, every computer must have an account on the domain.

There are significant risks to consider in the LAN Domain. Routers have access control lists (ACLs) used to control what traffic is allowed through them. Switches can also be programmed for specific functionality.

Routers and switches are commonly located in a wiring closet or server room. This ensures they are protected with physical security. If an attacker has unrestricted access to these devices, the ACLs could be modified. Additionally, an attacker could connect a wireless access point to capture and transmit all the traffic going through any of these devices.

Many organizations also practice port security as an added control. Port security ensures that only specific computers are able to attach to the network device. In other words, if an attacker brings in a computer, he will not be able to connect the computer to the network.

LAN-to-WAN Domain

The LAN-to-WAN Domain marks the boundary where the private network meets the public network. In this context, the public network is the Internet.

Many different types of attacks come from the Internet. The primary protection here is the use of one or more firewalls. Firewalls can examine traffic as it passes through and allow or block traffic based on rules.

Although most organizations have firewalls in place, the major concern here is the management of the firewalls. A common problem is too many firewall rules allowing too much traffic. The firewall should discriminate and allow only certain types of traffic.

Organizations commonly use hardware firewalls that can be very sophisticated. Administrators often need additional training to ensure they know how to manage and maintain them. Trained administrators understand the importance of limiting the number of firewall rules.

Remote Access Domain

The Remote Access Domain allows remote users to access the private network. Users can dial in if the remote access server is a dial-in server. You can also use a virtual private network (VPN). A VPN allows a user to access the private network over a public network, such as the Internet.

> **TIP**
>
> An older technique of locating remote access servers is war dialing. The attacker dials numbers randomly until a modem answers. Once the modem answers, the attacker attempts to log on.

If your organization utilizes remote access servers, you need to consider the risks. If you are using dial-in remote access servers, your systems are available from any phone. The attacker only needs to know the phone number.

If you are using VPN servers, the VPN server has an Internet Protocol (IP) address that is publicly available from anywhere on the Internet. It is susceptible to attacks from anywhere in the world.

You can use several different controls to protect servers in the Remote Access Domain.

Automatic callback is one method used with dial-in remote access servers. Imagine that Sally can work from home. Her account information includes her phone number. When she dials in, she is prompted to log on. As soon as she logs on, the remote server hangs up and calls her home number.

This increases security because even if an attacker learns Sally's credentials, the attacker can't use them for remote access. If the attacker dials in and logs on with Sally's credentials, the server hangs up and calls Sally's home.

Remote access policies are another control used with remote access. Policies are used to specify several conditions to ensure the connection is secure. For example, a policy could specify that only Layer 2 Tunneling Protocol (L2TP) connections are allowed. Additionally, Internet Protocol Security (IPSec) could be required to ensure the connection encrypted.

WAN Domain

The WAN Domain includes all systems that are accessible over a wide area network (WAN). This primarily refers to servers accessible over the Internet.

Servers available on the Internet have public IP addresses. They can be reached from any system on the Internet. This makes them easy targets.

A primary method of protection for systems in the WAN Domain is the use of a demilitarized zone (DMZ). A DMZ uses two firewalls. One firewall has direct access to the Internet. The other firewall has direct access to the internal network. The area between the two firewalls is the DMZ.

Although the DMZ doesn't stop an attacker from accessing a server, it can limit the attacker's access. For example, a Web server can be placed in the DMZ to host a Web site. Web servers host the Hypertext Transfer Protocol (HTTP). Secure Web servers also host the Hypertext Transfer Protocol Secure (HTTPS). The Well Known ports for HTTP and HTTPS are 80 and 443, respectively. You can configure the DMZ to allow traffic to the Web server using only ports 80 and 443. All other traffic directed at the Web server is blocked.

Additionally, these servers need to be kept up to date. When security patches are released, you should evaluate them as soon as possible. Test the patch to ensure it doesn't have any negative impacts. You can then deploy it to the servers.

> **NOTE**
>
> The WAN Domain can also include systems that are accessible over a WAN link that is semiprivate. For example, an organization can lease lines from a telecommunications company. Other customers share these lines. They aren't as public as the Internet. However, your systems are still susceptible to attacks from other customers leasing the same lines.

> **NOTE**
>
> Chapter 2 covered DMZs in greater depth. Figure 2-2 showed how a DMZ is configured and how public facing servers are placed within the DMZ.

System/Application Domain

The System/Application Domain includes any server-based applications. This can include e-mail servers. It can include database servers. It can include any server or system that has a dedicated application.

For example, Oracle Database hosts databases on a server. Microsoft Exchange is a popular e-mail server. Apache hosts Web applications on Web servers. Each of these applications is specialized. They have unique risks. They often require specialized knowledge to manage and configure. What's more, they require attention to detail to keep them secure.

A primary requirement to keep these systems secure is to ensure administrators have adequate training and knowledge. Additionally, configuration and change management practices are helpful. Configuration management ensures the systems are configured using sound security practices. Change management ensures that the configuration is not modified without adequate review.

System applications often have bugs. Vendors release security patches when they have identified the bugs. Administrators of these systems need to stay in tune with the vendor so that they're aware when patches are released. You should test patches to ensure they do not have any negative effects. You should then apply the patches.

Information Systems Security Gap

The information systems security gap refers to the difference between the controls you have in place and what you need. In a perfect world, the in-place controls will address all threats and vulnerabilities. However, threats and vulnerabilities are constantly changing.

A risk assessment (RA) provides a point-in-time report. It can be used to compare the existing threats and vulnerabilities against the in-place controls. Even if the last RA was perfect, it wasn't able to address the threats and vulnerabilities that emerged after the RA.

Chapter 8 presented the concept of a gap analysis report. This is often used when dealing with legal compliance. For example, if reviewing compliance with the Health Insurance Portability and Accountability Act (HIPAA) or the Sarbanes-Oxley Act (SOX), you could use a gap analysis report. The gap analysis report documents the security gap.

You should combine the gap analysis report with a remediation plan. The remediation plan identifies how the security gap is closed. In other words, it provides recommendations on what controls to implement.

Defense in Depth

Even if you have aggressive risk management and risk mitigation plans, there will usually be security gaps. It's almost impossible to have systems 100 percent secure 100 percent of the time.

However, **defense in depth** is a security practice that adds multiple layers of protection. These multiple layers overlap with one another. Even if a gap occurs in one layer, there is a greater chance that a system is protected from another layer.

As an example, AV protection often uses a three-pronged approach. You install AV software at the firewall to scan incoming data. You also install AV software on the e-mail server to scan for malicious attachments or scripts. As a third measure, you install AV software on all workstations and servers.

You might wonder why you should install AV software on desktop systems if the firewall and e-mail already scan for malware. The reason is because users could transmit a virus from a CD/DVD or USB flash drive.

In addition, although AV software protects desktop systems, you still need additional AV software to scan e-mail attachments. Malware is most commonly sent through e-mail. If you haven't installed AV software on the e-mail server, it will forward malware to clients. If a single system isn't up to date, or has a malfunction with the AV software, it will be infected. This infection could quickly spread.

Defense in depth is more expensive in the short run. However, defense in depth closes more security gaps and in the long run, it saves money.

The Growth of Compliance

Greed and corruption can seep in anywhere. This includes large organizations. When problems are discovered, people are outraged. They demand justice. In the United States, Congress enacts laws.

Compliance has become more prominent in the past few decades. In the 1960s, General Electric and Westinghouse were convicted of several antitrust regulations. They were part of a widespread bid rigging and price fixing conspiracy. Congress responded with the Foreign Corrupt Practices Act (FCPA) in 1977.

In 1991, the U.S. Federal Sentencing Guidelines for Organizational Ethics legislation was passed. It included provisions to punish organizations for criminal actions and deterrence incentives to detect and prevent crime.

The Enron scandal occurred in 2001. A group of executives used a variety of tactics over several years to hide billions of dollars in debt from failed deals and projects. Enron's stock price went from $90 per share to less than $1, resulting in about $11 billion in losses to investors. Several executives were indicted and sentenced to prison.

WorldCom executives also used a variety of tactics over several years to artificially inflate the company's value by around $11 billion. When the CEO was ousted in April 2002, things began to fall apart. The fraud was discovered in June 2002. WorldCom filed for bankruptcy in July 2002 and never repaid most of the creditors. Several of WorldCom's executives were also indicted and sentenced to prison.

Congress responded to these scandals with laws to expand the reliability of financial reporting for public companies. The Sarbanes-Oxley Act was one such law. It increased penalties for defrauding shareholders. It also imposed more stringent requirements for internal controls.

This is certainly not a complete history. There was much more fraud. There were many more scandals. However, it does provide a partial view of how corruption can grow, and how Congress reacts.

Corporate compliance has become so important in some organizations that a new position has been created. Many companies have a chief ethics compliance officer (CECO) or an ethics compliance officer (ECO).

Understanding and Assessing the Impact of Legal and Compliance Issues on Your Organization

Chapter 3 covered many of the IT-related laws and regulations that affect organizations. It's important that an organization knows what laws apply to them. Once these are identified, it's important to ensure that the organization is in compliance.

Noncompliance can have serious consequences. Some laws assess hefty fines on an organization. Other laws can result in jail time. Some can negatively affect an organization's ability to do business.

In this context, compliance is a mitigation control. You may remember from Chapter 9 that you implement controls to mitigate risk. They will reduce or neutralize threats or vulnerabilities to an acceptable level.

For example, HIPAA fines can be as high as $25,000 a year for mistakes. An internal compliance program can ensure these costly mistakes don't happen.

When assessing the impact of compliance issues in your organization, you should take two distinct steps. First, identify what compliance issues apply to your organization. Second, assess the impact of these issues on your business operations. These two topics are presented in the following sections.

Legal Requirements, Compliance Laws, Regulations, and Mandates

Although there are many laws and regulations that apply to IT, they don't all apply to IT. One of the important issues to understand first is which laws apply to which organization.

As a reminder, some of the key laws that apply to organizations are:

- Health Insurance Portability and Accountability Act (HIPAA)
- Sarbanes-Oxley Act (SOX)
- Federal Information Security Management Act (FISMA)
- Family Educational Rights and Privacy Act (FERPA)
- Children's Internet Protection Act (CIPA)
- Payment Card Industry Data Security Standard (PCI DSS)

The following sections identify how you can determine if a law applies to your organization. Some laws are very specific and narrow in scope. However, others, such as HIPAA, apply to a wide range of organizations.

Health Insurance Portability and Accountability Act (HIPAA)

HIPAA applies to any organization that handles health information. The obvious organizations that handle health information are hospitals and doctor's offices. However, HIPAA reaches much farther than the medical industry.

Health information includes any data that relates to the health of an individual. This includes a person's past, present, and future health. It includes their condition, physical health, or mental health. It also includes any past, present or future payments for health care.

If any organization creates or receives health information, it must comply with HIPAA. This includes employers. It includes health plan sponsors. It includes health care providers. It includes public health authorities, and more.

If your organization isn't involved in health care but it does provide a health plan, it falls under HIPAA.

Sarbanes-Oxley Act (SOX)

The SOX Act applies to any business that is required to be registered with the Securities and Exchange Commission. This is any publicly traded company. In other words, if someone can buy stock in your company, then SOX applies.

SOX establishes a set of standards. Even if they don't apply directly to private businesses, private businesses can use these same standards. If the organization faces legal issues later, they can point to their actions as good faith efforts to avoid the problems.

Federal Information Security Management Act (FISMA)

FISMA applies to all U.S. federal agencies. The goal is to ensure that federal agencies take steps to protect their data. If you work in a federal agency, FISMA applies.

The National Institute of Standards and Technology (NIST) is tasked by FISMA to develop standards, guidelines, and best practices to support FISMA. Special publications created by NIST for FISMA are available publically.

Family Educational Rights and Privacy Act (FERPA)

FERPA applies to all education institutions and agencies that receive funding under any program administered by the U.S. Department of Education (ED).

The obvious examples are any public schools from grades K through 12. However many other entities can receive funding from ED. This includes any school or agency offering preschool programs. It includes any institution of higher education. It can also include community colleges or any other education institution.

Funding is often indirect. Although public grade schools receive their funding directly from ED, other institutions receive their funding indirectly. ED provides student aid and grants for college. If a student receives this funding and uses the money to pay for college, the college is receiving ED funding.

Children's Internet Protection Act (CIPA)

CIPA applies to any school or library that receives funding from the U.S. E-Rate program. The Federal Communications Commission (FCC) sponsors the E-Rate program. It provides discounts for Internet access.

Schools and libraries are not required to use the E-Rate program. However, if they choose to take advantage of the discounts, they are governed by CIPA. The annual E-Rate application requires schools and libraries to certify they are complying with CIPA.

Payment Card Industry Data Security Standard (PCI DSS)

PCI DSS is not a law. Instead, it is a standard that was jointly created by several credit card companies. Any organization that accepts credit card payments over the Internet needs to comply.

> **TIP**
> PCI compliance and PCI DSS compliance mean the same thing.

Many credit card companies support PCI DSS. This includes Visa International, MasterCard Worldwide, American Express, Discover Financial Services, and JCB International,

Smaller companies can certify they are compliant by completing a self-assessment questionnaire. A qualified security assessor independently audits large organizations.

10

Planning Risk Mitigation

Assessing the Impact of Legal and Compliance Issues on Your Business Operations

Once you've determined your organization has compliance requirements, the next step is to determine the impact of these relevant issues on your organization. The impact is significantly different depending on the law or standard.

The following sections present potential impacts for some of the common laws and standards.

Health Insurance Portability and Accountability Act (HIPAA)

HIPAA affects a wide spectrum of a business. The cost of non compliance is high. Additionally, the steps required to comply can be complex depending on how much health related information an organization handles.

First, the penalties are severe if the rules aren't being followed. Organizations can be fined $100 per violation and up to $25,000 per year for mistakes. If someone knowingly obtains or releases data he or she shouldn't, the penalties can be as high as $50,000 and one year in prison. If data is obtained or disclosed under false pretenses, penalties can be as high as $100,000 and five years in prison. If data is obtained or disclosed for personal gain or malicious harm, penalties can be as high as $250,000 and 10 years in prison.

However, compliance can also be expensive. Organizations that handle health data must take specific steps to protect it. This includes any data that it creates, receives, or sends. It also includes protecting any of the systems that handle health data.

The responsibility to keep the data secure rests with the organization. The data must be protected while at rest. In other words, if it is stored on a hard drive or in a filing cabinet it must be protected. This can be done through access controls, or physical security depending on the type of data.

Use of health information is restricted. Employees who handle and review health information must be trained so they know the requirements. As an example, data cannot be released to a third party without the written consent of the patient.

Data must be protected when transmitted. When any health data is transmitted, it must be transmitted in a specific format.

The good news is that health plan providers are well versed in HIPAA. A company that outsources a health plan can also outsource handling of the health data.

For example, a health plan provider can be contracted to provide insurance to employees. Employees can then be directed to the health plan provider's Web site to enroll. When a health plan is managed in this manner, the provider hosts almost all the information. The company has very little data and its risks are limited.

Sarbanes-Oxley Act (SOX)

The business impact of SOX is a higher liability for the accuracy of data. High-level officers such as chief executive officers (CEOs) and chief financial officers (CFOs) must personally verify and attest to the accuracy of financial data.

Because of this, organizations are required to take extra steps to ensure the accuracy and integrity of the data. This includes implementing internal controls. It also requires both internal and external audits to verify compliance.

Compliance costs can be high. Congressman Ron Paul quotes a survey by Korn/Ferry International stating, "Sarbanes-Oxley cost Fortune 500 companies an average of $5.1 million in compliance expenses in 2004."

Federal Information Security Management Act (FISMA)

Because FISMA applies only to federal agencies, it does not affect the revenue of any organization. However, it can have a significant effect on operations.

A core requirement of FISMA is to identify, certify as compliant, and authorize for operation all IT systems in the organization. This process can be lengthy. One of the primary problems is the slow implementation of new systems.

FISMA encourages the use of baselines. As long as a system follows the same baseline as another system, it can be certified and authorized quicker.

> **▶ TIP**
>
> A baseline is any known starting point. If it's an IT system, a baseline represents the same hardware, software, and configuration as another system. For example, if one server has been authorized using a baseline, another server can be authorized much more quickly by using the same baseline.

Family Educational Rights and Privacy Act (FERPA)

FERPA requires covered organizations to share student records with students or their parents. If the student or parent makes the request, the school must comply.

Students or parents can request the correction of errors in the student's record. The school has an obligation to consider the request. However, the school isn't required to make all the changes a student asks for. For example, if a student requests a poor grade to be removed from a record, but the grade is accurate, the school isn't required to remove it.

> **▶ TIP**
>
> FERPA grants specific rights to parents of students under 18. However, when the student turns 18, these rights transfer to the student. The parents no longer have rights to the information without the student's knowledge and consent.

Students can grant access to their record to specific third parties. For example, a student may grant access when applying for admission to a college or university. Some specific third parties are automatically granted access to the records. Many school officials, for instance, do not need student permission to view the record.

The biggest impact this has on business operations is ensuring that employees know the rules. This can be done with training.

If a student under 18 requests access to the record, the employee should know the right belongs to the parent. If a parent of a 20-year-old requests access, the employee should know the right belongs to the student. Similarly, if a third-party requests access, the employee should know if access should be granted.

Children's Internet Protection Act (CIPA)

CIPA imposes several technical requirements on schools and libraries. They must be able to filter offensive content to ensure that minors aren't exposed to it. If the school or library cannot comply with CIPA, it risks losing all E-Rate discounts.

E-Rate funding provides discounts to schools and libraries for Internet access. Any school or library that requests discounts under the E-Rate program is required to certify that they comply with CIPA rules.

The first challenge is identifying offensive content. CIPA allows the school or library to define "offensive" using local standards. In other words, what is deemed offensive content in a library in one area of the country may be acceptable in a library in another area of the country.

Schools and libraries filter the content with a **technology protection measure (TPM)**. Figure 10-5 shows an example of a **proxy server** used as a TPM. A proxy server receives requests from clients for Web pages, retrieves the Web pages, and then serves the pages to the clients. It can also filter the requests to block content requests.

Users are able to access the Internet through the proxy server. All content requests are filtered using the content filter. If the content is acceptable, the page is retrieved and sent to the client. If the content is unacceptable, the content is blocked.

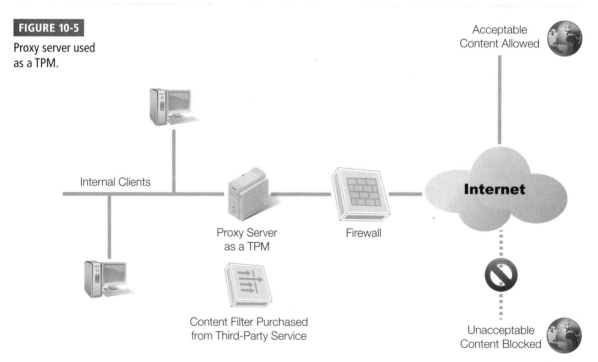

FIGURE 10-5

Proxy server used as a TPM.

Acceptable Content Allowed

Internal Clients

Proxy Server as a TPM

Firewall

Internet

Content Filter Purchased from Third-Party Service

Unacceptable Content Blocked

A proxy server commonly works with data provided by a third-party service. This third-party service provides a list of content to filter. The list is often in the format of specific Web site URLs. The proxy server uses this list to prevent the content from reaching the requesting computer.

Minors are defined as anyone under the age of 17. Their access should be restricted by the TPM.

However, anyone 17 years old or over should be able to use the computer without restrictions. For example, if an adult wants to use it, he or she can request that the TPM filter be removed. An administrator or librarian should be able to remove the filter in a timely manner.

Payment Card Industry Data Security Standard (PCI DSS)

PCI DSS is built around 6 principles and 12 requirements. These principles and requirements were documented in Chapter 3 and are listed here for completeness:

- **Build and Maintain a Secure Network**
  Requirement 1: Install and maintain a firewall.
  Requirement 2: Do not use defaults, such as default passwords.

- **Protect Cardholder Data**
  Requirement 3: Protect stored data.
  Requirement 4: Encrypt transmissions.

- **Maintain a Vulnerability Management Program**
  Requirement 5: Use and update antivirus software.
  Requirement 6: Develop and maintain secure systems.

- **Implement Strong Access Control Measures**
  Requirement 7: Restrict access to data.
  Requirement 8: Use unique logons for each user. Don't share usernames and passwords.
  Requirement 9: Restrict physical access.

- **Regularly Monitor and Test Networks**
  Requirement 10: Track and monitor all access to systems and data.
  Requirement 11: Regularly test security.

- **Maintain an Information Security Policy**
  Requirement 12: Maintain a security policy.

Notice that all of the principles and requirements are IT related. However, they reflect many common best practices. If your organization is already using best practices, PCI DSS won't have much effect on your business operations.

However, if your organization is not currently using common security practices, PCI DSS compliance may affect your budget and operations.

Translating Legal and Compliance Implications for Your Organization

Compliance implications can have far-reaching effects. Just as with other threats and vulnerabilities, you can have both direct and indirect losses.

For example, if your organization is fined $10,000 for mistakes related to HIPAA, the direct loss is $10,000. However, once this hits the news, your organization will have indirect losses.

The media may report that you mishandle health data. If your customers have health data stored with your organization, they may leave. Even if your customers don't have health data stored with your organization, they may be suspicious of how you handle other data. Similarly, employees may realize their data is mishandled. Valuable employees may leave.

Public relations (PR) campaigns can sometimes restore your organization's good name. However, PR isn't cheap. It takes talent to create effective campaigns. It also takes money to implement the campaigns. However, the money spent proactively will be far less than the costly damage shown above.

Assessing the Impact of Legal and Compliance Implications on the Seven Domains of a Typical IT Infrastructure

The seven domains of a typical IT infrastructure have been presented throughout this book, including earlier in this chapter. When evaluating legal and compliance implications, you can examine the impact of each of these domains:

- **User Domain**—For most compliance issues, the User Domain is affected the most. You need to train users to ensure they comply with the procedures. For example, HIPAA requires users to understand what data they can give out. CIPA requires librarians to know how to turn off the TPM for an adult. PCI DSS requires users to have unique logons.

- **Workstation Domain**—If employees will access covered data with their workstations, you need to examine the workstations. If HIPAA or SOX data is stored on the systems, you need to protect that data with access controls. Many companies use desktop PCs as point of sale (POS) systems. A POS system is an electronic cashier. These systems need to be compliant with PCI DSS guidelines. Any desktop system needs antivirus software installed.

- **LAN Domain**—The LAN needs to be secure to prevent attackers from capturing data. This includes HIPAA, SOX, and PCI DSS data. Encryption technologies may be required to ensure transmitted data is secure. This is especially true if your organization uses wireless networks. In the past, attackers captured details of wireless transactions while sitting in the parking lot of the business.

- **LAN-to-WAN Domain**—A firewall is used to protect a network here. PCI DSS specifically requires a firewall. A library may use a proxy server as a TPM to comply with CIPA. A proxy server has access to the Internet and the intranet. It would need additional security to protect it from external attacks.

- **Remote Access Domain**—Many organizations use VPNs to connect a main office and a remote office. If the VPN is used to transmit covered data, it should be examined to ensure it complies with the laws. For example, if HIPAA data is transmitted over the VPN it should be encrypted.

- **WAN Domain**—Some PCI DSS systems may have direct access to the Internet to transmit transaction data. These systems need additional protection. For example, transmissions need to be encrypted. Additionally, the systems need to be protected from attackers that may try to access data stored on the system.

- **System/Application Domain**—Health and financial data governed by HIPAA and SOX are often hosted on database servers. These servers need to be examined to ensure they comply. Access controls should ensure that least privilege principles are implemented. If a proxy server is used as a TPM for CIPA requirements, it needs a method to disable the TPM for an adult.

Assessing How Security Countermeasures and Safeguards Can Assist with Risk Mitigation

The primary purpose of countermeasures, safeguards, or controls is to mitigate risk. Controls are implemented at a point in time to reduce the risks at that time. However, things change. Threats change. Vulnerabilities change. Because of this, the effectiveness of controls can change. It's important to regularly assess controls to ensure they are effective.

> **TIP**
>
> The terms countermeasure, safeguard, and control are used interchangeably. Each is used to mitigate risk.

You can measure the effectiveness of a control by determining how well it meets its goals. A control will attempt to mitigate risk by:

- **Reducing the impact of threats to an acceptable level**—For example, the threat of a hurricane can't be stopped. However, a business continuity plan that identifies an alternate location for the business can reduce the threat.

- **Reducing a vulnerability to an acceptable level**—For example, some denial of service (DoS) attacks can take down unpatched servers. By keeping servers up to date with current patches, they are less vulnerable to known DoS attacks.

You may remember from Chapter 5 that a risk assessment (RA) is a point-in-time assessment. It will evaluate the threats and vulnerabilities at a specific time. An RA recommends controls based on the risks at the time. RAs should be repeated periodically.

Additionally, an RA should be repeated if the control is changed. For example, if you replace a hardware firewall with a different model, the original RA is no longer valid. You should redo it with the new hardware.

Understanding the Operational Implications of Legal and Compliance Requirements

Compliance requirements will often affect how systems operate. When considering the legal and compliance requirements, you'll need to consider how compliance may affect operations.

Consider the following examples:

- **HIPAA**—HIPAA requires the protection of any health-related data. When this data is stored electronically, it becomes easier to control using standard access controls in a network. You may choose to switch from paper-based records to computer-based records. This will affect how employees access data and may represent a change in operational procedures.

- **SOX**—SOX requires the protection of financial data. This data may be stored on a database server. If so, the database server is subject to additional controls that may not be required for other database servers. Administrators may need to take additional steps to protect the data. Users may need to take additional steps to access the data.

- **FISMA**—FISMA requires different procedures for government agencies to purchase and deploy systems. If you purchase different systems outside of the norm, the process to get them certified and authorized can be lengthy. This may affect the agency's ability to field new systems in a short period of time.

- **FERPA**—FERPA mandates access to educational records by students or parents. If the school has a large volume of these requests, it could affect regular operations. The school could choose to limit when access to records is granted.

- **CIPA**—CIPA requires that minors be protected from offensive content, but adults should be able to have unrestricted access. Librarians may not have had to manage systems in the past. However, they may need to be trained on how turn off the TPM for adult access.

- **PCI DSS**—If an organization is already conducting standard security practices, PCI DSS has little effect on normal operations. However, if the organization has weak security practices, PCI DSS standards could drastically change operations. Although this is good in the long run, it may be uncomfortable for users to get used to in the short term.

Identifying Risk Mitigation and Risk Reduction Elements for the Entire Organization

Although it's important to look at individual systems and functions for possible risks, it's also important to take a broader view. A macro view of the organization identifies how all the pieces fit together.

Most organizations have a security policy created by senior management. It lays out the philosophy of security in the organization and identifies big-picture security goals. You implement security controls based on direction from the security policy.

Some of the controls that have a macro view of the organization include:

- **Account management controls**—These controls ensure that account management is secure. With account management controls, you give each user a separate account. You disable accounts if the user leaves. You use password management policies for the accounts.

- **Access controls**—Although access controls are applied to individual systems, you create them using a global system. For example, Microsoft domains use Active Directory Domain Services as the basis for assigning permissions and controlling access. Most organizations create an administrative model that defines how to use groups to organize users. You then grant access permissions to the groups instead of the individual users. Least privilege is a core principle enforced with access controls.

- **Physical access**—It's just a matter of time before an attacker breaks into a system if he has unrestricted physical access to the system. Physical access controls are used to protect the valuable assets. They can include key locks, cipher locks, proximity cards, and closed-circuit television (CCTV) systems.

- **Personnel policies**—Personnel policies such as separation of duties and mandatory vacations are used to help prevent fraud. These policies aren't targeted at individuals. Instead, they're targeted at positions such as accounting positions where personnel have access to organizational monies.

- **Security awareness and training**—Some training is targeted for specific groups, such as management or administrators. Other training is given to all personnel. You can use training and awareness programs to raise the security awareness of all personnel.

There are many additional controls that you can review. However, the point is that you should not focus controls only on individual systems. A sound security program will have a mix of both broad and narrow security controls.

Performing a Cost-Benefit Analysis

The cost-benefit analysis (CBA) is a significant step when evaluating a control. You compare the cost of the control to the cost of the risk if it occurs. If the control costs more to implement than the cost of the risk, it isn't cost effective.

> ▶ **NOTE**
> Chapter 1 presented cost-benefit analysis topics in more detail.

You need to have two pieces of data to perform an effective CBA. You need to know the cost of the control. You also need to know the projected benefits of the control. The projected benefits can be calculated with the following formula:

Loss before control − Loss after control = Projected benefits

You can then determine if the control should be used with this formula:

Projected benefits − Cost of control

If the result is a positive value, the control is worthwhile. If the value is negative, the control costs more than the benefits and shouldn't be purchased.

For example, imagine you have a database server that is hosting a large database. Backups are completed regularly. However, you conducted a risk assessment that determined that backup copies are not stored off site. All of the backup tapes are stored in the same room as the backup server.

The risk is that a fire could destroy the server and all the backup tapes. By storing a copy of the backup tape at an alternate location, you can eliminate the risk.

You need to identify the value of the data. If this is a primary database for the organization, the value could easily be in the millions of dollars. For this example, imagine that the value is $1 million. A complete loss before the control is $1 million.

A company picks up your tapes weekly and stores them at an alternate location. The company can also rotate tapes in and out based on your needs. Imagine the cost for this service is $100 a month, or $1,200 a year.

If you subscribe to this service, the most you can lose is seven days' worth of data. If a fire destroys your building right before the most recent backup tape is picked up, you'll lose the last seven days. Imagine that the value of this week's worth of data is $10,000. You can now plug in the numbers for the formulas.

The loss before the control is $1 million. The loss after the control is $10,000. The cost of the control is $1,200.

Loss before control − Loss after control = Projected benefits

  $1,000,000 − $10,000 = $990,000

Projected benefits − Cost of control

  $990,000 − $1,200 = $988,800

These figures show the value of storing data offsite. They can be valuable when trying to get support to approve the purchase of the control. If you present a request to spend $1,200 annually without justification, the request may be denied. However, if you submit a request to prevent a potential $990,000 loss by spending $1,200, you can expect the request to be approved.

Best Practices for Planning Risk Mitigation Throughout Your Organization

When planning risk mitigation strategies for your organization, you can use several best practices. These include:

- **Review historical documentation**—This includes previous RAs and BIAs. It includes documentation on policies and procedures. It also includes any documentation on past security incidents. Although risks change, many of the threats and vulnerabilities will be the same.

- **Include both a narrow and broad focus**—You can identify specific risks and mitigation strategies for specific systems and functions. This is a narrow focus. However, you also must broaden the focus to include the entire organization. For example, training and awareness programs help ensure the entire organization recognizes the importance of security.

- **Ensure that governing laws are identified**—Take time to understand the laws. If you don't know what laws apply, you won't be compliant. If a law does apply to your organization, ensure you implement steps to become compliant.

- **Redo RAs when a control changes**—Risk assessments are completed at a point in time. If the control changes, the RA is no longer valid.

- **Include a cost-benefit analysis**—CBAs provide justification for controls and help you determine their value. Some CBAs clearly demonstrate that a control should be purchased. Other CBAs clearly demonstrate that a control isn't worth its cost.

CHAPTER SUMMARY

This chapter covered important elements of risk mitigation throughout an organization. You implement controls to mitigate risk by reducing the impact of threats, or by reducing vulnerabilities. You can measure the effectiveness of the controls against those two requirements. They should be most effective at preventing risk for any critical business operations in your organization.

Legal compliance issues have grown very important in recent years for IT. More laws and regulations apply, and the cost for noncompliance can be expensive. It's important to take the time to identify relevant laws and guidelines. Regulations can have varying impacts on your organization, and you should consider them when implementing supporting controls.

KEY CONCEPTS AND TERMS

Critical business function (CBF)
Critical success factor (CSF)
Defense in depth
E-Rate funding
Maximum acceptable outage (MAO)

Proxy server
Return on investment (ROI)
Service level agreement (SLA)
Technology protection measure (TPM)

CHAPTER 10 ASSESSMENT

1. A _____ is used to identify the impact on an organization if a risk occurs.

2. MAO is the minimal acceptable outage that a system or service can have before affecting the mission.

A. True
B. False

3. Your organization wants to have an agreement with a vendor for an expected level of performance for a service. You want to ensure that monetary penalties are assessed if the minimum uptime requirements are not met. What should you use?

A. MAO
B. BIA
C. SLA
D. IDS

4. What can be used to help identify mission-critical systems?

    A. Critical outage times
    B. Critical business functions
    C. PCI DSS review
    D. Disaster recovery plan

5. What can be used to remind users of the contents of the AUP?

    A. Logon banners
    B. Posters
    C. E-mails
    D. All of the above

6. Routers have _____ to control what traffic is allowed through them.

7. Which of the strategies below can help to reduce security gaps even if a security control fails?

    A. Access control implementation
    B. Critical business factor analysis
    C. Defense in depth
    D. Business impact analysis

8. How much can an organization be fined in a year for mistakes that result in noncompliance?

    A. $100
    B. $1,000
    C. $25,000
    D. $250,000

9. What determines if an organization is governed by FISMA?

    A. If it is registered with the Securities and Exchange commission
    B. If employees handle health-related information
    C. If it receives E-Rate funding
    D. If it is a federal agency

10. What determines if an organization is governed by HIPAA?

    A. If it is registered with the Securities and Exchange commission
    B. If employees handle health-related information
    C. If it receives E-Rate funding
    D. If it is a federal agency

11. What determines if an organization is governed by SOX?

    A. If it is registered with the Securities and Exchange commission
    B. If employees handle health-related information
    C. If it receives E-Rate funding
    D. If it is a federal agency

12. What determines if an organization is governed by CIPA?

    A. If it is registered with the Securities and Exchange commission
    B. If employees handle health-related information
    C. If it receives E-Rate funding
    D. If it is a federal agency

13. You've performed a CBA on a prospective control. The CBA indicates the cost of the control is about the same as the projected benefits. What should you do?

    A. Identify the ROI.
    B. Purchase the control.
    C. Cancel the purchase of the control.
    D. Redo the CBA.

14. Which of the following is a valid formula used to identify the projected benefits of a control?

    A. Loss after control − loss before control
    B. Loss before control − loss after control
    C. Cost of control + losses
    D. Cost of control /12

15. A CBA can be used to justify the purchase of a control.

    A. True
    B. False

Turning Your Risk Assessment into a Risk Mitigation Plan

O NCE THE RISK ASSESSMENT IS COMPLETE and approved, the next step is to create a risk mitigation plan. This plan will implement the approved countermeasures. If much time has passed since the risk assessment was completed, you may have to check some of the findings to ensure they are still valid. For example, some threats or vulnerabilities may have disappeared.

A significant part of the risk mitigation plan is the identification of costs. Ideally, the risk assessment will already have identified the costs, but some hidden costs may have been overlooked. If you discover additional costs, you'll need to recalculate the cost-benefit analysis. Lastly, it's important to follow up on the risk mitigation plan. This includes ensuring that all the approved countermeasures are implemented. It also includes ensuring the countermeasures mitigate the risks as expected.

Chapter 11 Topics

This chapter covers the following topics and concepts:

- What a review of a risk assessment is
- What translating a risk assessment into a risk mitigation plan entails
- How to prioritize risk elements
- What the verification of risk elements entails
- What a cost-benefit analysis for risk elements includes
- What implementing a risk mitigation plan includes
- How to follow up on a risk mitigation plan
- What best practices for enabling a risk mitigation plan are

Chapter 11 Goals

When you complete this chapter, you will be able to:

- Evaluate a risk assessment created for your IT infrastructure
- Describe the process to translate a risk assessment into a risk mitigation plan
- Discuss the importance of prioritizing risk elements
- Describe the process to verify what risk elements can be mitigated
- Perform a cost-benefit analysis for risk elements
- Describe the process of implementing a risk mitigation plan
- Describe the process to follow up on a risk mitigation plan
- List best practices for enabling a risk mitigation plan from a risk assessment

Review the Risk Assessment for Your IT Infrastructure

Once a risk assessment has been completed and approved, you can begin reviewing it for your IT infrastructure. Chapter 6 covered the process of performing a risk assessment. As a reminder, the risk assessment includes the following high-level steps:

- Identify and evaluate relevant threats.
- Identify and evaluate relevant vulnerabilities.
- Identify and evaluate countermeasures.
- Develop mitigating recommendations.

Next, management reviews the risk assessment. Management can approve, reject, or modify the recommendations. You then document the management decisions and include them in a plan of action and milestones document.

The following step is to translate the risk assessment into an actual risk mitigation plan. Before jumping into this, it's a good practice to review the risk assessment. When reviewing the risk assessment, you should pay special attention to the following key items:

- **In-place countermeasures**—The risk assessment may have addressed some of the countermeasures that are already being used. Some may need to be upgraded or reconfigured. Others may need to be replaced completely. If a countermeasure is to be replaced, you shouldn't remove the original countermeasure until the new one is ready to be installed.

- **Planned countermeasures**—A planned countermeasure is one that has been approved and has a date for implementation. Planned countermeasures are documented in the risk assessment. Review these countermeasures to determine their status. A countermeasure may have been installed since the risk assessment was published. It's also possible that the date the countermeasure will be implemented will affect the timeline for an approved countermeasure. You should document these countermeasures in the plan of action and milestones.

- **Approved countermeasures**—Approved countermeasures are the controls previously approved by management. They need to be added into the implementation pipeline. Some will be very easy to implement. Others may be complex and require extra steps. They may need to be purchased. They may need to be delegated. All will need to be tracked for completion.

Overlapping Countermeasures

Another important consideration when reviewing the plan is to determine if there is any overlap among the countermeasures. One mitigation countermeasure may resolve more than one risk. Additionally, some risks may be mitigated by more than one countermeasure.

The overlap may be purposeful or accidental. In other words, multiple countermeasures may be implemented for a single risk as a defense-in-depth strategy. This ensures that the risk is mitigated even if a countermeasure fails. An accidental overlap occurs when two or more countermeasures mitigate the same risk, but the overlap wasn't intentional. As long as the countermeasures aren't mitigating the same risk in the same way, this isn't a problem. However, you should be aware of any countermeasure overlaps.

If a countermeasure overlaps with another, check for conflicts. Although many security countermeasures work together, some countermeasures may cause problems for others.

For example, consider a vulnerability scanner and an intrusion detection system used to protect a server. You could configure the vulnerability scanner to scan this server on a daily basis. However, the intrusion detection system will likely alert on this scan. It will recognize the scan as a potential attack and provide notification. This notification could be an e-mail to a group of administrators.

In this example, the intrusion detection system alert is a false alert, or false positive. It requires an administrator to investigate and review the alert. Because the internal vulnerability scanner is causing the alert, it clearly isn't an actual attack. However, it still takes time to investigate.

This doesn't mean that either of the countermeasures should be avoided. However, there may be ways to avoid the conflict.

Perhaps you could program the intrusion detection system so that it doesn't alert on scans from this vulnerability scanner. It's possible that only a specific scan is detected. Perhaps you can program the scanner to skip this scan. If you can't avoid the conflict, you should at least educate personnel. Let them know what is causing the alert and stress that other alerts should be investigated thoroughly.

Attacks Ignored for a Full Weekend

A large network operations center had several countermeasures in place to detect attacks. These countermeasures provided notification to network operations center personnel on a large monitor viewable by all personnel.

On one weekend, an IDS alerted on a potential attack. One of the administrators investigated and realized it was a false alert. Three more alerts occurred in the next hour. Other administrators investigated. Each time they were false alerts.

These false alerts continued, but at some point in the next few hours, an actual attack started which also caused alerts. However, the administrators began to expect false alerts and gave all the alerts less and less attention. The IDS had become the IDS that cries wolf. When the real wolf was at the door, no one believed it. None of the alerts was recognized as valid.

When administrators came on duty Monday morning, they completed a review of activity and detected the actual attack. Luckily, the attack didn't take down any systems, but the attacker did gather reconnaissance data.

You should minimize false alerts, if possible. Personnel can get accustomed to seeing alerts and dismissing them without investigation. This activity of reducing false alerts is sometimes called "tuning the IDS." Without tuning, when a live attack occurs, personnel may dismiss it before even investigating.

As long as one countermeasure doesn't conflict with another, there is nothing wrong with having overlapping countermeasures. In fact, a defense-in-depth strategy encourages having more than one countermeasure for different risks. If one countermeasure fails or is circumvented, the other countermeasure will provide protection.

Matching Threats with Vulnerabilities

One of the methods you can use to determine if countermeasures overlap is to map the countermeasure to threat/vulnerability pairs. Chapter 1 covered matching threats with vulnerabilities to help determine a risk. You may remember the following formula:

$$\text{Risk} = \text{Threat} \times \text{Vulnerability}$$

A vulnerability is a weakness, and by itself it doesn't present a risk. Similarly, threats by themselves don't present a risk. A risk occurs when a threat exploits a vulnerability. Countermeasures either reduce or eliminate the impact of the threat or the vulnerability.

> ▶ **NOTE**
>
> Risk = Threat × Vulnerability isn't a mathematical formula. In other words, you don't assign numerical values to threats and vulnerabilities to determine a numerical value for risk. Instead, it shows that risks occur when both threats and vulnerabilities are combined.

> **FYI**
>
> Non-repudiation prevents individuals from denying they took an action. Audit logs include details on who performed an action by logging user names. Because the activity is logged, users can't deny they took the action. You lose effective non-repudiation if one user can use another user's account. The same goes for shared accounts where all team members use, for example, "admin." Some methods of logging include Internet Protocol (IP) addresses and computer names. This audit trail helps an investigator determine what actually happened.

For example, consider user accounts of terminated employees. As a best practice, accounts should be disabled when the employee leaves. This allows another employee to access the ex-employee's data. Once the data has been accessed, the account should be deleted.

Imagine a company that doesn't do anything to old accounts. Instead, they simply remain enabled. As long as the account is enabled, it can be accessed by anyone. Anyone with physical access and knowledge of the credentials can use the account.

If previous employees have physical access to the network, they can log on. Some networks will even allow them to log on remotely. They would have the same permissions as if they had never left the job. They could then access all of the same data as if they were an employee. They could read, modify, or delete the data.

Perhaps a previous employee still has friends on the job. The previous employee could give his or her credentials to a friend, and the friend could log on using the ex-employee's credentials.

At this point, you lose non-repudiation. If any of the activity is logged, it looks as if the ex-employee is taking the action. Imagine that Bob is an ex-employee but Sally learns his user name and password. Sally can log on as Bob. Audit logs may record what Sally does, but they record Bob's user name. This might send security personnel on a wild goose chase trying to determine how Bob gained access to the network.

In this situation, the vulnerability is that inactive accounts are still enabled. User accounts aren't managed, leaving them available even if they aren't needed. The threat is that a previous employee may log on and access the account, or someone else may use the account.

Identifying Countermeasures

You mitigate risks by adding countermeasures. Consider the risks from not disabling inactive accounts. You could choose to mitigate these risks with several countermeasures:

- **Create an account management policy**—An **account management policy** is a written policy that spells out exactly what should be done with accounts. The policy may cover much more than just ex-employee accounts. For example, it could also address the format used to create accounts, such as *firstname.lastname*. It could include requirements for an account lockout policy. It could include details for a password policy.

- **Create a script to check account usage**—You could task administrators with writing a script to identify inactive accounts. An inactive account could be defined as any account that hasn't been used in the last 30 days. The script could automatically disable the inactive accounts. It could also be scheduled to run automatically once a week, log the results, and e-mail the results to interested personnel.

- **Countermeasure physical access to employee areas**—You could control access to employee-only areas. This can be as simple as signs to discourage non-employees. You can also use physical locks, cipher locks, badges, or proximity cards.

Similarly, the risk assessment may determine that users are not using strong passwords or changing their passwords regularly. The vulnerability is that the passwords are weak. Password-cracking tools can easily crack weak passwords. The threat is that an attacker may use one of the many tools available to crack the weak password. Attackers can use the cracked passwords to log into a system or network.

The solution is to implement a **password policy**. A password policy is often part of an overall account management policy. You can enforce password policies using technical means. For example, Microsoft domains allow you to enforce strong password practices with Group Policy.

A password policy would specify the following:

> **TIP**
>
> Group Policy settings allow you to configure a setting once in a domain. This setting will then apply to all users and computers in the domain. If desired, you can also configure a Group Policy object to apply to specific users and computers. Once configured, Group Policy works the same with five users and computers as it does with 50,000 users and computers.

- **Password length**—Common recommended lengths are at least 8 characters for regular users and at least 15 characters for administrators. Although 15 characters may seem outrageous if you haven't used them, they are used. However, passphrases are commonly used instead of passwords. For example, a password could be IL0veR1$kM@n@gement. This is a complex 19-character password, but it isn't hard to remember.

- **Complexity**—The complexity refers to the mixture of characters. Complex passwords commonly have a mixture of at least three of the four character types. Character types are uppercase, lowercase, numbers, and special characters. Some requirements specify all four character types must be used. A complex password is more difficult to crack than a simple password.

- **Maximum age**—The maximum age identifies when the password must be changed. For example, a maximum age of 45 indicates the password must be changed at least every 45 days. Once the maximum age passes, the user is unable to log on until the password is changed.

- **Password history**—Some users will try to use one or two passwords. They use password 1 until they are forced to change the password and then they switch to password 2. When they are forced to change the password again, they switch back to password 1. They constantly swap back and forth between password 1 and password 2.

However, when password history is used, users are prevented from using a password they used before. When password history is used, it's common to remember the past 24 passwords. This prevents a user from reusing a password until he or she has used 24 other passwords.

- **Minimum age**—This prevents a user from changing his or her password until a minimum amount of time has passed. It's common to use one day as a minimum password age. This works with the password history. It prevents a user from changing a password right away to get back to his or her original password. With a password history set to 24 and the minimum age set to 1 day, a user would have to change the password every day for the next 25 days to get back to the original password. This makes it simply too difficult for a user to circumvent the intended policy. The user will instead comply with the intention of the policy, which is to change the password to a new password.

At this point, you can match the countermeasures with threat/vulnerability pairs. Table 11-1 shows the threat/vulnerability pairs matched to recommended countermeasures.

In the table, you can see that the account management policy is addressing two threat/vulnerability pairs. This can be valuable to know. If you recognize a single countermeasure is addressing multiple risks, you may decide to move the priority of the countermeasure higher.

Scripting as a Technical Countermeasure

Technical countermeasures don't have to be expensive. Some can be created at no cost with scripts, if your administrators have the expertise.

The difference between good administrators and great administrators is often the ability to write administrative scripts. Good administrators can get tasks done, but it often takes them longer. This is especially true for repetitive tasks. Great administrators can accomplish tasks much more quickly, and with very little effort.

One of the great benefits of scripts is that you can automate them. For example, imagine that you want to disable inactive accounts. You could write a script to identify and disable accounts that haven't been used in the last 30 days. You can then schedule that script to run every Saturday night. All accounts are automatically examined on a weekly basis and inactive accounts eliminated without any administrative effort.

Compare this to the administrator who can't script. The same tasks can still be accomplished. However, it will take time each week.

As administrators get more proficient with scripts, they can add additional bells and whistles. For example, it's possible for a script to log results or send an e-mail. After the script locates and disables inactive accounts, it can e-mail a list of accounts that were disabled.

Scripts can meet most administrative needs. A common saying among scripting administrators is "If you can envision it, you can script it."

TABLE 11-1 Matching threat/vulnerability pairs with countermeasures.		
THREAT	VULNERABILITY	COUNTERMEASURE(S)
Previous employee	Inactive accounts not disabled	Account management policy Script to deactivate accounts Restrict access to employees only
Weak passwords	Password-cracking tools launched by attacker	Account management policy Group Policy password policy

Translating Your Risk Assessment into a Risk Mitigation Plan

The next step is to translate your risk assessment into a risk mitigation plan. The mitigation plan will include the details on how and when to implement the countermeasures.

There are three important considerations when developing the mitigation plan. They are:

- Cost to implement the countermeasures
- Time to implement the countermeasures
- Operational impact of the countermeasures

Cost to Implement

You'll need to purchase many of the countermeasures you implement. It's important to be able to accurately identify the costs of these countermeasures. On the surface, the cost of the countermeasure may be simple to calculate. However, they are frequently hidden costs.

Costs can include the following items:

- Initial purchase cost
- Facility costs
- Installation costs
- Training costs

FYI

If you discover hidden costs, they may affect the decision to implement the countermeasure. If the difference between the original estimate and the actual cost is significant, the counter-measure may no longer be cost effective. In that case, the cost-benefit analysis should be redone. It the results show that the countermeasure changes the original cost-benefit analysis, the data should be presented to management. Management could decide to still go forward, or stop the purchase of the countermeasure.

One of the common problems that creep up in this stage is a lack of money. Ideally, the risk assessment accurately identified the cost of the countermeasure. However, if you discover new costs, you may have problems. The new cost may be beyond the original budgeted amount. This may move the cost of the countermeasure from a budgeted item to an unfunded requirement.

Unfunded requirements may simply have to wait until the next year for implementation.

Initial Purchase Cost

The cost of the initial purchase is the price of the product. For software, the cost is the retail price less any discounts given to the organization. For example, an organization could purchase a software vulnerability scanner. For hardware such as a router or server, the initial purchase cost is the price of the hardware.

Some countermeasures may be internally developed. For example, this chapter has mentioned scripts used as a countermeasure. If your organization has a talented administrator, he or she may be able to write the script easily. It won't take much time or prevent the completion of other tasks.

On the other hand, if scripting is a new function for the administrator, you may decide to calculate the labor costs. It will take a significant amount of time for the administrator to write the first script. Subsequent scripts become easier and easier to complete.

The initial purchase price is usually identified accurately in the risk assessment. If it's the purchase of a product, the price can be verified with the vendor.

Facility Costs

Facility requirements include space, power, and air conditioning. These requirements are sometimes overlooked. If they're needed but not identified, they can cause significant problems with your schedule. They may even affect the accuracy of the cost-benefit analysis.

> **NOTE**
>
> The figure shows spaces between the servers. These are open for the figure so that you can see the different components. However, in an actual bay, these spaces won't be there. Either the server and components are mounted right on top of each other, or metal plates are installed to cover the spaces. These plates help counteract the airflow through the bay.

Many people have the impression that a server room has unlimited space, but that's rarely the case. Servers are usually mounted in equipment bays. Equipment bays are about the width and depth of a home refrigerator and about six feet tall. Figure 11-1 shows how equipment is mounted in an equipment bay. Notice that the bays hold more than just servers.

The bay on the left has four large servers. They could be large 32-processor systems with 2 terabytes (TB) of memory. The bay on the right has seven smaller servers. These could be smaller four-processor systems with 32 gigabytes (GB) of RAM. The applications hosted on the servers dictate the size. For example, a database server hosting a very large database requires more resources than a file server used to host user files.

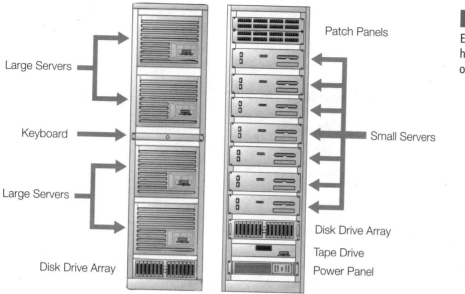

Large Servers

Keyboard

Large Servers

Disk Drive Array

Patch Panels

Small Servers

Disk Drive Array

Tape Drive

Power Panel

FIGURE 11-1

Equipment bays hosting servers and other components.

Equipment bays commonly host other components. For example, the figure shows patch panels, a disk drive array, a tape drive array, and more.

Now imagine that these are the only two bays in your server room. The mitigation plan calls for adding two additional servers. Where will they go? They won't fit into the existing bays. You either have to remove equipment from these bays or add another bay. If this requirement wasn't identified before, it will add additional cost for the countermeasure.

Besides space, you should also consider air conditioning and power requirements. AC units provide a certain level of cooling power. Consider a home. The AC unit needed to keep a 1,000-square-foot home cool is much smaller than one needed to keep a 3,000-square-foot home cool. Similarly, the AC unit used to keep two bays cool may not be able to keep three bays cool.

Power is another consideration. There are two things to consider with power—power capacity and power source.

First, you need to ensure that the room can support the additional power. Again, think of a home. If you connect multiple power adapters so you can plug 15 different kitchen appliances into a single outlet, you'll have problems. Circuit breakers will pop. Worse, you may start a fire. That single outlet has a limit. Similarly, a server room has a limit.

If the power supplied to the server room is already at its limit, you cannot support the additional servers and equipment bays until additional power is added. Routing additional power to the server room will add additional cost for the countermeasure.

Second, you may need to ensure the power is supplied by different sources. Failover clusters add additional servers for redundancy. If any single server fails in a failover cluster, another server will pick up the load, ensuring that the service continues to function. However, what if power fails? A power failure can be a single point of failure.

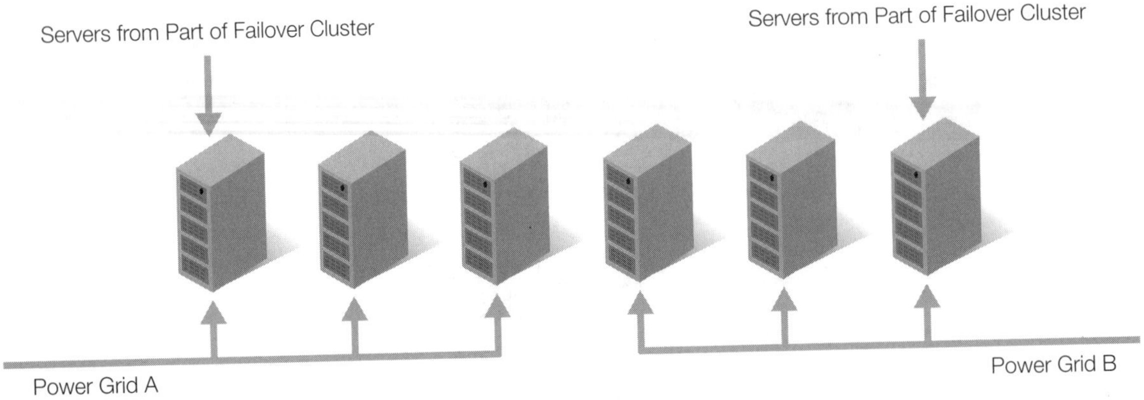

FIGURE 11-2

Failover cluster servers connected to different power grids.

Different servers in failover clusters are sometimes placed on different power grids. Consider Figure 11-2. In the figure, the equipment bays on the left are connected to Power Grid A. The equipment bays on the right are connected to Power Grid B. You could place some of the failover cluster servers in the bay on the far left and some of the servers in the bay on the far right.

If Power Grid A suffers a failure, the servers on Power Grid B will still operate. Of course, this configuration requires that your server room have power from different power grids. If it doesn't, you can consider alternatives. You could modify the power to bring power into the room from a different power grid. Some organizations place failover cluster servers in different locations to ensure that each is on a different power grid.

Another method of providing alternative sources is using a different **uninterruptible power supply (UPS)**. A UPS can be a simple portable unit you may use on your home computer. It can also be a full room filled with banks of batteries.

If power fails, the UPS will provide power for a short amount of time. For some less critical systems, a UPS allows a system to shut down logically. For critical systems, a UPS gives time for generators to power on and stabilize. After the generators stabilize, power is switched from the UPS system to the generators. The generators provide long-term power.

Most countermeasures won't require additional facility costs. However, if facility costs are required, the overall costs for the countermeasure will increase significantly. These additional costs may be so high that the cost-benefit analysis shows that it no longer makes fiscal sense to add the countermeasure.

Installation Costs

In-house administrators will install most countermeasures. However, some sophisticated countermeasures may require outside help. Occasionally, it's worth the extra expense to have the vendor install and configure the countermeasure so that you're sure it has been installed correctly. This decision is often dependent on the level of expertise you have on staff.

Consider a small school with a library. It has not received any E-Rate funding discounts from the Federal Communications Commission (FCC) in the past. These discounts subsidize the cost of Internet access. However, the library wants to apply for the discounts. They must comply with the Children's Internet Protection Act (CIPA). CIPA requires the library to filter the content to ensure that children are protected from offensive content.

The library could decide to purchase a proxy server to comply. The proxy server can be used with a subscription to filter offensive content. However, the school may not have the expertise to install and configure the proxy server easily. Instead of taking the chance of making mistakes and being on the wrong side of the CIPA law, the school could decide to outsource this.

In this example, the installation costs will add to the cost of the countermeasure.

Training Costs

Another overlooked cost is training. The new countermeasure may be the greatest thing since the invention of the personal computer. However, if no one knows how to operate it, it will sit in the corner gathering dust. Technical training can be quite expensive. It could cost as much as $3,500 to send a single administrator to a weeklong training session.

Many companies will also host training at your location. Costs may be as much as $20,000 to send a trainer to your site and train 15 or so people.

As you can see, technical training costs can quickly add up. As with other costs, they can significantly add to the total cost of a countermeasure. If training requirements haven't been identified before, you want to ensure they are identified before you start. In addition to the final cost, they may also affect the schedule. You may need to delay the implementation of the countermeasure until you're able to get personnel trained.

Time to Implement

The time to implement the countermeasure can vary widely. Some implementations can be completed within days or weeks. Others may take months. It's important to consider the entire process when identifying timelines.

For example, consider the creation of a written account management policy. On the surface, this may seem like a simple and quick procedure. If you're the security expert, you can probably draft an account management policy within a day. However, this is not *your* account management policy. All policies need senior management approval and buy-in. Your draft needs to be routed to senior management for review.

> **▷ TIP**
>
> A risk assessment includes a plan of action and milestones (POAM). Once you've identified the time and schedule for a countermeasure, you will need to update the POAM with this data. The POAM is a valuable tracking tool, especially for complex projects.

It's highly likely that management will want changes. Some may be stylistic and others may be content-related. However in order to get management buy-in, it needs to be their policy. The more changes they make, the more they own it. If a policy isn't edited at least once, be concerned. It could be that management really isn't buying into it.

A policy owned by management will be supported by management. If management doesn't support the policy, no one will.

▶ **TIP**

Tracking of any countermeasure is important. This doesn't have to be complex. It just has to be accurate. For example, if a policy is submitted to the CIO for review, you can document this with a comment in your POAM or other tracking document. The comment can be as simple as "submitted draft to CIO on April 14th."

Although management review of a policy may only take 20 minutes, it doesn't mean it will be done in the 20 minutes after you complete the first draft. Unless there's been a recent high-level security incident, a written security policy is not likely to be a top priority. It will take time to rise to the top of the manager's in-pile.

With all this mind, you may decide to estimate 30 days for the completion of the policy. You'll draft it in a day and submit it. It may take a couple of weeks to route through proper management personnel. You'll make changes and then resubmit it for final approval and signature. This may take another week or so before the policy is finally approved.

Some timelines could be much more complex. For example, imagine that Figure 11-3 represents your current Web server configuration. The Web server is in the demilitarized zone (DMZ) and accesses a back-end database hosted on a server. It supports an online business that has enjoyed explosive growth in the past two years. It's currently generating millions of dollars in revenue a year.

A recent outage resulted in tens of thousands dollars in lost sales. Combined with indirect costs, management estimates they lost over $100,000.

Management has approved an upgrade. You will purchase additional servers to create the configuration shown in Figure 11-4. You will also expand the Web server to a **Web farm**. The back-end database server will be protected with a failover cluster.

A Web farm is multiple servers using **network load balancing**. The first client connects to Web 1, the next client connects to Web 2, and so on. At any given time, each of the servers has about the same load. Web farms allow an organization to scale out easily.

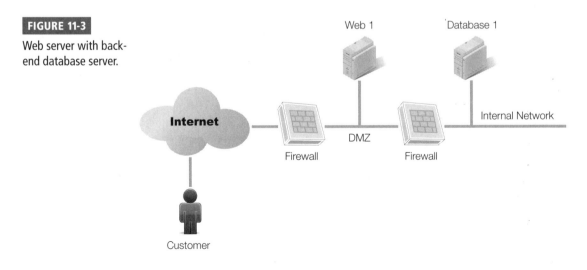

FIGURE 11-3

Web server with back-end database server.

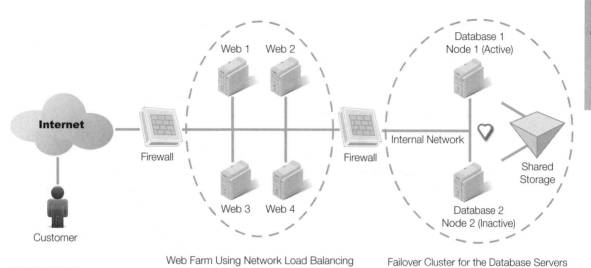

Web 1   Web 2

Web 3   Web 4

Internet

Customer

Firewall

Firewall

Internal Network

Database 1
Node 1 (Active)

Database 2
Node 2 (Inactive)

Shared
Storage

Web Farm Using Network Load Balancing

Failover Cluster for the Database Servers

FIGURE 11-4

Here a single Web server has been replaced by a Web farm.

For example, an administrator can add a server to the Web farm if there is a surge in demand. Additionally, if one of the servers in the Web farm fails, network load balancing ensures that clients aren't directed to the failed server.

Failover clusters were presented in Chapter 7. As a reminder, the failover cluster provides fault tolerance for the database server. Node 1 is active and Node 2 is inactive. Node 2 monitors the health of Node 1 by monitoring its heartbeat. If Node 1 fails, Node 2 takes over.

Clearly, there are differences between Figures 11-3 and 11-4. The new configuration adds four servers and two different technologies. It will require much more planning than the implementation of a written account policy.

There are several things to consider. The server room may not have equipment bay space. The added servers may exceed the power capabilities of the room. Air conditioning capacity may need to be added. Your timeline could include the following steps:

> **TIP**
>
> When a system or service has additional demand, you should be able to scale up or scale out. **Scale up** means that you add additional resources to a server. For example, you could upgrade the processor or add additional RAM. **Scale out** means that you add additional servers to the service. A Web farm with network load balancing supports scaling up without changing the core application. In this case, the core application is the Web application hosted on the Web servers.

- **Add additional equipment bay(s)**—The bay should be the same size as other bays and be installed the same way. This will ensure it takes full advantage of the existing air conditioning. This is assuming the room will support another bay. If not, your problem may be bigger.

- **Add additional air conditioning capacity**—You may need to add an additional unit, or upgrade the existing unit.
- **Add power from different power source**—If your facility supports it, you may choose to separate the power. For example, you can reroute power so that two of the Web servers and one of the failover cluster nodes are on different power. This helps prevent a loss of power from taking down the Web site.
- **Balance servers on different power grids**—If you add additional power sources, you may need to balance all the servers in the server room.
- **Purchase servers and hardware**—Additional servers need to be supported for the plan. The plan may require six additional servers, or four additional servers. The two database servers in the failover cluster need to have matching hardware. Additionally, they should be designed to work with a failover cluster. This usually requires purchasing dedicated servers. The old database server may work in the new Web farm. If desired, all the servers in the Web farm could be upgraded.
- **Provide training to administrators**—Configuring and administering failover clusters can become complex. If administrators haven't worked with a failover cluster before, they will need training. Network load balancing is easy to work with, but training may also be needed for it.

▶ **TIP**

All of this is time consuming and expensive. However, remember that a recent outage resulted in the loss of over $100,000. The cost is justified. Moreover, the countermeasure is needed to ensure the availability of the Web site that is generating so much revenue.

- **Install servers and configure**—How you do this may also depend on the experience of your administrators. The installation and configuration of the failover clusters may be outsourced. For example, companies that sell failover cluster solutions frequently provide installation support.
- **Test**—Before you go live, you want to ensure that the Web farm and failover cluster work as expected. There are bound to be some technical issues that need to be resolved. After testing shows the bugs have been worked out, you're ready to go live.
- **Implement**—The original configuration is switched over to the new configuration. You may use a phased implementation. For example, you may implement the Web farm first. Once it's stable, you can implement the failover cluster.

Operational Impact

There is often a tradeoff with security. The more secure you make a system, the harder it is to use. On the other hand, the easier it is to use, the less secure it is. In short, any countermeasure can have an impact on normal operations.

You should identify the operational impact as early as possible. You may be able to take steps to minimize this impact.

For example, you may be considering beefing up your firewall security. The goal is to minimize the traffic allowed through the firewall. You can implement an implicit deny philosophy.

An **implicit deny** philosophy starts by blocking all traffic. Only traffic that is explicitly allowed by a rule can pass through the firewall. Even if the firewall doesn't have a rule to explicitly deny certain traffic, it is implicitly denied.

The challenge is to identify what traffic is allowed. You can block all traffic and wait until people complain but that method is sure to impact operations.

A better method is to enable extensive logging on the existing firewall or router. You can then analyze this log to determine what traffic is passing through. You can import most logs into other tools for better analysis. For example, you can import a text log into a database to review the data. You'll be able to analyze the data in a database much easier than in a text file.

It's important to realize that just because traffic is going through the network, it doesn't mean it should be. For example, the written security policy may state that Network News Transfer Protocol (NNTP) traffic is restricted. NNTP uses port 119. A review of the traffic log may show a substantial amount of traffic using port 119.

Traffic that looks unfamiliar should be investigated. You shouldn't just block unfamiliar traffic without consideration. For example, you may have a lot of traffic using port 5678. Although this isn't familiar to you, it may be legitimate. Your company may have a line of business (LOB) application used for ordering parts and supplies from vendors. If you block this port, you'll block the application. Employees will no longer be able to use the LOB application to order parts and supplies. Clearly, that will have a detrimental effect on operations.

> **NOTE**
> NNTP newsgroups are often a source of malware. Attackers spam the newsgroups with infected malware, or with links to malicious Web sites. Uneducated users can cause problems for their computer or the network. Because of this, many networks prevent all NNTP traffic.

Prioritizing Risk Elements That Require Risk Mitigation

One of the ways that you can identify the most important countermeasures is by prioritizing the risk elements. Risks occur when a threat exploits a vulnerability. In other words, the risk elements are the threats and the vulnerabilities.

If you've taken the time to match the countermeasures with the threat/vulnerability pairs, this step is a little easier to complete. You'll only need to provide values for the threats and vulnerabilities.

Using a Threat/Vulnerability Matrix

The National Institute of Standards and Technology (NIST) Special Publication 800-30 provides guidelines on evaluating threats and vulnerabilities. Chapter 1 presented these in greater depth. As a reminder, Table 11-2 shows a sample threat/likelihood impact-matrix.

Threats can negatively affect confidentiality, integrity, or availability. You evaluate the severity of the threat by identifying the likelihood it will affect one of these. You evaluate the impact by determining the extent to which it will affect confidentiality, integrity, or availability.

TABLE 11-2 A threat/likelihood-impact matrix.			
	LOW IMPACT (10)	**MEDIUM IMPACT (50)**	**HIGH IMPACT (100)**
High threat likelihood 100 percent (1.0)	$10 \times 1 = 10$	$50 \times 1 = 50$	$100 \times 1 = 100$
Medium threat likelihood 50 percent (.50)	$10 \times .5 = 5$	$50 \times .5 = 25$	$100 \times .5 = 50$
Low threat likelihood 10 percent (.10)	$10 \times .1 = 1$	$50 \times .1 = 5$	$100 \times .1 = 10$

> **FYI**
>
> The numerical values assigned to the word values can be different if desired. For example, a low impact could be assigned a value of zero instead of 10. A high likelihood could be assigned a value of 90 percent instead of 100 percent. Additionally, you can have more than three data points and you can use different names. You can use something different from Low, Medium, and High. For example, you could use Low, Moderately Low, Moderate, Moderately Severe, and Severe.

Prioritizing Countermeasures

You can use the threat/vulnerability matrix to prioritize the risks and countermeasures. Risks with higher scores result in a higher loss and should be addressed before risks with lower scores.

You evaluate threats and vulnerabilities based on current in-place countermeasures. For example, if an organization was not using any antivirus software, there is a high likelihood that systems would become infected. If several systems became infected, the impact would also be high. A high likelihood of 100 percent times a high impact of 100 gives a score of 100.

However, you may have antivirus software installed on all your systems. In the past year, imagine that only one malware incident caused problems after a single user disabled the antivirus software. The malware tried to spread but was quickly detected by antivirus software on other systems. In this example, there is a low likelihood and a low impact giving a score of one.

Table 11-3 shows an example of how the threat likelihood impact-matrix can be used to prioritize threats. Each of the threats is assigned a likelihood and impact based on current countermeasures.

With this data, you can see the biggest current threats are the two with a score of 50:

- Attacks on DMZ servers
- Loss of data on key database server

You may choose to address the recommended countermeasures for these threats first.

The attacks on DMZ servers are a threat because these servers are updated only once every six months. Remember, these updates are intended to fix bugs and vulnerabilities that have been discovered since the software was released. If the bugs aren't fixed, the servers are vulnerable. Many attackers look for servers that do not have recent patches installed, giving this risk a high likelihood.

In this case, the solution is simple. You would implement a countermeasure to ensure that the servers are up to date. There are many ways this can be done. You should use the one recommended and approved in the risk assessment.

Similarly, there are a couple of holes in the backup procedures. First, backups aren't reliable. This could be because there is no backup plan or no backup procedures. It could be because test restores are never done to test the backups. A common countermeasure to fix this is to develop a backup plan. You could also develop backup procedures. The plan could include a requirement to perform test restores on a weekly basis.

TABLE 11-3 Threat scores used to prioritize threats.

THREAT	LIKELIHOOD	IMPACT	SCORE
Attacks on DMZ servers Servers in the DMZ are currently updated only once every six months.	High Value of 100 percent	Medium Value of 50	50
Loss of data on key database server Backups are currently done on the database server daily but recent restore attempts were not successful.	Medium Value of 50 percent	High Value of 100	50
Loss of data due to fire Backups are done regularly but stored in the server room.	Low Value of 10 percent	High Value of 100	10
Malware infection Antivirus software is currently installed on all systems.	Low Value of 10 percent	Low Value of 10	1

Test Restores as Part of a Backup Plan

A common management saying is that you can't manage what you can't measure. This includes the effectiveness of backups. However, you can measure the effectiveness of your backups by regularly performing test restores and tracking the success rate.

Test restores are frequently mandated as part of a backup plan. A test restore simply retrieves a backup tape and attempts to restore data from it. If the data can be restored, the test was successful. If the data cannot be restored, the test is not successful. An unsuccessful test should be investigated.

A test may be unsuccessful due to many reasons:

- **The tape could be old or corrupt**—You should reevaluate the length of time tapes are kept in rotation or consider purchasing higher quality tapes.
- **The tape drive could be faulty**—The problem needs to be fixed as soon as possible. If the drive is faulty, all of the backups are suspect.
- **The backup procedures could be faulty**—The procedures should be reviewed and corrected. If the procedures are incorrect, all of the backups could have problems.

Whatever the problem, the good news is that you've discovered it before a crisis. If actual data was lost and couldn't be restored, the problem would be much more serious.

Companies that measure backups often strive for a success rate of over 95 percent. Companies that don't measure the effectiveness of their backups could have a success rate anywhere from zero percent to 100 percent. They just don't know until data is lost if the data can be restored or not.

The threat scores aren't necessarily perfect. They do take a little human interaction to ensure that the organization's needs are met. For example, the threat of "loss of data due to a fire" has a score of 10. Just because this score is less than the two scores of 50 doesn't mean it can't be addressed earlier.

Management may decide that even though the score is low, the impact is sufficiently high that it needs to be addressed as soon as possible. The countermeasure for this threat is simple. Store a copy of backup tapes off site.

Verifying Risk Elements and How These Risks Can Be Mitigated

When converting the risk assessment into a risk mitigation plan, you may need to verify the risk elements. As mentioned previously, the risk assessment is a point in time assessment. However, things change.

If too much time has passed since completion of the risk assessment, it's important to verify the risk elements. In other words, you need to ensure the threats and vulnerabilities you're trying to mitigate still exist. Additionally, you'll need to verify the approved countermeasure can still mitigate the current risk.

You can use the same steps to verify the risk elements used in the risk assessment. For example, the risk assessment may have used a vulnerability scanner that discovered a SQL injection vulnerability. A penetration test could have been used to verify that the vulnerability could be exploited.

Imagine that it took three months for the risk assessment to be approved. You could then perform the same vulnerability scan to see if the vulnerability remained. If so, you could rerun the penetration test. If you can exploit the vulnerability, the risk remains.

However, in this example, it's possible that the vulnerability has been resolved. Application and database developers may have taken immediate steps to resolve the problem. Many programming techniques can mitigate this risk. None are that difficult. They are usually omitted simply because application developers are unaware of the risks.

The original solution may have been the purchase of a product. However, if the risk is no longer present, you shouldn't spend the money on the countermeasure.

In this example, it's worthwhile reevaluating the risk and the solution. You can interview the application developers to determine what they did to resolve the vulnerability. You can then evaluate the solution to determine its effectiveness.

> **NOTE**
>
> If the turnaround between approval of the risk assessment and the start of the mitigation plan is quick, this step is less important. The risk assessment would have identified the risk elements and recommended steps to mitigate them. Management then approved these steps.

> **TIP**
>
> One way to prevent SQL injection attacks is with the use of stored procedures to validate input. A stored procedure is a type of script or mini program used within a database application. Instead of using data entered by users directly, data is passed to a stored procedure. The stored procedure validates the data before it is used. The stored procedure rejects the type of invalid data used in a SQL injection attack.

You may even decide to recommend this solution as a countermeasure. You would write a policy to ensure that all code is written to ensure it isn't vulnerable to SQL injection attackers. You could also ensure that all applications are tested for SQL injection vulnerability prior to release.

Performing a Cost-Benefit Analysis on the Identified Risk Elements

A cost-benefit analysis (CBA) helps determine if you should use a countermeasure. If the benefits of a countermeasure are more than the costs, the countermeasure provides benefits. If the benefits of the countermeasure are less than the cost of the countermeasure, the countermeasure does not provide benefits.

If you have two possible countermeasures that will mitigate the same risk, you can complete two CBAs. Each of the CBAs will document the benefit of the individual counter-measures. You can then easily choose the countermeasure that provides the best benefits.

Calculate the CBA

Chapters 1 and 10 both presented details on how to perform a CBA. You start by identifying the losses you expect before, or without, the countermeasure. You then identify the losses you expect after implementing the countermeasure. This gives you the projected benefits. The formula is:

Loss before countermeasure − Loss after countermeasure = Projected benefits

Next, you identify the cost of the countermeasure. You then subtract the cost of the countermeasure from the projected benefits.

Projected benefits − Cost of countermeasure

If the result is a positive value, the countermeasure provides cost benefits. It the cost of the countermeasure is more than the benefits, it doesn't provide cost benefits. If the values are close to each other, you can calculate the return on investment (ROI).

The most important part of this process is identifying the costs and benefits. The goal is to identify both tangible and intangible values. If you don't accurately identify the costs and benefits, the CBA loses its value and may need to be redone.

It can take a significant amount of time to complete an accurate CBA. Because of this, you would not perform a CBA on every possible recommended countermeasure. For example, if an administrator can write a script to mitigate a risk, the countermeasure has almost zero cost. There's no need to perform a CBA for the administrator to write the script. On the other hand, a failover cluster can be very expensive. It adds servers and can add additional facilities costs.

A CBA Report

There is not a single format for a CBA report. However, it is valuable to create the CBAs consistently, especially within the same project.

For example, you may need to create two CBAs for different countermeasures that will mitigate the same risk. Management doesn't want to purchase both countermeasures. Instead, they want to determine which countermeasure will provide the greatest benefit. If both CBAs are completed using the same methods, and in the same format, the decision is easier.

The following elements are commonly included in any CBA report for a countermeasure:

- **Recommended countermeasure**—Identify the countermeasure in as much detail as possible. For example, if a failover cluster was recommended, the countermeasure would include the required purchases such as two matched servers and additional failover cluster hardware.

- **Risk to be mitigated**—Provide details of the threat/vulnerability pair that result in the risk. Include the likelihood and impact of the threat if a threat matrix method was used to prioritize the risk. If the countermeasure is eliminating a vulnerability, include an overview of how the reduction is accomplished. If the countermeasure is reducing a vulnerability, include an estimate of the success. For example, if the countermeasure is expected to reduce incidents from 10 a year to one a year, you would state it here.

- **Annual projected benefits**—Calculate direct and indirect benefits as an annual monetary value. Determine the benefits by calculating losses with and without the control. For example, imagine there's a 25 percent chance of a service failing once a year. When it fails, it results in a loss of $20,000. A countermeasure can reduce this risk to zero. The annual benefit is $20,000 × .25, or $5,000.

- **Initial costs**—State the initial costs to implement the countermeasure here. This would include the purchase price and any indirect costs. Indirect costs include items such as training and the cost to modify the environment. You may need to add power capability. You may need to upgrade air conditioning. You may need to tighten physical access countermeasures.

- **Annual or recurring costs**—Some countermeasures will require ongoing costs to maintain the countermeasure. For example, you could purchase a proxy server to filter Internet content. A proxy server can restrict users from going to specific Web sites. You can also purchase a subscription to a content filter company for specific categories. For example, if you don't want users going to gambling sites, you can subscribe to a service that will block access to such sites. Subscriptions have ongoing costs.

- **A comparison of the costs and benefits**—This is the primary purpose of the report. If the costs are less than the benefits, the countermeasure provides a benefit. If the costs are greater than the benefits, then the cost does not provide a benefit. If the results are close, you can calculate a ROI.

- **Recommendation**—Recommend the countermeasure if it provides a benefit. Don't recommend it if it does not provide a benefit.

Implementing a Risk Mitigation Plan

The next step is to implement the risk mitigation plan. This is where you put the counter-measures into place. When implementing a risk mitigation plan you should have two primary goals:

- Stay within budget
- Stay on schedule

Any project will have unknowns and surprises. However, advance planning will reduce these unknowns to a minimum. This is especially true for complex countermeasures. If you haven't completed adequate planning, you may find your project going over budget, or frequently delayed.

Either problem could cause management to change their mind on the value of the countermeasure. If it costs too much or takes too long to implement, the value of the countermeasure will be questioned.

Stay Within Budget

Consider the addition of a Web farm and failover cluster presented earlier in the chapter. These are being added to decrease outages, or increase availability of the Web site. This is an example of a complex countermeasure.

If your advance planning identified all of the costs to implement the plan, the project will be relatively smooth. However, if you did not identify any of the costs, the project will have problems. You could experience problems in any of the following areas:

- **Initial purchase costs**—The equipment will be expensive. Servers used in a failover cluster have specific technical requirements. If someone chose to cut costs and buy cheaper servers at the expense of the failover cluster requirements, you may see additional problems. It may take extensive testing to ultimately determine if the cheaper servers will be reliable in the failover cluster.

- **Facility costs**—The purchased servers may not fit in the existing equipment bays. The addition of the servers may overload the power fed to the room. Circuit breakers could pop, resulting in outages for other servers. Air conditioning may be inadequate. The room could overheat with additional servers in the room, resulting in equipment damage to existing servers. Any of these problems could be substantial if not addressed earlier.

- **Installation costs**—If your in-house personnel don't have the expertise to install the countermeasure, it may require additional expense for a professional installation. If not planned beforehand, this will delay the project. Technicians will try first. It'll only be after they expend valuable labor hours trying to install and configure the countermeasure before they realize they can't get it to work. Worse, their efforts may actually damage the countermeasure.

- **Training costs**—If technicians don't know how to operate the countermeasure, it may just sit in the corner gathering dust. Yes, it is a fancy new server that can do great and wonderful things, but if no one knows how to use it, it may stay in the box, or stay turned off after being installed in the bay. You face a delay in implementation until personnel are trained.

Any of these additional costs could easily bust the budget. If the cost of the countermeasure exceeds the allocated budget, management could decide to pull the plug on the countermeasure. Remember, each time an additional cost is identified, the CBA needs to be reevaluated. The original decision to implement the countermeasure was based on the original costs. As the costs go up, the value of the countermeasure goes down.

Stay on Schedule

An important consideration for any project is the schedule. Plan tasks to ensure they occur in a specific order. If any task is delayed, it may delay other tasks. These delays may affect the actual implementation date.

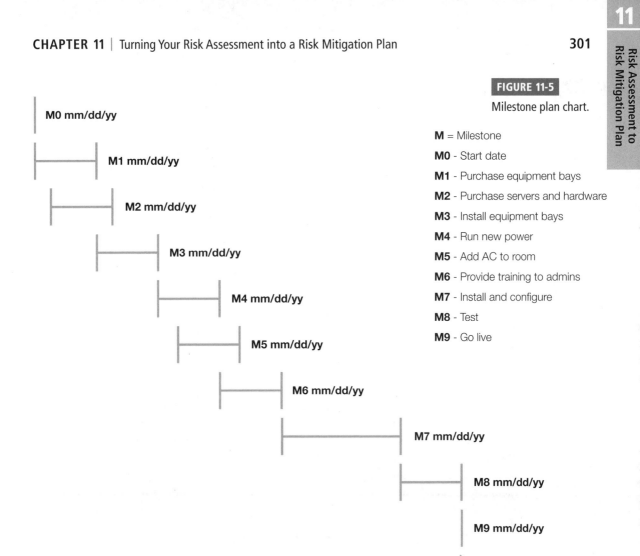

FIGURE 11-5

Milestone plan chart.

M = Milestone
M0 - Start date
M1 - Purchase equipment bays
M2 - Purchase servers and hardware
M3 - Install equipment bays
M4 - Run new power
M5 - Add AC to room
M6 - Provide training to admins
M7 - Install and configure
M8 - Test
M9 - Go live

One of the tools you can use to help you stay on schedule is a milestone chart. Figure 11-5 shows an example milestone chart for the Web server upgrade discussed in this chapter. Project management software is available that can be used to easily create a chart similar to this.

When using project management software, you can enter the milestone dates, and the length of any specific tasks. The software then allows you to display the data in multiple formats.

For example, Figure 11-6 shows the same project in a Gantt chart format. Once you enter the data into the project management software, it's relatively easy to show the data in an alternate format. Often it only requires a few clicks of the mouse.

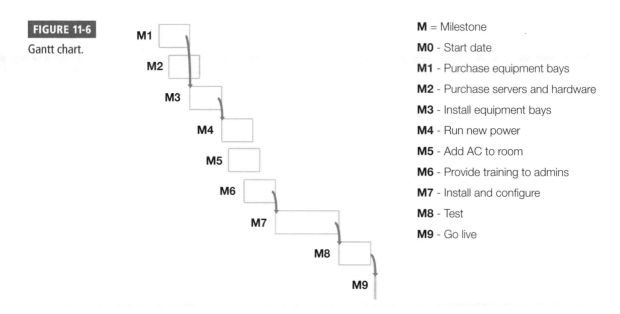

FIGURE 11-6

Gantt chart.

It's important to realize that some tasks are dependent on each other. For example, you need to install new equipment bays before you run power to the bays. The timing of the training is important. If it's provided too early, it won't be fresh when the technicians need to install the equipment. If it's provided too late, they may need to install the equipment without the training, or the project schedule could slip.

A critical path chart will show dependencies. Figure 11-7 shows an example of a critical path chart. If any of the items in the critical path slip, the entire project will be delayed. Managers need to pay much closer attention to items on the critical path than other items.

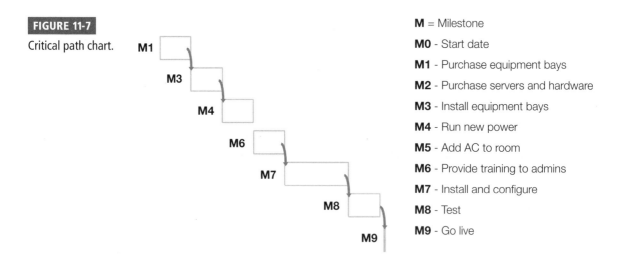

FIGURE 11-7

Critical path chart.

For example, milestones 2 and 5 are not on the critical path. The purchase of the servers and hardware, and the addition of AC to the room can be delayed. Of course, these can't be delayed indefinitely. When it's time to install and configure the servers, these milestones must be met. Early in the project, milestones 2 and 5 could be given less attention as the manager focuses on the critical path milestones.

The tools you use aren't as important as realizing there are tools available. For simple projects, you may be able to sketch out the schedule on a napkin. However, larger projects benefit from the more sophisticated project management tools available.

Following Up on the Risk Mitigation Plan

An important part of management is follow-up. You need to ensure that plans are implemented as expected. The risk management plan is no exception. When following up on risk mitigation plans, include the following two elements:

- Ensure countermeasures are implemented
- Ensure security gaps have been closed

Ensuring Countermeasures Are Implemented

The primary tool you'll use to ensure countermeasures are implemented is the POAM. The POAM is created with the risk assessment. However, the POAM is a living document. It is regularly updated. As the risk assessment transforms into a risk mitigation plan, the POAM document will expand.

The POAM will include all the approved countermeasures, and their timelines. A simple countermeasure may have only one or two milestones. However, a complex countermeasure could have multiple milestones. If you meet the milestones as expected, you have a much better chance of ensuring the schedule is met. In other words, you don't need to focus on the final date as much as you need to focus on the milestone dates.

> **NOTE**
>
> You may also create a separate POAM exclusively for the risk mitigation plan. For example, the POAM in the risk assessment may require the creation of a risk mitigation plan by a specific date. The most important point is that a method of tracking the implementation must exist.

If you miss a single milestone, the entire project may be delayed. As mentioned previously, the critical path chart can be invaluable in determining which milestones the project must complete in a timely manner.

When you use project management software to implement a countermeasure, you can often determine with a quick glance if it's on schedule. Project management software uses color-coded status symbols. For example, a green circle could indicate the project is on schedule. A yellow circle could indicate the project is slightly delayed. A red circle could indicate a severe delay.

Ensuring Security Gaps Have Been Closed

You should also ensure that the countermeasures are working as expected. Remember, the purpose of the countermeasure is to mitigate a risk. It should either reduce the impact of a threat, or reduce a vulnerability.

This is the same with any product. It should work as expected. You may watch an infomercial and become convinced that an advertised product will help you lose weight, or make you rich, or increase your health. However, when you receive it, if it doesn't perform up to expectations, you have wasted your money.

Not all countermeasures perform as expected. The only way you'll discover this is to do some testing and evaluation. Some countermeasures are easier to evaluate than others.

For example, imagine that a vulnerability scanner detected a vulnerability. The risk assessment then recommended a countermeasure to eliminate the vulnerability. After you implement the countermeasure, you can run the same vulnerability scan. If the risk isn't detected, the security gap has been closed. However, if the risk is still present, the security gap remains open. You'll need to take additional steps. You don't necessarily have to redo the risk assessment from the beginning, but you should address the gap.

Consider the Web farm and failover cluster example. The goal was to eliminate outages and increase availability. An outage will show that the solution isn't working. However, an outage will cost money in lost revenue. You can perform testing to measure the successful implementation of the countermeasure. Some tests and measurements you can use are:

- **Measure the load on the Web farm**—During normal operation, the load should be balanced among servers. You can measure the load using load-balancing software. You can also measure the resources on each individual server. The processor, memory, network card, and disk usage of each server should be about equal.

- **Remove a server from the Web farm**—This simulates the failure of a server in the Web farm. The failure of a single server should not affect the entire farm. In other words, if a server is removed from the Web farm, the other servers should pick up the load. Additionally, new clients should not be referred to the nonexistent server.

> **TIP**
>
> You can regularly swap nodes during the lifetime of a failover cluster. A common reason to do so is for maintenance. For example, you can update Node 2 while Node 1 is active. Later, you could bring Node 2 online and make it active. This allows you to take Node 1 down to update it.

- **Add a server to the Web farm**—If your Web site experiences more growth, you should be able to add another Web server to the Web farm. The network load-balancing software should then balance the load with the new server. This allows the Web farm to scale up. You can add additional clients to the service without changing the actual service.

- **Transfer nodes on the failover cluster logically**—Failover clusters include software that can be used to swap nodes. Node 1 could be active and Node 2 inactive. You can switch Node 2 to inactive and Node 1 active. If this is unsuccessful when done logically, it won't succeed if Node 1 actually fails.

- **Shut down the active node on the failover cluster**—If logical transfers work, you can simulate an actual failure of the active node. Failover clusters usually identify a specific procedure used to simulate a failure. The inactive node should sense the failure and failover. The inactive node should become active. If the test fails, you can quickly switch back with minimal impact on the operations. Testing of failover clusters can affect the service provided by the failover cluster. Testing should be done during a slow period and with a lot of forethought and planning. One of the primary considerations is the ability to return the system to normal if the system fails.

Remember, the goal of any testing and evaluation is to ensure that the countermeasure has acceptably closed the security gap. If the security gap isn't closed, management needs to be informed of the remaining, or residual risk. Management may decide the gap has been closed satisfactorily. They may also decide that you need to identify an additional countermeasure to further mitigate the risk.

Best Practices for Enabling a Risk Mitigation Plan from Your Risk Assessment

The following list identifies several best practices you can follow when enabling a risk mitigation plan from a risk assessment:

- **Stay within scope**—The mitigation plan is derived from the risk assessment. In other words, the scope of the mitigation plan should not go outside the scope of the risk assessment. If you don't manage the scope, the costs can easily get out of countermeasure.

- **Redo CBAs if new costs are identified**—You commonly complete a cost-benefit analysis for a countermeasure as part of the risk assessment. If the CBA identifies any costs that weren't identified in the original CBA, the accuracy of the CBA is in question. You should redo the CBA with the accurate costs.

- **Prioritize countermeasures**—You should prioritize countermeasures based on their importance. A common way to identify the high-priority countermeasures is by scoring them with a threat/vulnerability matrix. You should implement high-priority countermeasures first.

- **Include current countermeasures in analysis**—When scoring countermeasures, ensure that current countermeasures are considered. For example, a threat may have a high impact but an in-place countermeasure has reduced this to a low impact. When evaluating a threat, consider the in-place countermeasure and assign a low impact to the threat.

- **Control costs**—Costs should stay within the allocated budget. Any change in the costs can affect the CBA. If additional costs are too high, the value of the counter-measure may be significantly reduced.

- **Control the schedule**—When the schedule is delayed, costs frequently go up. Also, remember that the countermeasure is mitigating a risk. Additionally, the longer the implementation is delayed, the longer the organization remains at risk.
- **Follow up**—Ensure that approved countermeasures have been implemented. Additionally, ensure that the countermeasures mitigate the risk as expected.

CHAPTER SUMMARY

This chapter covered many of the details you'll consider when turning a risk assessment into a risk mitigation plan. You'll start with a thorough review of the countermeasures. This often includes matching threats with vulnerabilities. It's important to identify all the costs associated with the countermeasures. At this stage, you may need to dig a little deeper to uncover any hidden costs. If the costs change, you'll need to consider redoing a cost-benefit analysis.

If much time has passed since the risk assessment was approved, you'll need to verify that the risk elements still exist. Additionally, you'll want to double-check to ensure the countermeasure will mitigate the risk. Two key goals while executing the plan are to stay within budget and stay on schedule. Last, you can follow up to ensure that the approved countermeasures are implemented, and that they actually mitigate the risks as expected.

KEY CONCEPTS AND TERMS

Account management policy
Implicit deny
Network load balancing
Password policy
Scale out

Scale up
Uninterruptible power supply (UPS)
Web farm

CHAPTER 11 ASSESSMENT

1. A(n) _____ countermeasure has been approved and has a date for implementation.

2. A single risk can be mitigated by more than one countermeasure.

  A. True
  B. False

3. The formula for risk is Risk = _____.

4. What would an account management policy include?

  A. Details on how to create accounts
  B. Details on when accounts should be disabled
  C. Password policy
  D. A and B only
  E. All of the above

5. What could a password policy include?

  A. Length of password
  B. List of required passwords
  C. User profiles
  D. All of the above

6. The _____ plan will include details on how and when to implement approved countermeasures.

7. You are reviewing a countermeasure to add to the mitigation plan. What costs should be considered?

  A. Initial purchase costs
  B. Facility costs
  C. Installation costs
  D. Training costs
  E. All of the above

8. Which of the following are considered facility costs for the implementation of a countermeasure?

  A. Installation and air conditioning
  B. Installation and training
  C. Power and air conditioning
  D. Power and training

9. An account management policy needs to be created as a mitigation countermeasure. You will write the policy. What's a reasonable amount of time for this to be completed and approved?

  A. 20 minutes
  B. One day
  C. One month
  D. One year

10. What can you use to determine the priority of countermeasures?

  A. Cost-benefit analysis
  B. Threat/vulnerability matrix
  C. Disaster recovery plan
  D. Best guess method

11. A risk assessment was completed three months ago. It has recently been approved, and you're tasked with implementing a mitigation plan. What should you do first?

  A. Verify risk elements.
  B. Purchase countermeasures.
  C. Redo risk assessment.
  D. Redo the CBA.

12. You are evaluating two possible countermeasures to mitigate the risk. Management only wants to purchase one. What can you use to determine which countermeasure provides the best cost benefits?

  A. Threat/vulnerability matrix
  B. Threat/vulnerability score
  C. CBA
  D. CIA

13. You are performing a cost-benefit analysis. You want to determine if a countermeasure should be used. Which of the following formulas should you apply?

  A. Loss before countermeasure − Loss after countermeasure
  B. Loss after countermeasure − Loss before countermeasure
  C. Projected benefits − Cost of countermeasure
  D. Cost of countermeasure − Projected benefits

14. Of the following, what should be included in a cost-benefit analysis report?

  A. Recommended countermeasure
  B. Risk to be mitigated
  C. Costs
  D. Annual projected benefits
  E. A and C only
  F. All of the above

15. A POAM can be used to follow up on a risk mitigation plan.

  A. True
  B. False

PART THREE

Risk Mitigation Plans

Mitigating Risk with a Business Impact Analysis

AN IMPORTANT PART of a business continuity plan (BCP) is a business impact analysis (BIA). The BIA is largely a data collection process. You can gather data through several methods. These include interviews, surveys, meetings, and more. After the data is collected, you can analyze it to determine which functions and resources are critical.

Once you've identified the critical functions and resources, you can identify acceptable outage times. The maximum acceptable outage (MAO) for a resource drives the recovery objectives. The two primary recovery objectives to focus on are recovery time objectives (RTOs) and recovery point objectives (RPOs).

Chapter 12 Topics

This chapter covers the following topics and concepts:

- What a business impact analysis is
- What the scope of a business impact analysis is
- What the objectives of a business impact analysis are
- What the steps of a business impact analysis are
- What mission-critical business functions and processes are
- How business functions and processes map to IT systems
- What best practices for performing a business impact analysis are

Chapter 12 Goals

When you complete this chapter, you will be able to:

- Define a business impact analysis
- Identify the scope for a business impact analysis
- Identify objectives for a business impact analysis
- Map business functions and processes to IT systems
- List best practices for performing a business impact analysis

What Is a Business Impact Analysis?

A business impact analysis (BIA) is a study used to identify the impact that can result from disruptions in the business. It focuses on the failure of one or more critical IT functions.

Another way of thinking of a BIA is that it helps you identify the systems critical to the survival of an organization. As a reminder, survivability is the ability of a company to survive loss due to a risk. Some losses are so severe that they can cause the business to fail if they aren't managed.

Chapter 10 introduced BIAs and included several terms relevant to BIAs, including:

> **TIP**
>
> The BIA includes systems critical to the company's survivability. However, lesser systems can also be included. In other words, a company may have significant problems if e-mail capabilities are lost for a week. However, the company wouldn't necessarily fail. Still, e-mail may be considered important enough to include in a BIA.

- **Maximum acceptable outage (MAO)**—The MAO identifies the maximum acceptable downtime for a system. If the MAO is exceeded, the mission of the organization is affected. The MAO directly affects the recovery time.

- **Critical business functions (CBFs)**—Any functions considered vital to an organization. If a CBF fails, the organization will lose the ability to perform essential operations, such as sell products to customers. If the organization cannot perform the function, it will lose money.

- **Critical success factors (CSFs)**—Any element necessary to perform the mission of an organization. An organization will have a few elements that must succeed in order for the organization to succeed. For example, a reliable network infrastructure may be considered a CSF for many companies today. If the network infrastructure fails, all other business functions may stop.

The BIA isn't intended to include all IT functions. Instead, the BIA helps the organization identify the critical IT systems and components. You identify the critical systems and components by identifying the critical business functions. Non-critical business functions are not included.

This brings up an important question: What is a critical IT function?

> **TIP**
>
> A "stakeholder" is any individual or group that has a stake or interest in the success of a project. This includes executives and managers that have a stake in the success of their department or division. In other words, they want to ensure success in their area of responsibility.

Any stakeholder can determine that a business function is critical. If the stakeholder determines that the loss of the function will cause an unacceptable loss, it is a critical function. The stakeholder makes this decision based on experience and opinion. This isn't a light decision. Once the function is designated as critical, the stakeholder needs to dedicate resources to protect it. Resources can include money and personnel.

Additionally, a law could dictate that a function be considered critical. For example, consider the Health Insurance Portability and Accountability Act (HIPAA). HIPAA mandates the protection of health-related information. Access controls and other protection measures could be considered critical to ensure HIPAA compliance.

The BIA is largely a data-gathering process. You receive input from stakeholders, users, process owners, and others in the organization. You can gather the data from interviews. You can create questionnaires or surveys. You can also review available reports. You can use any method that will give you information on the target system.

It's important to realize that the BIA doesn't provide solutions. Instead, it's part of a larger business continuity plan (BCP). The BIA provides input into the BCP. The BCP does include solutions. For example, the BCP may provide recommendations for controls to reduce the impact of an outage.

Additionally, it's worth comparing a BIA against a risk assessment (RA). The RA looks at threats and vulnerabilities. When a threat exploits a vulnerability, a risk occurs. The RA has a primary goal of reducing the risk. It can be reduce the risk by reducing or eliminating the vulnerability. It can also reduce the risk by reducing the impact of the threat.

The BIA doesn't address the threats or vulnerabilities. Instead, it just looks at the effect if there is an outage. Although the focus of a BIA is primarily on disaster recovery, the BIA's output can also be used in an RA. In other words, if you're trying to determine what systems to evaluate with an RA, you can consider the output of a BIA. At the very least, the BIA identifies and prioritizes the critical systems.

Similarly, if you've already completed an RA, you can use that data to help with the BIA. One of the first steps in an RA is to identify assets. This helps you identify the assets that are important to the organization.

Collecting Data

Because the BIA is a data-gathering process, you should consider the different methods used to gather the data. There are multiple methods available.

Seven Steps of Contingency Planning

The National Institute of Standards and Technology (NIST) has published Special Publication (SP) 800-34. SP 800-34 is titled "Contingency Planning Guide for Information Technology Systems." Contingency planning helps an organization identify measures to recover services after an emergency or disaster. SP 800-34 includes information on BIAs.

SP 800-34 identifies seven steps of contingency planning. The seven steps are:

1. Develop the contingency planning policy statement.
2. Conduct the business impact analysis.
3. Identify preventative controls.
4. Develop recovery strategies.
5. Develop an IT contingency plan.
6. Plan testing, training, and exercises.
7. Plan maintenance.

As you can see, the BIA is part of the overall contingency planning. As the second step, it drives much of the contingency planning. You only need to plan contingencies for systems identified as critical by the BIA.

You can conduct interviews with key personnel. You can improve the results with a little forethought. Plan the interviews. Make sure the people you're interviewing have the time to answer your questions. Make sure you're ready with the right questions. Remember, your questions should focus on CBFs and the MAO of supporting resources.

Another method is to use questionnaires, forms, or surveys. Keep these limited and focused. In other words, focus on only one process at a time. If the form is too long, people may not have the time needed to answer it. If it's shorter, you'll get more usable information. These can be paper-based or computer-based. For example, you could use a SharePoint Web site to gather and compile the data.

You can also host meetings or conference calls. A benefit of this format is that multiple people can interact, and your results may be much richer. However, it may be quite difficult to gain consensus. This is especially true if you're trying to identify the priority of different systems.

Varying Data Collection Methods

Nothing says that you can only use one data collection method. Feel free to vary your methods. Some people may have a lot of information and an interview may be appropriate. However, just because you interview one person does not mean you have to interview everyone.

If people are already weighed down with a large number of meetings, they may resent another meeting for a BIA. On the other hand, they may welcome the opportunity to fill out an online form at their leisure.

Defining the Scope of Your Business Impact Analysis

As with any project, it's important to define the scope of a BIA early in the process. The scope defines the boundaries of the plan. Defining the scope helps ensure that the BIA is focused. It ensures that you analyze the correct functions.

The scope is affected by the size of the organization. For a small organization, the scope of the BIA could include the entire organization. For larger organizations, it may include only certain areas. For example, a BIA may include only the online sales division of a large business.

> **TIP**
>
> You should also consider the budget when identifying the scope. If the organization is large enough, you can hire a security consultant to assist with the BIA. However, if the budget is limited, this may not be possible.

Consider Figure 12-1. It shows an online Web server with a back-end database. The BIA could focus only on the critical functions needed to support this Web server. Based on the figure, the systems needed to support online sales are the Web server, the firewalls, and the database server. Notice that this is only the phase when a customer purchases a product. It doesn't include the shipment of the product.

Figure 12-2 shows the elements of the product shipment phase. There are distinct differences in the functions needed for these two phases. Additionally, there are distinct differences in the MAO of each. The MAO for the Web site is much shorter.

Consider a customer who is ready to purchase a product. If the Web site is down, the sale is lost. It doesn't matter if the Web site was down for only five minutes. If it's down when the customer visits, the customer can't make the purchase.

On the other hand, if you have problems at the warehouse, the impact isn't immediate. You could have outages for hours without any impact. Even if an outage lasts a full day, it may result in only a slight delay in shipment, which isn't critical.

FIGURE 12-1

Online Web server with back-end database.

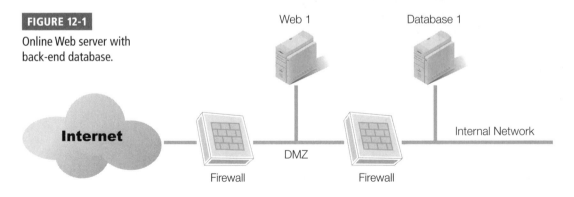

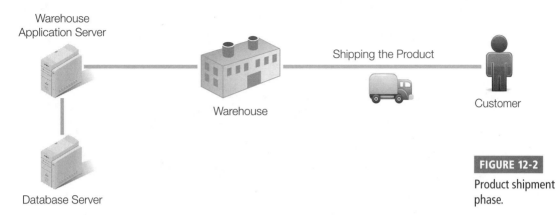

Warehouse
Application Server

Shipping the Product

Customer

Warehouse

Database Server

FIGURE 12-2

Product shipment
phase.

This doesn't mean you shouldn't include the shipment phase in the BIA. Instead, the point is that you should specifically identify the scope. Consider this scope statement:

The scope of the BIA will cover the functions of the Web site.

One person conducting a BIA may interpret this to mean only the purchase phase. If the intent of the BIA is to include both the purchase and shipment phases, the BIA would then be incomplete. Another person may interpret it to mean both the purchase and shipment phases. If the intent were to have the BIA cover only the purchase phase, money would be wasted doing both.

This scope statement is clearer:

The scope of the BIA will cover the functions of the Web site during the customer purchase. This includes all functions that support a customer's visit and purchase. The shipment phase is not included in this BIA.

If you wanted to include the shipment phase, you could modify the scope statement as follows:

The scope of the BIA will cover all functions of the online Web site. This includes all functions that support a customer's visit and purchase. It also includes all functions that support the shipment of the product.

Objectives of a Business Impact Analysis

The overall objective of the BIA is to identify the impact of outages. More specifically, the goal is to identify the critical functions that can affect the organization. After identifying these, you can identify the critical resources that support these functions.

Each resource has a MAO and an impact if it fails. The ultimate goal is to identify the recovery requirements. Figure 12-3 shows these overall steps. You gather input from process owners and experts. This helps you identify the CBFs. You then identify the critical resources that support the critical business functions. You then identify the impact and MAO of the resources. The MAO is used to determine the recovery requirements.

FIGURE 12-3

Objectives of a BIA.

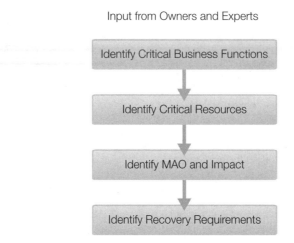

An indirect objective of the BIA is to justify funding. After you've identified the recovery requirements in the BIA, the BCP will identify controls. If the impact is high, it is cost effective to spend money to prevent the outage.

NIST SP 800-34 includes a diagram similar to Figure 12-4. This shows the direct relationship between costs and time. Look at the line that ends with Cost to Recover. The upfront costs are high to reduce the impact of the disaster. Even if the disaster lasts a long time, the costs to recover from the disaster are low.

The other line shows the Cost of Disruption. Little money is spent on prevention. As time passes after a disaster, more and more money is lost due to lost revenue and other consequences.

The goal is to find the optimum point. This is the balance where you can spend the minimum amount on prevention while still being able to minimize the costs of disruption.

The following sections cover the objectives of a BIA in more detail.

FIGURE 12-4

Relationship of costs.

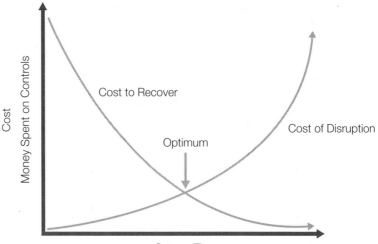

Identify Critical Business Functions

Unless you own the process, it's not always apparent what the critical functions are. For example, if you are the security expert, you may not know the critical functions of a Web site. The Web server is the obvious component, but there are others.

By interviewing or surveying the experts, you can gain insight into all the components that support the Web server. It's often worthwhile to use this data to identify the specific steps for the process. For example, the following bullets detail the steps for a customer's online purchase. It also includes the steps after the purchase.

▷ TIP

By identifying CBFs first, you use a top-down approach. You will ultimately drill down to the critical IT services and infrastructure. If you try a bottom-up approach, you're likely to miss important elements. In other words, you don't start with a server and then try to determine what functions it supports. You start with the CBFs.

- **The customer visits the Web site**—The customer uses any Web browser to access the Web site. The Web site is hosted on a Web server located in the demilitarized zone (DMZ). A firewall provides access to the Web site with a layer of security.

- **The customer browses the product catalog**—Users can search for specific products. The Web site sends queries to a back-end database. The database server is on the internal network behind a second firewall. The database results are included in a Web page that is sent back to the customer.

- **The customer picks a product**—While browsing, the customer can place any product into his or her shopping cart.

- **The customer checks out**—When the customer is ready to purchase the product, he or she clicks the Checkout button. This starts a secure session. Previous customers can log on to access previously used information, such as their address and credit card numbers. This information is stored on a back-end database server behind the second firewall. New customers are prompted to enter their customer data. This data is then stored on the back-end database server. After the order is completed, the customer is sent an acknowledgement e-mail.

- **A message is sent to the order processing application**—The database server sends a message to the order processing application. A different server in the internal network hosts the order processing application.

- **Order is processed**—The order processing application tracks the order until the customer receives it. If inventory levels are low, it will automatically order products to replenish the stock. It sends the customer's order to a warehouse application for shipping. It also accepts status data from the warehouse application. If a shipment is delayed, it sends a notification to the customer. When the order is shipped, it sends a follow up e-mail to the customer. It tracks the shipment with the carrier to ensure the order is successfully delivered.

12

Business Impact Analysis

▷ NOTE

This isn't the only way the process could be designed. The product database could be hosted on a server in the DMZ so data can be retrieved more quickly. The customer database could be hosted separately in the internal network. The DMZ could be designed differently. There are many possibilities. This is why it's important to ask the experts. They will know how it's configured.

In this example, the critical business functions are:

- The customer accessing the Web site
- The Web server accessing the database server
- The order-processing application receiving and processing the order

With this information, you can identify the critical resources.

Identify Critical Resources

The critical resources are those that are required to support the CBFs. Once you've identified the CBFs, you can analyze them to determine the critical resources for each.

Following the example of the Web site, you can see how to identify critical resources from the CBFs. One of the CBFs identified earlier was the customer accessing the Web site. The following IT resources are required to support this function:

- Internet access
- The Web server
- The Web application
- Network connectivity
- The firewall on the Internet side of the DMZ

The second CBF is the Web server's ability to access the database server. The database server hosts product information. It also hosts customer information. The customer information is used when a customer makes a purchase and to target advertising for the returning customer. The following IT resources are required to support this function:

- The Web server
- The Web application
- The database server
- Network connectivity
- The firewall on the internal side of the DMZ

The third critical function is the order processing application. It needs to receive orders from the database server. It also needs to be able to track the order until delivery. The following IT resources are required to support this function:

- The server hosting the order processing application
- The database server
- Warehouse application
- Network connectivity
- Internet access

In many instances, there will be overlap in the critical resources. In other words, a critical resource required for one function may also be required for another function. For example, the Web server is required for two of the functions.

Recovery Without a BIA

Imagine the recovery steps after a disaster without a BIA. What systems should you restore first? What CBFs should you restore first? Will there be any order to the recovery?

Employees will likely have systems they're comfortable with and will try to start them first. Of course, while they're doing so, managers may redirect them. The managers may have pet projects and want them up first. If the employee changes direction, an executive may redirect them again. An executive may have a favorite system and want it up first.

It's entirely possible that none of these systems is critical to the survivability of the organization. However, that won't stop the employee from focusing on one of them first.

Starting a system because it's what you know isn't what the business needs. Starting pet projects or favorite systems isn't what the business needs. Instead, the systems that support critical business functions should be started first. These are identified in the BIA.

The time to perform a BIA is before the disaster. If you have specified priorities in writing, they will be used. However, if you don't have any documentation, there's no telling what will happen. One thing is certain. You can't expect cool heads to prevail during or after the disaster.

Additionally, facility support is required for each of these functions. This includes power, heating, and air conditioning. For example, uninterruptible power supplies and generators will ensure systems are operational even if power is lost.

You may choose to list the resource one time for all the functions, or with each function. In the case of IT resources, it's a good idea to list each of the resources for each of the functions. However, it is acceptable to compile a separate list of the facility resources that apply to all functions.

For example, all IT resources require facility support. You could list these requirements one time as follows:

- **Power**—Uninterruptible power supplies and generators required to ensure systems are operational even if power is lost.

- **Heating and air conditioning**—Heating and/or air conditioning is required to ensure all systems can operate.

Identify MAO and Impact

Once you've identified the critical business functions and the IT resources that support them, you turn your attention to the MAO and impact. The maximum acceptable outage (MAO) is sometimes referred to as the maximum tolerable period of disruption (MTPD).

The MAO helps you determine which CBFs you need to recover and restart as soon as possible after a disaster. It identifies the specific resources needed to restart the CBF. It also tells you how soon you need to recover these systems.

TABLE 12-1 Example critical levels and recovery objectives.	
IMPACT VALUE LEVEL	**MAXIMUM ACCEPTABLE OUTAGE AND IMPACT**
Level 1 Business functions must be available during all business hours. Online systems must be available 24 hours a day, 7 days a week.	Two hours Any outage will have an almost immediate impact on the business.
Level 2 Business processes can survive without the business function for a short time.	One day If the outage lasts more than a day, it will have an impact on the business.
Level 3 Business processes can survive without the business functions for one or more days.	Three days The outage won't have an impact on the business, even if the outage lasts as long as three days.
Level 4 Business processes can survive without the business functions for extended periods.	One week The outage won't have a significant impact on the business unless it lasts longer than a week.

> **NOTE**
>
> The values assigned are internal. In other words, the values and recovery objectives used by one organization can be completely different from those used by another organization.

The impact on the business is monetary, but it doesn't need to be expressed as money. Instead, the impact is often expressed as a relative value such as High, Medium, and Low. It can also be expressed as a number such as 1 through 4.

Once you identify the impact level, you can match it with a MAO. Table 12-1 shows an example of how impact value levels are defined in an organization. Each level is matched to the MAO to identify how long the system can be down before the impact is felt.

When calculating the MAO for an organization, it's important to consider both direct and indirect costs.

Direct Costs

The direct costs are usually easier to calculate. Some of these costs are readily apparent. Others you may not have considered. The following list shows some of the direct costs:

- **Loss of immediate sales and cash flow**—This is the most obvious loss. During the outage, you won't be able to sell your products or services. You will lose the normal cash flow from these sales.
- **Equipment replacement costs**—If equipment is damaged it will need to be repaired or replaced. Depending on the equipment, these costs can be substantial.
- **Building replacement costs**—If a building is lost due to a fire or natural disaster, it will need to be rebuilt or replaced. While insurance covers most of the costs, it will rarely cover all the costs. The organization will have to make up the difference.

Loss of Share Value After Disaster

If an organization is a publicly traded company, you should also consider the share price. Millions of investor dollars can be lost in a short time.

Noted author Andrew Hiles wrote that the share price of a corporation drops by 5 to 8 percent within the first few days after a disaster.[1] Disasters can happen anywhere to any corporation. How well the corporation recovers determines the recovery of the stock.

Organizations that recover decisively also see their stocks recover. Within 100 days, these stocks not only regain their price, but often show gains of about 10 to 15 percent. Organizations that do not recover well find a new low for their stock price. Their stock sometimes rallies at about 75 days after the disaster, but then settles at about 15 percent below its pre-disaster level.

The organizations that recover are better prepared for the disasters. Their successful recovery doesn't happen by accident. They have talented leaders. They also have comprehensive disaster preparedness plans.

- **Penalty costs for late delivery**—Service level agreements (SLAs) specify expected levels of service. SLAs often impose penalties if the service is not met. These penalties should be calculated as direct costs for an outage.

- **Penalty costs for noncompliance issues**—Some laws impose penalty costs for noncompliance. If a failure will result in noncompliance with a law, this cost should be included.

- **Costs to re-create or recover data**—Data lost during an outage needs to be re-created or restored. Some data may need to be re-created manually. Other data may be recoverable using existing backups. You may have labor costs associated with recovering data.

- **Salaries paid to staff who are idled due to outage**—If an outage prevents normal work, workers will still be on the clock. In other words, you'll be paying workers to perform jobs they can't perform.

Indirect Costs

It is a little harder to identify indirect costs. However, their value also affects the impact value. The following list shows some of the indirect costs to consider:

- **Loss of customers**—Customers who can't purchase from you may purchase from your competitor. They may find the experience satisfying and never come back. It costs a significant amount of money to attract new customers.

- **Loss of public goodwill**—The outage may cause your organization to look less desirable. Consider personally identifiable information (PII). If an outage results in the compromise of PII, customers may distrust you. If credit card data of customers is compromised, they may no longer do business with you.

- **Costs to regain market share**—When customers and goodwill are lost, the company loses market share. The competitors increase market share. Most companies realize it's much easier to keep a customer than it is to attract a new one.

- **Costs to regain positive brand image**—If the company's brand is tarnished, steps need to be taken to repair it. It takes a lot of advertising money to repair a tarnished reputation. Some companies never recover.

- **Loss of credit, or higher costs for credit**—When an outage affects a company's cash flow, it can also affect the company's credit rating. A lower credit rating results in higher costs. Worse, a company may lose existing credit.

- **Lost opportunities during recovery**—While your organization is dealing with the outage, resources are occupied. These same resources may have been working on projects to attract new business. The new business becomes a lost opportunity.

Identify Recovery Requirements

The recovery requirements show the time frame in which systems must be recoverable. They also identify the data that must be recovered. For example, it may be acceptable for some data to be lost. Other data loss is not acceptable.

There are two primary terms related to the recovery requirements. They are **recovery time objective (RTO)** and **recovery point objective (RPO)**. Although the RTO applies to any systems or functions, the RPO applies only to data. More specifically, the RPO addresses data housed in databases.

> **TIP**
>
> Although lower RTOs are achievable, they are much more expensive. When interviewing stakeholders it's important to connect the cost with the RTO. For example, you can ensure that a database is recoverable up to the moment of failure, even if an earthquake hits. This requires a separate site, separate servers, and immediate data replication. All of this is expensive. Once stakeholders recognize the costs, they may give you a different RTO.

The RTO is the time in which the system or function must be recovered. The RTO would be equal to or less than the MAO. For example, if the MAO is one hour, the RTO would be one hour or less.

The RPOs identify the maximum amount of data loss an organization can accept. This is the acceptable data latency. For example, a database may record hundreds of sales transactions a minute. The organization may need to recover this data up to the moment of failure. This would be expensive. Another database may import data once a week. You'd only need to restore the data since the last import to ensure nothing is lost. This is less expensive.

Another way of thinking of RTO and RPO is as time critical and mission critical. The RTO identifies the time when the system is restored. The RPO identifies data that is mission critical. Some processes must be delivered in a timely manner, requiring a short RTO. Other processes can be delayed, as long as all of the data is recovered.

Recovering Databases

There is a wide range of choices when determining recovery options for a database. Some databases require you to be able to recover the data up to a moment in time. Other databases may allow you to recover the data from a week ago. It depends on the how the data is used and updated.

For example, a database used for online transaction processing (OLTP) may record sales. As a back-end database for an online Web server, every minute of data is important. Databases use transaction logs to record transactions. The combination of these transaction logs and regular backups allows you to restore data up to the moment of failure.

Advanced recovery models replicate data from one server to another. The transaction log updates the database on one server. The log is then copied to the other server. The copied log updates the database on the second server. Even if the entire server becomes corrupt, the second server has all of the data since the last copied transaction log. If you want to ensure you lose no more than five minutes of data, you copy the log to the other server every five minutes.

Consider another database that holds product data. It is updated once a week by importing data. You can back up the data once a week and be safe. If the database becomes corrupt, you can restore it from the week-old backup and have all the data. Even if you backed it up before the import, you could easily import the data after the database is restored to recover all the data.

After you've identified the MAO, it becomes easy to identify the recovery time objectives. Table 12-2 shows the recovery objectives added to the impact levels and MAO. Notice that the recovery objective is directly related to the MAO.

You may be wondering about Impact Value Level 4. If an organization can do without a function for up to a week, why include it in the BIA at all? You can think of this level as minor desirable functions. Although the organization won't fail without them, it will be able to operate with less problems. For example, an organization may not use Internet access for mission-critical tasks. However, it may make other jobs easier when available.

The RPO isn't calculated directly from the MAO. Instead, you'll need to interview personnel to determine what data loss is acceptable.

Acceptable data loss is variable. A database used to record sales can't accept much data loss. It's common to measure acceptable data loss in minutes, such as 15 minutes. Every minute of data loss represents lost sales revenue.

On the other hand, other databases may not change as much. Additionally, their changes may be manually reproduced. If there aren't many changes and they can easily be reproduced, you can accept more data loss. For example, consider a database that is manually updated about five times a week. The updates have a paper trail that shows what needs to be reproduced. You could easily accept data loss in the database of a week. Because the updates have a paper trail, you can restore the database and then reproduce the updates.

TABLE 12-2 Critical levels and recovery objectives.

IMPACT VALUE LEVEL	MAXIMUM ACCEPTABLE OUTAGE	RECOVERY OBJECTIVE
Level 1 Business functions must be available during all business hours. Online systems must be available 24 hours a day, 7 days a week.	Two hours Any outage will have an almost immediate impact on the business.	Two hours or less Functions in this category must be recovered in less than two hours.
Level 2 Business processes can survive without the business function for a short amount of time.	One day If the outage lasts more than a day, it will have an impact on the business.	24 hours or less Functions in this category must be recovered within 24 hours
Level 3 Business processes can survive without the business functions for one or more days.	Three days The outage won't have an impact on the business even if the outage lasts as long as three days.	72 hours or less Functions in this category must be recovered within 72 hours
Level 4 Business processes can survive without the business functions for extended periods.	One week The outage won't have a significant impact on the business unless it lasts longer than a week.	Seven days or less Functions in this category must be recovered within one week

The Steps of a Business Impact Analysis Process

The majority of the work of a BIA is gathering data. You'll need to gather data surrounding the critical business functions within the scope of the BIA.

Once the data is gathered, you'll complete some analysis. The end stage is the publication of the BIA report. Some organizations may want you to include recommendations to meet recovery times. However, that is not technically part of a BIA. Recommendations for controls normally come after the BIA.

The overall steps of a BIA are:

1. Identify the environment.
2. Identify stakeholders.
3. Identify critical business functions.
4. Identify maximum downtime.

5. Identify critical resources.
6. Identify recovery priorities.
7. Develop BIA report.

Although these steps identify the actions to take, you can combine them or order them differently. The most important point to remember is that the goal of the BIA is to identify the critical resources and recovery priorities. The actual steps to get there can be different from one organization to another.

> **TIP**
>
> Note that the BIA is not concerned with identifying or implementing recovery methods. However, the BIA is an important prerequisite. You can't begin looking for recovery methods until you know what you need to recover.

Identify the Environment

The first step identifies the overall IT environment. This means having a good understanding of the business function. This includes the number of customers and the number of transactions. If sales revenues are generated, you should know the sales amounts.
The sales revenue translates to lost sales during an outage.

It is possible to perform a BIA on a critical business function that doesn't generate sales revenue. For example, e-mail is a critical business function for many organizations. An e-mail system may serve 5,000 employees. It could pass tens of thousands of e-mails daily. Even though it doesn't generate any direct sales revenue, it may be considered critical.

At this point, you may not know what is critical. Instead, you take the time to get a big picture of what IT systems exist within the scope of the BIA. Depending on the scope of the BIA, this step could include collecting diagrams and technical documentation. This documentation helps you determine which components are critical.

It's possible to complete a BIA on the entire organization, or only portions of the organization. For example, consider a small company with less than 100 users. You could complete the BIA on the entire company.

On the other hand, consider a company with several offices spread throughout the country. Instead of doing one enormous BIA, you could do several. You could do individual BIAs for any of the small offices. Additionally, you may do separate BIAs for different functions within the organization. For example, you could do a single BIA for online sales, another for database support, and so on.

After completing this step, you'll have a better idea of what systems may be included in the BIA. You'll also be able to identify the possible stakeholders.

Identify Stakeholders

Stakeholders are those individuals or groups that have a direct stake or interest in the success of a project. For example, a vice president of sales would have a direct stake in the success of sales. Stakeholders know what systems are critical.

A stakeholder can help ensure that you have adequate resources available. This includes simple matters, such as ensuring personnel are available for interviews for the BIA. It also includes the larger issues when it comes time to identify the MAO.

Individual stakeholders can determine that any system is critical. Any losses suffered from the system outage are their responsibility. Additionally, any resources dedicated to protect the systems are their responsibility. Because these are their responsibilities, their opinions matter the most.

Identify Critical Business Functions

The critical functions are those that will have a direct impact on the profitability or survivability of an organization.

Some BIAs are designed to focus on a critical function from the beginning. For example, a BIA could be commissioned specifically for an online Web site. If this is the case, you'll start with a clear picture that your focus is on the Web site and the functions that support it. Still, you'll need to identify the processes involved.

Another BIA may be focused on a remote office. You'll need to identify what is done at the remote office first. It's possible that the majority of the work can be done offline. For example, a remote office may provide presentations to client sites on a regular basis. It's possible the people there could do so even if all the IT functions are lost for a week or more. In this case, none of the functions would be considered critical.

On the other hand, a remote office may sell products or services. The remote office may need constant connectivity with the main office during business hours. If connectivity is lost, the people there can't close a sale. If they generate a lot of revenue, this may be considered a critical function.

Identify Critical Resources

Critical resources are the resources needed to support the critical systems and the critical system processes. These could include hardware, such as servers or routers. They could also include software, such as the operating system and applications.

When identifying critical resources, it's important to include the supporting infrastructure. For example, imagine a Web server that must be operational 24 hours a day, seven days a week. It also needs facility support. This could include power, heating, and air conditioning. If a critical system requires support personnel for operations, you should include items such as food and potable water as critical resources.

It's also important to identify critical personnel. Any system has several key personnel integral to its success. These could be executives. They could be managers, supervisors, or administrators. They could also include key customers or vendors.

Consider the online Web server with the back-end database presented earlier. It would include the following systems:

- Web server
- Database server
- Internal firewall
- External firewall

It's important to interview the experts to identify the critical systems. Consider e-mail services within a Microsoft domain. The obvious systems are any of the e-mail servers. However, within a Microsoft domain, several additional servers are critical. These include a domain controller (DC). They include a DC that's also a global catalog server. They also include a domain name system (DNS) server used to locate these other servers. If any of these are unavailable, e-mail will not work.

Identify Maximum Downtime

The maximum downtime is the maximum acceptable outage (MAO). Once you identify the critical resources, you'll be able to identify the MAO for each of them.

In addition to identifying a MAO, you should usually include an impact statement. The impact statement identifies the effect of the loss. You can state the impact directly by identifying what cannot be done in case of a loss. You can also state the impact in monetary terms.

For example, e-mail services may be critical. However, the organization may be able to continue to operate for as long as eight hours before suffering a serious impact. On the other hand, a Web server generating $60,000 in revenue an hour loses as much as $1,000 in direct sales a minute. The maximum downtime for this Web server could be identified as five minutes.

Table 12-3 shows an example output for this step.

TABLE 12-3 MAO and impact for specific resources.

RESOURCE	MAO	IMPACT
Web server	Five minutes	Loss of significant direct sales revenue and indirect losses Five minutes of downtime results in a loss of about $5,000 in direct sales
Database Server	Five minutes	Loss of significant direct sales revenue and indirect losses Users will still be able to browse the Web site Five minutes of downtime results in a loss of about $5,000 in direct sales
E-mail server	Eight hours	Loss of primary communications within the company Loss of primary communications with vendors and customers

TABLE 12-4 Critical systems and their priorities.	
SYSTEM	**PRIORITY**
Web server	1
Database server	1
E-mail server	2
Desktop PCs	5

Identify Recovery Priorities

This part of the BIA identifies the most important critical systems, and the least important critical systems. The highest priorities are assigned based on the shortest MAOs. For example, consider a system that will have an impact after five minutes of downtime compared to another system that can be down for eight hours before an impact occurs. Clearly, the system with a five-minute MAO should be recovered first.

The output of the BIA at this stage can be as simple as a list of the critical systems with priorities. You can use numerical priorities such as 1, 2, 3, and so on. You can also categorize the priorities. For example, the most important systems can have a category of High. Other categories could be listed as Medium and Low.

Table 12-4 shows how recovery priorities could be listed for some of the servers mentioned in this chapter. This table is using a scale of 1 to 5 with 1 as the highest priority. Desktop PCs are added as the lowest priority.

Develop BIA Report

The BIA report compiles the data you've collected. SP 800-34 includes a template that you can use as a guide for the BIA. It includes the following sections:

- **Preliminary system information**—This includes generic information such as the organization, the system name, and system documentation.
- **System points of contact (POCs)**—These are the experts on the system. They are the ones who provided the input into the BIA. They can also be queried with any follow up-questions. You may include both internal and external POCs depending on the scope of the BIA.
- **System resources**—List the specific resources here. These include the hardware and software. They can also include any personnel or other resources.
- **Critical roles**—Some POCs may have critical roles related to a system. If so, you can identify them here. Again, this will make it easier for follow-up.
- **Table linking critical roles to critical resources**—This table matches the personnel to the systems. For example, if e-mail services are considered critical, you would match the e-mail POC to this system.

BIA Reports Are Popular

Once you complete the BIA, you may find that many people want to see it. This is especially true if the BIA looks at more than a single function. Many people want to know what the CBFs are. The BIA provides an overall picture of the organization that isn't commonly understood.

Many people suggest that the disaster recovery and security people have more knowledge of the details of a business than most employees do. Executives have a good overall view. However, other employees often know their area well, but don't have a good idea of other areas. The BIA provides that view.

Executives may consider the BIA confidential. With this in mind, you should ensure that it's acceptable to give the BIA out before doing so.

- **Table identifying resources, outage impact, and acceptable outage time**— This table lists each critical resource you've identified in the BIA. For each resource, include the impact of an outage and the MAO. This is one of the most important elements of the BIA.
- **Table identifying recovery priority of key resources**—This table lists the recovery priority. The priority scale you use is internally developed. It could be numerical such as 1, 2, 3 and so on. It could use words such as High, Medium, Low, and so on.

Identifying Mission-Critical Business Functions and Processes

An important step in the BIA is identifying the mission-critical business functions and processes. This is not always an easy task. One of the most important points to remember is that the experts have the key information. You'll need to use different data collection methods to get this information.

Mission-critical business functions are any functions that are considered vital to an organization. They are derived from critical success factors, or CSFs. CSFs are any elements necessary to perform the mission. CSFs are a limited number of areas where successful results will ensure success for the organization.

Consider figure 12-5. Processes are the underlying actions that contribute to the CSFs. In other words, certain processes result in successful CSFs. Successful CSFs result in successful CBFs.

Consider a company that generates the majority of revenue from online sales. Sales from the Web site are a CBF. However, you can't say the company needs to sell products to be successful. You have to identify the underlying factors and actions needed to sell products.

FIGURE 12-5

Key processes, CSFs, and CBFs.

Imagine a company that sells widgets online. Some of the underlying CSFs could be:

- Best widgets available
- Motivated employees
- Customer satisfaction
- Effective advertising

Different processes support each of these CSFs. For example, some of the processes that support customer satisfaction are:

- Satisfying buying experience
- Competitive pricing
- On-time delivery

Many companies document these processes with work flows. If work flows exist, they can easily be used to determine the steps in the processes. If they don't exist, you should still be able to document the steps in a process.

On-time delivery is an important process that supports customer satisfaction. You may want to document this to identify the resources involved.

Consider Figure 12-2 shown earlier in the chapter. It shows the elements involved in the product shipment phase.

The actual workflow could be:

1. Orders are sent to the warehouse database.
2. The warehouse application identifies new orders.
3. The application notifies warehouse workers of new orders, including the location of the product.
4. Warehouse workers retrieve the product.
5. Warehouse workers package and ship the product.

With this knowledge, you can now identify the critical resources required for on-time delivery. They include:

- Database server hosting database
- Communication between database server and Web server
- Application server hosting application
- Employees in the warehouse
- Shipment method

TABLE 12-5 Critical systems and their priorities.

SYSTEM	PRIORITY
Database server	2
Warehouse application server	2
Connection to Web server	3

Mapping Business Functions and Processes to IT Systems

Once you've identified the critical business functions and processes, you need to map them to the actual IT systems. You can then determine the recovery options.

If you consider the example used for shipment of products, you have three primary systems. First, employees access the warehouse application. If it fails, they can't identify the products to ship. Second, the warehouse application accesses a database. If the database server fails, the same problem occurs. The employees can't identify the products to ship. Last, you need a link between the Web server accepting the orders, and the database server. If this fails, new orders can't be shipped.

You can then identify the priority of these systems. You can use the same scale as earlier in this chapter. A priority of 1 is the highest priority. A priority of 5 is the lowest priority. If the database server or the warehouse application servers are down, shipments can't occur. However, some delay in shipments is acceptable.

If the connection with the Web server is broken, new orders aren't passed to the warehouse. However, the warehouse workers can still process existing orders.

Best Practices for Performing a BIA for Your Organization

When performing BIAs, you can use several different best practices. The following list shows many of these:

- **Start with clear objectives**—Make sure you and anyone involved with the BIA understands the scope of the BIA. This is best defined in writing. Many projects get off track simply because individuals have a different understanding of the requirements.

- **Don't lose sight of the objectives**—In addition to the scope statement, remember that the purpose of the BIA is to identify the critical functions, critical systems, and MAO. This data is used to determine the recovery priorities.

- **Use a top-down approach**—Start with the CBFs and drill down to the IT services that support them. If you start with the servers, you'll miss important elements that are needed for the success of the CBFs.

- **Vary data collection methods**—When collecting data, ensure you match your method to the organization's practices. You may be able to get solid data from individual interviews with some people. You may not be able to get access to others for individual interviews. In the latter case, questionnaires may be useful. BIA data collection can sometimes benefit from group discussions. These can be conducted via a conference call or from a meeting or workshop.

- **Plan interviews and meetings in advance**—Data gathering is an important part of the BIA. You want to ensure that the attendees have enough time to give you the data you need. If they're rushed or you aren't prepared, you won't get the data you need.

- **Don't look for the quick solution**—The BIA will take time. It takes time to collect the data. It takes time to evaluate the data. It takes time to identify priorities. Shortcuts are likely to overlook critical functions or processes.

- **Consider the BIA as a project**—All normal project management practices apply. Set milestones and track the progress.

- **Consider the use of tools**—Many tools are available that can assist with the completion of disaster preparedness projects. These include tools that can help with a BIA.

Consider Tools

Some tools are available that may assist in completing the BIA. For example, BIA Professional is one of several tools sold by Sungard Availability Services.

BIA Professional includes tools that can help you gather and compile information. It guides you through the process from beginning to end.

It includes Web-based surveys. You can design the questions that will branch off based on users' answers. In other words, users who don't have direct knowledge of a specific process won't be asked questions about the process.

Once you've created the questions, you can send the experts links to the surveys. They can answer the questions from anywhere via the Internet.

BIA Professional is a part of Sungard's overall Continuity Management Solution suite of tools. Alternative tools available include ReliaSoft's BlockSim and Factonomy 4BIA.

CHAPTER SUMMARY

The BIA is a valuable tool that can help identify critical systems and resources. Once you've identified them, you can then identify the MAO for resources. The impact of the outage and the MAO is then used to determine recovery priorities. Some systems may need to be up and operational almost immediately after a disaster. Other systems can be down for days at a time. The BIA identifies which systems are which.

Two important terms related to the BIA are the recovery time objective (RTO) and recovery point objective (RPO). The RTO helps identify systems that are time critical. The RPO helps identify systems that hold data that is mission critical.

KEY CONCEPTS AND TERMS

Recovery point objective (RPO)
Recovery time objective (RTO)

CHAPTER 12 ASSESSMENT

1. The _____ identifies the maximum acceptable downtime for a system.

2. Stakeholders can determine what functions are considered critical business functions.

   A. True
   B. False

3. The BIA is a part of the _____.

4. What defines the boundaries of a business impact analysis?

   A. MAO
   B. BCP
   C. Recovery objectives
   D. Scope

5. What are two objectives of a BIA? (Select two.)

   A. Identify minimum acceptable outage.
   B. Document new policy.
   C. Identify critical resources.
   D. Identify critical business functions.

6. You are working on a BIA. You are calculating costs to determine the impact of an outage for a specific system. When calculating the costs, you should calculate the direct and _____ costs.

7. You are working on a BIA. You want to identify the maximum amount of data loss an organization can accept. What is this called?

   A. BIA time
   B. Maximum acceptable outage
   C. Recovery time objectives
   D. Recovery point objectives

8. You have identified the MAO for a system. You now want to specify the time required for a system to be recovered. What is this?

   A. BIA time
   B. Maximum acceptable outage
   C. Recovery time objectives
   D. Recovery point objectives

9. Which of the following statements is true?

   A. The RPO applies to any systems or functions. However, the RTO only refers to data housed in databases.
   B. The RTO applies to any systems or functions. However, the RPO only refers to data housed in databases.
   C. Both the RTO and RPO apply to any systems or functions.
   D. Neither the RTO nor RPO apply to data housed in databases.

10. You are working on a BIA. You are calculating costs to determine the impact of an outage for a specific system. Which one of the following is a direct cost?

   A. Loss of customers
   B. Loss of public goodwill
   C. Loss of sales
   D. Lost opportunities

11. What type of approach does a BIA use?

   A. Bottom-up approach where servers or services are examined first
   B. Top-down approach where CBFs are e xamined first
   C. Middle-tier approach
   D. Best-guess approach

12. Mission-critical business functions are considered vital to an organization. What are they derived from?

   A. Critical success factors
   B. Critical IT resources
   C. Executive leadership
   D. Employees

13. You are performing a BIA for an organization. What should you map the critical business functions to?

   A. Personnel
   B. Revenue
   C. Replacement costs
   D. IT systems

14. Of the following choices, what are considered best practices related to a BIA?

   A. Start with clear objectives.
   B. Use different data collection methods.
   C. Mitigate identified risks.
   D. A and B only
   E. All of the above

15. A cost-benefit analysis is an important part of a BIA.

   A. True
   B. False

ENDNOTE

1. Hiles, Andrew. "Business Impact Analysis: What's Your Downside?" (Rothstein.com, 2006). *http://www.rothstein.com/articles/busimpact.html* (accessed April 24, 2010).

Mitigating Risk with a Business Continuity Plan

BUSINESS CONTINUITY PLANS (BCPs) are an important element of risk management. They help an organization plan for a major disruption or disaster and ensure that critical business functions (CBFs) continue to operate. The business impact analysis (BIA) sets the stage for the BCP by identifying CBFs. The BCP coordinator then develops the BCP to support these CBFs. The BCP coordinator has assistance from one or more BCP teams and team leads.

Activities happen in different phases if a disruption occurs. The first phase is the notification/activation phase, called by the BCP coordinator. The second phase is the recovery phase, where CBFs are recovered and returned to full operation. The final phase is the reconstitution phase, where the organization returns to normal operations. In order for a BCP to succeed, personnel need to be trained, and the BCP needs to be tested and exercised. Additionally, the BCP needs to be reviewed regularly and kept up to date.

Chapter 13 Topics

This chapter covers the following topics and concepts:

- What a business continuity plan (BCP) is
- What the elements of a BCP are
- How a BCP mitigates an organization's risk
- What best practices for implementing a BCP are

Chapter 13 Goals

When you complete this chapter, you will be able to:

- Define a BCP
- Identify the elements of a BCP
- Describe the purpose of a BCP
- Identify key responsibilities of personnel related to a BCP
- Describe the procedures in the notification/activation phase of a BCP
- Describe the procedures in the recovery phase of a BCP
- Describe the procedures in the reconstitution phase of a BCP
- Identify the different types of testing and exercises used for a BCP
- Describe how a BCP mitigates an organization's risk
- Identify different steps used to maintain the BCP
- List best practices for enabling a risk mitigation plan from a risk assessment

What Is a Business Continuity Plan (BCP)?

A business continuity plan is a plan designed to help an organization continue to operate during and after a disruption. The disruption can be manmade or a natural disaster. The goal is a continuation of operations.

BCPs can address any type of disruption or disaster. Organizations that operate by a southern coast plan for hurricanes. Businesses in the heartland's "tornado alley" plan for tornadoes. Californians plan for earthquakes. Everyone plans for fires.

Disruptions can also be from attacks or failures. If a critical server goes down, it doesn't matter what caused it to go down. It could have been from an attacker on the Web. It could have been a malware infection. It could have been a hardware or software failure. If it's a critical business function, the BCP needs to ensure that plans are in place to get it operational as soon as possible.

> **TIP**
>
> You can limit the scope of the BCP to certain parts of an organization. For example, it could include just a specific location, or specific critical business functions. However, the BCP is focused on the overall business functions rather than individual IT systems.

The scope of the BCP includes a global view of the organization. It includes the IT systems, the facilities, and the personnel. This is not to say that all elements of an organization must continue to operate during a disruption. Instead, it means that the BCP examines all elements. The BCP then identifies the elements that are mission-critical and need to continue to operate. Non-mission-critical elements that do not need to continue aren't addressed by the BCP.

Mission-critical systems are any systems identified as critical to the mission of the organization. Mission-critical can also apply to functions or processes. Mission-critical systems and activities are necessary to keep the organization functioning.

A business impact analysis (BIA) is included as part of a BCP. Chapter 12 covered BIAs in more depth. The BIA has several key objectives that directly support the BCP. These include:

- **Identify critical business functions (CBFs)**—A CBF is any function considered vital to an organization. If the CBF fails, the organization will lose the ability to perform mission-critical operations.

- **Identify critical processes supporting the CBFs**—The critical processes are the steps or actions taken to support CBFs.

- **Identify critical IT services supporting the CBFs, including any dependencies**—This includes the servers and other hardware necessary to support critical processes. Many services have dependencies. For example, an application server may need a database server to remain operational.

- **Determine acceptable downtimes for CBFs, processes, and IT service**—The BIA defines this as maximum acceptable outage (MAO). When considering the BCP, you should also determine if there are different MAOs for different times of the year. For example, a database server may be critical for end-of-year processing but not critical at other times.

All of this comes together in the BCP to align the organization's priorities. The BIA identifies the mission-critical systems, applications, and operations. The BCP provides the plan to ensure that they continue to operate even if a disaster strikes.

Similarly, the BCP includes disaster recovery plans. These help the organization restore IT services after the disaster. Any organization can create its BCP using procedures that match its needs. However, the overall steps of a BCP are:

- Charter the BCP and create BCP scope statements.
- Complete business impact analysis (BIA).
- Identify countermeasures and controls.
- Develop individual disaster recovery plans (DRPs).
- Provide training.
- Test and exercise plans.
- Maintain and update plans.

Elements of a BCP

BCPs are large, comprehensive documents. They include many elements and often cover many contingencies. There isn't a single format that will cover all requirements for all organizations. However, some guides suggest the inclusion of certain elements.

Business Continuity Versus Disaster Recovery

Business continuity (BC) and disaster recovery (DR) are not synonymous. They are two separate but related processes. Some people confuse them and use the terms interchangeably. However, they are not the same.

BC covers all functions of a business. It ensures the entire business can continue to operate in the event of a disruption. It includes a BIA. It also includes DR plans as attachments of the BCP.

DR is largely a function of IT. It includes the elements necessary to recover from a disaster. This includes elements such as backups, recoveries, and restores. DR can also be broader and include elements such as alternate sites. However, the DR plan is a part of the larger BCP.

For example, consider a bank that operates on a coast threatened by hurricanes. Customers use the bank's Web site to do online banking. If a hurricane hits, the bank wants to ensure that its Web site will continue to be available. The BCP could include a DR that includes the steps needed to recover the Web site.

Weather services provide warnings at certain hourly periods. In other words, when a hurricane is expected to hit within 72 hours, a warning is issued. The BCP could designate specific steps at 72 hours, 48 hours, and 24 hours. The DR would provide details on how to move the Web site to an alternate location.

The BCP may address other non-technical elements of the hurricane. For example, when should the bank close? When should the vault be locked? Should guards remain inside? Are there any other security precautions to take?

After the disaster passes, both the BC and DR plans would have different goals, but they would work together. Again, the BC is focused on getting the overall business functions back to normal. The DR is focused on restoring and recovering IT functions.

For example, the following sections are often included in a BCP:

- Purpose
- Scope
- Assumptions and planning principles
- System description and architecture
- Responsibilities
- Notification/activation phase
- Recovery phase
- Reconstitution phase
- Plan training, testing, and exercises
- Plan maintenance

The following sections describe the contents of these sections.

Purpose

The purpose of the BCP is to ensure that mission-critical elements of an organization continue to operate after a disruption. The disruption can be any event that has the potential to stop operations. You implement the BCP when a disruption occurs or is imminent. The BCP then stays in place until the restoration of normal operations.

You maintain only critical business functions during the disruption. In other words, you don't continue to do business as usual during a disaster. The BIA identifies the CBFs and their priorities. The BCP ensures that all the elements are in place to maintain these CBFs.

The BIA also includes acceptable outage times. Some CBFs may need to be kept operational with minimal outage. Other CBFs may have lower priorities. Depending on the recovery time objectives identified in the BIA, these lower priority CBFs may be down for hours or even days.

Scope

Just as with any project, you need to define the scope of the BCP. The success of the project is dependent on personnel understanding the tasks.

If there is no scope statement, two problems can occur. First, the desired tasks aren't finished. In other words, the BCP will be incomplete. Second, scope creep can occur. Scope creep happens when the project keeps taking on additional tasking. For example, the intended scope may cover a single location, but instead the BCP includes research and recommendations for five locations.

The scope statement can include several key items. For example, they could include the location, the systems, the employees, and the vendors. Only the critical systems identified in the BIA should be included. Include employees who are necessary to support the critical systems. Identify employees by title or position rather than name. If parts or supplies can be obtained only from a single source, the vendor could be included in the BCP.

Although a BCP will take a global view of the organization, it doesn't have to cover the entire organization. For example, it could cover only specific locations. Consider a company with a main office in Atlanta and regional offices in Chicago, Los Angeles, and Miami. The company could create four separate BCPs. One BCP would be for each location.

Individual departments or divisions may have smaller threats that need to be addressed from a business continuity perspective. However, it's common for these departments to use contingency planning or redundancy measures. You wouldn't address these smaller threats with separate BCPs.

Assumptions and Planning Principles

Every BCP needs to include some basic assumptions and planning principles. These are very helpful in the initial development of the BCP. They are also useful in the implementation phases.

> **TIP**
>
> These assumptions and principles will drive much of the decision-making process. They need to be accurate. For example, if you assume that you'll never lose power, you won't plan for alternate power sources. However, if a disruption does result in a power loss, the rest of the plan will be useless.

You can review and assess assumptions and principles in several different categories. These categories include the incidents you plan to address in the plan. They also include elements such as strategy, priorities, and required support. The following sections provide guidance for these areas.

A key planning principle is the length of time you expect to continue operations under the BCP before returning to normal operations. For example, consider a hurricane. The company could plan on continuing operations under the BCP for seven days following a hurricane.

Seven days then becomes a guiding principle for many other elements. You'll need seven days of supplies. If you're using generators, you'll need seven days of fuel. You'll need seven days of food and water for personnel.

Incidents to Be Included and Excluded

Many BCPs identify specific incidents that are included and excluded. In other words, the BCP may be designed to address specific disruptions due to hurricanes or earthquakes. It may also be designed to address generic incidents, such as power loss from any cause.

Consider an organization that is in a hurricane-prone area. You'll have many hours if not days of advance notice before the hurricane hits. Safety precautions and preparedness steps are well known for hurricanes. Anything that can blow away should be stored inside. Expect wind damage. For some areas, expect flooding.

Now compare this to an organization in an area prone to earthquakes. You don't have any notice. One moment everything is calm. The next moment buildings are collapsing. Depending on the severity of the quake, damage can range from very little to mass destruction.

The responses to each of these incidents are very different. If you know what incidents the BCP will be used to respond to, you'll have a better idea of what steps to include.

On the other hand, some incidents are generic. For example, your BCP could include plans to provide backup generator power to the organization if power is lost. You could use these steps no matter how the power was lost. You could also include plans to relocate to another location if one location is not usable. Again, it doesn't matter why the location is unusable. It could be due to fire, flood, tornado, earthquake, or something else.

Strategy

The strategy of the BCP identifies some of the key elements of the plan. This includes elements such as location, notification, transportation, and more.

If your organization is in a single location, the strategy is to address this single location. However, if the organization is in several locations, you'll need to identify a strategy for each location.

For example, you may decide that key IT resources will be centrally located and maintained. Consider a large university with many buildings spread across an expansive campus. Instead of maintaining operations at each building, the BCP could identify specific resources to maintain at one or more central buildings.

If an incident has occurred, or is imminent, you'll need to notify BCP team members. It's important to identify how to notify all key players. Many organizations use phone trees. One person starts the process. This person calls several key people such as team leads. These individuals call people on their lists. Eventually, everyone is notified.

Transportation may be a concern. If members will need transportation from one area to another, you should address this need in the BCP. You could designate company vehicles for shuttling personnel as needed. Additionally, if you need to move equipment, you'll need to identify how you will move it.

Supplies are an important concern if you need them for continued operation. For example, if the company will need supplies to continue producing a product, you need to ensure they are on hand.

> **TIP**
>
> Having supplies on hand for continued production may conflict with other organizational principles. For example, many organizations use a just-in-time philosophy. Parts and supplies arrive when needed. Stocking seven days of supplies at all times for the BCP ties up funds in inventory. In addition, some supplies need to be rotated to ensure they don't expire or become outdated.

Utilities such as water, power, and gas are needed. If your strategy is to be able to continue to operate on the BCP plan for seven days, you'll need to supply your own utilities for seven days.

Communications is another concern. Typical communications are often interrupted during a disruption. Land-based phone lines may not function, and in some situations, cell-based phones are also disrupted. Many organizations use push-to-talk cell phones. These work as cell phones and as walkie-talkies.

The benefit of the push-to-talk phones is that they don't require external resources. They simply broadcast on a frequency. As long as the other cell phone is in reach, it will get the message. One approach is to purchase many of these push-to-talk phones and issue them to key players during the first phase of the plan.

> **TIP**
>
> It's not a good idea to depend heavily on technology during some business disruptions. For example, if e-mail is the only method of communication for the BCP, communication could easily be cut off during a disruption. Without this communication, a whole host of other problems could arise.

Priorities

The BIA identifies critical business functions, critical resources, and their priorities. It's common to reaffirm these priorities in the BCP.

The BCP will ensure that efforts focus on returning the top priority systems first. These top priority systems will have the most resources dedicated to them.

Required Support

The BCP requires support during every stage. To begin with, the BCP requires management support. If it's not supported by management, you won't be able to get the required input and support from personnel. You won't be able to get the required funding. Without support from top-level management, the BCP is doomed to fail.

▶**TIP**

Ensure steps are taken to provide for families of employees. This is especially true if employees need to stay on site during the disruption. You don't want employees to have to choose between taking care of their families or the organization in an emergency.

Later in this chapter, responsibilities are listed for individuals and teams. Clearly, it's important that these teams provide support to the BCP and are supported in their endeavors.

During the notification/activation phase, all personnel need to respond as quickly as possible. Some personnel may be identified as mission-critical and will need to remain at the site during the emergency.

System Description and Architecture

The BCP identifies critical business functions that need to remain operational during the disruption. Each of these CBFs has individual systems that support it. It's important to ensure that you have current descriptions and documentation on these systems.

This documentation needs to be detailed enough to identify the critical system, and the supporting architecture. If the documentation isn't available, or is out of date, maintaining and recovering the CBFs becomes much more difficult.

While documenting the CBF systems for the BCP, you can also look for elements that you may need to address in the recovery plan. For example, documentation may show that a system must maintain connectivity via a wide area network (WAN) link to stay operational. If the plan doesn't include an alternative, this WAN link becomes a single point of failure.

For example, consider Figure 13-1. This shows a WAN link connecting a database server at the headquarters office to a remote location. If the WAN link fails, the CBF fails. Therefore, the WAN link must stay operational.

On the other hand, Figure 13-2 shows an alternative. The original WAN link is used the majority of the time. If it fails, the modem is used. Although the modem will be substantially slower than the WAN link, it may meet the needs during a disruption.

The following sections identify some common documentation to include with the BCP.

FIGURE 13-1

Database servers connected via WAN link.

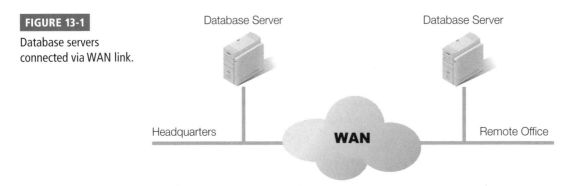

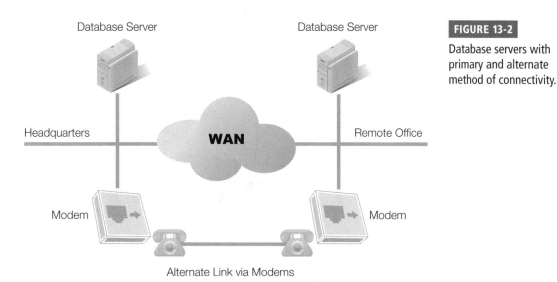

FIGURE 13-2

Database servers with primary and alternate method of connectivity.

Overview

The overview section provides a description of the CBF. It describes it in big-picture terms. For example, consider the following description of a critical database hosted at headquarters of an organization:

> Headquarters hosts the Sales database on a database server. This database is critical to several different business functions.
>
> - Management at headquarters uses this database to identify and track sales throughout the company.
> - Ordering and production personnel use this database to order and track products shipped to stores.
> - Employees at any store query the database to determine if an item is in stock locally or at another store. The database hosts inventories within each store.
>
> Sales at each store are recorded on the store's local database. Each store database synchronizes with the headquarters database server once an hour.

> **NOTE**
>
> In this example, the database server hosted at headquarters is critical. As described, there is no indication that the store database servers are critical. In other words, a store database server could fail without affecting the headquarters database. However, in another situation, it's possible that the database server at each store location is critical. In this case you could include all of them in the same BCP, or you could create a BCP for each store.

With this description, you understand that each location has a database. This database is synchronized with the database at headquarters. It doesn't provide details but does provide enough information for anyone to understand the big picture.

FIGURE 13-3

Database servers
connected between
stores and headquarters.

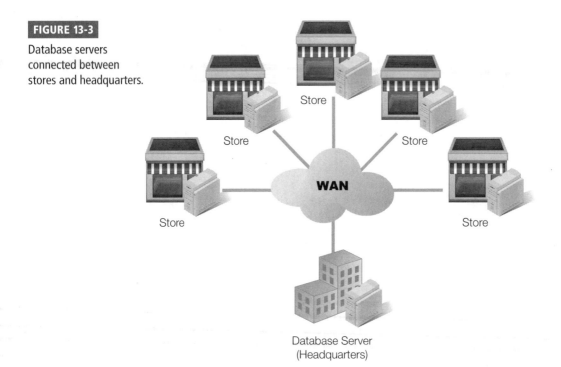

Database Server
(Headquarters)

Functional Description

The functional description provides more details of the systems. It builds on the overview.

Many systems interact with other critical systems, so it's valuable to include figures whenever possible. As an example, consider Figure 13-3. This shows a diagram for the database described in the overview section. It shows how each of the outlying stores connects to headquarters over the WAN links.

The description would provide more details. This would include the store names and the store locations. It would include details on the WAN links. If there were redundant WAN links, it would describe them.

Details on the headquarters server are also important. This description should include the server name, the operating system, and the database application used. For example, the server could be running Windows Server 2008 with SQL Server 2008.

If the server includes any fault-tolerance capabilities, you'd mention it here. For example, a two-node failover cluster allows one server to fail without affecting the services provided by the database. Servers may also include redundant array of inexpensive disk (RAID) configurations. With RAID, drives can fail but the system will continue to operate.

Sensitivity of Data and Criticality of Operations

The BCP includes information on the sensitivity of the system's data. It also includes details on the criticality of the system operations.

Chapter 7 described the importance of classifying data. Any organization will have some secret or proprietary data. Some data may be classified as private and used only within the organization. Other data may be public and freely available. The classification determines the level of protection required for the data.

If the system houses data, you need to ensure that the data is protected according to its level of classification. With this in mind, the BCP needs to document the sensitivity of the data. In the midst of an emergency, security precautions aren't at the forefront of everyone's mind. However, if the sensitivity is documented in the BCP, people will know what precautions to take.

TIP

You may remember that the primary objective of a security system is to protect confidentiality, integrity, and availability. Consider the loss of any of these when documenting this section in the BCP. For example, what will happen if the organization loses the availability of data or a system?

For example, a database may collect customer information including credit card data. It may also include sales data for all its stores. The organization could classify this data as private or proprietary. If you move the database server, you will need to take steps to protect the data during transit at both the original and alternate locations.

Consider the data hosted on the headquarters database server in the previous example. Because this data includes sales data, the server very likely holds customer data, including credit card information. It likely also holds actual sale amounts, which most organizations try to keep private whenever possible.

Criticality of operations identifies the impact if the IT service fails. Criticality is usually documented in the BIA, but is repeated in the BCP so that it's clear. It can be a simple statement. For example, you could use the following statement for the headquarters database server mentioned in the previous example:

> If the database server fails, outlying stores will not be able to query the database for products. They won't be able to verify the product is in their store or another store. If store servers are unable to synchronize with the headquarters server, they will queue the sales data on their systems until it can be sent.

> Ordering of new products will be delayed, since the sales of existing products will be unknown. Additionally, management will not have current data available. This can affect decisions on many levels.

Identifying Critical Equipment, Software, Data, Documents, and Supplies

The BCP should list all the critical components for the system. There are two reasons for including this data. First, it makes it clear which components are needed for the CBF. Second, it provides a list that you can use to restore the system from scratch.

This list includes any equipment, such as servers, switches, and routers. Because the servers may need to be rebuilt from scratch, the BCP should list the operating system and any applications needed to support the system. If an image is used to rebuild servers, it will list the version number.

Data can include a database hosted on the system. It can also include any type of files, such as documents or spreadsheets. Last, the list can include any needed supplies. This can be simple office supplies, such as printer paper and toner. For some systems, it can include technical supplies, such as special oils for machinery or tools needed for maintenance.

Whenever possible, the location of these items should be included. Some organizations create "crash carts" that include all the components needed to rebuild a system. Crash carts include CDs or DVDs for operation systems, applications, or images. They also include basic instructions for building or rebuilding systems.

Telecommunications

Required connectivity with other systems is an important element to document in the BCP. Connectivity can be from the internal network. It can be via the Internet. It can be via dedicated WAN lines. Communication can also be via simple phone lines.

External connections often use lines from telecommunications companies. Internet service providers (ISPs) often provide more than just access to the Internet. They can also lease lines used for WANs and virtual private networks (VPNs).

Document any required communication links. For example, if a database receives updates from other databases using VPN lines, include it. Just as important, if the system can operate without specific telecommunications lines, identify what is optional.

Responsibilities

Just as within a project, it's important to lay out responsibilities within a BCP. When you assign responsibilities, this makes things clear to all concerned. When tasking is not completed or behind schedule, it is easier to get it back on track.

Employees in the organization will fill specific roles in a BCP. This includes the BCP program manager, the BCP coordinator, BCP team leads, and BCP team members.

This section covers these roles and responsibilities. It also covers some of the other key personnel who may be included in the BCP.

BCP Program Manager

A BCP program manager (PM) usually manages multiple BCP projects within a large organization. For example, a large organization could have multiple locations and BCPs for each location. A BCP coordinator manages a BCP. The BCP program manager ensures that each BCP is progressing as expected. The PM can use traditional project management skills to manage these BCPs. For example, every BCP has a start date, milestones, and end date for the development stage. Additionally, each will have dates for the reviews to start. These reviews will also have milestones and end dates.

The BCP PM is responsible for ensuring that each of the BCPs is on track. Depending on the hierarchy of the organization, the BCP PM may not have any authority over the individual BCP coordinators. This requires exceptional communication skills on the part of the PM.

Other organizations may have a specific department of project managers. Personnel in this department have specialized project management skills. Lead program managers oversee several PMs. In this situation, the BCP PMs have direct authority over the BCP coordinators.

BCP Coordinator

The BCP coordinator is in charge of a specific BCP. This individual can have two roles depending on the stage of the BCP:

- Before the BCP is completed and activated, this person is responsible for developing and completing it.

- When the BCP is completed and activated, the BCP coordinator is responsible for declaring the emergency and activating the BCP.

When an emergency is declared, the BCP coordinator contacts appropriate teams or team leads. For example, if an emergency management team is used, the BCP coordinator will contact the emergency management team lead.

BCP Teams

A BCP can't be planned, implemented, and executed by a single person. Instead, teams are put together to help the process. There are several possible teams you can put together to help.

If your organization is small, you may have a single BCP team. This single BCP team has the responsibilities of all the individual teams mentioned in the following sections. Members have different levels of expertise. Some members will be more active during different phases than others. Larger organizations have multiple teams with different goals and responsibilities.

Although different teams have different goals, members need some common skills and abilities. Most importantly, they need to work together. When picking members, ensure they have the ability to work with others. One member who can work with others and get the job done is better than numerous "experts" who excel at finding fault and who rarely complete a team project.

Three commonly used teams are the **Emergency Management Team (EMT)**, the **Damage Assessment Team (DAT)**, and the **Technical Recovery Team (TRT)**. These teams are described as follows:

- **Emergency Management Team**—This team is composed of senior managers. They have overall authority for the recovery of the system but also work closely with the BCP coordinator. At this point, there is the potential for a conflict. Who's in charge? The BCP coordinator or the EMT lead? The BCP identifies who makes the ultimate decisions. For example, the BCP coordinator may be in charge until the EMT lead shows up and then authority passes to the EMT lead. Either way, the EMT works closely with the DAT to identify damage. The EMT also works closely with the BCP coordinator to determine the response.

- **Damage Assessment Team**—This team assesses the damage and declares the severity of the incident. The members primarily collect and report data but don't take action. The exception is if they identify personnel that need assistance.

Preserving the health and safety of personnel is always a top priority. The team can include IT personnel, facility personnel, and any other personnel overseeing resources. Team members report to the emergency management team. The BCP may designate specific forms to be used by this team to report their findings. For example, a damage assessment form would allow the members to document the location and severity of damage they discover.

- **Technical Recovery Team**—The technical recovery team is responsible for recovering the critical IT resources. Remember, during the disruption you will recover and restore only the IT resources identified in the BIA. The members of the technical recovery team will need skills directly related to the resource they are recovering. For example, if team members need to restore a database server, they need knowledge of how to do so.

Key Personnel

The BCP may identify additional personnel who have other responsibilities. These personnel would vary from one organization to another. They could include:

- **Critical vendors**—If specific supplies or other resources are needed from a critical vendor, the BCP would identify their responsibilities. A critical vendor could be a vendor that is the sole source for a specific part of product that you sell. It could also be a vendor that will deliver emergency supplies within a certain time. For example, you could contract with a vendor to deliver potable water to the site anytime a hurricane is within 36 hours of striking. Service level agreements (SLAs) may be in place with the vendor to ensure they provide the service when needed.

- **Critical contractors**—Many companies have contractors on staff in addition to full-time employees. Contractors can be full-time workers supplementing the staff, or part-time workers fulfilling a specific need. If you expect contractors to have specific roles in the BCP, you should identify them. For example, some contractor positions may be mission-critical, requiring the workers to work on site through any type of disruption. Identify the specific responsibilities of these contractors in the BCP.

- **Telecommuters**—Telecommuters often work from home. As long as the organization is fully operational, this usually works. However, during a disruption, the telecommuters may not be able to access the organization's resources and may not be able to accomplish any work. The organization may want these employees to access resources at a different location. Alternately, these workers may have skills that will help the organization get through the disruption and they may need to report to the work site. The BCP documents what the organization expects of these workers during a disruption.

Order of Succession and Delegation of Authority

In some disasters, the key personnel may not be available. For example, the chief executive officer (CEO) may want to be informed by the BCP coordinator prior to activating the BCP. However, what if the CEO is on vacation in another country? Whom should the BCP coordinator notify instead?

The BCP would include an order of succession to address these types of situations. You can also think of this as a chain of command. An organization could designate the order of succession as follows:

- CEO
- Chief information officer (CIO)
- Vice presidents (VPs) in the following order: service delivery, sales, marketing
- Department directors in the following order: service delivery, sales, marketing

If the CEO or the CIO were on site, he or she would be contacted first. If the CEO or CIO isn't there, the VP of Service Delivery is contacted. Notice that if both the VPs of Service Delivery and Sales are there, the order of succession specifies that the VP of Service Delivery is first.

Similarly, you may want to identify what authority you can delegate. Decisions made during a major crisis can affect the organization for years afterwards. The BCP may specify that either the CEO or CIO must make some decisions, even if he or she isn't on site. If the CEO or CIO isn't reachable, these decisions can then be delegated based on the order of succession. If authority is not delegated, personnel on site may not be able to reach an executive, so decisions can't be made. The inaction may cause more damage than making a decision that is less than perfect.

Notification/Activation Phase

The BCP coordinator declares the notification/activation phase. This is the point when the disruption has occurred or is imminent. Comparing hurricanes and earthquakes shows how this phase can differ depending on the disruption.

Weather forecasters are able to give warnings several days in advance for many hurricanes. Although the forecasts aren't 100 percent accurate, they do provide advance warning for an organization to prepare in case it does hit. You can write the BCP so that different steps are taken at different stages.

For example, Table 13-1 shows what actions to take at different stages. In the table, the time frames are identified with a specific stage or level code. This stage is internal and indicates what actions to take when that code is reached. This is not a complete list, but it does give you an idea of how different actions are taken at different times.

An earthquake doesn't give any notification. Instead, it just hits. What's more, after a major earthquake hits, you can expect many aftershocks.

> **NOTE**
>
> Time frames are sometimes reported differently by different sources. For example, one TV station may say a hurricane will make landfall in 75 hours. Another TV station says it will hit in 72 hours. The BCP coordinator will be the authority to declare when a specific hurricane stage is reached.

13

Business Continuity Plan

TABLE 13-1 Hurricane checklist.	
TIME FRAME	**ACTIONS**
96 hours Hurricane Stage 4	Inform all personnel that a hurricane can hit within 96 hours. Begin general cleanup outside to ensure that materials that can become projectiles in hurricane-force winds are moved inside. Review steps and responsibilities for other stages.
72 hours Hurricane Stage 3	Review supply list. Ensure that all needed supplies are on hand. For buildings susceptible to flooding, begin sandbagging activities. Review steps and responsibilities for other stages.
48 hours Hurricane Stage 2	Release nonessential personnel to take care of their homes and families. Test backup generators. Notify the hurricane crew that they are on call and when they should report to the site.
24 hours Hurricane Stage 1	Bring in the hurricane crew that will stay throughout the hurricane. Release all other personnel.

With this in mind, the BCP for an earthquake will have a much different notification/activation phase. You could even write the BCP so that personnel are required to take specific actions when it hits, without being formally notified. For example, the response team members could immediately report to their lead for direction.

The BCP coordinator will still activate the BCP. This ensures that everyone is notified. However, if an earthquake hits, it will be obvious to anyone in the area what happened.

Notification Procedures

> **TIP**
>
> Issuing the BCP coordinator a cell phone is a justifiable expense in this instance. The BCP coordinator should be reachable at any time of day or night to respond to major disruptions or disasters.

Notification procedures can vary from one organization to another. However, the most important step is to ensure that the BCP coordinator is notified of any disruption or disaster covered by the BCP. If a disruption or disaster occurs during working hours, the BCP coordinator will probably be on the scene quickly. If it's after hours, the BCP coordinator should be tracked down and contacted.

It's common to use some type of phone tree to notify the teams and team members. For example, the BCP coordinator could notify the team leads for the EMT, DAT, and TRT. Team leads can all notify all the members of their teams.

Damage Assessment Procedures

The Damage Assessment Team (DAT) is responsible for assessing the damage and reporting the damage to the BCP coordinator. The team's primary goal is to identify the extent of the damage as quickly as possible.

Again, the time when the DAT goes into action is dependent on the disruption. If it's a hurricane, the members will assess the damage inside the building as the storm hits. For example, they will assess internal flooding and leaks due to storm damage as they occur. When the storm has passed and it's safe to go outside, the DAT will assess the damage externally. If it's an immediate disaster such as an earthquake, the DAT will go into action as the members are called.

Data is passed to the EMT team lead and the BCP coordinator. They work together to determine the extent of the damage based on all the reports, and steps to take.

The EMT team lead will then make a determination on what to do. If critical operations can continue to operate on site, the TRT will begin recovery operations. If damage is extensive and critical operations cannot continue in the same location, operations may need to be moved at an alternate location.

> **TIP**
>
> BCPs will already have determined alternate locations. Chapter 14 presents hot sites, warm sites, and cold sites in more detail.

Plan Activation

Although the BCP coordinator is responsible for activating the BCP, there are some criteria. In other words, the BCP coordinator doesn't just make the decision based on a hunch.

For example, the following items are valid reasons to activate the BCP:

- Safety of personnel
- Damage to the building affecting critical business functions
- Loss of operations of one or more critical business functions
- Specific criteria identified in the BCP, such as a hurricane warning or an earthquake

Specific responsibilities when the plan is activated include:

- **BCP coordinator**—The BCP coordinator's primary responsibility after activating the plan is ensuring everyone is aware that it's activated. This includes anyone involved in the plan. The BCP coordinator will notify team leads. The coordinator's responsibility also includes notification of senior management personnel, such as the CEO or CIO.
- **EMT Lead**—The EMT lead coordinates the actions of the EMT. The team lead also works closely with the DAT lead and the BCP coordinator.

- **EMT**—The EMT works with the DAT and TRT as directed by the EMT. Members of this team also interact with personnel outside the organization. For example, a member of this team will talk to the press and ensure the organization presents an image of being "in control" as much as possible. If the organization looks as if it is in chaos, public trust may be lost, affecting the goodwill of the company for years to come.
- **DAT Lead**—The DAT lead coordinates the actions of the DAT. The team lead also works closely with the EMT lead and the BCP coordinator.
- **DAT**—The DAT gathers all the information on the disruption or disaster. The goal is to provide specific details on what is damaged and the extent of the damage. Whenever possible, the team tries to determine if the site is recoverable. This information is reported to the DAT lead.

If the site is not recoverable within a certain period of time, operations may need to move to an alternate location. The BCP coordinator, EMT lead, and DAT lead work together to determine possible recovery solutions based on available data.

Alternate Assessment Procedures

In some instances, the DAT may not be able to assess the damage directly. If necessary, the team can do an indirect assessment based on the available information.

For example, when hurricane Katrina hit the Gulf Coast in 2005 many organizations had to evacuate. Additionally, personnel were not able to return right away. However, images shown on TV showed the extent of the damage in the area. A company may not have seen its building directly, but saw damage to buildings near them. Executives knew that they weren't returning to operations in the original building anytime soon.

Personal Location Control Form

Many organizations use a notification roster. This form identifies the name and contact information of appropriate personnel. It can be used in many different ways. The primary purpose is to contact personnel when necessary.

For example, consider a plan that is being implemented for an imminent disaster, such as a hurricane. This form can be used to phone all personnel and make sure they know what is happening, and what their responsibilities are.

This same form can be used by the BCP coordinator to locate and talk to any of the team leads. Similarly, any of the team leads can use it to contact personnel on his or her team. The format can be as simple as that shown in Table 13-2.

TABLE 13-2 Personal location control form.

NAME	PHONES		E-MAIL
Darril Gibson	Cell	xxx-xxx-xxxx	Darril@sy0-201.com
	Home	xxx-xxx-xxxx	
	Work	xxx-xxx-xxxx	

Recovery Phase

The next step after the activation phase is the recovery phase. This is when the Technical Recovery Team members go to work. They have several goals, including:

- Restore temporary operations to critical systems
- Repair damage done to original systems
- Recover damage to original systems

Once the TRT has completed its job, the critical operations will be functioning. Remember though, the TRT does not focus on recovering and restoring all operations. Instead, the TRT only focuses on the CBFs identified in the BIA.

It's common for TRT members to use specific disaster recovery plans (DRPs) to recover individual systems. For example, the BCP may designate a Web site and database server as critical. A DRP could be included as an attachment to the BCP, showing how to recover and restore these services.

Recovery Planning

The success of the recovery phase is based on the recovery planning done beforehand. As someone once said, "It wasn't raining when Noah built the Ark." In other words, it's too late to plan when the disaster strikes. The plans must be made earlier.

Recovery planning often takes the format of a disaster recovery plan (DRP). Chapter 14 covers DRPs in more detail. In short, the DRP will identify the steps and procedures to restore and recover systems after an incident.

Recovery Goal

The recovery goal is dependent on several factors. The goal could be to recover a portion of the functionality of a CBF. For example, a database may need to be operational so that it can accept some updates and some queries. However, it may not need to be able to support the full load of normal operations.

On the other hand, the recovery goal could be much more complete. For example, an organization may have services provided at one location. When a disaster strikes, it may need to restore all functionality at another location.

The TRT will perform the work to achieve the recovery goals. The DRP guides the work, but it is possible that the work will be in phases, depending on the depth of the recovery. This is especially true when operations have to be relocated to a different location.

Technical Recovery Team Lead

The TRT lead will oversee the work done by the TRT. This lead will need to be very familiar with existing DRPs and may even have authored them.

This person will need to coordinate all the activities of TRT. The lead will also need to keep the EMT lead and BCP coordinator informed of the progress.

Technical Recovery Team

The TRT performs the recovery work. The extent of its work will depend on the extent of the damage. It will also depend on whether or not operations are moved.

For example, a hurricane could have caused water damage in the server room. On-site personnel may have limited the amount of damage by quickly killing the power and moving the servers before the water reached them. Recovery could be as simple as cleaning up the water damage, moving the servers back, and rebooting them.

On the other hand, an earthquake could have destroyed the building. The servers are now buried beneath the rubble. Recovery is much more complex. The servers need to be recovered and restored at an alternate location. The offsite backups will need to be retrieved and shipped to the alternate locations. The servers will need to be configured and data restored.

The success of the TRT is often dependent on the advance work done with the DRP. Additionally, moving operations from one location to another is a huge project. You should expect problems. If this plan has never been tested and personnel have never been trained, expect more problems.

Reconstitution Phase (Return to Normal Operations)

The last stage is the reconstitution phase. This is where you return functions to normal. This includes both the critical functions and the non-mission-essential functions.

This phase begins when one of two things occurs:

- The damage at the original location is repaired
- Management decides to move operations permanently to an alternate location

Original or New Site Restoration

If damage at the original location is extensive, management may decide to move operations. This decision will involve many factors.

Consider if critical business operations were moved to a regional office as an alternate location. A fire damaged the original location. The DAT determined that the original building was uninhabitable unless it was rebuilt. Now management must decide where to relocate operations.

Even though critical operations are at the alternate location, they may not be able to support the non-critical operations. Management could decide to move all operations to a new site and restore them there. On the other hand, the damage could have been only minor. The critical operations would then need to be moved soon from the alternate location back to the original location.

Either way, the TRT will perform the primary work. This team is most familiar with the DRPs and the steps that need to be taken to restore the functions.

If operations move to a new location, the TRT will be involved. If the operations move back to the original location, the TRT will also be involved.

Move Least Critical Functions First

When moving CBFs from an alternate location back to the original location, you should move the least critical functions first. This helps ensure the most critical functions aren't interrupted.

When functions are restored at the original location, you'll likely have some problems. It may not go smoothly at first. However, if you're moving the least critical functions first, only the least critical functions will be affected.

After you get the kinks out of the process, you can move the more critical functions.

Concurrent Processing

Concurrent processing has operations running at two separate locations at the same time. Imagine that a disruption caused operations to move to an alternate location. After the disaster, you'll rebuild systems at the primary location. Many experts recommend operations at both locations for three to five days. This will ensure that the primary location systems are running smoothly.

For example, imagine a disaster forced the organization to move operations to an alternate location. CBFs are running successfully. The TRT has been working hard and now has the CBFs running at the original location as well. The team says it's ready to switch over.

However, instead of switching over completely, you can run operations at both sites at the same time. In many systems, it's possible to gradually move the load from the alternate location to the original location. If undiscovered bugs begin to appear in the original location, you still have the alternate location running. You can easily switch back.

An organization will often keep the alternate location up and operational until it is sure the original location is operational. After all functionality is tested and confirmed, operations are switched over completely.

> **NOTE**
>
> Not all systems will support concurrent processing. If it's possible, use concurrent processing. However, some systems may present technical challenges that prevent you from running both systems at the same time.

Plan Deactivation

You deactivate the BCP once everything is normalized. There are a few things to consider at this stage. First, just returning the original site to operations doesn't necessarily mean that everything is normalized. For example, if you moved operations to an alternate location, you'll need to clean things up there.

The alternate location may have started with all the equipment you needed. On the other hand, you may have shipped multiple servers, routers, and switches there. You'll need to return all the equipment. The goal is to return it to how it was before the disruption. Even better, use the Boy Scout rule and leave it a little better than you found it.

An important consideration is data. If any data was moved to the alternate location, you need to ensure it is not left there. After a major disaster, management sometimes decides to leave some hardware staged at the alternate location. However, if data is left on these systems, it presents an unnecessary risk. It could be retrieved by anyone who has physical access to the alternate location.

Again, the technical recovery team will be responsible for these steps. It's worthwhile to include a checklist in the BCP to ensure that nothing critical is overlooked.

Plan Training, Testing, and Exercises

Although creating the BCP plan is a huge step, it's not enough. You need to take steps to train personnel about the plan. You also need to take time to test and exercise the plan. The overall goals of these steps are:

- Training: Teach people details about the BCP.
- Testing: Show that the BCP will work as planned.
- Exercises: Show how the BCP will work.

BCP Training

The primary people to train for the BCP are the members of the teams. They should have a good understanding of what their actual responsibilities are when the BCP is activated. The BCP coordinator is responsible for ensuring all personnel are trained.

Remember, each of the BCP teams has different responsibilities. You don't need to train all the teams on all of their responsibilities at the same time. You could do several training sessions as follows:

> **TIP**
>
> Because team leads will need to interact with each other, you can have each of the team leads attend all team training. For example, the DAT lead could attend the EMT and TRT training sessions, in addition to the DAT training.

- **Training session for all teams**—This gives everyone an overall idea of the plan, and how each one fits into its success.
- **EMT training**—This training is targeted at members of the EMT. It identifies their specific responsibilities.
- **DAT training**—This training is targeted at members of the DAT. It stresses the importance of the assessment and identifies tools or checklists to use.
- **TRT training**—This training is targeted at members of the TRT. It includes reviews of each of the individual disaster recovery plans.

Training should be conducted at least annually. If the BCP or systems change, training will need to be done more often. For example, if a critical system identified in the BCP is replaced, the BCP needs to be modified. Subject matter experts update the DRP. Members of the TRT will then need training on the new DRP.

BCP Testing

BCP testing should be completed at least annually. The goal of the testing is to show that the steps within the BCP are achievable. In other words, it shows that the plan will work. It also provides team members an opportunity to walk through the steps of the plan.

Testing may include the following steps:

- **Test individual steps within each phase of the BCP**—This requires a line-by-line review of the BCP. Procedures such as performing a recall can be tested only by retrieving the recall roster and calling people on it.

- **Test all disaster recovery plans**—This ensures that the steps in the DRP can be completed as written. For example, a DRP may identify steps to rebuild and recover a database server. An administrator will follow the DRP on an offline system to determine if the steps succeed.

- **Locate and test alternate resources**—If the plan identifies alternate locations or alternate resources, identify and test them. For example, if the plan identifies an alternate location, test the alternate location to see if it can actually support the critical business functions.

Testing should reveal any problems or deficiencies with the plan. This includes any problems with the steps, resources, or personnel. You should resolve any problems as soon as possible.

BCP Test Exercises

The primary purpose of BCP exercises is to show how the BCP will work. BCP exercises should be challenging but realistic. Additionally, tests should present problems that are solvable.

> **TIP**
>
> BCP exercises should not affect normal mission operations. Any steps that will affect operations can be tested with a simulation.

In addition to testing the capabilities of the BCP, an exercise will also build the confidence of participants. If an actual emergency occurs, people will think back to the exercise. If everything failed, they won't feel very confident about the plan during the emergency. They may even abandon or try to circumvent it during an emergency.

Many organizations use a phased approach toward exercising a plan. Instead of doing a full-scale exercises at first, they perform tabletop and functional exercises.

Tabletop Exercises

A tabletop exercise brings all the members together to talk though the process. Think about all the team members sitting around a conference room table. The BCP coordinator then presents a scenario to the team members.

Team members identify what they'd do to respond to the scenario. Remember, at this point the BCP is written and has been approved. Ideally, the team member responses would match what the BCP says. However, in this setting participants may place themselves in the actual situation and identify different problems.

You can do multiple scenarios as tabletop exercises. For example, one scenario may be a weather-related event, such as a hurricane. The BCP coordinator can identify the stage and team leads, or members can respond by identifying what they'll do. Another scenario can be more immediate, such as a fire that occurs in the middle of the night.

It's important to document the exercise. You can have someone who isn't a member of any of the BCP teams document and evaluate the exercise. This outside perspective can be valuable in ensuring that all the issues are addressed.

> **NOTE**
>
> The primary difference between testing and a functional exercise is that testing is done without a time frame. In other words, you give team members advance notice to perform a test, and they can take their time to perform it. An exercise is more immediate. You don't give team members any advance notice. Make sure you document the amount of time it takes to complete the exercise.

Functional Exercises

A functional exercise evaluates specific functions within the BCP. For example, imagine that the BCP identifies an alternate location for some critical functions. You can perform a functional exercise to restore and recover all the critical resources at the alternate location.

Functional exercises can be less dramatic and resource intensive. For example, you can simply initiate the recall roster. This exercise verifies that the recall roster is accurate and identifies how long it will take to complete the recall.

Just as with a tabletop exercise, it's important to document the results of the functional exercise. The BCP coordinator or someone who isn't a member of any of the BCP teams can do this.

Full-Scale Exercises

A full-scale exercise is more realistic than either tabletop or functional exercises. It simulates an actual disruption of critical business functions. Team members aren't sitting around a table discussing what they'd do. Instead, they take action.

Full-scale exercises require many resources to complete. The primary resource is personnel. However, full-scale exercises provide the most realistic view of how team members will respond to an actual emergency.

Just as with other exercises, it's important to document the results. Depending on the breadth of the plan, you may have several outside observers document what they see. Additionally, you should gather input from the team members when the exercise is complete. They will likely have insight into what elements of the BCP worked. They may also have ideas to improve the BCP.

You can then compile and document this data into a single report. Just as with other types of exercises, you should address any issues. This may require modification of the BCP.

TABLE 13-3 BCP version control page.			
DATE	**AUTHOR**	**VERSION**	**COMMENTS**
xx / xx / xx	Individual or group making the change	Current version of the document such as 1.1, 2.0, and so on	Comments about the changes made to the document

Plan Maintenance

The BCP coordinator is responsible for the BCP plan. This also includes reviews and updates of the BCP. There are several specific reasons to update the BCP, such as:

- Changes to the IT infrastructure
- Regular updating, such as annually
- After testing or exercises

BCP Plan Revisions Tracking

All revisions to the BCP need to be documented. This ensures that people can easily tell if the document has been modified, and they have the most up-to-date version. Many organizations use a simple version control page. For example, Table 13-3 shows an example of a version control page.

In addition to documenting the change in the version control page, you should also ensure that all relevant parties know about the change. For example, if changes directly affect the EMT members, they should know what those changes are.

BCP Updates Based on Changes Within the IT Infrastructure

You should review the BCP when any substantial changes occur within the IT infra-structure. This includes especially any changes to critical systems.

For example, imagine a single server used to host a Web server and a database for online sales. The BCP includes a DRP to recover this server if a disaster occurs. If you upgrade this system to a four-node Web farm with back-end database servers in a two-node failover cluster, the change is substantial. The original BCP and DRP don't address this new configuration. If you need to move these servers to an alternate location, the BCP and DRP simply won't provide much help. In this example, you should ensure that the BCP is reviewed. You then upgrade the BCP and DRP to reflect the changes.

Organizations that have change management procedures in place make this review much easier. The BCP coordinator can simply review approved change requests periodi-cally to determine when changes have occurred. It's also possible to include a check item in the change management review. For example, you may require that the TRT lead verify that the change won't affect the BCP or any DRPs. Many changes are inconsequential and don't require a change to the BCP.

BCP Annual Updates and Content Refreshment

The BCP coordinator is responsible for reviewing the BCP at least annually, even if there are no known changes. This review ensures the BCP still addresses and meets all of the organization's requirements. It includes a review of the BIA to ensure that critical business functions haven't been modified and are still considered critical. It includes operational and security requirements. It includes a review of any of the individual processes, such as recalls, and more technical procedures such as DRPs.

The review process can be separate from the rewriting process. For example, you can task a member of the TRT to review a specific DRP that is included as an attachment of the BCP. The review may identify changes to the system that make the DRP out of date. The TRT member should report the results of the review back to the BCP coordinator, and the review is then complete. Finally, the BCP coordinator would have the TRT lead update the DRP.

The BCP coordinator should route changes through appropriate personnel. In other words, if a change directly affects the TRT, the changes should be routed through the TRT lead for input. Additionally, all affected personnel should be notified of the change when it's complete. For example, all TRT members should be notified of a change approved by the TRT lead and the BCP coordinator.

BCP Testing

The review of the BCP should also include information from training, testing, and exercises. You'll learn a lot of valuable information during each of these activities. Some of the procedures in the BCP will work well. Others will need to be improved by updating the BCP.

Ideally, you would update the BCP soon after the report from these events is completed. However, you can also include a review of these reports in the annual review of the BCP. This review ensures that all the issues identified in the training, testing, and exercises are resolved.

▶ **TIP**

Serious losses have caused entire companies to fail when they didn't have a BCP. Andrew Hiles in *The Definitive Handbook of Business Continuity Management* writes that between 60 and 90 percent of companies that lost a key facility but didn't have a BCP completely failed within 24 months. The BCP is like insurance. You always want to have it but never want to use it.

How Does a BCP Mitigate an Organization's Risk?

BCPs mitigate an organization's risk by ensuring that the organization is better prepared for disasters. If a disaster occurs, the organization meets it with the benefit of forethought and planning. On the other hand, if an organization doesn't have a BCP, managers must make spur-of-the-moment decisions.

Pilots are often praised for their ability to react coolly in the face of disaster. For example, Captain Chesley "Sully" Sullenberger realized his best option was to land a jetliner in the Hudson River in 2009 and calmly said into the microphone "We're gonna be in the Hudson." Why so calm?

Pilots train for disasters so many times that they know what needs to be done. Even amidst a crisis, they calmly identify the best steps to take to reduce the impact of disasters.

On the other hand, if a pilot never trained for a disaster and suddenly had two jet engines go dead, he'd be tempted to try anything to get things going again. Much of the energy would be wasted on attempting actions that can't succeed or will make matters worse.

Similarly, the BCP helps an organization plan and train for disasters. No one wants to see a disaster hit. However, if a disaster does arrive, the organization is much better prepared to address it directly if a BCP is in place.

Best Practices for Implementing a BCP for Your Organization

When implementing a BCP, you can use several different best practices. The following list shows many of these:

- **Complete the BIA early**—Ensure the BIA is done early in the process for the BCP. Without the BIA, you won't know what systems are critical. You also won't know what priority to use to recover the systems.

- **Exercise caution when returning functionality from alternate locations**— When restoring functionality from an alternate location to the primary location, consider these best practices:

  - Restore least critical functions first to the primary location. This allows you to get the bugs out of the process without affecting critical functions.
  - Use concurrent processing after a disruption. If systems have been rebuilt at the primary location, run them for three to five days before cutting off the services at the alternate location.

- **Review and update the BCP regularly**—The BCP coordinator should review and update the BCP at least annually. If critical systems are changed or modified between annual reviews, the BCP should be reviewed when those changes or modifications occur.

- **Test all the individual pieces of the plan**—This includes basic procedures, such as recalls. It also includes the more detailed procedures documented in DRPs.

- **Exercise the plan**—Verify the plan works by performing test exercises. These exercises should not affect normal operations.

CHAPTER SUMMARY

This chapter covered the details on BCPs. The primary purpose of a BCP is to ensure that an organization can continue to operate after a disruption or disaster. The BCP includes details on the CBFs, including what needs to be done to keep them operating. Many different individuals and teams share responsibilities. The BCP program manager oversees all BCPs, and the BCP coordinator manages one or more BCPs. Multiple teams with individual team leads also provide support to the BCP coordinator during development of the BCP and implementation of a BCP.

A BCP has three primary phases. In the notification/recovery phase, the BCP coordinator initiates the activity. In the recovery phase, critical systems are recovered and restored. In the reconstitution phase, normal operations are restored when the disaster has passed. Make sure that BCP team members and leads are trained on the BCP. Additionally, use testing and exercises to ensure the completeness of the BCP. The BCP coordinator is responsible for regularly updating the BCP. This includes regular updates, and additional ones when warranted.

KEY CONCEPTS AND TERMS

Mission-critical

Emergency Management Team (EMT)

Damage Assessment Team (DAT)

Technical Recovery Team (TRT)

CHAPTER 13 ASSESSMENT

1. A(n) _____ is a plan that helps an organization continue to operate during and after a disruption or disaster.

2. Business continuity and disaster recovery is the same thing.

   A. True
   B. False

3. You want to ensure that a BCP includes specific locations, systems, employees, and vendors. You should identify these requirements in the _____ statement.

4. What is the purpose of a BCP?

   A. To identify critical business functions
   B. To reduce or eliminate threats
   C. To ensure mission-critical elements of an organization continue to operate after a disruption
   D. All of the above

5. What does a BCP help to protect during and after a disruption or disaster?

   A. Confidentiality, information, and authentication

   B. Certifications, identities, and accreditations

   C. Mission essential and non-mission-essential BCFs

   D. Confidentiality, integrity, and availability

6. The _____ is responsible for declaring an emergency and activating the BCP.

7. After a BCP has been activated, who has overall authority for the recovery of systems?

   A. EMT

   B. DAT

   C. TRT

   D. CAT

8. After a BCP has been activated, who will assess the damages?

   A. BCP coordinator

   B. EMT

   C. DAT

   D. TRT

9. After a BCP has been activated, who will recover and restore critical IT services?

   A. BCP coordinator

   B. EMT

   C. DAT

   D. TRT

10. What are the three phases of a BCP?

   A. Activation/notification, transfer, recovery

   B. Activation/notification, recovery, reconstitution

   C. Recovery, renewal, reconstitution

   D. Transfer, recovery, notification,

11. A major disruption has forced you to move operations to an alternate location. The disruption is over and you need to begin normalizing operations. What operations should you move back to the original location first?

   A. Least critical business functions

   B. Most critical business functions

   C. Non-mission-essential personnel

   D. Mission-essential personnel

12. A major disruption has forced you to move operations to an alternate location. The disruption is over and you need to begin normalizing operations. You have rebuilt several servers at the primary location. What should you do?

   A. Test the servers and then turn off the servers at the alternate location.

   B. Bring the servers online and turn off the alternate location servers.

   C. Run the servers concurrently with the alternate location for three to five days.

   D. Test the servers for three to five days before bringing them online.

13. What can you do to show that the BCP will work as planned?

   A. BCP planning

   B. BCP training

   C. BCP testing

   D. BCP exercises

14. What types of exercises can demonstrate a BCP in action? (Select three.)

   A. Tabletop exercises

   B. Functional exercises

   C. Pull-the-plug exercises

   D. Full-scale exercises

15. Once a BCP has been developed, it should be reviewed and updated on a regular basis, such as annually.

   A. True

   B. False

13

Business Continuity Plan

Mitigating Risk with a Disaster Recovery Plan

DISASTERS HAPPEN. You can't prevent them. The best you can do is prepare for them. A disaster recovery plan (DRP) helps organizations prepare for disasters. When they strike, the DRP mitigates the short-term and long-term damage.

When developing a DRP, there are several factors to consider that are critical to its success. This includes elements that must be provided by management. It includes what the DRP developers need. It also includes an understanding of several primary concerns. These primary concerns include recovery time objectives and the need for alternate locations. Every DRP must have a budget. Without any funding, the DRP is sure to fail.

DRPs can have different elements within them. However, several elements are commonly included. DRPs start by defining the purpose and scope of the DRP. They identify what disasters the DRP will address. DRPs also include detailed steps and procedures that identify how to recover the organization in response to a disaster. Once they are written, DRPs need to be tested. Additionally, they need to be regularly reviewed and updated. This chapter covers all of these concepts.

Chapter 14 Topics

This chapter covers the following topics and concepts:

- What a disaster recovery plan (DRP) is
- What critical success factors are
- What the elements of a DRP are
- How a DRP mitigates an organization's risk
- What best practices for implementing a DRP are

Chapter 14 Goals

When you complete this chapter, you will be able to:

- Describe the need and purpose of a disaster recovery plan
- Define critical success factors for a DRP
- Identify what management must provide to ensure the success of the DRP
- Identify what DRP developers need to ensure the success of the DRP
- Describe recovery time objectives as they are used in the DRP
- Define and contrast cold sites, hot sites, and warm sites
- Define a redundant backup site
- Describe the access concerns when planning for an alternate location
- Describe the purpose of the disaster recovery financial budget
- Identify the different elements of a DRP
- Describe the contents of recovery steps and procedures used in the DRP
- Identify the different types of testing used for a DRP
- Identify different steps used to maintain the DRP
- Describe how a DRP mitigates an organization's risk
- List best practices for implementing a DRP

What Is a Disaster Recovery Plan (DRP)?

A disaster recovery plan is a plan to restore a critical business process or system to operation after a disaster. You can use the DRP to respond to a wide range of disasters. This includes weather events such as hurricanes, tornadoes, and floods. It includes natural events such as earthquakes. It includes fires from any source.

You can also use the DRP to rebuild systems after hardware or software failures. If a critical system crashes, operations stop. Although this isn't as big a disaster as an earthquake, it is a disaster for this system. You can use the DRP to recover the system and restore operations.

Disaster recovery occurs after a disaster. It will bring a system back into service after it has failed. The specific steps and procedures for disaster recovery are documented in the DRP. One or more DRPs are included in the BCP.

> **TIP**
>
> Chapter 13 presented business continuity plans (BCPs). BCPs are plans for the overall business. In comparison, the DRP targets specific systems and is an element of the BCP.

Fault Tolerance Is Not Disaster Recovery

Many organizations provide fault tolerance for systems. Fault tolerance helps ensure systems continue to operate even after a failure of a component. However, fault tolerance and disaster recovery are not the same thing.

For example, a redundant array of inexpensive disks (RAID) provides fault tolerance for disks. If a disk in the system fails, the fault is tolerated and the system continues to operate. However, if a disaster destroys the server, the fault-tolerant RAID system can't overcome this failure. You need to be able to rebuild the server and restore the lost data for disaster recovery.

Similarly, fault tolerance doesn't negate the need for backups. If a server is protected by a RAID system, backups still need to be done. The RAID protects against a failure of a disk. However, if the server catches fire, or a catastrophic failure destroys all disks, data on the RAID is lost. Without a backup, the data will be lost forever.

Both fault tolerance and disaster recovery techniques are necessary. Fault tolerance increases the availability of systems even when an isolated outage occurs. Disaster recovery provides the procedures to recover systems from outages after a major failure.

You may see disaster recovery planning described with many different terms, but they all mean essentially the same thing. Instead of the term DRP, you may see:

- Contingency planning
- Business resumption planning
- Corporate contingency planning
- Business interruption planning
- Disaster preparedness

Earlier chapters presented several terms related to DRPs. It's important to understand these to fully understand a DRP. These include:

- **Critical business function (CBF)**—Any function considered vital to an organization. If the CBF fails, the organization will lose the ability to perform critical operations necessary to meet its mission. Individual IT systems and services support CBFs.
- **Maximum acceptable outage (MAO)**—The maximum amount of time a system or service can be down before affecting the organization's mission. This directly affects the required recovery time. In other words, a system must be recoverable before the MAO time is reached.
- **Recovery time objectives (RTO)**—The time when a system or function must be recovered. The RTO is equal to or less than the MAO. For example, if the MAO is 10 minutes, the RTO is 10 minutes or less.

- **Business impact analysis (BIA)**—A study that identifies the CBFs and MAOs. It identifies the impact to the business if one or more IT functions fails. Additionally, it identifies the priority of different critical systems.
- **Business continuity plan (BCP)**—A comprehensive plan that helps an organization prepare for different types of emergencies. The goal is to ensure that mission-critical functions continue to operate even after a disruption or disaster strikes. The BCP includes a BIA. It also includes one or more DRPs.

Need

Every organization that has a critical mission needs to plan for disasters. If the operations that support the mission stop, the business stops. Unless an organization can do without critical business systems for a long period of time, a DRP is needed.

The time to plan for a disaster is before the disaster, not during it. Once the disaster occurs, it's too late to determine which systems are critical. It's too late to determine which critical systems are more important than others. It's also too late to identify the best methods to restore and recover the most important systems.

However, if the BCP identifies the critical systems and the DRP provides details on how to recover these systems, the organization is ready to respond. Without the DRP, the organization may not be able to recover.

Purpose

Most DRPs include a purpose statement. This helps identify the goals of the DRP. The DRP often has multiples goals or purposes. These include:

- **Saving lives**—The protection and safety of personnel is always important. If any steps are required to protect personnel, the DRP will identify these steps. This includes preparation steps before an impending disaster, such as a hurricane. It includes steps to take as a disaster is occurring. It also includes steps to take after a disaster strikes.
- **Ensuring business continuity**—The DRP includes procedures to restore CBFs if a disaster occurs. The purpose of these procedures is to ensure that mission-critical operations continue to function during and after a disaster.
- **Recovering after a disaster**—The DRP also addresses processes to recover the organization after the disaster has passed. This would include normalizing any CBFs moved to an alternate location. It may also include normalizing non-critical functions.

DRPs are often written to target different phases of the disaster. One phase identifies the steps and procedures to restore CBFs as soon as a disaster strikes. This may include moving CBFs to an alternate location. Another phase identifies the steps and procedures to normalize operations. This phase returns operations to the original location. A single DRP can address both phases.

Critical Success Factors

The success of a DRP depends on several critical success factors (CSFs). A CSF is an element necessary for the plan's success. For example, any organization has several CSFs that must be successful to ensure the success of the organization. Similarly, DRPs have CSFs. Without these factors included in the DRP, it has less chance to succeed.

Elements that are critical to the success of a DRP include:

- Management support
- Knowledge and authority for DRP developers
- Identification of primary concerns, such as recovery time objectives and alternate location needs
- A disaster recovery budget

The following sections explore these disaster recovery plan CSFs in more depth.

What Management Must Provide

Like risk management and security plans, DRPs require the support of management. Some support can be as simple as publicly endorsing the plan. Other support can be much more material, such as providing funds.

Management support doesn't guarantee success of a DRP. Other elements are necessary. However, without management support, a DRP is likely to fail. If management doesn't support the DRP, others within the organization won't support it either.

> **TIP**
>
> There's a difference between being a boss and a leader. The boss has a position of authority and directs people to complete tasks. People complete the tasks for the boss because they are told to do so. The leader influences others to achieve a common goal and excel in their performance. The leader has, or at least understands, the overall vision and helps others see how they can contribute to its success. People complete the tasks for the leader because they share the vision.

Resources

The primary resource that management provides is labor. You need personnel to create, test, and update the DRP. These personnel can be in-house employees. They can also be outside consultants that are specialists in disaster recovery.

You also need financial support from management. For example, if you need an alternate location, you'll be able to secure one only with financial support. If backups are needed, you'll need funding for backup tapes or other backup media.

Leadership

Management must also provide leadership to support any DRP. Leaders understand the importance of the DRP and know that its success can only be achieved with combined teamwork. Leaders help disaster recovery and business continuity teams recognize the value of the DRP.

Management helps teams identify project priorities. For example, if a DRP includes multiple DRPs, management helps identify which ones are more important than others. If a single DRP has multiple objectives, management can help the authors identify priorities within the DRP. More resources will be given to the highest priorities in a DRP or child DRPs.

It's also important for management to lead by example. If management wants others to support the requirements of the DRP, it must support it also. If management wants others to give the DRP their time and attention, managers must provide their time and attention to it when needed.

All of this translates into support. When management supports the efforts of the disaster recovery team, the overall disaster recovery process has a much better chance to succeed.

What DRP Developers Need

The developers of the DRP need some specific knowledge and authority to succeed. You can't just task some system subject matter experts (SMEs) and expect them to be able to write a DRP. Neither can you simply task some disaster recovery experts and expect them to be able to write a DRP.

> **▶ TIP**
>
> Many companies hire outside consultants to help with the development of DRPs and BCPs. These consultants can work with management and the SMEs to ensure that the DRPs meet the needs of the organization.

Instead, you need personnel with combined skills. The DRP developers need to have an understanding of disaster recovery. They also need to have an understanding of how the organization functions. They can often work with individual SMEs to identify specific steps for systems.

Knowledge of Disaster Recovery

The DRP team must have an understanding of disaster recovery in general. They should understand what a BIA is. They should know what a BCP is. They should also understand how a DRP fits in with a BIA and a BCP.

As a reminder, the BIA identifies the critical systems and prioritizes them. The BCP includes both BIAs and DRPs. DRPs provide details to restore specific systems. Some DRPs address system recovery of CBFs immediately after a disruption. Other DRPs address system recovery of all business functions after a disaster has passed.

If the DRP developer doesn't understand the purpose of the DRP, or how it fits in the overall business continuity plan, the focus of the DRP is lost.

Knowledge of How the Organization Functions

It's critical to understand how the organization functions to write the DRP. For example, the DRP for a military base will be much different from the DRP for a small business. The military base would require some support 24 hours a day, seven days a week. The small business may require support only from 9:00 to 5:00, Monday through Friday.

In addition to the operating hours, any organization has specific processes in place. The DRP developer needs to understand these processes. Some are critical. Either they will need to be supported by the DRP, or the DRP can assume that they will remain operational. Other processes are not critical and should not be relied on for the DRP.

For example, one organization may have both uninterruptible power supplies (UPSs) and generators in place. These units provide continuous power to critical systems even if commercial power is lost. The DRP may include steps to ensure that fuel is on hand to last a specific amount of time when a disaster occurs.

Another organization may use cloud computing for some CBFs, such as data services. If so, service level agreements (SLAs) will be in place to ensure that a third-party vendor keeps these operational. The DRP doesn't need to address these services.

Authority

DRP developers need some authority when creating the DRP. Before the DRP can be written, the developer needs to gather data. This is especially true if the developer is not an SME. To succeed, the DRP developer needs authority to interview experts who understand the systems.

If the DRP crosses departmental lines, the DRP author needs to make decisions that can affect multiple departments. With this in mind, the DRP author needs management support to make the initial decisions.

Primary Concerns

There are several primary concerns that the DRP should address. It's important for the DRP developer to have a clear idea of these as the DRP is being developed. One important concern is recovery time objectives. These objectives identify the critical nature of the DRP. Some systems need to be restored almost immediately. Others can be offline for days before they are recovered.

It's also important to have a clear idea which off-site resources are needed. At a minimum, a copy of backups needs to be stored off-site. Additionally, the DRP may also address the use of alternate locations for operations. These topics are explored in the following sections.

Recovery Time Objectives (RTOs)

The recovery time objectives identify when a system must be recovered. This is derived from the maximum acceptable outage identified in the BIA. Outages longer than the MAO will have a significant negative effect on the organization. In other words, if the outage isn't resolved within the RTO, the mission is impacted.

An MAO could be 60 minutes, 24 hours, or something different. However, this number drives the RTO. For example, if the MAO is 60 minutes, the DRP needs to be written to meet an RTO of less than 60 minutes. If the MAO is 24 hours, the RTO needs to be less than 24 hours.

This helps amplify the importance of a BIA. If you're writing a DRP before a BIA has been developed, you'll have extra steps to take. It's hard to simply guess what the RTO should be if the BIA hasn't been completed.

Off-Site Data Storage, Backup, and Recovery

Performing backups of critical data is an integral part of any recovery plan. Data will be lost. You can count on it as surely as you can count on the sun rising every morning. If you can't restore the data, the result can be catastrophic to the organization.

Backup plans are often included as a part of the DRP. They are derived from backup policies. The backup policy identifies details, such as what data should be backed up and how long to keep backup data. The backup plan identifies the steps to take to back up and restore the data.

Backups are primarily focused on data. However, in some situations you may need to back up programs. For example, if your organization develops applications, you'll need to ensure that backups of these applications are available. Naturally, the source code should be kept secure, but backups should be kept.

Another critical element of backups is ensuring that copies of backups are stored off-site. All of the backups should not be stored in the same location as the servers. If a fire destroys the building, it destroys the servers and also destroys all of the backups. On the other hand, if copies of backups are stored in a separate location, you'll always have the ability to restore your data even if a fire completely destroys your building.

Restore Horror Stories

The goal of backing up data is to be able to restore it. That seems obvious enough. However, there's an endless stream of horror stories in which backups can't be restored. In other words, an organization consistently performs backups. However, when a restore is needed, the organization discovers the backups are corrupt and can't be restored.

One organization required daily backups of a critical database. Backups were scheduled to occur in the middle of the night. Each morning, technicians removed the tape that held the backup and inserted a new tape. They then labeled and stored the backup tape.

Then the inevitable happened. The database became corrupt. No problem, they thought, because they have backups. They retrieved these backup tapes and discovered that most of the backups had not succeeded in over a month. The problem was new tapes. These new tapes were rotated into the mix but none of the backups to these new tapes succeeded. Ultimately, they were able to find a good tape. It restored most of the database, but a lot of data was lost. Forever.

You can easily avoid this common problem by performing test restores. A test restore attempts to restore data from a recent backup. If the test succeeds, the backup is good. If the test doesn't succeed, the backup process needs to be addressed. Many backup plans include details and scheduling for test restores.

FIGURE 14-1

Data backups from
data replication.

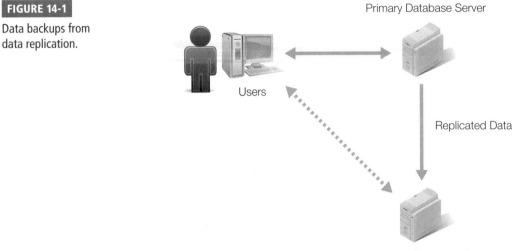

FIGURE 14-1

Data backups from
data replication.

> **TIP**
>
> There are multiple methods of
> replicating data from one database
> server to another. You can create
> mirrored servers and have them
> both online. You can create standby
> servers with one online but the other
> offline, accepting the replicated
> data. You can also create complex
> replication models with distributors,
> publishers, and subscribers.

You don't always have to perform traditional backups
to ensure you have copies of your data. You can use other
technical processes, too. For example, database applications such as Oracle and Microsoft SQL Server support
data replication.

Consider Figure 14-1. Users access a primary database
server for data. However, this primary server is also replicating data to a secondary server. This secondary server
has up-to-date data each time replication occurs. If the
primary server fails, you can bring the secondary server
online to take over for the primary server. You can also
control how often replication occurs. This ensures that
you can meet the RTO for the system.

The following two terms identify different types of redundant transfers. These are
often used as part of an overall disaster recovery plan:

- **Electronic vaulting**—This method transfers the backup data to an off-site location.
  Electronic vaulting transfers the data over wide area network (WAN) links or tunnels
  through the Internet.
- **Remote journaling**—This method starts with full copies of the data at the remote
  location. It then sends a log of the changes from the primary location to the
  secondary location. These changes are applied as a batch to the secondary location.
  After they are applied, the secondary location is up to date.

Slight variations of remote journaling are possible with databases. These include database
mirroring and database shadowing techniques.

TABLE 14-1 Comparison of cold, warm, and hot sites.

CAPABILITIES AND COSTS	COLD SITE	WARM SITE	HOT SITE
Time to bring the site online	Longest	Balanced	Shortest; minutes or hours
Equipment located at the site	None; only facilities such as space and power	Most equipment needed to support the CBFs	Most, if not all, of the equipment needed to support the CBFs
Expense to maintain the site	Lowest to maintain	Balanced	Highest cost
Testing capabilities of the site	Hardest to test	Balanced	Easiest to test

Alternate Locations

Many companies need to ensure that their business stays in operation even if a significant disruption occurs. For example, businesses working along the San Andreas Fault in California have an almost constant threat of an earthquake. If an earthquake hits, the business location may not be able to function in the same location.

If it's important for an organization to continue to operate even if a major disaster occurs, you need to identify alternate locations. These alternate locations can be in a different building, a different city, or even a different state. It depends on the type of disaster you're preparing for. For example, if a fire destroys a building, an alternate location in the same city will work. If you're preparing for an earthquake, you'll need an alternate location in a different city or possibly in a different state.

There are three types of alternate locations: cold sites, warm sites, and hot sites. Each site must have the capability to host the critical data and programs of the primary location. However, each has different costs and initial capabilities. As an introduction, Table 14-1 provides an overview of cold, warm, and hot site capabilities.

Cold Site. A **cold site** is an available building. It has electricity, running water, and restrooms, but none of the equipment or data needed for critical operations. It may have raised floors if needed to support a server environment. However, it does not include any equipment, data, or applications.

For example, an organization could rent space in a different building to prepare for a major disaster. If a disaster occurs, they would move the equipment and data to this location and set up the CBFs there. Obviously, it would take a lot of work to move and set up the equipment.

Cold sites are inexpensive to maintain. They are just empty buildings. However, it is very difficult and costly to test a cold site.

14

Disaster Recovery Plan

Hot Site. A **hot site** includes all the equipment and data necessary to take over business functions. A hot site will be able to assume operations within hours and sometimes within minutes. It usually has personnel at the location 24 hours a day, seven days a week.

Hot sites are expensive to maintain. However, some newer technologies make them a little easier to manage. **Cloud computing** and **virtualization** are two newer technologies that are sometimes used with hot sites. Cloud computing is a general term for anything that involves hosting services over a public network, such as the Internet.

Consider Figure 14-2. Several services are hosted using cloud computing. Each of these services is accessible over the Internet. The physical location of the services doesn't matter. As long as the service consumers are able to access the Internet, they are able to access the service.

This can be useful for hot sites. For example, if critical operations need to be managed from a regional office instead of from headquarters, the transfer can be almost seamless. Both locations already have access to the critical services. You may only need to move personnel to the regional office.

> **TIP**
>
> Third-party vendors often provide services to organizations via cloud computing. In other words, the organization contracts with another organization to host the service. The first organization doesn't need to manage the service. Instead, the organization has an SLA with a third-party vendor that provides the service.

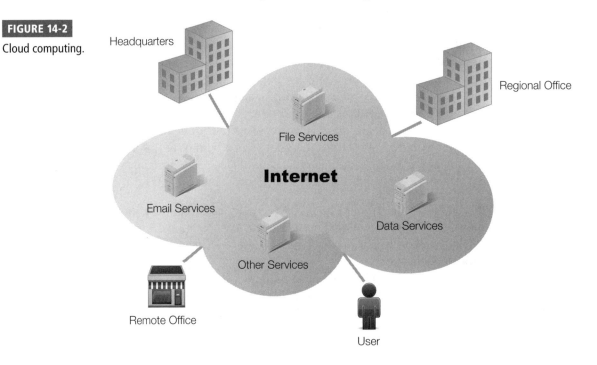

FIGURE 14-2

Cloud computing.

Time Clock Services Provided via Cloud Computing

Many organizations have switched to cloud computing for tracking employee work hours. An Internet-based Web server hosts a time clock application. Employees then use a Web browser to log on and record hours.

Some of these services allow employees to record the number of hours worked for any given day. Others require employees to log on when they report to work and "punch in." Before they leave, employees log on and "punch out." These Web sites are often configured so that they are accessible only from the employee location. In other words, employees are unable to punch in and out from home.

At the end of the pay period, a supervisor approves the hours. The data is then turned over to accounting to process paychecks.

This significantly reduces the time that an organization spends managing payroll. Additionally, because this is a primary function of the organization providing the service, that company is able to do it efficiently and for a low cost.

Virtualization is another technology that can be useful for hot sites. You can host multiple virtual servers on a network within a single physical server. Each virtual server runs on the network just as if it's a physical server.

Consider Figure 14-3. SRV1 is the physical server. It is hosting servers SRV2, SRV3, SRV4, and SRV5. All five servers work and behave as if they are on the network as separate servers. You would install additional resources on SRV1. It would have multiple processors, a significant amount of RAM, and fast hard drives. Each virtual server would be allocated some of these resources.

Once you create a virtual server, you can easily move it from one physical server to another. The virtual server consists of a few files stored on the physical server. Admittedly, these files are quite large. However, you can shut down the virtual server, copy the files to another physical server, and start the virtual server there.

You can transfer virtual server files over a WAN link if you have adequate bandwidth. If not, a high-capacity universal serial bus (USB) drive is an option. Just copy the virtual server files to the USB drive, plug it in to a new physical server, and copy the files to the physical server.

Virtual servers also require less facility support. If you're hosting four servers on a single physical server, you don't need as much physical space as you would for five servers. Additionally, these five servers draw less power and require less air conditioning.

FIGURE 14-3

One physical server hosting four virtual servers.

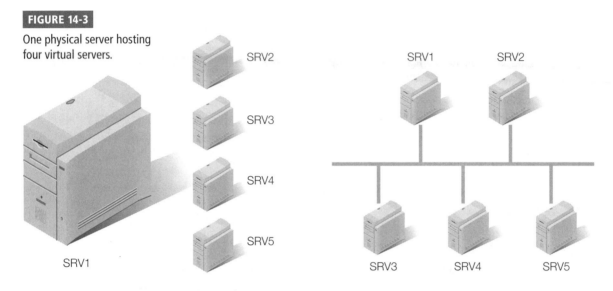

Warm Site.   A **warm site** is a compromise between a cold site and a hot site. It includes most or all of the equipment needed, but data is not usually kept up to date. The equipment is maintained in an operational state. If a disaster occurs, the systems are updated with current data and brought online.

Warm sites are often fully functioning sites for non-critical business functions. In other words, they are used for regular business normally. When a disaster occurs, non-critical functions stop and the site is used for critical business functions.

One of the main benefits of the warm site is that management is able to match the desired cost with an acceptable amount of time for an outage. In other words, if a longer MAO is acceptable, management can balance the costs to match the desired amount of time it will take to bring the warm site online.

Redundant Backup Site.   It's also possible to outsource your data recovery site. Instead of maintaining the alternate location, you can contract with a third-party vendor to host your data and services in a redundant backup site. If a disaster occurs, you can switch the critical services over to the alternate location. This often has minimal impact on operations.

Fully redundant backup sites have the ability to host all the data and services. These can be used as both the primary and secondary environments. In this scenario, you outsource hosting of all of your data and services on the third-party vendor's primary location. If a disaster occurs, the vendor is responsible for switching over to the secondary environment.

User Access.   It's important that your users have access to data and services if you move to an alternate location. To meet this need, you have to understand user behavior. In other words, you need to understand how users are using the data and services.

If users access services over the Internet, you simply need to ensure that the alternate location includes Internet access. You also need to ensure that the alternate location has the needed bandwidth.

However, your users may normally access the services internally or via private WAN links. If so, you need to ensure that the alternate location can get the data to the users. This may require additional WAN links at the alternate location.

Management Access.   Management may also need access to data and services during the disaster. In many instances, management represents just another user. If you provide user access, you've provided management access.

However, in some instances, management may have specific needs. Some data may be time-sensitive. For example, if it's close to the end of the fiscal year, certain data must be accessible to management for reporting requirements.

It's important to identify specific needs of management. If these are addressed in the DRP, these needs can be met.

Customer Access.   You need to ensure that customers have the access they require. Customer access needs vary from one organization to another. It depends on how customers normally access the organization's network, and what customer expectations are during a disaster.

Consider a local bank. The majority of banking may be done at the bank's location. However, more and more customers use online banking today. If a disaster hits, customers can use the online site for many of their banking needs. The DRP should ensure that the bank's Web site could continue to function even if a major disruption affects the physical location of the bank.

Today, many organizations have Web sites. Most of those organizations outsource their Web site hosting. In other words, the Web site isn't hosted on a server at the organization's location. Instead, organizations rent space on a Web server, and the hosting provider hosts the Web site. In this example, the hosting provider is responsible for disaster recovery.

However, this doesn't mean that the Web site shouldn't be considered. What if a disaster affected the Web site hosting provider? How would this affect your organization? Low-cost hosting providers often don't have significant disaster recovery processes in place. Both minor and major disruptions take down Web sites on a regular basis.

Disaster Recovery Financial Budget

The last critical success factor to consider for a DRP is money. It's impossible to successfully develop and implement a DRP without a budget. A budget ensures that you have money to pay for preparation, and for executing a DRP if a disaster strikes.

There are multiple costs to consider when preparing for disasters. These include:

- **Backups**—Although most operating systems include backup software, it usually does only the basics. Most organizations purchase third-party backup software that is easier to use and has more capabilities. Additionally, backup media, such as multiple backup tapes, can be expensive. If you need to back up more data, the cost goes up.

- **Alternate locations**—Any type of alternate location costs additional money. As mentioned previously, hot sites are the most expensive while cold sites are the least expensive. The site you choose depends on multiple factors, including your available budget.

- **Fuel costs during a disaster**—If an organization needs to be able to generate power for extended periods, someone must purchase fuel for the generators. The BCP identifies assumptions, such as how long critical operations need to function without outside support like commercial power. This information helps determine how much fuel to purchase.

- **Food and water during a disaster**—If personnel need to support the systems during the disaster, they need food and water. The amount you need depends on how many people will stay at the location and how many days you expect them to stay there.

- **Emergency funds right after a disaster**—Funds are often needed right after a disaster for unforeseen circumstances. Your budget should include funding for these expenses, if needed. Additionally, you need to ensure these funds are accessible when the disaster hits.

In addition to establishing the budget, you also need to identify who can release the funds. This is especially true for any monies needed during and immediately after the disaster. You could identify who has authority to release the funds in the DRP, or in the BCP.

Elements of a DRP

There are no specific rules that identify what must be in a DRP. You can add and remove sections and elements to meet your needs. However, many elements are commonly included. These are:

- Purpose
- Scope
- Disaster/emergency declaration
- Communications
- Emergency response
- Activities
- Recovery steps and procedures
- Critical business operations
- Recovery operations
- Critical operations, customer service, and operations recovery

In addition to including these elements in the DRP, you should also test and maintain it. Testing verifies that the procedures are valid. Additionally, the DRP should be regularly reviewed and updated to ensure it stays current. The following sections explore these elements in greater depth.

Eight R's of Recovery Planning

Some DR experts list the eight R's of recovery planning. These eight R's provide a good overview of the recovery planning process. The eight R's are:

- **Reason for planning**—The scope and purpose sections address the reasons for the DR. They address personnel safety and the critical business functions.

- **Recognition**—When the disaster is recognized, it is "declared." Personnel are notified and a decision is made to activate the plan.

- **Reaction**—Management and DR personnel respond to the emergency. They assess damage and decide which steps to take next.

- **Recovery**—DR personnel follow procedures to recover critical systems. If necessary, they activate alternate locations.

- **Restoration**—DR personnel restore CBFs to full operation. This can include restoration of facility resources, such as power. It includes restoration of connectivity such as local area network (LAN) and WAN connections. It also includes restoration of the systems that support the CBFs.

- **Return to normal**—After the disaster has passed, DR personnel return the systems to normal operations. This could include moving from generator power to commercial power. It could entail moving functions from the alternate location back to the primary location.

- **Rest and relax**—Ensure your DRP responders have time off after the incident. Take time to thank the people who helped the organization survive the disaster.

- **Re-evaluate and re-document**—Identify the things that went well and the things that can be improved. Document any lessons learned. Review any weaknesses or deficiencies in the plan. Use this data to update the plan.

Purpose

The DRP starts with a simple statement identifying its purpose. DRPs are often written to support an individual function, service, or system. You could write a DRP to restore a single database server to functionality after a disaster. It would include the steps necessary to recover the database server after the failure.

You could also write the DRP to restore several servers that work together to host a service. For example, a Web site could be supported by many different elements. This includes several Web servers in a Web farm and several database servers in a failover cluster. If a disaster took down the Web site, the DRP would include steps to either restore or recover all of these elements.

Either way, the purpose of the DRP needs to be defined early in the process and included in the final product. When considering the purpose, you should consider the following activities:

- **Recovery**—Immediately after a disruption in services, you should be able to recover a system. This includes a complete system rebuild, if necessary. It also includes recovery of all the data. The RTO defines the maximum length of time this should take.
- **Sustaining business operations**—CBFs need to continue to operate even during a disaster. You can use multiple methods to ensure these CBFs can continue. This could include a fully redundant data center, alternate locations, or redundant data sites. The method used should match the needs of the service and the available budget.
- **Normalization**—Once the disaster has passed, the systems need to be normalized. This means different things depending on what was done to sustain business operations. For example, if you used alternate locations, normalization includes moving the CBFs back to the original location.

Scope

The scope of any project helps identify the boundaries. It helps all parties understand what is covered and what is not covered. Without an identified scope, well-meaning people can cause the project to grow and expand. This is commonly known as scope creep.

The purpose of the DRP drives the scope. In other words, based on the purpose of the DRP, you can identify what elements should be included and what should not. Although the included elements may be obvious to some, you would still identify them in the DRP.

When developing the scope, you should consider the following areas:

- **Hardware**—Hardware includes servers and network devices necessary to support them. You may want to ensure that replacement servers are available on-site or at another location. You may also need to include support equipment. This can be generic office equipment or spare parts for the critical servers.
- **Software**—All software needed to support the CBFs needs to be considered. This includes operating systems and applications. Many organizations use imaging technologies. An "image" is an exact replica of a computer's operating system, applications, settings, and other files. IT personnel might capture an image of a generic server every few months. When a system crashes, IT personnel use this image to quickly restore a server's operations.
- **Data**—Data considerations are essential to include in the scope of the plan. This includes a backup plan that identifies backups and restores if data is needed for CBFs. The recovery point objectives (RPOs) identify the amount of data loss that is acceptable. The RPO depends on the value of the data.
- **Connectivity**—Connectivity to the service consumers should also be included. This could include users, managers, and customers, depending on who the consumers are. Connectivity could be redundant Internet service provider (ISP) links to the Internet or redundant WAN links.

Disaster/Emergency Declaration

When a disaster or emergency occurs, or is imminent, the DRP is implemented. As a reminder, the DRP is a part of the BCP. Usually, the overall BCP is activated first. Then, based on what the DRP does, the DRP is activated to support the overall BCP.

As an example, a hurricane could be approaching. The BCP coordinator could activate the BCP when the hurricane is 96 hours out. The DRP might specify that when the hurricane is 36 hours out, a recovery team be deployed to an alternate location to prepare the equipment for transfer. In this example, the DRP is activated when it's determined that the hurricane is within 36 hours of striking.

The point is that the DRP should clearly state what causes it to be activated. Activation could result in the recall of personnel and the movement of equipment. When it's time to take these steps, by all means do so. However, taking these steps before they are necessary can result in wasted money.

Consider the hurricane again. Hurricanes don't always travel in a straight line. A hurricane that is 96 hours away from striking can easily turn. Instead of hurricane-force winds, your location might just get some rain. You don't want to activate the DRP just because of rain.

Communications

Several communications elements are important to the success of a DRP. These include:

- **Recall**—The DRP should identify all personnel who should be notified when the DRP is activated. This includes any personnel who have any responsibilities within the DRP. It also includes senior management personnel. Phone trees are often included as part of the BCP and can be used for this purpose.

- **Users**—Users may need to be notified if the DRP affects them. For example, critical business operations may not include some routine functions that users expect. They should be notified about what services are not available due to the disaster. You can do this notification before the disaster, with a reminder to the user during the disruption.

- **Customers**—If the disruption affects customers, they should be notified. For example, an online Web site may be moved to an alternate location, causing it to be down for a short period. The Web site could post a single page indicating that the DRP is being implemented in response to a disaster and that the Web site will be operational again within a specific time. Customers will understand this much better than an error message when they try to visit the Web site.

- **Communications plan**—DRPs often include both primary and alternate communications plans. These ensure that personnel are able to communicate during an outage. The plans may be IT-based, such as e-mail or instant messenger. They could include cell phones or walkie-talkies. They could even include specific meeting times in a central location set up as a "war room" instead of using electronic communications.

Emergency Response

The DRP could include an emergency response element. This is used for short-fused disasters. For example, an earthquake will strike without warning. Tornadoes strike with very little warning. Similarly, a fire could result in a disaster that requires an emergency response.

Emergency response steps could include:

- Recall and notification of personnel
- Damage assessment
- Plan activation
- Implementation of specific steps and procedures

Depending on the location of your organization, you could write the DRP to address specific disasters. For example, many organizations on the East Coast of the United States have DRPs that cover hurricanes. The DRP would include many preparation steps, but the emergency response steps wouldn't appear until much later.

Activities

The Emergency Response section identifies several emergency response steps to take, such as recalling personnel and assessing the damage. The DRP also identifies other activities to take in response to the disaster.

A primary activity of any DRP is ensuring that personnel safety has been addressed. Ensuring personnel safety and the protection of life should always be at the forefront of any DRP. In other words, the clear message should be *people* first, *things* next.

Activities defined in the DRP depend on the purpose and scope of the DRP. If the DRP addresses the recovery of a single system, the activities are limited and focused. If it addresses a large, complex system, many more activities will be required.

If you have warning of the disaster, activities may include preparing the environment. This is possible with weather-related events, such as hurricanes and other serious storms. However, many other disasters don't provide any warning.

When alternate locations are used, a primary activity is preparing the alternate location. A cold site requires the most work. You'll need to move all the required equipment to the alternate location, set it up, and configure it. This will result in a flurry of activity to prepare. The activity section for a cold site will be quite extensive.

On the other hand, activities required to set up a hot site will be minimal. You may designate personnel in a flyaway team to go to the hot site to take over operations. You'll need to identify how, and when, the cutover to the hot site will occur.

A warm site presents a compromise between a hot site and a cold site. The activities to get the warm site up and operational depend on how much equipment and data are normally staged at the alternate location. The activity section can be quite extensive if the warm site is more of a cold site than a hot site.

Recovery Steps and Procedures

The recovery steps and procedures describe all the specific actions required to recover systems or functions. This section often includes multiple procedures. For example, you could have a separate procedure for each critical function. Different personnel will be recovering separate systems, so the procedures could all be implemented at the same time.

Recovery steps and procedures usually include specific recovery plans and backup plans.

Recovery Plans

The recovery plan identifies steps for rebuilding and recovering a system after a disaster. Recovery plans often include steps for recovering a system from scratch. This includes installing the operating system and all applications. If data is needed, the plan specifies how to restore the data.

For example, a database server could be running an Oracle database on a Microsoft Windows Server operating system. The recovery procedure would start with instructions for installing the Windows operating system. After installation, the procedure would describe how to install Oracle. Last, the procedure would describe how to restore the database.

It should be clear in the recovery plan which steps must be completed before moving on to the next step. In other words, data shouldn't be restored to a server until after the operating system and application have been successfully installed.

It's possible to capture an image of a server hosting Oracle. If the server crashes, the image can be installed on a system. It will include the operating system, the fully configured Oracle application, and the data that was on the system when the image was captured. IT personnel will have to update the data from a recent backup. Restoring the image is much quicker than reinstalling everything from scratch.

> **TIP**
>
> If you image servers, you may need to recapture the image periodically. For example, if the operating system or application has been updated or modified, the original image won't have the changes. You have either to recapture the image after a change is made, or to ensure that the changes are reapplied after the image is restored on a server.

Backup Plans

If data needs to be restored, you must have an effective backup plan. One of the first steps is to identify critical data. Critical data is data that supports CBFs. This can be large databases. Data can also be any other types of files that are critical.

The backup plan identifies several elements including:

- The data to back up
- Backup procedures for data
- Length of time to keep the data
- Types of backups, such as regular, electronic vaulting, or remote journaling
- Off-site storage location, including how to retrieve a backup during a disaster
- Testing of restore procedures and schedules
- Disaster restore procedures

> **TIP**
>
> A DRP ensures that backup plans exist for critical data. However, an organization may have backup plans that protect other data in the organization.

The RPOs identify the amount of data loss that is acceptable for any data. The RPO is considered in the backup plan. If the RPO is a short period of time, such as minutes instead of hours or days, backups must be performed more frequently. If the RPO is a longer time, you can schedule backups less often.

For example, consider a high-volume database. The RPO could be 10 minutes, indicating that no more than 10 minutes of data loss is acceptable. The transaction log for the database can be backed up every 10 minutes to ensure that the last 10 minutes of data can be restored. This transaction log backup is restored after the other database backups are restored.

Critical Business Operations

The DRP also identifies critical business operations. These are supported by critical business functions. Specific servers and services in turn support CBFs. As a reminder, a CBF is any function that is considered vital to the organization. If the organization loses the ability to perform the CBF, it loses the ability to perform critical business operations. By identifying critical business functions, the DRP helps ensure that the critical servers and services continue.

As an example, consider Figure 14-4. It shows a Web farm connected to a back-end database. The Web servers in the Web farm host an application that sells products online. In this example, the critical business operation is sales of products.

Several critical business functions support the sale of products. First, the Web farm hosts the Web application. One CBF is serving Web pages to clients. Users can access the Web site, and the Web farm ensures that one of the servers serves the pages to the clients.

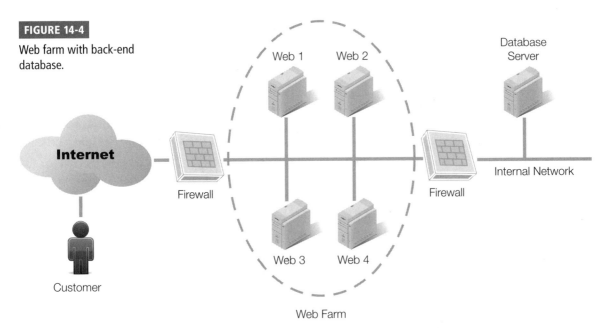

FIGURE 14-4

Web farm with back-end database.

Additionally, the back-end databases host the product database that is queried to build the pages.

Once a customer decides to buy, an additional CBF comes into play. Existing customer data is retrieved from the database. New customer data is gathered and stored. Once a customer purchases the product, a CBF works with a bank to be paid. Another CBF ensures that the product is shipped. All of these CBFs are in support of the critical business operation of product sales.

Looking back at Figure 14-4, you can see that several servers are needed to support some of these CBFs. Specifically, the Web servers in the Web farm and the back-end database server are all needed. The DRP would ensure that these servers are included.

Recovery Procedures

Specific recovery procedures are identified for all the servers and services in the DRP. You can create separate written documents for each procedure. The procedures will be different for each of the systems being recovered.

These procedures are one of the most important elements of the DRP to test. Although many of the steps in the DRP may be generic in nature, these recovery procedures are often very technical.

In addition, you should ensure that anyone could follow the steps in these procedures. During a disaster, you never know who is available. Your best administrators may be away on travel or otherwise unable to get to the business location. The people recovering the critical systems may be mid-level or junior technicians.

> **TIP**
>
> Recovery operations begin after the DRP has been activated and damage has been assessed. Recovery focuses on measures necessary to restore IT capabilities and repair damage. The goal is to restore the critical operational capabilities at either the original location or an alternate location.

In addition to ensuring the recovery procedures have been written and tested, you should also consider contingencies. What should recovery personnel do if certain recovery steps don't work? For example, recovery personnel may be working to recover WAN or LAN access. If the server requires specific access to the Internet or another server, the procedure should state the network bandwidth and connectivity requirements of the alternate site.

Critical Operations, Customer Service, and Operations Recovery

The DRP identifies critical business operations and CBFs to support. However, it is often important to specify other elements of the business to recover.

For example, will you stop customer service activities when a disaster occurs? Alternatively, will customer service activities move? If you provide customer service via phone, you may be able to easily switch the functions to another location. On the other hand, if your organization does very little customer service, you may not consider it critical enough to recover during the disaster. You could provide a simple notification to customers. For example, you might post a notification on the organization's Web page. You could also record a short message on the phone system.

Similarly, you may have other operations that need to be recovered. These may not necessarily be considered a part of any CBF, but management may still consider them important enough to recover. For example, some personnel may be working on critical research projects. Although the research isn't critical for current cash flow, management may want to ensure it can continue to operate. In this situation, the systems and services for research will need to be recovered.

This section can also provide another look at normal operations. While preparing the DRP, you should review what is considered a CBF and what is not. It may be apparent when looking at day-to-day operations that some operations are critical, yet they were omitted from the DRP. You should add these operations.

Testing

It's important to test DRPs to ensure they perform as expected. Remember, the DRP is written to restore CBFs. Testing of the DRP should not affect operations of these CBFs. The goal of the tests is to identify any problems or omissions in the DRP.

Like a BCP, you can use different testing methods to test a DRP. The following are common testing methods:

- **Desktop exercise**—In a desktop exercise, participants meet in a conference room setting. Participants talk through the steps of the DRP. This is similar to a tabletop exercise used in a BCP.

- **Simulation**—A simulation goes through the steps and procedures in a controlled manner. The goal is to ensure that the DRP can be completed in the order presented. Simulations may test portions of the DRP without testing them all. For example, you could just restore data at an alternate location to ensure this procedure works.

- **Full-blown DRP test**—The full-blown DRP test goes through all of the steps and procedures as if an actual disaster were occurring. It also helps you determine the actual time required to complete each step and procedure. The full-blown DRP test has the most potential to disrupt operations. Plan a full-blown test so that it has a minimum effect on operations.

You should thoroughly document the results of all tests. Include any lessons learned, mistakes, or weaknesses uncovered during testing. You can then use this documentation to improve the DRP. It's common to update the DRP if testing identifies any deficiencies.

One of the benefits of testing is that it will give you an accurate time frame when restoration can occur. For example, consider a database server. One administrator may think it can be rebuilt and restored in 30 minutes. Another administrator may estimate it will take as long as four hours. Actually rebuilding and restoring the server will give you an accurate time of how long it takes. A checklist is helpful for tracking the time frame for individual steps. The checklist may look similar to Table 14-2.

TABLE 14-2 Recovery times checklist.		
STEP	**START TIME**	**END TIME**
Locate server and install operating system		
Install applications on server		
Locate backup tape and restore data		
Notify DRP coordinator of completion		

Maintenance and DRP Update

The DRP needs to be regularly reviewed and updated. This ensures that it is ready when needed. IT systems are regularly updated and upgraded. Any of these changes to the IT systems could affect the usability of the DRP.

Most organizations have change management processes in place. These processes ensure that changes to systems are reviewed before the change occurs. Additionally, they ensure that changes are documented. DRP developers should be involved in this process. This ensures they are aware of system changes. When a change is proposed, the DRP developer should review the change to determine if it affects the DRP.

The review should include the following elements:

- **Systems**—Verify that the systems covered by the DRP have not been changed since the last review. This includes any significant changes that may affect how they are recovered. Even smaller changes should be investigated to determine if the DRP is affected.

- **Critical business functions**—Verify that the DRP covers the CBFs and that priorities have not changed. An organization can change, resulting in some CBFs becoming more important than others.

- **Alternate sites**—If you will need alternate sites, ensure the designated sites still support the DRP. Ensure that changes to the alternate sites don't adversely affect the DRP. If possible, you should visit these alternate sites while reviewing the DRP to determine if they still meet your needs.

- **Contacts**—Ensure that contact information is accurate. This includes contact information for management personnel that need to be notified. It also includes re-call information used in the phone trees.

14

Disaster Recovery Plan

Just as with other documents, it's important to track changes to the DRP. The DRP should include a change page or version control page. This page will identify when the change was made, who made the change, and what the change was.

How Does a DRP Mitigate an Organization's Risk?

DRPs reduce risk by reducing the impact of disasters. The disaster is the threat, which you can't stop. If an earthquake, tornado, or hurricane is going to hit, you can't stop it. However, you can reduce the impact of the threat by being prepared. The DRP helps you prepare. It helps you mitigate both the short-term and long-term damage.

For example, the DRP can help you reduce the length of an outage after a disaster. Organizations that have a DRP in place are able to handle disasters much more easily than organizations without DRPs. Of course, the existence of a DRP doesn't guarantee success. It does increase your odds if a disaster strikes your organization.

With a disaster recovery plan, you'll be much better prepared to recover critical business functions. A cold site takes a lot of work to put together when you plan for it. You'll have to move all the equipment, set it up, and configure it. With some extra resources and preplanning, you could plan to use a warm site. However, with no planning, the job will be twice as hard.

In addition to being more difficult, having no DRP will mean you'll experience more errors and problems. The DRP helps you to apply critical thinking to problems before they occur. It allows you to logically think through what you'll do. You can talk through the problems with experts. You can test the plan. Without a DRP, you'll be thrown into the middle of a crisis without any of these benefits. With luck, the disaster won't destroy the business.

Best Practices for Implementing a DRP for Your Organization

When implementing DRPs, you can use several different best practices. The following list shows many of these:

- **Ensure BIAs have been completed**—BIAs identify critical business functions. The critical business functions are used to identify the critical business operations and critical servers and services.
- **Start with a clear purpose and scope**—The purpose and scope statements help ensure the DRP stays focused. Resources are wasted when steps and procedures are taken that are outside the scope of the DRP.

- **Review and update the DRP regularly**—You should review the DRP at least annually. If you change critical systems covered by the DRP, you should review the DRP to determine if the changes affect it.
- **Test the DRP**—Testing ensures that you can implement the DRP as expected. When testing the DRP, it should not affect normal operations.

It's often worthwhile to use a checklist to ensure that you have addressed all the relevant concerns. You can use the following checklist before, during, and after the creation of a DRP to identify your preparedness.

- Is your organization's BIA up to date? If your BIA is more than one year old, update the BIA first.
- Have any systems covered by the BIA changed since the BIA was completed? If so, the BIA needs to be revised.
- Are critical business functions defined? Is it clear what systems need to be recovered first?
- Does the DRP specify the level of service to provide for the CBFs? In other words, if the business must continue to operate during a disaster, does the DRP identify which services to restore?
- Are specific responsibilities assigned? Do departments or individuals know what is expected of them at different times during an emergency?
- Is it clear what hardware, software, and data should be recovered? Does the DRP include any necessary support equipment needed to support the CBFs?
- Does the DRP include a backup plan? Does this backup plan include a testing element for test restores? Does the DRP include steps to use for data restores?
- Are backups stored off-site? Are the off-site backups easily accessible if a disaster occurs?
- Is there a communication plan? Does it have alternate methods of communication?
- Are alternate sites required? What type of alternate site is desired? Does the budget allow for the desired site?
- Are facility needs considered? This includes UPS and backup power. It also includes heating and air conditioning systems.
- Have support services been addressed? For example, if you need backup generators, is enough fuel on hand to support the organization during the disaster? Is there enough food and water to support on-site personnel during the disaster?
- Are personnel trained on the DRP? Do they know what their responsibilities are before, during, and after a disaster?
- Has the DRP been tested? Have the procedures been tested to verify the work as expected?
- Is the DRP reviewed at least annually? Is it updated as needed when elements within it are affected?
- Are changes to the DRP tracked?

CHAPTER SUMMARY

This chapter covered important elements of risk mitigation with a disaster recovery plan. It defined a DRP, including its purpose. Several factors are critical to the success of a DRP. Management must provide both resources and leadership. DRP developers need to understand disaster recovery concepts and how an organization operates. The DRP must address several primary concerns. The RTOs identify the time by which a CBF must be returned to operation. When necessary, you can move CBFs to alternate locations. A hot site can be used within minutes or hours but is the most expensive to implement. A cold site is simply a building with electricity, water, and other facility support. It's the least expensive, but the most difficult to test. A warm site is a compromise between the two. Another critical success factor is a budget. DRPs must have funding to succeed.

DRPs can include different elements. It's common to start with purpose and scope statements to ensure these are clear to all parties. Identifying the scope helps prevent scope creep. DRPs will include specific steps and procedures. When the disaster strikes, use the steps and procedures in the DRP to recover the systems. You should test DRPs to verify they work as planned. Additionally, you need to update DRPs periodically and in response to changes.

KEY CONCEPTS AND TERMS

Cloud computing	Hot site
Cold site	Virtualization
Disaster recovery	Warm site

CHAPTER 14 ASSESSMENT

1. A(n) _____ is a plan used to restore critical business functions to operation after a disruption or disaster.

2. A DRP has multiple purposes. This includes saving lives, ensuring business continuity, and recovering after a disaster.

A. True
B. False

3. Disaster recovery and fault tolerance are the same thing.

A. True
B. False

4. A _____ is an element necessary for success. For example, the success of a DRP depends on elements such as management support and a disaster recovery budget.

5. A business impact analysis (BIA) includes a maximum allowable outage (MAO). The MAO is used to determine the amount of time in which a system must be recovered. What term is used in the DRP instead of the MAO?

   A. Critical business function (CBF)
   B. DRP action item (DRPAI)
   C. Recovery action item (RAI)
   D. Recovery time objective (RTO)

6. A certain DRP covers a system that hosts a large database. You want to ensure that the data is copied to an off-site location. What could you use?

   A. Data replication
   B. Electronic vaulting
   C. Remote journaling
   D. All of the above

7. A copy of backups should be stored _____ to ensure the organization can survive a catastrophic disaster to the primary location.

8. You are considering an alternate location for a DRP. You want to minimize costs for the site. What type of site would you choose?

   A. Cold site
   B. Warm site
   C. Hot site
   D. DRP site

9. You are considering an alternate location for a DRP. You want to ensure the alternate location can be brought online as quickly as possible. What type of site would you choose?

   A. Cold site
   B. Warm site
   C. Hot site
   D. DRP site

10. You are considering an alternate location for a DRP. You want to use a business location that is already running non-critical business functions as the alternate location. This location has most of the equipment needed. What type of site is this?

    A. Cold site
    B. Warm site
    C. Hot site
    D. DRP site

11. Which of the following elements are commonly included in a DRP?

    A. BCP, BIA, communications, recovery steps and procedures
    B. BCP, backup plans, recovery steps and procedures
    C. Purpose, scope, communications, recovery steps and procedures
    D. Purpose, scope, CIRT activation, recovery steps and procedures

12. You are considering using a hot site as an alternate location. You want to consider different technologies to keep the data updated and decrease the time it will take for the hot site to become operational. What are some technologies that may help?

    A. Data replication
    B. Cloud computing
    C. Virtualization
    D. All of the above
    E. A and B only

13. Of the following, what is critical for any DRP?

    A. Third-party backup software
    B. Budget
    C. Alternate locations
    D. Fuel for generators

14. Your organization has created a DRP but it hasn't been tested. Which of the following methods can you use to test it?

    A. Desktop testing
    B. Simulation testing
    C. Full-blown DRP testing
    D. All of the above

15. Once a DRP has been created, it's not necessary to update it.

    A. True
    B. False

Mitigating Risk with a Computer Incident Response Team Plan

C OMPUTER SECURITY INCIDENTS can result in the loss of confidentiality, integrity, or availability of data or services. Attackers will attack. Incidents will happen. However, you can be prepared with computer incident response teams (CIRTs). These teams are trained and have the knowledge and expertise to reduce the damage resulting from attacks. Their actions are guided by a CIRT plan.

The primary purpose of a CIRT plan is to help an organization prepare for incidents and mitigate the damage. The plan identifies members based on their roles and responsibilities. It includes policy statements related to incidents, such as if CIRT members are authorized to attack back. It also includes detailed information on how to handle incidents.

Chapter 15 Topics

This chapter covers the following topics and concepts:

- What a computer incident response team (CIRT) plan is
- What the purpose of a CIRT is
- What the elements of a CIRT plan are
- How a CIRT plan can mitigate an organization's risk
- What best practices for implementing a CIRT plan are

What Is a Computer Incident Response Team (CIRT) Plan?

A **computer incident** is a violation, or imminent threat of a violation, of a security policy or security practice. It includes any adverse event or activity that affects the security of computer systems or networks. These adverse events affect the organization's security. They may result in loss of confidentiality, integrity, or availability.

The terms "computer incident" and "computer security incident" mean the same thing and are used interchangeably. For example, some organizations have CSIRTs and CSIRT plans instead of CIRTs and CIRT plans.

An imminent threat of violation is an incident that is about to occur. This commonly refers to emerging threats, such as viruses or worms that are rapidly spreading. Even if the organization isn't infected now, it will be if action is not taken quickly.

FYI

You may see the term Computer Emergency Response Team (CERT) in place of CIRT. CERT® is a registered trademark, and it refers to the federally funded CERT Coordination Center (CERT/CC). CERT/CC is a part of Carnegie Mellon University (CMU). CERT/CC is different from the United States-CERT (US-CERT) that coordinates defense and responses to cyberattacks in the United States. If an organization uses the term "CERT," it is infringing on CMU's trademark. Terms such as CIRT, IRT, or CSIRT are more common.

In the context of this chapter, an event is any observable occurrence within a system or network. This includes any activity on the network, such as users accessing files, or data transmitted over the network. Not all events are incidents. Adverse events are events with a negative result. This could include any types of attacks on systems or networks.

Multiple types of computer incidents can affect an organization. These include:

- **Denial of service (DoS) attack**—An attack that prevents a system from providing a service. A DoS attack comes from a single attacker. A distributed denial of service (DDoS) attack comes from multiple systems.

- **Malicious code**—Any type of malicious software or **malware**. This includes viruses, worms, Trojan horses, and other types of software intended to infect a system. Viruses and other malware that are replicating and causing harm to computers are "in the wild."

- **Unauthorized access**—This occurs any time an attacker is able to access data without authorization. It can be from different types of social engineering attacks. It can also be from technical attacks used to gain access or control to systems. Unauthorized access often results in loss of confidentiality.

- **Inappropriate usage**—This occurs when employees or internal users violate acceptable use policies (AUPs) or other internal policies. It can be as simple as a user going to a malicious Web site identified as off-limits in the AUP. It could be a user copying proprietary data from a secure system to an insecure system. It could be a user installing peer-to-peer (P2P) software on his or her system when this is prohibited in the AUP.

- **Multiple component**—This is an incident that includes two or more incidents at the same time. For example, malware could infect a system. The malware is then used to launch a DoS attack on other systems.

> **TIP**
>
> An organization may define a security incident internally. This definition is more specific and may be slightly different depending on the needs of the organization.

A **computer incident response team (CIRT)** is a group of people that will respond to incidents. The CIRT team can be designated in advance. It can also be formed as needed. For example, a large organization may have a group of security professionals designated as the CIRT. When an incident occurs, the CIRT responds. A smaller organization may not have a formal CIRT. Instead, when an incident occurs, IT professionals respond to the incident as an informal CIRT.

The **CIRT plan** is a formal document that outlines an organization's response to computer incidents. It formally defines a security incident. It may also designate the CIRT team. The following sections outline the purpose and elements of a CIRT plan.

Purpose of a CIRT Plan

The purpose of the CIRT plan is to help an organization prepare for computer incidents. Preparation helps the organization identify potential incidents. Security personnel can then identify the best responses to reduce the potential damage.

This is similar to the purpose of a disaster recovery plan (DRP). By taking the time to create a plan, you're able to apply critical thinking to potential problems. You can logically think through the expected issues. You can get the advice of experts and research the best types of responses.

However, if you don't have a plan, you won't have any of these benefits. In this case, when the incident occurs, responders will use trial-and-error techniques. These may succeed. On the other hand, they may allow the attacker to continue and cause significantly more damage to the organization.

A CIRT plan outlines the purpose of the response effort. In general, the purpose is to identify the incident as fully as possible. The answers to the five Ws are a good starting point. The five Ws are *what*, *where*, *who*, *when*, and *why*. For good measure, add in *how* it occurred.

The *what* identifies what type of attack occurred. It could be a DoS attack, a malware attack, unauthorized access, or inappropriate usage. Understanding what happened helps you to determine the impact and prioritize the response. CIRT plans often include tools to determine the impact and the priority of the attack.

> **NOTE**
>
> The "Incident Handling Procedures" section later in this chapter shows some examples of tools to determine the impact and priority of incidents. Table 15-1 shows an example of effect rating definitions. Table 15-2 shows an example of criticality rating definitions. Table 15-3 shows an example of incident impact ratings.

Next, identify *where* the attack occurred. You'll see symptoms on at least one system that raised the alarm. However, you should also check to see if the attack affected other systems. If more than one system is affected, you may need to reassess the impact and priority.

If possible, you'll want to identify *who* launched the attack. Logs are very useful for this. You can check audit logs for systems. You can also check firewall and router logs. If the user authenticated, the logs will identify the user account used for the attack. If the attack was from an external source, the logs will identify an external Internet Protocol (IP) address. You can block the attack by blocking this IP address.

> **technical TIP**
>
> Attackers often hijack other systems to launch attacks. Zombies within botnets can be commanded to launch an attack. Additionally, an attacker can simply drive around until an open wireless network is located. The attacker can then use this network to launch the attack. Attacks traced back to this wireless network won't identify the actual attacker, but instead the wireless network. By the time you trace the attack back to the IP address, the actual attacker will be long gone.

Identifying *when* an attack occurred is much more than just identifying when the symptoms were discovered. Attackers often perform reconnaissance before an attack. Log entries may show that the reconnaissance attacks occurred several times over the past week from the same source.

Answering *why* attackers attacks helps to understand their motive. Attackers in the past often attacked out of boredom. Sometimes they just did it for the same reason George Mallory wanted to climb Mount Everest—"because it's there." However, attackers today are often motivated by greed. They are trying to monetize the attacks. They want to steal data they can convert into money.

As an example, one famous set of attackers regularly stole credit card data. They used this data to create fake credit cards. They hired women to shop at malls. These women

The Growth of Incidents

Back in 1988, it was news when a computer on the Internet was attacked. The Morris worm hit the Internet in November 1988. CERT was created at CMU to respond, and CERT began counting incidents.

Figure 15-1 shows the growth of incidents over the years. In 1988, there were eight incidents. In 1998, there were 3,734 incidents. In 2003, there were 137,529 incidents. The last year that CERT at CMU reported the number of incidents was in 2003. If the number of incidents were still tracked and reported today, they would be off the chart. It's no longer news that computers are attacked. Unless you never turn the computer on or keep it completely isolated, it will be attacked. You can count on it.

The names of these incidents have morphed over the years. The terms cyberattacks and cyberterrorism are commonly used. Cyberattacks and cyberterrorism are significant threats on the Internet today.

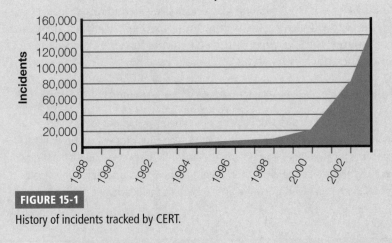

FIGURE 15-1

History of incidents tracked by CERT.

bought as much as they could in a lavish shopping spree spending tens of thousands of dollars with the fake credit cards. The women took the goods out to a truck in the mall's parking lot. A "fence" bought the goods at reduced prices and then promptly sold them elsewhere.

Attackers may also be motivated by espionage. Both corporate espionage and international espionage are vigorously alive on the Internet today. Spies regularly try to gather as much data about competing organizations or other countries as possible.

Last, identify *how* the attack occurred. This helps to identify the vulnerabilities that exist in this system. Once you understand how the attack succeeded, you can then identify how to prevent it in the future. In other words, identifying how the attack succeeded helps you identify controls or countermeasures to prevent future attacks.

Elements of a CIRT Plan

CIRTs can have several different elements. There are no specific requirements stating that certain elements must be included. However, a CIRT commonly includes information on the membership of the CIRT and policy information. It may also include details on communications methods, and incident response procedures. The following sections outline these common elements.

> **NOTE**
> This section isn't intended to indicate that these are the only elements of the CIRT plan. Neither is it intended to say that these elements must exist. The CIRT plan will meet the needs of the organization, and organizations differ widely.

CIRT Members

Although a CIRT plan identifies CIRT members, these members will probably be involved before the creation of the CIRT plan. Specifically, they will help create it. CIRT members include IT and security professionals who understand the risks that threaten networks and systems.

There are different models that you can use for a CIRT. The National Institute of Standards and Technology (NIST) regularly releases special publications (SPs). NIST SP 800-61 identifies the following three models:

> **NOTE**
> The members of the CIRT are usually identified by title, rather than by name within the plan.

- **Central incident response team**—Organizations in a single location can use a single team. This team will respond to all incidents. It's also possible to have a single team to cover multiple locations. This team will have remote access to all locations. It will also be available at any time to provide flyaway support, if needed.
- **Distributed incident response teams**—If the organization has major computing facilities in multiple locations, multiple teams can be used. In this example, each location will have a single team. It's recommended that these teams be centrally managed. For example, if the organization has multiple regional locations with teams at each location, personnel at the headquarters location will still centrally manage the teams.

- **Coordinating team**—This team includes senior personnel who provide advice to other teams. It doesn't have any authority over the other teams. However, when incidents occur at outlying locations, this team has the expertise to provide assistance.

Roles.   CIRT members often hold one or more specific roles in the team. The goal is to ensure that the team includes members from several different areas. Some of the roles held by the team members are:

- **Team leader**—This individual is responsible for the team's actions. He or she is usually a senior manager with expertise in security. However, some CIRTs identify the first team member that arrives on the scene as the team leader. This person takes charge of the incident and directs other member activities.

- **Information security members**—These individuals could be experts on boundary protection. This includes firewalls and routers on the edge of the network. They are able to identify the source of breaches and recommend solutions. These members could also be experts in intrusion detection systems (IDSs) and other systems that include audit logs and audit trails.

- **Network administrators**—Network administrators understand the details of a network. They understand what systems are connected and how they're connected. They also understand what systems are accessible from the Internet. They know what normal traffic flow is and can recognize abnormal traffic.

- **Physical security**—Because attackers can be social engineers and might be on company property, physical security personnel need to be represented on the team. They know what physical security controls are used, and where they are used. They also know the different types of surveillance methods used within the organization, such as what cameras are running, and what cameras are recording.

- **Legal**—Legal personnel provide advice on the organization's legal responsibilities and legal remedies. This can be before, during, and after an incident. The legal team understands what legal actions are possible against the attackers, and requirements necessary to pursue legal actions.

- **Human resources (HR)**—If the attack originated from an employee, HR needs to be involved. HR understands what the policies are and enforcement methods that are available. For example, if an employee violates the AUP, the first offense may result in a formal written warning. A second or third offense may result in termination. HR personnel would know if the employee had been previously warned.

- **Communications**—Public relations (PR) personnel become the face of the organization if the incident becomes public. They help to present an image of resolve, even if everything is not quite under control. If PR reps aren't used, there is the risk of team members expressing frustration or confusion about the attack. This can present a poor image to customers, vendors, and stockholders of the organization.

Responsibilities.   The incident response team has several responsibilities. These involve helping develop the plan, helping respond to incidents, and helping document the incidents. Each member of the team has special skills and responsibilities to the team. However, the team as a whole also has specific responsibilities.

Some of the primary responsibilities of the CIRT include:

- **Develop incident response procedures**—These can be generic procedures to respond to any types of incidents. They can also be detailed checklists for different types of incidents. For example, there may be one checklist for malware infections. There could be another checklist for a DoS attack.

- **Investigate incidents**—When an incident occurs, the CIRT is responsible for responding. Depending on the priority and impact of the incident, a single team member may respond. For high priority, high impact incidents, the entire team may respond.

- **Determine cause of incidents**—One of the goals of the investigation is to determine the cause. By understanding the cause, the CIRT is better able to determine the best response. For example, imagine a user brings in an infected universal serial bus (USB) flash drive from home. After plugging it into the system, the antivirus (AV) software detects and quarantines it. The cause was from the user transferring the virus from home to the work computer via the USB drive. This type of incident has caused many organizations to outlaw USB flash drives on their networks.

- **Recommend controls to prevent future incidents**—CIRT members often know the best solution to prevent the same incident again. Even if they don't know it already, they have the expertise and experience to research it. The control may be as simple as upgrading the security policy. It could be more complex and require the purchase and installation of hardware or software. Either way, the CIRT members provide the recommendation.

- **Protect collected evidence**—Evidence should not be modified when it's collected. Police officers don't walk through the blood at a crime scene, because that would affect the evidence. Similarly, CIRT members should not modify the evidence. They don't access files. They don't turn off the computers until the contents of RAM is captured, if the contents are desired. They use bit copy tools to copy hard drives to get a complete copy without modifying the data.

- **Use a chain of custody**—CIRT members are responsible for managing the evidence as soon as they collect it. A "chain of custody" helps ensure that the evidence presented later is the same evidence collected originally. The chain of custody should be established when evidence is seized and maintained throughout the life of the evidence. This chain of custody log documents who had the evidence at any moment. It also documents when the evidence is secured in a semipermanent storage location.

The CIRT plan at any organization may spell out the previous responsibilities. Additionally, if the organization has other responsibilities expected of the CIRT, they can be included in the CIRT plan. For example, members may be expected to subscribe to different security bulletins, or otherwise ensure that they stay aware of current risks.

Computer Forensics

Computer forensics has become much more prevalent in recent years. Just as forensics experts on TV's CSI series can discover hidden details from a crime scene, computer forensics experts can discover hidden details on computers.

A computer forensic investigation generally has three phases:

- **Acquire the evidence**—The data is collected. It's important that data not be modified during this phase. Toolkits capture data on systems. For example, a bit copy tool can create a complete image of a hard drive without modifying a single bit on the hard drive. It's important that people responding to the scene first do not access any files or turn the system off.
- **Authenticate the evidence**—Chain of custody forms track the evidence. They verify that the data is protected and controlled after it is collected. This verifies that the evidence is trustworthy. If a chain of custody is not used, the evidence may not be admissible in court. Instead, the evidence is considered tainted.
- **Analyze the evidence**—This is where the data is inspected and viewed. If the data includes files on a disk, a copy of the disk is used. If the original data needs to be verified, another copy from the original disk can be created.

Computer forensics is a growing field among computer professionals. Forensics isn't restricted to the police. Many IT professionals expand their security knowledge and become experts in computer forensics.

Accountabilities.   The CIRT is also accountable to the organization to provide a proactive response to any incident. Although incidents can't be avoided, the team is expected to minimize the impact of any incident.

Organizations often invest a lot of time and money in team members. The goal is to ensure they are trained and capable of handling the incidents. However, serious incidents don't happen often. That doesn't mean team members don't think about security very often. The team members are expected to keep up to date on security threats, and possible responses. This requires dedication on the part of each of the team members.

CIRT Policies

A CIRT plan also includes CIRT policies. These may be simple policy statements, or they could be appendixes at the end of the plan. These policies provide the team with guidance in the midst of any incident.

One of the primary policies to consider is whether CIRT members can attack back or not. In other words, during the investigation of an incident, a team member may have the opportunity to launch an attack on the attacker. Should this be done?

The answer is almost always a resounding "No!" First, there may be legal ramifications. If someone steals from you, you can't use that as excuse to steal from him or her.

If you are caught, you can be prosecuted. A defense of "but he did it first" won't impress a judge. Similarly, even if the attacker broke laws attacking your network, it doesn't give you justification to break laws to attack back.

You also run the risk of escalating the incident between your organization and the attacker. If someone bumps into you on a busy street, you could both say "excuse me" and the incident is over. Even if the other person is rude and purposely bumped into you, if you say "excuse me" and move on, the incident is over. However, if you turn on the person, flail your arms, push, and yell, the incident is not over. Instead, it escalates into a conflict. The result may depend on which party is willing to cause the most harm to the other.

Similarly, if an attacker attacks your network and fails, he may just move on to an easier target. He may have been looking for an easy mark, and your network looked like a target of opportunity. However, if you attack the attacker, you escalate the incident. He may now consider it personal. He might not care if it takes every waking moment of his time. He is now intent on breaking into your network and causing as much damage as possible.

With this in mind, it's worthwhile considering how many work hours an attacker may spend attacking. If there are personal gains such as millions of dollars at stake, 12-hour days and 80-hour works are doable in the short term. Similarly, if he has a personal vendetta against an organization that had the audacity to attack him, he may devote all his working time to satisfy the vendetta.

This is not to say that an organization should never attack back. Police, government, and military agencies may have specific units that are trained to attack. These attacks may gather evidence on criminal activities. They may be purposeful cyberwarfare against a government's enemies. However, if this isn't the specific mission of your unit, you should not attack back.

Other policies included in the CIRT may include policies related to evidence, communications, and safety.

You may need to use evidence collected during an investigation to prosecute people in the future. However, there are specific rules that govern the collection and storage of evidence. The CIRT plan can include policies to define these rules.

Communications with media can be challenging for anyone who doesn't have experience in this. However, a CIRT should have a PR person. A simple policy may state that the only person who may talk to the media about any incident is the PR person. If the media queries anyone else, the response is to refer the query to the public relations office or the specific PR person.

Although computer incidents aren't as dangerous as disasters, such as hurricanes or earthquakes, there could be some danger involved. A CIRT plan often states that the safety of personnel is most important. Actions should not be taken that may risk the safety of any personnel.

Incident Handling Process

A CIRT plan identifies the incident handling process. This can be a large part of the plan depending on how detailed the plan is. NIST SP 800-61 is the "Computer Security Incident Handling Guide." It outlines four phases of an incident. Figure 15-2 shows these four phases as an incident response life cycle.

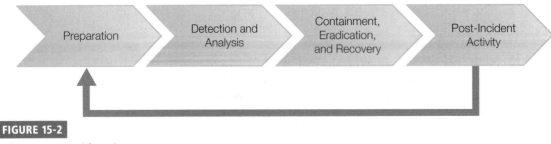

FIGURE 15-2

Incident response life cycle.

The four phases outlined in NIST SP 800-61 are described as follows:

- **Preparation**—This involves creating a CIRT plan, defining incidents, and creating CIRTs. The team members are trained and have specific roles and responsibilities. They know how to recognize, contain, and mitigate incidents.

- **Detection and analysis**—This phase uses different controls to detect incidents. It includes intrusion detection systems (IDSs) and AV software. Some detected events may not actually be incidents. You need to investigate and analyze events to determine if they are actual incidents, or false positives.

- **Containment, eradication, and recovery**—Once an incident is detected it needs to be contained as quickly as possible. This can be as simple as removing the cable from the network interface card (NIC) on the affected system. The source of the attack is then removed. For example, if a system is infected with malware, quarantine or remove the malware. You can then return the system to normal operations.

- **Post-incident recovery**—This includes an after-action review. You examine the incident and the response to determine if there are any lessons to be learned. The goals are to determine if the response was as effective as possible, and if the response can be improved. When warranted, modify the CIRT plan to include these lessons.

The individual steps of these phases can be different depending on the type of incident. However, even though the individual steps are different, the phases are the same.

> **NOTE**
>
> Botnets often include tens of thousands of computers. Cybercriminals manage the botnets and rent access to them to other criminals. For example, an attacker can rent access to them to launch a DDoS attack on a specific server.

Handling DoS Attack Incidents.   DoS attacks attempt to prevent a system or network from providing a service. They often try to overwhelm a system by consuming its resources. Any system has four primary resources. These are the processor, memory, disk, and bandwidth. When these resources are responding to the attack, they can't be used for normal operations.

A DDoS attack is launched from multiple systems. These systems are often controlled in a botnet. Consider Figure 15-3. This shows multiple zombies or clone computers that have been infected by malware. They are now controlled by an attacker from a command and control center. When the command is issued, each of the zombies attacks.

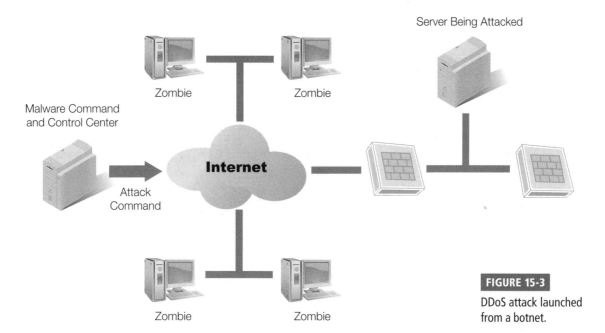

FIGURE 15-3

DDoS attack launched from a botnet.

DoS attacks attack a single system with a public IP address. There are several indications that a DoS attack is occurring. These include:

- Users report system unavailability
- Intrusion detection system alerts on the attack
- Increased resource usage on the attacked system
- Increased traffic through the firewall to the attacked system
- Unexplained connection losses
- Unexplained system crashes

You can confirm a suspected attack by reviewing available logs. System logs include information on system activity. Firewall logs can show network traffic to the system. Additionally, logs gathered by the IDS can identify many specific types of attacks.

The response depends on the type of attack. If the attack is due to a vulnerability, such as an unpatched system, that should be the primary response—fix the vulnerability. In this case, patch the system. You can block many attacks at the network firewall. You can block other attacks at the system firewall.

Many IDS systems include automated response capabilities. They can change firewall rules to block specific types of traffic. For example, if the attack is Internet Control Message Protocol (ICMP)–based, you can configure the firewall to block ICMP traffic. If the attack is a Syn flood attack that is holding the third packet of a TCP handshake, you can configure the firewall to block traffic from the attacking IP.

> **NOTE**
>
> Chapter 8 described the Syn flood attack, or TCP Syn flood, in detail. Although this is an older DoS attack, it is still used on the Internet.

15

Computer Incident
Response Team Plan

If an IDS system doesn't automatically respond to the attack, you can make the changes manually. The goal is to identify the source of the attack and modify the firewall rules to block the traffic. You can modify basic packet filtering rules on routers or firewalls. You can block traffic based on IP addresses, ports, and some protocols, such as ICMP.

It's also possible to get your Internet service provider (ISP) to assist with the response. The ISP can filter the traffic so the attack doesn't even reach your network.

Handling Malware Incidents.   Malware incidents are the result of any malicious software, such as viruses and worms. There are many types of malware, and new ones appear daily. Some of the varieties include:

- **Viruses**—Viruses attach themselves to applications and execute when the application executes. Viruses have three phases: replication, activation, and objective. Their first goal is to replicate to other applications. At some point, they activate to launch the objective. The virus payload is launched as the objective. This is the most dangerous part of the program. It is where the virus inflicts damage on the system or network. In some cases, the objective can be to contact a control server in a botnet to download additional malware.

- **Worms**—Worms are self-replicating programs. They don't need a host application as a virus does. They can also travel over networks. Worms commonly have a virus component. They travel over the network using the worm component and then, when they arrive at a system, they install a virus.

- **Mobile code**—This includes different types of malware that is executed when a user visits a Web site or opens an e-mail. Some of the languages and methods used are Java, ActiveX, JavaScript, and VBScript.

- **Trojan horses**—A Trojan horse appears to be one thing but is another. For example, it may look like a game or a screen saver. However, once it's installed, the malware is also installed. Some Trojan horses will keep the malicious software installed even if you uninstall the original application.

The primary protection against malware is antivirus software. Many organizations use a three-pronged approach. AV software is installed on all the systems in the organization. Because the majority of viruses are delivered via e-mail, AV software is installed on the

> **FYI**
>
> Trojan horses are named after the wooden horse in Greek mythology. This wooden horse looked like a gift from the gods to the people of Troy. Residents of Troy rolled the horse through the gates to the city and partied all day and night celebrating their good fortune. When the city slept, hidden attackers climbed out of the horse. They opened the gates and let the attacking army in. The army promptly sacked the city of Troy. The lesson is the same today as it was then. Beware of gifts from unknown sources.

e-mail server. Last, AV software is often installed at the boundary of the network. This is where the intranet meets the Internet and can filter all traffic for potential malware.

Additionally, signature files on the AV software must be updated regularly. Most organizations use automated techniques to install the AV software. These automated techniques also update the signatures regularly.

A secondary protection is training and education. Many users are unaware of how malware is delivered. They also don't recognize the extent of damage possible from malware. Routine training educates users about the types of malware threats. Users should also be educated on what to do if malware infects their system.

Some organizations create checklists that identify what a user should do if his or her system is infected. These checklists are posted where users can regularly see them. The first step after identifying the virus is to contain the threat. The checklist may direct the user to remove the NIC.

If an e-mail server is infected, isolate the e-mail server until the malware is contained. Depending on the extent of the malware, this may require you to shut down the e-mail server and rebuild it. It could also mean you simply remove the cable at the NIC until you remove the malware.

> **▶ TIP**
> NIST SP 800-83, "Guide to Malware Incident Prevention and Handling," includes details on how to address malware incidents.

Last, many organizations configure Web browsers and e-mail readers to prevent the execution of malicious mobile code. For example, Microsoft domains can use Group Policies to configure all the systems in the network. You can set Group Policy settings once to restrict execution of scripts or unsigned ActiveX controls on all user systems.

Handling Unauthorized Access Incidents. An unauthorized access incident occurs when a person gains access to resources, even when that person is not authorized access. Although this can be accidental, the focus is on attackers gaining access to data or systems. Attackers can gain access through social engineering or technical attacks.

Once they gain access, attackers try to exploit the access. Even if the attacker has only limited initial access, privilege escalation techniques allow the attacker to gain additional access. Some examples of unauthorized access incidents include:

- Attacking and defacing a Web server
- Uploading or downloading data from a File Transfer Protocol (FTP) server
- Using an unattended workstation without permission
- Viewing or copying sensitive data without authorization
- Using social engineering techniques to collect organization data
- Guessing or cracking passwords and logging on with these credentials
- Running a packet sniffer like Wireshark to capture data transmitted on the network

The majority of these types of attacks originate from attackers outside the organization. Attackers often access servers or other internal resources through the Internet. Internet-facing servers are most vulnerable to Internet-based attacks.

One of the basic protection steps you can take is to ensure that all servers are hardened. Chapter 2 presented basic steps to harden a server. These included:

- **Reduce the attack surface**—If services are not used, disable them. If protocols are not used, remove them. If an attacker launches an attack using a protocol that isn't installed, the server is protected.

- **Keep systems up to date**—Bugs and vulnerabilities can cause security vulnerabilities. As they are discovered, software vendors release patches and updates. Apply these updates regularly to protect the systems.

- **Enable firewalls**—Firewalls filter traffic to ensure that unwanted traffic does not reach vulnerable systems. Network-based firewalls provide one layer of protection for the computers in the network. Host-based firewalls provide another layer of protection. Both types of files should be enabled.

- **Enable IDSs**—Intrusion detection systems detect attacks. A passive IDS detects the attack and then provides notification. An active IDS can modify the environment and stop attackers before any damage is done.

Additionally, basic access controls provide protection. These ensure that all users must authenticate on the network before access is granted. Additionally, the principle of least privilege ensures that users only have access to the data they need and no more.

Attackers from outside the network won't have any access by default. However, this doesn't prevent an attacker from using social engineering tactics to discover network credentials. Social engineers trick or con the users into giving up valuable information, such as their user names and passwords. The attacker can then use this information to launch an attack.

> **TIP**
>
> Attackers commonly scan systems to determine what ports are open. Many protocols use well known ports. If the port is open, the attacker realizes the port is probably running on the server. For example, if port 80 is open, Hypertext Transfer Protocol (HTTP) is probably running on the server. This indicates the server is probably a Web server. Attackers use other techniques to verify it is a Web server, and if possible, the Web server brand.

You can detect unauthorized access incidents through several methods. IDSs often provide warnings about reconnaissance activity before an attack. For example, an attacker may scan a server for open ports to determine what protocols are running. Data gained in the reconnaissance attack is later used in the access attack.

Educated users can report social engineering attempts. A social engineer uses conning and trickery to get a user to give up secrets. Informed users can recognize these attempts and report them to administrators. Of course, uneducated users often give up the secrets without realizing what they've done.

Some attacks are not detected. In other words, an attacker may reach in, access data in a database and then disappear. Even if it is logged, the actual event may go undetected. It isn't until later that you realize that a problem has occurred. The stolen data may be research and development data that is now being used by a competitor. The stolen data may be customer credit information. It may not be until customers complain that you actually discover the problem.

The response depends on the attack. However, just as with other attacks, containment is important. If you detect the attack in progress, the goal is to isolate the affected system. You don't necessarily have to isolate the system from all users. Instead, you can isolate the system from the attacker. For example, you can modify firewall rules to block the attacker's IP address.

If the problem is due to a compromised account, you can disable the account. If the account is an elevated account, such as one with elevated permissions, you should check to see if other accounts were created with this one. For example, an attacker may steal the credentials of an administrator account. Right after logging on, the attacker creates another account with administrative permissions. Even if you lock out the first account, the attacker can still use the second account.

Handling Inappropriate Usage Incidents. Inappropriate usage incidents occur when users violate internal policies. These incidents aren't usually as serious as external incidents. However, depending on the activity, the incidents can be quite serious and result in loss of money for the organization.

Some examples of inappropriate usage include users who:

- Spam coworkers
- Access Web sites that are prohibited
- Purposely circumvent security policies
- Use file-sharing or P2P programs
- Send files with sensitive data outside the organization
- Launch attacks from within the organization against other computers

> **TIP**
>
> It's estimated that as many as 80 percent of the incidents that result in business losses are the result of internal attacks. Internal users have the most access to data and can cause the most damage. The importance of these incidents should not be overlooked or minimized.

One of the first things to do to help prevent these incidents is to have a security policy. The security policy should include an AUP, or the AUP should be separate. The AUP identifies what is acceptable usage and what is not acceptable usage.

For example, the AUP may specify that using e-mail to advertise a personal business is prohibited. Using the Internet to access gambling or pornographic sites may also be prohibited. Similarly, the policy often prohibits the use of anonymizer sites. Most proxy servers can detect and block access to anonymizers.

---

technical TIP

An **anonymizer** site attempts to hide a user's activity. The user visits the anonymizer site and then visits other sites through this site. The anonymizer retrieves the Web pages, but serves them as if they originated from the anonymizer site. For example, a user could visit a gambling site via the anonymizer. If the internal proxy server tracked the user's activity, it would identify the traffic from the anonymizer but not the traffic from the gambling site. Many organizations consider just the use of an anonymizer as a serious offense.

Marine One Helicopter Plans Shared with Iran

In 2008, a government contractor inadvertently shared the plans for the new Marine One helicopter with everyone on the Internet. Marine One is the helicopter used to shuttle the president. Air Force One is the plane used to transport the president.

The contractor installed a P2P application on a computer used at home and at work. At some point, plans for the Marine One helicopter and other secret data made their way onto the contractor's computer. The user was probably not aware of it, but the P2P application was sharing data on the user's computer—even the secret data that included plans for Marine One. This is classic data leakage. The P2P program shares data on the system without the user's knowledge.

Personnel of Tiversa, a private company, discovered the data on the Internet during the summer of 2008. They promptly reported it to the contractor. The contractor notified the Navy and the White House. Tiversa provided all the data they had to all the parties. Then, in 2009, the same data appeared on a computer in Iran. This is when it hit the news. Tiversa again discovered it, and reported it.

Notice that even though the data was first leaked in the summer of 2008, it wasn't reported in the media until 2009. How much other data is compromised but never reported in the news? How much other data is lost but simply never discovered?

Most organizations prohibit the use of P2P software. Users often think it's to control piracy. However, the real reason is the extreme risks related to data leakage.

The use of P2P programs to download or share pirated music, videos, or programs is also included in many AUPs. One of the main problems with P2P programs is **data leakage**. Data leakage occurs when the P2P network shares user data without the user being aware of it. A user could have a file with personal data, such as credit card information, that is being shared on the Internet without the user's being aware of it. Similarly, the user could be sharing proprietary data if a P2P program is installed on the user's computer.

You can discover inappropriate usage incidents through many different methods. These include logs and reports by other users.

Firewalls and proxy servers log all the traffic going through them. You can scan these logs to determine if users are violating the policies. Additionally, you can configure an IDS to automatically detect and report this activity. Once you detect a user, you can gather additional information to determine all of the user's activities.

Another way to detect inappropriate usage is through other users. Other users may receive spam from an employee advertising his or her business or promoting a religion. Other employees may view inappropriate images on an offender's computer. The organization responds to the incident when notified by these employees.

The primary response is based on the existing policies. This includes the security policy and the AUP. If policies don't exist, they need to be created. If an employee violates the policy, the employee is at fault. However, if a policy doesn't exist, the organization may be at fault.

In addition to having policies, it's worth stating the obvious: They must be enforced. Some organizations go through the motions of creating policies. However, when it comes time to enforce them, they look the other way. Employees quickly realize that there are dual policies. One is written but not followed. The other is unwritten and is the norm.

Handling Multiple Component Incidents.   A multiple component incident is a single incident that includes two or more other incidents. These incidents are related to each other, but this isn't always apparent right away. For example, imagine a user receives an e-mail with a malware attachment. When the user opens the attachment, it infects the user's system. This is the first incident.

The malware has three objectives. First, it releases a worm component that seeks out computers on the network and infects them. This is the second incident.

Next, it contacts a server on the Internet that is managing a botnet. In this role, the infected system acts as a zombie. It waits for a command from the botnet control server and then does whatever it's commanded to do.

Because the infected system has infected other systems on the network, you could easily have multiple systems that are infected. Each of these systems is looking for other systems to infect, and acting as a zombie ready to perform the bidding of the botnet.

Next, imagine that the botnet control server issues a command to all the infected systems. It directs them to launch an attack on a server on the Internet. All the zombies in your network attack. This is the third incident.

From the perspective of the attacked server, it looks as if your organization is attacking. The party being attacked may query your ISP and report your attacks. Your ISP may then threaten to discontinue your service. Notice that the ISP contact may be the first indication that you have a problem. Before then, the problem may not have been noticeable.

In this case, the primary protection is AV software and ensuring the AV software is up to date. Up-to-date AV software reduces the likelihood that systems are infected. Up-to-date AV software doesn't guarantee you won't be infected, however. It simply reduces the likelihood. You're always susceptible to new and emerging threats.

Anomaly-based intrusion detection systems may notice the increased activity on the network. An anomaly-based IDS starts with a baseline of normal activity. When activity increases outside the established threshold, the IDS alerts on the anomaly.

> **TIP**
> A behavior-based IDS is the same as an anomaly-based IDS. Both start with a baseline of regular activity. Activity is monitored and compared with the baseline.

When a multiple component incident is discovered, it's important to identify the root cause. In the preceding example, the root cause is the initial malware. If the root cause can be removed, you may be able to eliminate the other issues. However, any one of the individual components in a multiple component incident can take on a life of its own. In other words, a single component can launch another multiple component incident.

The Organization's Reputation

Communication outside the organization is important to understand too. If the media hear about an incident, you'll need to know how to respond. Negative publicity can destroy the reputation of the organization. Even if the organization is responding admirably, if this isn't presented to the media accurately, the result is negative.

The best method is to enlist the help of your public relations people. Ideally, the CIRT will include a PR person. Additionally, all personnel should understand that all media queries should go through this PR person.

Communication specialists know how to communicate effectively. Even in the midst of a major incident, they are able to present the organization in a favorable light. This is not to say that they know all the answers or give all the answers. However, they do know how to give honest, positive answers.

A technician may say something like "This worm hammered us. I've never seen so many servers down before. I don't know how we'll get them back up."

The PR person may say. "We have been attacked. We have several controls in place, but the attack appears to be very sophisticated and simultaneously hit several elements of our network. Our computer incident response team is on the scene. Even as we speak, they are investigating the source of the problems and resolving them."

Both statements are accurate. However, the first statement presents an image of chaos or being out of control. Although the technician's statement may be accurate, it has the potential to adversely affect the organization's reputation. The PR statement is also accurate. However, it preserves the organization's reputation.

Communication Escalation Procedures

When an event is determined to be an incident, it is declared an incident. This is also known as escalation. One of the first steps to take when an incident is declared is to recall the CIRT members. This can be done by a phone tree or any other type of traditional recall.

Additionally, incidents can get worse. For example, the initial report may have been a virus on a user's computer. However, the CIRT member may discover that the malware is being delivered from the e-mail server to every client in the network. What looked like a small problem now has the potential to become catastrophic. In this case, the CIRT member can escalate the response. The full CIRT can be activated to respond.

Communication is very important during the incident. It's important to remember that communication may be hampered during the incident. For example, e-mail or instant messenger systems can fail during an incident. If these are the primary methods of communication with no backup plan, communication will be challenging.

Chapter 14 mentioned similar communication problems. Solutions used for DRPs can also be used for computer incidents. For example, CIRT members can be issued push-to-talk phones or walkie-talkies. It's also possible to set up a war room for face-to-face communications. The war room could be staffed constantly, and team members could report findings to personnel there.

Incident Handling Procedures

When an incident is suspected, you can use a checklist to guide your actions. Checklists can be included in the CIRT plan as procedures to use in response to incidents. IT professionals who are first notified of a potential incident can use these checklists. CIRT members can also use the checklists when responding to incidents.

> **NOTE**
> The checklists in this section are derived from information in NIST SP 800-61, "Computer Security Incident Handling Guide."

Although checklists can't be created to respond to every possible incident, they can be tailored to the different types of incidents. For example, you can create a generic checklist to match most incidents. You can then create other checklists to identify what do to for the different types of incidents.

Calculating the Impact and Priority.   One of the important steps when handling an incident is to identify the impact and priority of the incident. The CIRT plan can include tools to help personnel determine the impact and priority. Members can then refer to these tools for clarification during the incident.

For example, data in Table 15-1 identifies the effect of the attack. A CIRT member compares the actual effect of the risk to the definition. This provides a value or a rating. For example, imagine that an organization has multiple locations spread around the country. No effect on any locations is a minimal effect. A severe effect on a single location is a medium effect. A severe effect on multiple locations is considered critical. Each of these ratings is assigned a numerical value.

> **NOTE**
> The definitions, values, and ratings used in these examples can be expanded to fit any organization. For example, you could have five values and ratings instead of three. You can use different values, different ratings, and even different definitions based on your needs.

The values in Table 15-1 are used to determine both current and projected effects. For example, a DoS attack may be launched against one of several Web servers in a Web farm. The effect may be minimal as long as only a single server is being attacked. However, if the attack isn't resolved soon, it may affect all the servers in the Web farm. The projected effect may be considered medium.

TABLE 15-1 Effect rating definitions.

DEFINITION	RATING	VALUE
No effect on any locations or the critical infrastructure	Minimal	10
Severe effect on a single location or minimal effect on multiple locations	Medium	50
Severe effect on multiple locations	Critical	90

15

Computer Incident
Response Team Plan

TABLE 15-2 Criticality rating definitions.		
DEFINITION	**RATING**	**VALUE**
Non-critical systems	Minimal	10
Systems that are mission critical to a single location	Medium	50
Systems that are mission critical to multiple location	Critical	90

You can use Table 15-2 to determine how critical the attack is. This is determined based on the importance, or criticality, of the systems.

You can then use the data from tables 15-1 and 15-2 to determine an overall score. For example, the data from an incident may be:

- **Current effect rating**—Minimal. Score of 10. This will be used for 25 percent, or one quarter of the overall impact score. ($10 \times .25 = 2.5$)
- **Projected effect rating**—Medium. Score of 50. This will be used for 25 percent, or one quarter of the overall impact score. ($50 \times .25 = 12.5$)
- **Criticality rating**—Medium. Score of 50. This will be used for 50 percent, or one-half of the overall impact score. ($50 \times .50 = 25$)

You can then use the following formula to determine the impact:

(Current effect rating $\times .25$) + (Projected effect rating $\times .25$) + (Criticality rating $\times .50$)

$10 \times .25 + 50 \times .25 + 50 \times .50$

$2.5 + 12.5 + 25$

Incident impact score $= 40$

After you've identified the incident impact score, you can then rate the impact of the incident. Table 15-3 shows a sample incident rating table. Note that a score of 40 indicates that the incident has a Medium impact rating.

TABLE 15-3 Incident impact rating.	
SCORE	**RATING AND PRIORITY**
0 to 25	Minimal, low priority
26 to 50	Medium, medium priority
51 to 100	Critical, high priority

Using a Generic Checklist.   Once you've identified how to calculate the impact and priority, you can then focus on checklists. The following checklist is a sample generic checklist:

- **Verify that an incident has occurred**—This verification ensures that the event is an actual incident. Verify that it is not a false positive. For example, some intrusion detection systems send an alert on unusual activity when the activity is not an actual incident.

- **Determine the type of incident**—Determine if the incident is a DoS, malware, unauthorized access, inappropriate usage, or a multiple type of incident. Some incidents may require specialists. If a checklist exists for an incident that requires a specialist, retrieve it from the CIRT plan.

- **Determine the impact or potential impact of the incident**—Determine the extent of the attack. For example, it could be a virus affecting a single workstation. It could be a worm affecting multiple servers. It could be a DoS attack taking down a primary Web server that is generating over $20,000 an hour in revenue. If the impact is high, the resulting response will be a high priority.

- **Report the incident**—If you aren't a member of the CIRT, report the incident to a member of the CIRT. Include the impact and severity of the incident, if possible. If you are a member of the CIRT, consider reporting the incident to management. High impact incidents should be reported as soon as possible. Lower priority incidents can be reported after they have been contained.

- **Acquire any available evidence on the incident**—Ensure that the evidence is preserved. If evidence is collected, ensure that it is secured so it can't be modified. Establish a chain of custody as soon as evidence is collected. This should include the time, date, and name of the person who is receiving the evidence. If the evidence is passed from one person to another, or into storage, update the chain of custody. It's also important to ensure that the evidence is not modified. Do not access any files or turn off the system. If files are accessed, the evidence is modified. If the system power is turned off, data in the memory is lost.

- **Contain the incident**—Ensure the incident can't spread to other systems. Isolate the system. You can do this by removing the NIC from the system, or disabling the NIC. If multiple systems are affected, isolate the network. This can be done by isolating all the systems on the network, or by isolating the network devices. For example, a router could be turned off or modified to isolate a subnet.

- **Eradicate the incident**—Identify the exploited vulnerabilities. Determine steps to reduce the weaknesses. If malware was involved, take steps to remove it. If the attack was on a public facing server, determine how to harden the server to prevent another attack.

- **Recover from the incident**—Once the incident has been eradicated, return systems to normal operation. Depending on the system and the damage, you may be able to simply reboot the system. You may also need to rebuild the system completely, or reapply a system image. If the system is rebuilt, ensure it is patched and up to date before returning it to operation. Also, ensure that the system is operating normally.

15

Computer Incident
Response Team Plan

- **Document the incident**—Documentation includes many elements. Ensure an after-action report is documented that describes the incident. This includes all the details gathered during the incident. It also includes all the steps taken to eradicate and recover from the incident. If a chain of custody was created, ensure it is maintained with any collected evidence. This evidence may be needed later.

The following sections show information that you can use in checklists for other types of incidents. CIRT members can use either the generic checklist or the specific type of checklist when responding to an incident.

Handling DoS Attack Incidents.   If the attack is a DoS attack, you can use a checklist designed to address DoS attacks. You can design the checklist as a standalone checklist or in conjunction with the generic checklist.

Consider the following items when creating a checklist for DoS attacks:

- **Containment**—Halt the DoS attack as soon as possible. You may be able to add filters at routers or firewalls to block the traffic based on the IP address, port, or protocol used in the attack. If you're unable to block it in your network, your ISP may be able to help. You should disconnect the server only as a last resort. Once it's disconnected, the service is stopped, which is the primary objective of the DoS attack.

- **Eradication**—Identify vulnerabilities that allowed the DoS attack. It could be because the server wasn't adequately hardened. For example, there may be unused protocols installed on the system. The server may not have up-to-date patches. After identifying the vulnerabilities, take steps to mitigate them.

- **Recovery**—Determine if there is any long-term damage on the server and repair it. The attack may have installed malware. Consider performing a malware scan with updated AV software. After recovery, test the system to ensure it is operating normally.

Handling Malware Incidents.   If an incident was the result of malicious software, you can take several additional steps. These are in addition to the steps in the generic checklist. If desired, you can create a specific checklist for malware incidents. You could also use a separate checklist for malware, or combine items into the generic checklist.

Consider the following items when creating a checklist for malware incidents:

- **Containment**—Identify all the infected systems and disconnect them from the network. Identify why the AV software didn't detect the malware. For example, the AV software may have been disabled, or the AV signatures may have been out of date. Update AV signatures and ensure the AV software is enabled. If necessary, configure firewall or router rules to block the malware from being transmitted to or from the infected system.

- **Eradication**—Run full scans on the systems. AV vendors such as Symantec and McAfee often host pages that show detailed steps to remove multipartite viruses and other advanced malware. If necessary, perform individual steps to remove all elements of the malware from the system. Disinfect, quarantine, or delete infected files.

- **Recovery**—Replace any files that were deleted or quarantined and are needed for system operation. Verify the system is no longer infected. If multiple steps were required to clean the system, consider running another full scan before returning the system to operation.

> **NOTE**
>
> A multipartite virus is a virus that uses multiple infection methods. It often requires more steps or complex procedures to eradicate than simpler malware.

Handling Unauthorized Access Incidents.   You can take several steps in response to unauthorized access incidents. Just as with other types of incidents, you can create separate checklists to cover unauthorized access incidents. You can also supplement the generic checklist with a checklist for unauthorized access incidents.

Consider the following items when creating a checklist for unauthorized access incidents:

- **Containment**—If the attack is discovered in process, identify the attacked system and isolate it from the network. You can do this by pulling the NIC cable or disabling the NIC. You can also use a host-based firewall to block all traffic while logging all attempts to connect. Determine if other systems were attacked. Attackers that succeed when attacking one system will usually try to attack other systems in the same network. Contain other systems, if necessary.

- **Eradication**—Identify the weaknesses that allowed the attack to succeed. Ensure that all the steps to harden the server have been completed and haven't been modified. Ensure that strong passwords are being used. Consider changing the passwords on the system. Check to see if additional accounts were created during the attack that may be used to access the system at another time. If you identify additional unneeded accounts, disable them and consider deleting them.

- **Recovery**—After the vulnerabilities have been resolved, reconnect the systems and verify they are operational. Test the systems to ensure they are operating as expected. Consider adding additional monitoring such as an IDS to identify future incidents as soon as possible.

When creating a follow-up report of unauthorized access, you need to consider the data that was accessed during the attack. If it was private customer data, such as credit card data, your organization may have specific liabilities associated with the incident. Determine the liabilities and include this in the report. Management will be responsible for determining how to handle these liabilities.

Handling Inappropriate Usage Incidents. Inappropriate usage incidents need specific responses to mitigate their effects. You can combine these steps with the steps in a generic checklist, or create a separate checklist to address inappropriate usage incidents individually.

As a reminder, an inappropriate usage incident occurs when an internal user is violating the organization's policies. Consider the following items when creating a checklist for inappropriate usage incidents:

- **Containment**—Consider disabling the user's account until management takes action. For example, if a user is sending religious materials to everyone in the organization, you can disable the user's e-mail access. You can also disable the user's account. It's worth noting that an employee is unable to perform regular work duties if network access is disabled. This does bring immediacy to the problem for both the user and the user's supervisor.

- **Eradication**—Some organizations require users to complete specific training before their access is returned. Other organizations require supervisors to document the activity in the employee's record. If the employee is a repeat offender, or the incident is considered severe enough, the employee may be terminated. For example, imagine if a user installed P2P software on an employer-owned computer that resulted in the loss of valuable research and development data through data leakage. The employer may terminate the employee immediately.

- **Recovery**—If the account was disabled, you would enable it after the appropriate action has been completed. For example, after the employee completes training, or HR informs you the incident is documented, you would enable the account. If the employee is terminated, the account should be disabled or deleted based on organization policy.

How Does a CIRT Plan Mitigate an Organization's Risk?

The CIRT plan helps an organization prepare for incidents. When prepared, the organization is able to respond to the incidents much quicker and with focused action.

One of the primary benefits of the CIRT plan is the identification of CIRT members. The plan identifies these individuals so that the organization knows who they are. Additionally, individuals on the team know their roles and responsibilities.

Once the plan and the members are identified, the organization has a better understanding of the skills needed. The members can be trained to ensure they have the skills needed to support the requirements.

Without the plan, IT and security professionals don't have the benefit of time to analyze their response. They may pull the NIC cable to stop a DoS attack on a server. Although this stops the attack, it also prevents the server from performing the expected service. Uninformed administrators may leave an infected system on the network, allowing it to infect other systems. A well-meaning administrator may launch an attack back on an attacker. This attack may be detected, resulting in the attacker launching a series of stronger and stronger attacks.

Best Practices for Implementing a CIRT Plan for Your Organization

When implementing a CIRT plan for your organization, you can use several best practices. The following list shows some of these:

- **Define a computer security incident**—Incidents are interpreted differently by different organizations. When you define the incident in the CIRT plan, it is clear to all parties. Employees and CIRT members have a clear understanding of which events are incidents.

- **Include policies in the CIRT plan to guide CIRT members**—These policies can be related to CIRT members attacking back at attackers. They can include statements regarding the use of chain of custody, or otherwise protecting evidence. They can include policies related to communications and safety. The policies included in the plan depend on what is important to the organization.

- **Provide training**—Ensure the CIRT members are trained, and that end users are trained. The CIRT members should understand their responsibilities. They should also know the best way to respond to different types of incidents. Users should also be trained. All personnel should understand the threats, as well as basic steps they can take to mitigate the threats.

- **Include checklists**—The checklists can be formal step-by-step checklists that must be performed in a specific order. They can also be informal bullet statements designed to help ensure the CIRT members don't overlook key data. You can include generic checklists or checklists targeted toward specific types of incidents.

- **Subscribe to security notifications**—There are many security bulletins you can sign up for. These provide e-mails describing different types of threats, including new emerging threats. Chapter 2 described several mail list bulletins you can sign up for through US-CERT. You can view them here: *https://forms.us-cert.gov/maillists*.

CHAPTER SUMMARY

This chapter covered computer incident response teams (CIRTs) and CIRT plans. Organizations should expect attacks that result in computer security incidents. Several types of incidents exist. Denial of service attacks try to prevent a system from providing a service. Malicious software attacks include viruses, worms, Trojan horses and other types of malware. Unauthorized access incidents result when individuals gain access to data that they shouldn't have access to. Unauthorized access can be from technical attacks or social engineering tactics. Inappropriate usage incidents result when employees or internal users violate the organization's policies. Some incidents have multiple components.

A CIRT can respond to the attack and mitigate the effects. The CIRT plan identifies organizational policies. For example, a policy may explain the conditions where a CIRT member can attack the attacker. It will certainly include procedures or checklists to use when responding to different types of incidents. Through preparation and training, the CIRT plan helps an organization mitigate the risks associated with incidents.

KEY CONCEPTS AND TERMS

Anonymizer
CIRT plan
Computer incident

Computer incident response
   team (CIRT)
Data leakage
Malware

CHAPTER 15 ASSESSMENT

1. A(n) _____ is a violation of a security policy or security practice.

2. All events on a system or network are considered computer security incidents.

   A. True
   B. False

3. An administrator has discovered that a Web server is responding very slowly. Investigation shows that the processor, memory, and network resources are being consumed by outside attackers. This is a _____ attack.

4. A user has installed P2P software on a system. The organization's policy specifically states this is unauthorized. An administrator discovered the software on the user's system. Is this a computer security incident? If so, what type?

   A. This is not a computer security incident.
   B. This is a form of inappropriate usage.
   C. This is a form of unauthorized access.
   D. This is a form of malware.

5. Some malware can execute on a user's system after the user accesses a Web site. The malware executes from within the Web browser. What type of malware is this?

   A. Virus
   B. Worm
   C. Trojan horse
   D. Mobile code

6. A malicious virus is replicating and causing damage to computers. How do security professionals refer to the virus?

   A. In the open
   B. In the containment field
   C. In the jungle
   D. In the wild

7. What is the greatest risk to an organization when peer-to-peer software is installed on a user's system?

   A. Loss of copyrights
   B. Piracy of the organization's copyrighted material
   C. Data leakage
   D. DoS attacks

8. Only police or other law enforcement personnel are allowed to do computer forensic investigations.

   A. True
   B. False

9. A log has shown that a user has copied proprietary data to his computer. The organization wants to take legal action against the user. You are tasked with seizing the computer as evidence. What should you establish as soon as you seize the computer?

   A. Chain of command
   B. Forensic chain
   C. Permission from the user
   D. Chain of custody
   E. All of the above

10. Many steps are taken before, during, and after an incident. Of the following choices, what accurately identifies the incident response life cycle?

    A. Preparation, deletion and analysis, eradication and recovery, and post-incident recovery
    B. Detection and analysis, containment, backup and eradication, and post-incident recovery
    C. Preparation, detection and analysis, containment, eradication and recovery, and post- incident recovery
    D. Preparation, detection, deletion and analysis, containment and recovery, and post-incident recovery

11. In general, it's acceptable for members of a CIRT to take actions to attack attackers. This is one of the normal responsibilities of a CIRT.

    A. True
    B. False

12. After an incident has been verified, you need to ensure that it doesn't spread to other systems. What is this called?

    A. Spread avoidance
    B. Containment
    C. Incident response
    D. Impact and priority calculation

13. Which of the following may be included in a CIRT plan?

    A. Policies
    B. Definition of incidents
    C. CIRT member responsibilities
    D. Incident handling procedures
    E. All of the above
    F. C and D only

14. Attackers attempt a DoS attack on servers in your organization. The CIRT responds and mitigates the attack. What should be the last step that the CIRT will complete in response to this incident?

    A. Attack the attacker.
    B. Contain the threat.
    C. Document the incident.
    D. Report the incident.

15. Several types of malicious code exist. Malware that appears to be one thing but is actually something else is _____.

Answer Key

CHAPTER 1 Risk Management Fundamentals

1. D   2. B   3. B   4. A and C   5. Intangible value   6. B   7. B   8. D
9. CVE   10. A   11. D   12. Transfer   13. A, B, and C   14. D   15. C

CHAPTER 2 Managing Risk: Threats, Vulnerabilities, and Exploits

1. D   2. A   3. B   4. C   5. D   6. C   7. B   8. A   9. A   10. E   11. A
12. B   13. C   14. The MITRE Corporation   15. A

CHAPTER 3 Maintaining Compliance

1. C   2. D   3. A   4. C   5. B   6. A   7. D   8. A   9. A   10. A
11. B   12. C   13. A   14. 5   15. D

CHAPTER 4 Developing a Risk Management Plan

1. E   2. E   3. D   4. C   5. B   6. A   7. A and B   8. B   9. D
10. A   11. C   12. A   13. C   14. D   15. C

CHAPTER 5 Defining Risk Assessment Approaches

1. E   2. Assessment   3. B   4. Quantitative risk assessment   5. C   6. A
7. B   8. Qualitative   9. Quantitative   10. B   11. Quantitative   12. Qualitative
13. D   14. A and B   15. E

CHAPTER 6 Performing a Risk Assessment

1. A   2. E   3. E   4. B   5. D   6. A   7. Administrative   8. Technical
9. Physical   10. C   11. A   12. B   13. B   14. C   15. B

CHAPTER 7 Identifying Assets and Activities to Be Protected

1. A   2. B   3. E   4. E   5. Job   6. E   7. C   8. A   9. D
10. Mission-critical   11. D   12. A   13. B   14. C   15. B

CHAPTER 8 Identifying and Analyzing Threats, Vulnerabilities, and Exploits

1. Natural   2. A   3. C   4. A, B, C, and D   5. D   6. Vulnerability   7. C
8. C   9. A   10. D   11. Access controls   12. D   13. A   14. B   15. B

CHAPTER 9   Identifying and Analyzing Risk Mitigation Security Controls

1. Control or countermeasure   2. A   3. C   4. B   5. D   6. Access
7. C   8. C   9. A   10. D   11. Certification authority (CA)   12. D
13. A   14. B   15. A

CHAPTER 10   Planning Risk Mitigation Throughout Your Organization

1. Business impact analysis (BIA)   2. B   3. C   4. B   5. D
6. Access control lists (ACLs)   7. C   8. C   9. D   10. B   11. A
12. C   13. A   14. B   15. A

CHAPTER 11   Turning Your Risk Assessment into a Risk Mitigation Plan

1. In-place   2. A   3. Threat X Vulnerability   4. E   5. A   6. Mitigation
7. E   8. C   9. C   10. B   11. A   12. C   13. C   14. F   15. A

CHAPTER 12   Mitigating Risk with a Business Impact Analysis

1. Maximum acceptable outage (MAO)   2. A   3. Business continuity plan (BCP)
4. D   5. C and D   6. Indirect   7. D   8. C   9. B   10. C   11. B   12. A
13. D   14. D   15. B

CHAPTER 13   Mitigating Risk with a Business Continuity Plan

1. BCP or business continuity plan   2. B   3. Scope   4. C   5. D
6. BCP coordinator   7. A   8. C   9. D   10. B   11. A   12. C   13. C
14. A, B, and D   15. A

CHAPTER 14   Mitigating Risk with a Disaster Recovery Plan

1. Disaster recovery plan (DRP)   2. A   3. B   4. Critical success factor (CSF)
5. D   6. D   7. Off-site   8. A   9. C   10. B   11. C   12. D   13. B
14. D   15. B

CHAPTER 15   Mitigating Risk with a Computer Incident Response Team Plan

1. Computer incident or computer security incident   2. B
3. Denial of service (DoS) or distributed DoS (DDoS)   4. B   5. D
6. D   7. C   8. B   9. D   10. C   11. B   12. B   13. E   14. C
15. A Trojan horse

Standard Acronyms

3DES	triple data encryption standard		**DMZ**	demilitarized zone
ACD	automatic call distributor		**DoS**	denial of service
AES	Advanced Encryption Standard		**DPI**	deep packet inspection
ANSI	American National Standards Institute		**DRP**	disaster recovery plan
AP	access point		**DSL**	digital subscriber line
API	application programming interface		**DSS**	Digital Signature Standard
B2B	business to business		**DSU**	data service unit
B2C	business to consumer		**EDI**	Electronic Data Interchange
BBB	Better Business Bureau		**EIDE**	Enhanced IDE
BCP	business continuity planning		**FACTA**	Fair and Accurate Credit Transactions Act
C2C	consumer to consumer		**FAR**	false acceptance rate
CA	certificate authority		**FBI**	Federal Bureau of Investigation
CAP	Certification and Accreditation Professional		**FDIC**	Federal Deposit Insurance Corporation
			FEP	front-end processor
CAUCE	Coalition Against Unsolicited Commercial Email		**FRCP**	Federal Rules of Civil Procedure
			FRR	false rejection rate
CCC	CERT Coordination Center		**FTC**	Federal Trade Commission
CCNA	Cisco Certified Network Associate		**FTP**	file transfer protocol
CERT	Computer Emergency Response Team		**GIAC**	Global Information Assurance Certification
CFE	Certified Fraud Examiner			
CISA	Certified Information Systems Auditor		**GLBA**	Gramm-Leach-Bliley Act
CISM	Certified Information Security Manager		**HIDS**	host-based intrusion detection system
CISSP	Certified Information System Security Professional		**HIPAA**	Health Insurance Portability and Accountability Act
CMIP	common management information protocol		**HIPS**	host-based intrusion prevention system
			HTTP	hypertext transfer protocol
COPPA	Children's Online Privacy Protection		**HTTPS**	HTTP over Secure Socket Layer
CRC	cyclic redundancy check		**HTML**	hypertext markup language
CSI	Computer Security Institute		**IAB**	Internet Activities Board
CTI	Computer Telephony Integration		**IDEA**	International Data Encryption Algorithm
DBMS	database management system		**IDPS**	intrusion detection and prevention
DDoS	distributed denial of service		**IDS**	intrusion detection system
DES	Data Encryption Standard			

IEEE	Institute of Electrical and Electronics Engineers
IETF	Internet Engineering Task Force
InfoSec	information security
IPS	intrusion prevention system
IPSec	IP Security
IPv4	Internet protocol version 4
IPv6	Internet protocol version 6
IRS	Internal Revenue Service
(ISC)²	International Information System Security Certification Consortium
ISO	International Organization for Standardization
ISP	Internet service provider
ISS	Internet security systems
ITRC	Identity Theft Resource Center
IVR	interactive voice response
LAN	local area network
MAN	metropolitan area network
MD5	Message Digest 5
modem	modulator demodulator
NFIC	National Fraud Information Center
NIDS	network intrusion detection system
NIPS	network intrusion prevention system
NIST	National Institute of Standards and Technology
NMS	network management system
OS	operating system
OSI	open system interconnection
PBX	private branch exchange
PCI	Payment Card Industry
PGP	Pretty Good Privacy
PKI	public-key infrastructure
RAID	redundant array of independent disks
RFC	Request for Comments
RSA	Rivest, Shamir, and Adleman (algorithm)
SAN	storage area network
SANCP	Security Analyst Network Connection Profiler
SANS	SysAdmin, Audit, Network, Security
SAP	service access point
SCSI	small computer system interface
SET	Secure electronic transaction
SGC	server-gated cryptography
SHA	Secure Hash Algorithm
S-HTTP	secure HTTP
SLA	service level agreement
SMFA	specific management functional area
SNMP	simple network management protocol
SOX	Sarbanes-Oxley Act of 2002 (also Sarbox)
SSA	Social Security Administration
SSCP	Systems Security Certified Practitioner
SSL	Secure Socket Layer
SSO	single system sign-on
STP	shielded twisted cable
TCP/IP	Transmission Control Protocol/Internet Protocol
TCSEC	Trusted Computer System Evaluation Criteria
TFTP	Trivial File Transfer Protocol
TNI	Trusted Network Interpretation
UDP	User Datagram Protocol
UPS	uninterruptible power supply
UTP	unshielded twisted cable
VLAN	virtual local area network
VOIP	Voice over Internet Protocol
VPN	virtual private network
WAN	wide area network
WLAN	wireless local area network
WNIC	wireless network interface card
W3C	World Wide Web Consortium
WWW	World Wide Web

Glossary of Key Terms

A

Acceptable use policy (AUP) | A policy that informs employees what is considered acceptable use for IT systems and data. Banners and logon screens are sometimes used to remind personnel of the policy.

Accept | One of the techniques used to manage risk. When the cost to reduce the risk is greater than the potential loss, the risk is accepted. A risk is also accepted if management considers the risk necessary and tolerable for business.

Account management policy | A written policy created to ensure that user and computer accounts are managed securely. It identifies details for creating accounts, such as using a firstname. lastname format. It specifies what to do with unused accounts. It can also include requirements for account lockout and password policies. This written policy is usually enforced with a technical policy.

Administrative security control | Control in place from the rules and guidelines directed by upper-level management.

Advanced Encryption Standard (AES) | The standard defined by NIST for symmetric encryption. It is fast, efficient, and commonly used to encrypt data on drives, including universal serial bus (USB) flash drives.

Affinity diagram | A method used to create lists of threats, vulnerabilities, or response plans. It starts with a large topic such as a problem statement. It then narrows the problem to individual sources.

Annual loss expectancy (ALE) | Total expected loss from a given risk for a year. ALE is calculated by multiplying SLE X ARO. ALE is part of a quantitative risk assessment.

Annualized rate of occurrence (ARO) | Number of times loss from a given threat is expected to occur in a year. It is used with the SLE to calculate the ALE. ARO is part of a quantitative risk assessment.

Anonymizer | A Web site used to hide a user's activity on the Internet. The user visits the anonymizer site and then requests pages from other sites. The anonymizer retrieves the Web pages and serves them as if they are served from the anonymizer site.

Asset management | Used to manage all types of assets. Asset management includes more detailed information than an inventory management system. For example, it would include installed components, hardware peripherals, installed software, update versions, and more.

Asset valuation | The process of determining the fair market value of an asset. You can determine the value of the asset from the actual cost. You can also determine the value based on what the asset provides to the organization.

Attack surface | How much can be attacked on a server. Every additional service or protocol running or enabled increases the attack surface. By disabling services or protocols that are not needed, you reduce the attack surface.

Attorney General (AG) | A state or federal position. A state AG represents the state in all legal matters. The U.S. AG is the head of the U.S. Department of Justice.

Audit trail | A series of events recorded in one or more logs. Audit trail events record who, what, where, and when. They can be in operating system logs like the Microsoft Security log, or application logs like a firewall log.

Audit | A check to see if an organization is following rules and guidelines. A vulnerability assessment audit checks to see if internal policies are followed.

Availability | Ensuring that data or a service is available when needed. Data and services are protected using fault tolerance and redundancy techniques.

Avoid | One of the techniques used to manage risk. A risk can be avoided by eliminating the source of the risk or eliminating the exposure of assets to the risk. A company can either stop the risk activity or move the asset.

B

Blacklist | A list used in a spam filter to block e-mail. It is a list of e-mail addresses or e-mail domains. You add the addresses or domains to the blacklist to ensure that e-mail from these sources is always marked as spam.

Brainstorming | A creative method used to generate a large number of ideas on a topic. Participants are encouraged to mention any idea that comes to mind. Ideas are recorded without judgments.

Buffer overflow | A common exploit used against public-facing servers. Buffer overflow can occur when an attacker sends more data or different data than is expected. Attackers can use it to gain additional privileges on the system.

Business continuity plan (BCP) | A comprehensive plan that helps a company prepare for different types of emergencies. The goal is to ensure that mission-critical functions continue operate even after a disaster strikes.

Business impact analysis (BIA) | Part of the BCP. It identifies the impact to the business if one or more IT functions fails.

C

Capability Maturity Model Integration (CMMI) | A process improvement approach to management. It includes six levels from 0 to 5. Level 0 indicates a process doesn't exist. Level 5 indicates the process is very mature and effective.

Cause and effect diagram | Also known as Ishikawa diagram or fishbone diagram. It is used to show the relationships between causes and problems.

Certificates | Files that are used for security. Uses include identification and encryption. Certificates can be issued to users or systems. These certificates are then presented to other entities. A certificate includes a public key that is shared with others. The public key is matched with a private key that is always kept private.

Certification authority (CA) | An entity that issues and manages certificates. A CA can be public or private. Public CAs are accessible on the Internet. Private CAs are internal to an organization. Certificates are used by users and systems for security purposes, such as identification and encryption.

Change management | A formal process requiring that changes be made only after they have been reviewed and submitted. This reduces outages caused by unauthorized changes.

Children's Internet Protection Act (CIPA) | A U.S. law passed in 2000. It requires schools and libraries receiving E-Rate funds to filter some Internet content. The primary purpose is to protect minors from obscene or harmful images.

CIRT plan | A formal plan created by the organization to respond to computer incidents. It includes a definition of a computer incident. It also formally designates the CIRT.

Cloud computing | A technology that allows an organization to access required services over a public network, such as the Internet. Organizations often contract with third-party vendors to provide services using cloud computing.

Cold site | An alternate location used for disaster recovery. This site is an available building. It has electricity, running water, and restrooms. None of the equipment or data is staged at a cold site. It is inexpensive to maintain. However, a cold site takes a lot of effort to get functional. Additionally, it is very difficult to test a cold site. Other alternate locations are warm sites and hot sites.

Common Vulnerabilities and Exposures (CVE) | Database of vulnerabilities maintained by the MITRE Corporation. MITRE works in conjunction with the U.S. Department of Homeland Security to maintain the CVE. The list includes over 40,000 items.

Compliance | When an organization is complying with relevant laws and regulations, it is said to be in compliance. Many organizations have programs in place to ensure that they remain in compliance.

Computer incident response team (CIRT) | A group of people who will respond to incidents. The CIRT can be a formal team designated in advance. It can also be an informal team created after an incident occurs.

Computer incident | Also known as a computer security incident. It is any activity that threatens the security of the computer systems. It affects the organization's security. It may result in loss of confidentiality, integrity, or availability.

Confidentiality | Protecting data from unauthorized disclosure. Data is protected using access controls and encryption technologies.

Configuration management | Standards used to ensure that systems are configured similarly. Additionally, you can perform compliance auditing regularly to ensure that systems have not been improperly modified.

Continuous monitoring | A philosophy centered on the principle that security requires continuous effort. You put controls into place. Later, you perform checks and audits to ensure they are still working as expected.

Control | An action or change put in place to reduce a weakness or potential loss. A control is also referred to as a countermeasure.

Control Objectives for Information and related Technology (COBIT) | A framework of good practices for IT management. COBIT is well respected and frequently used. It is organized into four domains. They are: 1) Plan and Organize, 2) Acquire and Implement, 3) Deliver and Support, and 4) Monitor and Evaluate.

Corrective control | A class of control identified by its function. It attempts to reverse the effect of an exploited vulnerability. For example, antivirus software can work as a corrective control if it detects an infected file.

Cost-benefit analysis (CBA) | A process used to determine how to manage a risk. If the benefits of a control outweigh the costs, the control can be implemented to reduce the risk. If the costs are greater than the benefits, the risk can be accepted.

Countermeasure | A security control or safeguard. It is put into place to reduce a risk. It reduces the risk by reducing the vulnerability or threat impact.

Critical business function (CBF) | Any function considered vital to an organization. If the CBF fails, the organization will lose the ability to perform a critical operation necessary for the businesses mission.

Critical path chart | A chart of critical tasks in a project. If any task in the critical path is delayed, the entire project will be delayed.

Critical success factor (CSF) | An element necessary for the success of an organization. CSFs often contribute to CBFs.

D

Damage Assessment Team (DAT) | A team that collects data after a disruption to determine the extent of the damage. The DAT collects data on damage to systems and facilities. The DAT reports the data to the EMT. The EMT, DAT, and TRT are teams designated by the BCP.

Data leakage | A result of peer-to-peer (P2P) programs. P2P programs are commonly used to download pirated music, movies, and applications. Users are often unaware that the P2P programs also share data on their systems. Data leakage occurs when data on a user's system is shared without the user's knowing it.

Data mining | The process of retrieving data from a data warehouse. Data mining allows decision-makers to view the data from different perspectives. Decision-makers can also use data mining to make predictions about future behavior or outcomes.

Data warehousing | The process of gathering data from different databases and storing them centrally. An extract, transform, load (ETL) process is used. Data is extracted from the original database. It is then transformed to match the target database. Finally, it is loaded into the target database.

Defense in depth | A security principle used to provide multiple layers of controls. Even though one control may provide protection, additional controls are added to provide stronger protection. A defense in depth strategy ensures a risk is mitigated even if one control fails.

Demilitarized zone (DMZ) | A buffer zone separating the Internet from the internal network. A DMZ is often created with two separate firewalls. You then place public-facing servers such as Web servers or e-mail servers in the DMZ.

Denial of service (DoS) | An attack designed to prevent a system from providing a service. A DoS attack is launched from a single client.

Department of Defense (DoD) Information Assurance Certification and Accreditation Process (DIACAP) | A risk management process applied to U.S. DoD systems. It is fully documented in DoD instruction 8510.1. Systems must go through a formal certification and accreditation process before being authorized to operate.

Department of Homeland Security (DHS) | A major department in the U.S. government. It is charged with protecting the United States from threats and emergencies.

Detective control | A class of control identified by its function. It will detect when a vulnerability is being exploited. An intrusion detection system (IDS) is an example of a detective control.

Digital signature | A method used for identification. Digital signatures use certificates issued by a CA. A hash of a message is created. The hash is encrypted with the sender's private key. If the receiver can decrypt the encrypted hash with the sender's public key, it has been verified that it was encrypted and sent with the sender's private key. Only the sender has the private key.

Disaster recovery | The procedures to bring a system back into service after it has failed. Disaster recovery occurs after a disaster. Disaster recovery steps are documented in a disaster recovery plan that is a part of a business continuity plan.

Disaster recovery plan (DRP) | A plan used to recover a system or systems after a disaster. The DRP is part of the BCP.

Distributed denial of service (DDos) | A DoS attack launched from multiple clients at the same time. DDoS attacks often include zombies controlled in a botnet.

Due care | Taking reasonable steps to protect against risks.

Due diligence | Taking a reasonable amount of time and effort to identify risks. The person or organization conducting due diligence investigates risks in order to understand them.

E

Emergency Management Team (EMT) | A team composed of senior management personnel, who have overall authority during a disruption or disaster. The EMT, DAT, and TRT are teams designated by the BCP.

E-Rate funding | A program in place that provides discounts to schools and libraries for Internet access. Any school or library that requests discounts under the E-Rate program must comply with CIPA rules. CIPA mandates the filtering of Internet content for children under 17 years of age.

Exploit | The act of initiating a vulnerability. It occurs when a command or program is executed to take advantage of a weakness. Some examples are buffer overflows, DoS attacks, and DDoS attacks.

Exploit assessment | An attempt to discover what vulnerabilities an attacker can exploit. Exploit assessments are also called penetration tests.

Exploit testing | Testing that tries to exploit vulnerabilities. Vulnerability testing identifies potential vulnerabilities, and exploit testing determines if the vulnerabilities can actually be exploited. Exploit testing can take down systems.

Exploit Wednesday | The day after Patch Tuesday. After patches are released, attackers attempt to reverse-engineer the patches to learn the vulnerabilities. They then create attacks to exploit the vulnerabilities before the patches are widely applied.

F

Failover cluster | A technology used to ensure a service can continue to run even if a server fails. A failover cluster has at least two servers. One server is active. The second server is inactive but available to take over if the active server fails.

Family Educational Rights and Privacy Act (FERPA) | A U.S. law passed in 1974. It mandates the protection of student records. This includes any records with education or health data. Any institution receiving federal funds for education is covered by this law.

Federal Deposit Insurance Corporation (FDIC) | A federal agency created in 1933. The FDIC provides insurance for depositor funds in FDIC banks. The goal is to promote confidence in U.S. banks.

Federal Information Security Management Act (FISMA) | A U.S. law passed in 2002. FISMA requires federal agencies to protect IT systems and data. Additionally, agencies must have annual inspections. These annual inspections provide independent evaluations of security programs.

Federal Trade Commission (FTC) | A federal agency created in 1914. Its primary goal is to promote consumer protection. It also works to prevent unfair methods of competition.

Fiduciary responsibility | A relationship of trust between two entities. A fiduciary could be a person who is trusted. The fiduciary has a responsibility to uphold this trust.

Firewall | A firewall filters traffic. Rules are configured on the firewall to define what traffic is allowed and what traffic is blocked. A network firewall is a combination of hardware and software. Individual systems can include a single software-based firewall

Firewall appliance | A self-contained firewall solution. It includes hardware and software to provide security protection for a network.

Firewall policy | A document that identifies what traffic to allow or block. A firewall policy is often used to implement rules on the firewall.

G

Gantt chart | A bar chart used to show a project schedule. Gantt charts are commonly used in project management. Gantt charts can be used in risk management plans.

Gap analysis | A report created by comparing exploits that should be controlled, with the exploits that are controlled. Any uncontrolled exploits represent a gap in the security. A gap analysis is often performed when an organization is trying to comply with legal requirements such as HIPAA.

Gramm-Leach-Bliley Act (GLBA) | A law passed in 1999. It applies to financial institutions. The financial privacy rule and the safeguards rule apply to IT security. Companies need to tell customers how customer data is used. Additionally, the companies need to take steps to protect financial data.

Group Policy | An automated management tool. You can configure a setting once and it will apply to all users or computers equally. It is much more efficient than configuring the setting on individual computers.

H

Hardening a server | The act of making a server more secure from the default. Defaults are changed. The attack surface is reduced. The system is kept up to date.

Health Insurance Portability and Accountability Act (HIPAA) | A U.S. law passed in 1999. It mandates the protection of health information. Any organization handling any type of health information must comply with this law. This includes health care providers. It also includes employers offering health plans.

Host-based intrusion detection system (HIDS) | An intrusion detection system that is installed on a single host such as a workstation or server. Any intrusion detection system detects intrusions and attacks.

Hot site | An alternate location used for disaster recovery. This site includes all the equipment and data necessary to take over business functions in a short period of time. A hot site will be able to assume operations within hours and sometimes within minutes. Hot sites are very expensive to maintain. Other alternate locations are cold sites and warm sites.

I

Impact | The amount of the loss resulting from a threat exploiting a vulnerability. The loss can be expressed in monetary terms or a relative value. The impact identifies the severity of the loss. Impact is derived from the opinions of experts.

GLOSSARY

Implicit deny | A philosophy applied to routers and firewalls. All traffic is blocked unless it is explicitly allowed. For example, port 80 can be opened to allow HTTP traffic with a firewall rule. If there are no other rules, no other traffic is allowed. Even though the firewall doesn't have a rule explicitly denying traffic on port 77, it is still denied.

Information Technology Infrastructure Library (ITIL) | A group of books developed by the United Kingdom's Office of Government Commerce. These books document good practices that can be used in IT networks.

In-place countermeasure | A countermeasure that is currently installed. Countermeasures can be in place or planned.

Intangible value | Value that isn't directly related to the actual cost of a physical asset. Intangibles can include future lost revenue, client confidence, and customer influence.

Integrity | Ensuring data or IT systems are not modified or destroyed. Hashing is often used to ensure integrity.

Intellectual property (IP) | Data created by a person or an organization. It can include creative works such as literary, musical, or artistic. It can also include industrial designs, trademarks, inventions, and patents.

Intentional threats | Acts that are hostile to the organization. Intentional threats come from criminals, vandals, disgruntled employees, hackers, and others.

International Electrotechnical Commission (IEC) | An international standards organization. The IEC focuses on electrical, electronic, and related technologies. The IEC works with the ISO on some standards. The IEC published IEC 31010 Risk Management—Risk Assessment Techniques.

International Organization for Standardization (ISO) | An international standards organization. Three risk-related documents that ISO published are ISO 27002, ISO 31000, and ISO 73.

Intrusion detection system (IDS) | A system that can monitor a network and send an alert if an intrusion is detected. Both host-based IDS (HIDS) and network-based IDS (NIDS) systems are commonly used. A passive IDS logs and alerts on events. An active IDS can block a detected attack.

Inventory management | Used to manage hardware inventories. Basic information is included, such as model numbers, serial numbers, and locations.

J

Job rotation | Rotating employees through different jobs. This results in additional oversight for past transactions. It can help prevent or reduce fraudulent activity such as collusion. Job rotation can also increase technical expertise on specific systems.

L

Least-privilege principle | A security principle that grants users only the minimum rights and permissions needed to perform their job. This is similar to the need-to-know principle. However, the need-to-know principle focuses only on permissions for data, not rights.

M

Malware | Malicious software. This includes viruses, worms, Trojan horses, or any other type of malicious software.

Mandatory vacation | Requiring employees to take an annual vacation of at least five consecutive days. While the employee is on vacation, someone else must perform the job. This increases the likelihood that illegal activities will be discovered.

Maximum acceptable outage (MAO) | The maximum amount of time a system or service can be down before affecting the mission. This directly affects the required recovery time. In other words, a system must be recoverable before the MAO time is reached.

Milestone | A scheduled event for a project. It indicates the completion of a major task or group or tasks. Milestones are used to track the progress of a project.

Milestone plan chart | A graphical representation of major milestones. It shows the time relationship of milestones to each other. It also shows dependencies, if any.

Mission-critical | Any system, function, or process identified as critical to the mission of the organization. Mission-critical systems and activities are necessary to keep the organization functioning.

Mitigate | One of the techniques used to manage risk. Mitigation is also known as risk reduction. Vulnerabilities are reduced by implementing controls or countermeasures.

N

National Cyber Security Division (NCSD) | A division of the Department of Homeland Security. NCSD and Department of Homeland Security work together with private, public, and international parties to secure cyberspace. They particularly focus on America's cyber assets.

National Institute of Standards and Technology (NIST) | A division of the U.S. Department of Commerce. Its mission is to promote U.S. innovation and industrial competiveness. The Information Technology Laboratory (ITL) is within NIST. ITL publishes special publications that are widely used in IT risk management.

Need-to-know principle | A security principle that grants users access only to the data they need to perform their job. This is similar to the least-privilege principle. However, the least-privilege principle includes rights and permissions, while the need-to-know principle focuses only on permissions for data.

Network load balancing | A technology that allows a load to be shared among multiple servers. As new clients connect, they are directed to the server that has the least load. Load-balancing is used in Web farms.

Non-repudiation | Used to prevent someone from denying they took an action. Audit logs record details of who, what, where, and when on events. If an audit log records an action by a user after the user logs on, the user cannot believably deny the action. Digital signatures are also used for non-repudiation.

Operational impact | The impact of a security control on operations. Countermeasures frequently consume resources. These resources can impact normal operations if not controlled.

P

Password policy | A written or technical policy that specifies security requirements for passwords. Requirements include length, age, and complexity. For example, a password policy may specify that passwords are at least eight characters and must be changed every 90 days. Complexity requirements specify the use of uppercase, lowercase, symbols, and numbers.

Patch management | Ensuring that patches are deployed when needed. Software regularly develops bugs. When that happens, vendors release patches to correct the problems. Patch management ensures that appropriate patches are deployed. Many bugs present serious security risks, so if the patches aren't deployed, the systems become vulnerable.

Patch Tuesday | The day that Microsoft releases patches for Microsoft products. Patch Tuesday is the second Tuesday of every month.

Payment Card Industry Data Security Standard (PCI DSS) | An international standard used to protect credit card data. These requirements are set by the PCI Security Council. Merchants are required to comply with the standards.

Penetration testing | Testing performed to see if a vulnerability can be exploited. Penetration testing is done after a vulnerability assessment. It can be invasive and can take systems down.

Physical controls | Controls that restrict physical access to areas or systems. Examples include locked rooms, guards, and cameras.

Physical security control | A control that controls the physical environment. It includes locks and guards to restrict physical access. It also includes heating and cooling systems to control the environment.

Plan of action and milestones (POAM) | A document used to track activities in a risk management plan. A POAM assigns responsibility for specific tasks. It also makes it easier for management to follow-up on the tasks.

Planned countermeasure | A countermeasure this is planned to be added at some point in the future. Countermeasures can be in place or planned.

Preventative control | A class of control identified by its function. A preventative control will attempt to prevent the risk from occurring. For example, an unneeded protocol is removed from a server to harden it. Any attacks on this protocol are now prevented on this server.

Principle of least privilege | See least-privilege principle.

Principle of need to know | See need-to-know principle.

Probability | Used in a qualitative risk assessment. It refers to the likelihood that a risk will occur. A risk occurs when a threat exploits a vulnerability. It is derived from the opinions of experts.

Profitability | The ability of a company to make a profit. Profitability is calculated as revenues minus costs. Risk management considers both profitability and survivability.

Proxy server | A server used to accept requests from clients for Internet access, retrieve the Web pages, and serves them back to the client. Proxy servers can filter requests so that clients cannot access Web pages. A proxy server can be used as a technology protection measure for CIPA.

Q

Qualitative risk assessment | A subjective method used for RAs. It uses relative values based on opinions from experts. A qualitative RA can be completed rather quickly. Qualitative RAs do not have predefined formulas.

Quantitative risk assessment | An objective method used for RAs. It uses numbers such as actual dollar values. Quantitative RAs require a significant amount of data that can sometimes be difficult to obtain. The data is then entered into a formula.

R

RAID | An acronym for redundant array of independent disks. It is also called redundant array of inexpensive disks. Multiple disks are used together to provide fault tolerance. A fault can occur with a disk and the system can tolerate it and continue to operate.

Reasonableness | A judgment test that a company can apply to determine if the risk should be managed. If a reasonable person would expect the risk to be managed, it should be managed.

Recovery point objective (RPO) | The maximum amount of acceptable data loss for a system. The RPO can be as short as under one minute, or up to the moment of failure. It can be longer, such as a day or week. The RPO is dependent on the value of the data, and the ability to reproduce it.

Recovery time objective (RTO) | The time in which a system or function must be recovered. The RTO would be equal or less than the maximum acceptable outage (MAO). For example, if the MAO is 10 minutes, the RTO would be ten minutes or less.

Residual risk | The risk that remains after controls have been applied. This is also referred to as acceptable risk. Residual risk is expressed in the following formula: Residual risk = Total risk − controls.

Return on investment (ROI) | A value that determines the monetary benefits of purchasing or improving a system. If the cost of a control is close to the annual projected benefits, the ROI can be calculated to determine if the control will be valuable over the lifetime of the control.

Risk | An uncertainty that may lead to a loss. Losses occur when a threat exploits a vulnerability. Risk is often expressed as: Risk = Threat × Vulnerability.

Risk assessment (RA) | A process used to identify and evaluate risks based on an analysis of threats and vulnerabilities to assets. Risks are quantified based on their importance or impact severity. These risks are then prioritized.

Risk management | The practice of identifying, assessing, controlling, and mitigating risks. Techniques to manage risk include avoiding, transferring, mitigating, and accepting the risk.

Risk statement | A statement used to summarize a risk. Risk statements often use an "if/then" format. The "if" part of the statement identifies the elements of the risk. The "then" portion of the statement identifies the result.

Rules of Behavior | A document users must read before accessing a system. It identifies what they can and cannot do on the system. OMB Circular A-130

Appendix III mandates the use of rules of behavior for agencies under the OMB. It is also called an acceptable use policy (AUP) in most private organizations.

S

Safeguard | Another term for a control. Safeguards and controls are used to mitigate risk. They can mitigate the risk by reducing the impact of the threat. They can also mitigate the risk but reducing the vulnerabilities.

Safeguard value | The actual cost of the safeguard or control. This data can be used to complete a cost-benefit analysis.

Sarbanes-Oxley Act (SOX) | A U.S. law passed in 2002. It applies to any publicly traded company. Senior officers and board members are directly responsible for the accuracy of data. If data is misreported they can be fined and go to jail.

Scale out | A method of increasing capability by adding additional servers to a service. Efficient scale out techniques don't require the modification of the core application. For example, an additional server can be added to a Web farm without changing the core Web application. The load is then spread equally among the servers.

Scale up | A method of increasing capability by adding additional resources to a server. You can scale up a server by adding additional RAM, or upgrading the processor.

Scope | The boundaries of a risk management plan. It defines what the plan should cover. Defining the scope helps prevent scope creep.

Scope creep | A problem with projects resulting from uncontrolled changes. Scope creep should be avoided. It results in cost overruns and missed deadlines.

Script kiddie | An attacker without much knowledge about programming and the potential harm it may cause. The idea is that some hacking tools are so easy to use, a kid can use them.

Securities and Exchange Commission (SEC) | A federal agency that regulates the securities industry. Securities include stocks, options, and other securities. Any publicly traded company or company that trades securities needs to comply with SEC rules.

Security policy | A written policy created by senior management. It identifies resources and plans to implement security in the organization. It will usually include individual policies such as a password policy, an acceptable use policy, and a firewall policy.

Separation of duties | A principle that ensures that a single person does not control all the functions of a critical process. It is designed to prevent fraud, theft, and errors.

Service level agreement (SLA) | A document that identifies an expected level of performance. It can specify the minimum uptime or the maximum downtime. It is often written as a contract between a service provider and a customer. An SLA can identify monetary penalties if the terms aren't met.

Service pack (SP) | A group of updates, patches, and fixes that apply to a specific operating system. Most SPs are cumulative. They include all the updates, patches, and fixes since the operating system was first released.

Single loss expectancy (SLE) | Total loss resulting from a single incident. The loss is expressed as a dollar value. It will include the value of hardware, software, and data. It is used to help calculate ALE (ALE = SLE × ARO). SLE is part of a quantitative risk assessment.

Single point of failure (SPOF) | The failure of any single component that can result in the total loss of a system. An SPOF is typically addressed by adding redundancy. For example, a disk drive can be protected with a RAID configuration. In addition, failover clusters remove servers as a single point of failure.

Sniffer | A tool used to capture traffic on a network in order to analyze it. Wireshark is a free packet analyzer that can be used as a sniffer. If data is sent in clear text, the captured traffic can easily be read.

Social engineering | Tactics used to trick people into revealing sensitive information or taking unsafe actions. Social engineering tactics include conning people over the phone or in person. It also includes phishing and other technical tactics.

Spear phishing | A phishing attempt that targets a specific company. It often looks as if it came from someone within the company and is more successful against unaware employees.

GLOSSARY

SQL injection attack | An attack on a Web site that accesses a database. The attacker uses Structured Query Language (SQL) code to retrieve or modify data in the database. You can prevent SQL injection attacks with sound development practices.

Stakeholder | An individual or group that has a stake, or interest, in the success of a project. A stakeholder has some authority over the project. Additionally, a stakeholder can provide resources for the project.

Survivability | The ability of a company to survive loss due to a risk. Some losses can be so severe they will cause the business to fail if not managed.

SYN flood attack | A common DoS attack, where the attacker withholds the third packet in a three-way handshake. When the attacker does this repeatedly in a short time period, the server's resources are consumed and the server can crash.

T

Tangible value | The actual cost of an asset.

Technical controls | Controls that use technology to reduce vulnerabilities. Examples include anti-virus software, intrusion detection systems, access controls, and firewalls.

Technical Recovery Team (TRT) | A team responsible for recovering critical systems after a disruption or outage. The BIA identifies the critical systems. The EMT, DAT, and TRT are teams designated by the BCP.

Technical security control | A technical security control uses computers or software to protect systems. The control provides automation.

Technology protection measure (TPM) | A requirement of CIPA. A TPM will filter offensive content on school and library computers. This ensures that minors are not exposed to the offensive content. A TPM can be disabled if an adult needs to use the computer.

Threat assessment | A process used to identify and evaluate potential threats. The goal is to identify as many potential threats as possible. These threats are then evaluated to determine the likelihood of the threat.

Threat | Any activity that represents a possible danger. This includes any circumstances or events with the potential to adversely impact confidentiality, integrity, or availability of a business's assets.

Threat modeling | A process used to identify possible threats on a system. Threat modeling attempts to look at a system from the attacker's perspective.

Threat/vulnerability pair | When a threat exploits a vulnerability, this results in a harmful event or a loss.

Total risk | The amount of risk when the affected asset value is known. Total risk is often expressed as: Total Risk = Threat × Vulnerability × asset value.

Transaction | A database term. Transactions allow several database statements to succeed as a whole, or if any single statement fails, the entire transaction fails. Failed transactions are not applied to the database.

Transfer | One of the techniques used to manage risk. The risk is transferred by shifting responsibility to another party. This can be done by purchasing insurance or outsourcing the activity.

U

Uncertainty level | A method of indicating the accuracy of data. Data consistency is evaluated to determine a level of certainty. You can then calculate the uncertainty level as 100 minus the percentage of certainty.

Unintentional threats | Threats that don't have a perpetrator. They include threats in the following categories: environmental, human, accidents, and failures.

Uninterruptible power supply (UPS) | A battery or bank of batteries used to provide immediate power to systems if power fails. UPS units are intended to provide short-term power. This gives a system enough time to shut down gracefully, or switch over to a long-term power source.

United States Computer Emergency Readiness Team (US-CERT) | Part of the National Cyber Security Division. The US-CERT provides response support and defense against cyber attackers. Their focus is on the protection of federal government resources. They also collaborate and share information with state and local governments, and other public and private sectors.

V

Version control | A process that ensures that changes to files are controlled and tracked. Version control is often used with application development. Programmers check out a module or file, make their changes, and then check the file back in.

Virtualization | A technology that allows a single physical server to host multiple virtual servers. Virtualization saves money in hardware and facility costs. Additionally, virtualization can be used for disaster recovery because a virtual server can be copied as a file and easily moved to a different location.

Vulnerability | A weakness or exposure to a threat. The weakness can be weakness in an asset or the environment. A vulnerability can be mitigated with a control.

Vulnerability assessment | A process used to discover weaknesses in a system. The assessment will then prioritize the vulnerabilities to determine which weaknesses are relevant.

W

Warm site | An alternate location used for disaster recovery. This site is a compromise between a cold site and a warm site. It usually includes most of the equipment needed for operations. However, data will need to be updated. Management is able to match the desired cost with an acceptable amount of time for an outage by using a warm site. Other alternate locations are cold sites and hot sites.

Web farm | A group of multiple servers used to host a single Web site. A Web farm allows a service to easily support more clients by just adding an additional server. If a server in the Web farm fails, clients will not be directed to the server. This provides a measure of fault tolerance.

Whitelist | A list used in a spam filter to allow e-mail. It is a list of e-mail addresses or e-mail domains. You add the addresses or domains to the whitelist to ensure that e-mail from these sources is not marked as spam.

GLOSSARY

References

Armstrong, Michael. *Handbook of Management Techniques*, revised 3rd ed. London: Kogan Page Limited, 2006. http://common.books24x7.com.proxy.itt-tech.edu/book/id_18795/book.asp (accessed April 16, 2010).

Biegelman, Martin T., and Daniel R. Biegelman. *Building a World-Class Compliance Program: Best Practices and Strategies for Success*. Hoboken, NJ: John Wiley & Sons, 2008. http://common. books24x7.com.proxy.itt-tech.edu/book/id_24339/book.asp (accessed April 13, 2010).

Bosworth, Seymour, M. E. Kabay, and Eric Whyne, eds. *Computer Security Handbook, Fifth Edition*. (Hoboken, NJ: John Wiley & Sons, 2009). http://common.books24x7.com.proxy.itt-tech.edu/ book/id_29816/book.asp (accessed March 31, 2010).

Burtles, Jim. *Principles and Practice of Business Continuity: Tools and Techniques*. Brookfield, CT: Rothstein Associates, 2007. http://common.books24x7.com.proxy.itt-tech.edu/book/ id_21623/book.asp (accessed April 29, 2010).

Carnegie Mellon University's Software Engineering Institute, Computer Emergency Response Team (CERT). "CSIRT FAQ," April 1, 2008. http://www.cert.org/csirts/csirt_faq.html (accessed May 9, 2010).

Contesti, Diana-Lynn, Douglas Andre, Eric Waxvik, Paul A. Henry, and Bonnie A. Goins. *Official (ISC)² Guide to the SSCP CBK*. Boca Raton, FL: Auerbach Publications, Taylor & Francis Group, 2007.

Correll, Sean-Paul, and Luis Corrons. "The Business of Rogueware: Analysis of the New Style of Online Fraud." http://www.pandasecurity.com/img/enc/The Business of Rogueware.pdf (accessed February 8, 2010).

Dinsmore, Paul C., and Jeannette Cabanis-Brewin, eds. *The AMA Handbook of Project Management, Second Edition*. New York: AMACOM, 2006. http://common.books24x7.com.proxy.itt-tech .edu/book/id_11943/book.asp (accessed February 25, 2010).

DoD 8510.1. Defense Information Systems Agency (DISA). http://iase.disa.mil/diacap/ ditscap-to-diacap.html#diacap (accessed February 19, 2010).

Dolewski, Richard. *System i Disaster Recovery Planning*. Lewisville, TX: MC Press, 2008. http:// common.books24x7.com.proxy.itt-tech.edu/book/id_28338/book.asp (accessed May 6, 2010).

Federal Communications Commission. "Children's Internet Protection Act (CIPA)," September 9, 2009. http://www.fcc.gov/cgb/consumerfacts/cipa.html (accessed February 16, 2010).

Federal Trade Commission. "Gramm-Leach-Bliley Act, The," n.d. http://www.ftc.gov/privacy/ privacyinitiatives/glbact.html (accessed February 16, 2010).

Federal Trade Commission. "Offices and Bureaus," 2010. http://www.ftc.gov/ftc/offices.shtm (accessed February 17, 2010).

Fletcher, Franklin. "Business Impact Analysis." (Global Information Assurance Certification, February 6, 2007). http://www.giac.org/resources/whitepaper/planning/122.php (accessed April 25, 2010),

Forrester Consulting. "The State of PCI Compliance," a study commissioned by RSA, the security division of EMC, September 2007. http://www.rsa.com/solutions/PCI/ar/RSA_AR_State_of_PCI_Compliance.pdf (accessed February 18, 2010).

Gregory, Peter. *IT Disaster Recovery Planning for Dummies*. Hoboken, NJ: John Wiley & Sons, 2008. http://common.books24x7.com.proxy.itt-tech.edu/book/id_20419/book.asp (accessed April 26, 2010).

Harris, Shon. *All-In-One CISSP Exam Guide, Fourth Edition*. San Francisco: McGraw-Hill, 2008.

Hiles, Andrew, ed. *The Definitive Handbook of Business Continuity Management*, 2nd ed. John Wiley & Sons [UK], 2007. http://common.books24x7.com.proxy.itt-tech.edu/book/id_24299/book.asp (accessed March 28, April 19, and April 27, 2010).

Hiles, Andrew N. *Enterprise Risk Assessment and Business Impact Analysis: Best Practices*. Brookfield, CT: Rothstein Associates, 2002. http://common.books24x7.com.proxy.itt-tech.edu/book/id_8576/book.asp (accessed March 2, April 12, and April 19, 2010).

ISACA. *Cybercrime Incident Response and Digital Forensics*. Rolling Meadows, IL: ISACA, 2005. http://common.books24x7.com.proxy.itt-tech.edu/book/id_30836/book.asp (accessed May 10, 2010).

ITT Tech Virtual Library> Main Menu> Books> Ebrary>

    Andersen, Erling, S., Kristoffer V. Grude, and Tor Haug. *Goal Directed Project Management: Effective Techniques and Strategies*, 3rd ed. London: Kogan Page, Limited, 2004. Chapter 5, "Global planning-milestone planning," pp. 67–94.

    Foster, James, C., Vitaly Osipov, and Nish Bhalla. *Buffer Overflow Attacks: Detect, Exploit, Prevent*. Rockland, MA: Syngress Publishing, 2005. Chapter 1, "Buffer Overflows: The Essentials."

    Gibson, Darril. *SQL Server 2005 Database Developer All-In-One Exam Guide*. San Francisco: McGraw-Hill, 2008. "SQL Injection Attacks," pp. 473–477.

    Rollins, Steven C., and Richard Lanza. *Essential Project Investment Governance and Reporting: Preventing Project Fraud and Ensuring Sarbanes-Oxley Compliance*. Boca Raton, FL: J. Ross Publishing, 2004. Chapters 1, 2, and 24.

Krutz, Ronald L., and Russell Dean Vines. *The CISSP and CAP Prep Guide: Platinum Edition*. Hoboken, NJ: John Wiley & Sons, 2007. http://common.books24x7.com.proxy.itt-tech.edu/book/id_17100/book.asp (accessed May 6, 2010).

Leung, Linda. "What's Your Certification Worth?" Global Knowledge, 2010. http://www.globalknowledge.com/articles/generic.asp?pageid=2595&country=United+States (accessed February 18, 2010).

Manley, Anthony D. *Security Manager's Guide to Disasters: Managing Through Emergencies, Violence, and Other Workplace Threats*. Boca Raton, FL: Auerbach Publications, 2009. http://common.books24x7.com.proxy.itt-tech.edu/book/id_30500/book.asp (accessed March 31, 2010).

Martin, Bryan C. "Disaster Recovery Plan Strategies and Processes," ver. 1.3. SANS Institute, 2002. http://www.sans.org/reading_room/whitepapers/recovery/disaster-recovery-plan-strategies-processes_564 (accessed May 11, 2010).

McCallister, Erika, Tim Grance, and Karen Scarfone. National Institute of Standards and Technology Special Publication 800-122 (NIST SP 800-122), "Guide to Protecting the Confidentiality of Personally Identifiable Information (PII)." Gaithersburg, MD: United States Department of Commerce, 2009.

Mell, Peter, Karen Kent, and Joseph Nusbaum. National Institute of Standards and Technology Special Publication 800-83 (NIST SP 800-83), "Guide to Malware Incident Prevention and Handling." Gaithersburg, MD: United States Department of Commerce, 2005.

Mell, Peter, Tiffany Bergeron, and David Henning. National Institute of Standards and Technology Special Publication 800-40 (NIST SP 800-40), "Creating a Patch and Vulnerability Management Program." Gaithersburg, MD: United States Department of Commerce, 2005.

MITRE Corporation. "Risk Management Toolkit," n.d. http://www.mitre.org/work/sepo/toolkits/risk/index.html (accessed February 27, 2010).

National Institute of Standards and Technology (NIST). "Federal Information Security Management Act of 2002 (Title III of E-Gov)," in H. R. 2458-48, December 2002. http://csrc.nist.gov/drivers/documents/FISMA-final.pdf (accessed February 15, 2010).

National Institute of Standards and Technology (NIST). Special Publication 800-53 Revision 3 (NIST SP 800-53 rev 3), "Recommended Security Controls for Federal Information Systems and Organizations." Gaithersburg, MD: United States Department of Commerce, 2009.

Paul, Ron. "Repeal Sarbanes-Oxley!" U.S. Congress. http://www.house.gov/paul/congrec/congrec2005/cr041405.htm (accessed April 13, 2010).

PCI Security Standards Council. "PCI Quick Reference Guide," 2008. https://www.pcisecuritystandards.org/pdfs/pci_ssc_quick_guide.pdf (accessed February 18, 2010).

Peltier, Thomas R., Justin Peltier, and John A. Blackley. *Managing a Network Vulnerability Assessment*. Boca Raton, FL: Auerbach Publications, 2003. http://common.books24x7.com.proxy.itt-tech.edu/book/id_5973/book.asp (accessed April 6, 2010)

Perrin, Richard. *Real World Project Management: Beyond Conventional Wisdom, Best Practices and Project Methodologies*. Hoboken, NJ: John Wiley & Sons, 2008. http://common.books24x7.com.proxy.itt-tech.edu/book/id_24330/book.asp (accessed February 28, 2010).

Peters, Sarah. Executive Summary in "CSI Computer Crime and Security Survey 2009." Computer Security Institute. http://www.gocsi.com/2009survey (accessed February 8, 2010).

Ross, Ron, Marianne Swanson, Gary Stoneburner, Stu Katzke, and Arnold Johnson. National Institute of Standards and Technology Special Publication 800-37 (NIST SP 800-37), "Guide for the Security Certification and Accreditation of Federal Information Systems." Gaithersburg, MD: United States Department of Commerce, 2004.

Sarbanes-Oxley Act (U.S. House of Representatives. Office of the Law Revision Counsel, January 5, 2009). http://uscode.house.gov/download/pls/15C98.txt (accessed February 16, 2010).

Scarfone, Karen, Tim Grance, and Kelly Masone. National Institute of Standards and Technology Special Publication 800-61 rev 1 (NIST SP 800-61 rev 1), "Computer Security Incident Handling Guide." Gaithersburg, MD: United States Department of Commerce, 2008.

Schweitzer, Douglas. *Incident Response: Computer Forensics Toolkit*. Indianapolis, IN: Wiley Publishing, 2003. http://common.books24x7.com.proxy.itt-tech.edu/book/id_6056/book.asp (accessed May 10, 2010).

Sharpe, Cat, ed. *How to Conduct a Cost-Benefit Analysis*. Alexandria, VA: ASTD Press, 1998. http://common.books24x7.com.proxy.itt-tech.edu/book/id_6588/book.asp (accessed April 16, 2010).

Sisco, Mike. *IT Asset Management*. Columbia, TN: MDE Enterprises, Inc., 2002. http://common.books24x7.com.proxy.itt-tech.edu/book/id_10959/book.asp (accessed March 18, 2010).

Snedaker, Susan. *The Best Damn IT Security Management Book Period*. Burlington, MA: Syngress Publishing, 2007. http://common.books24x7.com.proxy.itt-tech.edu/book/id_25442/book.asp (accessed April 11 and May 7, 2010).

Stoneburner, Gary, Alice Goguen, and Alexis Feringa. National Institute of Standards and Technology Special Publication 800-30 (NIST SP 800-30), "Risk Management Guide for Information Technology Systems." Gaithersburg, MD: United States Department of Commerce, 2002.

Sungard.com, 2010. http://www.availability.sungard.com/ITSolutions/software/Pages/biaprofessional.aspx (accessed April 26, 2010).

Swanson, Marianne, Amy Wohl, Lucinda Pope, Tim Grance, Joan Hash, and Ray Thomas. National Institute of Standards and Technology Special Publication 800-34 (NIST SP 800-34), "Contingency Planning Guide for Information Technology Systems." Gaithersburg, MD: United States Department of Commerce, 2002.

Swiderski, Frank, and Window Snyder. *Threat Modeling*. Redmond, WA: Microsoft Press, 2004. Chapter 2, "Why Threat Modeling?" http://common.books24x7.com.proxy.itt-tech.edu/book/id_10484/book.asp (accessed March 13, 2010).

Tassey, Gregory, Ph.D. "The Economic Impacts of Inadequate Infrastructure for Software Testing." National Institute of Standards and Technology, May 2002. http://www.nist.gov/director/prog-ofc/report02-3.pdf (accessed April 8, 2010).

Tipton, Harold F., and Kevin Henry, eds. *Domain 1—Information Security and Risk Management. Official (ISC)² Guide to the CISSP CBK*. Boca Raton, FL: Auerbach Publications, 2007. http://common.books24x7.com.proxy.itt-tech.edu/book/id_30425/book.asp (accessed March 4, 2010).

Tipton, Harold F., and Kevin Henry, eds. *Official (ISC)² Guide to the CISSP CBK*. Boca Raton, FL: Auerbach Publications, 2007. http://common.books24x7.com.proxy.itt-tech.edu/book/id_30425/book.asp (accessed March 8, 2010).

Tipton, Harold F., and Micki Krause. *Information Security Management Handbook*, 6th ed. Boca Raton, FL: Auerbach Publications, 2007.

U.S. Department of Education. "Legislative History of Major FERPA Provisions," February 11, 2004. http://www2.ed.gov/policy/gen/guid/fpco/ferpa/leg-history.html (accessed February 16, 2010).

U.S. Department of Health and Human Services. "Health Insurance Portability and Accountability Act of 1996." Public Law 104-191, June 25, 2007. http://aspe.hhs.gov/admnsimp/pl104191.htm (accessed February 16, 2010).

U.S. Department of Health and Human Services, Centers for Disease Control and Prevention. "Business Continuity Plan (BCP) Format Guide Version 1.0," 2007. http://csrc.nist.gov/groups/SMA/fasp/documents/incident_response/BCP_Format_Guide_07112007.doc (accessed April 29, 2010).

U.S. Department of Justice. "Justice Department Announces New Intellectual Property Task Force as Part of Broad IP Enforcement Initiative," February 12, 2010. http://www.justice .gov/opa/pr/2010/February/10-ag-137.html (accessed February 17, 2010).

U.S. Office of Management and Budget. "Appendix III to OMB Circular No. A-130, Security of Federal Automated Information Resources." http://www.whitehouse.gov/omb/circulars _a130_a130appendix_iii/ (accessed April 8, 2010).

Vacca, John R., ed. *Computer and Information Security Handbook.* San Francisco: Morgan Kaufmann Publishers, 2009. http://common.books24x7.com.proxy.itt-tech.edu/book/ id_32165/book.asp (accessed March 31, 2010).

Wrobel, Leo A., ed. *Business Resumption Planning*, 2nd ed. Boca Raton, FL: Auerbach Publications, Taylor & Francis Group, 2009. http://common.books24x7.com.proxy.itt-tech .edu/book/id_26404/book.asp (accessed May 7, 2010).

Index